Azure for Developers

Second Edition

Implement rich Azure PaaS ecosystems using containers,
serverless services, and storage solutions

Kamil Mrzygłód

BIRMINGHAM—MUMBAI

Azure for Developers

Second Edition

Copyright © 2022 Packt Publishing

Group Product Manager: Rahul Nair
Publishing Product Manager: Meeta Rajani
Senior Content Development Editor: Sayali Pingale
Technical Editor: Arjun Varma
Copy Editor: Safis Editing
Book Project Manager: Aishwarya Mohan
Proofreader: Safis Editing
Indexer: Tejal Daruwale Soni
Production Designer: Sinhayna Bais
Marketing Co-ordinator: Nimisha Dua
Senior Marketing Co-ordinator: Sanjana Gupta

First published: November 2018

Second edition: August 2022

Production reference: 1260822

Published by Packt Publishing Ltd.
Livery Place
35 Livery Street
Birmingham
B3 2PB, UK.

978-1-80324-009-1

www.packt.com

To Klaudia – for putting confidence in me.

Contributors

About the author

Kamil Mrzygłód is a skilled software developer, architect, and Microsoft Azure MVP. He is focused on delivering fast, reliable, and flexible cloud solutions based on the Microsoft Azure platform. He has spoken at multiple conferences and meetups, working on **open source software** (**OSS**) projects and driving workshops for different people and companies. In recent years, he has developed an interest in Azure serverless architectures, data analysis, and big data components. Currently, he works as an independent cloud consultant for various clients. His current goal is to make the world of cloud computing as accessible as it can be so that it's possible to lower the learning curve of this technology and help others start using it.

> *"I would like to take an opportunity and thank the whole team working on the new edition of this book for their professionalism and constant feedback. You made the book as good as it is now."*

About the reviewer

Jay Freeman has worked in the IT industry for over 25 years and has been helping organizations to transform the way they work by adding value and helping to deliver on time development practices, software and cloud architecture, and agile practices.

He has worked for some of the largest organizations in retail, finance, Formula One, automotive, education, transport, and specialist security firms, which gives him a great breadth of knowledge across many areas.

These days, Jay focuses mainly on helping organizations either migrate their on-premises infrastructure and data to the cloud or with the architecting and designing of existing cloud deployments to achieve maximum security and performance, while keeping costs to a minimum.

> *"I have been extremely fortunate over many years to have been able to work with some of the most experienced people and largest companies, which has helped me progress. I have spent many late nights learning new technologies, which I have always had a real passion for, from the age of 11 when I wrote my first program on a Commodore C64. Families of IT professionals don't always get as much time with us as they would like, so I want to thank my wife for really supporting me on my late nights and early mornings and both my boys for understanding that daddy can't always play."*

Table of Contents

Preface   xix

Who this book is for	xix	Download the color images	xxi
What this book covers	xix	Conventions used	xxii
To get the most out of this book	xxi	Get in touch	xxii
Download the example code files	xxi	Share Your Thoughts	xxiii

Part 1: PaaS and Containers

1

Web Applications in Azure – Azure App Service

Technical requirements	3	Dev / Test App Service plans	31
Creating and deploying an Azure App Service resource	4	Production App Service plans	32
		Isolated App Service plans	33
Creating an Azure App Service resource using the Azure portal	4	Isolated V2 plan	34
Creating an Azure App Service resource using Visual Studio	13	Securing App Service resources using different security providers	34
Deploying Azure App Service resources using the Azure CLI	19	Configuring authentication in the Azure portal	34
Creating Azure App Service resources using VS Code	22	Configuring networking for Azure App Service	38
Working with different operating systems and platforms	26	The Networking blade	38
Selecting an operating system	26	Access Restrictions	40
Selecting different platforms	28	Private endpoints	40
		VNet integration	41
Choosing the right App Service plan and exploring what its features are	30	Summary	42
		Questions	42
		Further reading	43

2

Using Azure Container Registry for Storing and Managing Images

Technical requirements	45	Granting permissions for pulling/pushing images	54
Different hosting options for Azure Container Registry	46	Tagging and versioning	56
Deploying ACR with the Azure portal	47	Zone redundancy and geo-replication	59
Deploying ACR using the Azure CLI	49	ACR Tasks	62
Registries, repositories, and images	51	Summary	65
Working with repositories and images	52	Questions	65
		Further reading	66

3

Deploying Web Applications as Containers

Technical requirements	67	Azure Kubernetes Service – a managed Kubernetes service	81
Different ways of hosting containerized applications	68	Kubernetes and managed cluster basics	81
Azure App Service – a web app for containers	73	Azure Kubernetes Service deployment	84
Preparing an application	73	Application deployment	86
Using a container image in an Azure App Service plan	78	Summary	92
		Questions	92
		Further reading	93

4

Using Azure Container Instances for Ad Hoc Application Hosting

Technical requirements	95	Security baseline and considerations	104
Provisioning and configuring a service	96	Summary	107
Container groups as the main unit of work	100	Questions	108
		Further reading	108

5

Building a Search Engine with Azure Cognitive Search

Technical requirements   109

Creating an Azure Cognitive
Search instance   110
Using the Azure portal   110

A full-text search in Azure Cognitive
Search   116
Sending a request   117

Linguistic analysis in a
full-text search   121
Analyzers in Azure Cognitive Search   121

Indexing in Azure Cognitive Search   125
Importing more data   125

Cognitive Search – adding AI to
the indexing workload   128
Configuring cognitive skills   128

Summary   131
Questions   131
Further reading   132

6

Mobile Notifications with Notification Hubs

Technical requirements   133
Reasons to use Notification Hubs   134
Challenges for application design   134

Push notification architecture   136
Direct connection   136
Queued communication   137
Triggered communication   138

Registering a device within
Notification Hubs   139
Notification Hubs device registration   139

Sending notifications to
multiple vendors   145
Sending a test notification   145
Using the SDK to send a notification   149

Sending a rich content notification
through Notification Hubs   150
Creating and sending a rich content
notification   151

Summary   152
Questions   152
Further reading   153

Part 2: Serverless and Reactive Architecture

7

Serverless and Azure Functions

Technical requirements	157	The features of Azure Functions	178
Understanding Azure Functions	157	Platform features	179
Being "serverless"	158	Security	180
The concepts of Azure Functions	160	Monitor	182
Scaling	164	host.json	183
		Publish	184
Configuring the local environment for developing Azure Functions	165	Integrating functions with other services	185
Starting with Azure Functions locally	166	The Function file	185
		Input/output bindings	188
Creating a function	171	Summary	190
Using Visual Studio Code	171	Questions	190
Using the Azure portal	174	Further reading	191

8

Durable Functions

Technical requirements	193	Eternal and singleton orchestrations, stateful entities, and task hubs	205
What is Durable Functions?	194		
Orchestrations and activities	194	Eternal orchestrations	205
Orchestration client	195	Singleton orchestrations	206
Orchestration history	196	Stateful entities	208
		Task hubs	208
Working with orchestrations	198	Advanced features – instance management, versioning, and high availability	209
Sub-orchestrations	200		
Timers, external events, and error handling	201	Instance management	209
		Versioning	211
Timers	201	High availability	212
External events	202		
Error handling	203		

Summary   215
Questions   215
Further reading   215

9

Integrating Different Components with Logic Apps

Technical requirements   217
What is Azure Logic Apps?   218
Azure logic apps – how they work   218
Azure Logic Apps – advantages   220

Connectors for logic apps   221
Connector types   222

Creating logic apps and integrating
services   224
Creating logic apps in the Azure portal   224

Working with Azure logic apps in Visual
Studio Code   230

B2B integration   233
Starting B2B integration in Azure Logic Apps   233

Integrating with virtual networks   234
Summary   236
Questions   236
Further reading   236

10

Swiss Army Knife – Azure Cosmos DB

Technical requirements   239
Understanding Cosmos DB   240
Creating a Cosmos DB instance in the portal   240
Pricing in Azure Cosmos DB   243

Partitioning, throughput,
and consistency   245
Partitions in Azure Cosmos DB   246
Throughput in Azure Cosmos DB   247
Consistency in Azure Cosmos DB   248

Azure Cosmos DB models and APIs   250
SQL   250
MongoDB   251
Graph   251
Table   252
Cassandra   253

Capacity, autoscale,
and optimization   253
Container throughput   253
Database level throughput   254
Firewall and virtual networks   255
Azure Functions   256
Stored procedures   257
User-defined functions and triggers   259
Autoscale in Azure Cosmos DB   261

Using change feed for
change tracking   262
Summary   265
Questions   266
Further reading   266

11

Reactive Architecture with Event Grid

Technical requirements	267	Event Grid schema	282
Azure Event Grid and reactive		The CloudEvents schema	284
architecture	268	Custom schema	285
Reactive architecture	268	**Receiving and filtering events**	**285**
Topics and event subscriptions	270	EventGridTrigger in Azure Functions	286
Connecting services through Azure		Testing Azure Event Grid and Azure Functions	286
Event Grid	274	**Summary**	**288**
Creating Azure Event Grid in the Azure Portal	274	**Questions**	**289**
Azure Event Grid security	277	**Further reading**	**289**
Creating a subscription	278		

Using different schemas in Event Grid 282

Part 3: Storage, Messaging, and Monitoring

12

Using Azure Storage – Tables, Queues, Files, and Blobs

Technical requirements	293	Querying data in Table storage	303
Using Azure Storage in a solution	294	Table API in Azure Cosmos DB	305
Different Azure Storage services	294	**Implementing fully managed file**	
Different types of storage accounts	294	**shares with Azure Files**	**306**
Securing Azure Storage	295	Azure Files concepts	306
Replication	296	Working with Azure Files	306
Storing structured data with Azure		Blob storage versus Azure Files	308
Storage tables	297	**Using queues with Azure Queue**	
Creating an Azure Storage service	298	**Storage**	**309**
Managing Table storage	299	Queue Storage features	309
Storing data in Table storage	302	Developing an application using Queue Storage	309

Using Azure Storage blobs for object storage   311

Blob storage concepts   312
Inserting data into Blob Storage   313
Containers and permissions   316

Blob storage – additional features   319

Summary   320
Questions   320
Further reading   321

13

Big Data Pipeline – Azure Event Hubs   323

Technical requirements   323

Azure Event Hubss service and concepts   324
Azure Event Hubss concepts   324
Azure Event Hubss durability   327

Working with Azure Event Hubss   328

Creating an Azure Event Hubss instance in the Azure portal   328
Working with Azure Event Hubss in the portal   329
Developing applications with Azure Event Hubs   332

Federation – events replication   340

Azure Event Hubs security   342

Private Link   342
Resource isolation   342
IP filters and networking   342

Azure Event Hubs Capture feature   344

What is an Azure Event Hubs Capture?   344
Enabling Event Hub Capture   345

Summary   350
Questions   350
Further reading   350

14

Real-Time Data Analysis – Azure Stream Analytics   351

Technical requirements   351
Introducing Azure Stream Analytics   352

Stream ingestions versus stream analysis   352
Azure Stream Analytics concepts   353

Defining available input and output types   354

Creating an Azure Stream Analytics instance in the Azure portal   355

Querying data using the Azure Stream Analytics query language   361

Writing a query   361

Event ordering, checkpoints, and replays   364

Event ordering   364
Checkpoints and replays   366

Common query patterns   367

Multiple outputs	367	**Summary**	**368**
Data aggregation over time	367	**Questions**	**369**
Counting unique values	368	**Further reading**	**369**

15

Enterprise Integration – Azure Service Bus

Technical requirements	**371**	**Advanced features of Azure**	
Azure Service Bus fundamentals	**372**	**Service Bus**	**385**
Azure Service Bus versus other messaging		Dead lettering	385
services	372	Sessions	386
Azure Service Bus and Azure Queue Storage	373	Transactions	387
Azure Service Bus in the Azure portal	374	**Handling outages and disasters**	**388**
Queues, topics, and relays	377	DR	388
Azure Service Bus design patterns	379	Handling outages	390
Developing solutions with the Azure Service			
Bus SDK	379	**Summary**	**392**
Azure Service Bus security	**383**	**Questions**	**392**
MI	383	**Further reading**	**393**
RBAC	384		

16

Using Application Insights to Monitor Your Applications

Technical requirements	**395**	**Monitoring different platforms**	**401**
Using the Azure Application		.NET	401
Insights service	**395**	Node.js	404
Logging data in the cloud	396	Azure Functions	405
Azure Application Insights fundamentals	397	**Using the Logs module**	**406**
Creating an Azure Application Insights		Accessing the Logs module	407
instance in the portal	399		

Automating Azure Application
Insights   410
Alerts   410

Summary   415
Questions   416
Further reading   416

17

SQL in Azure – Azure SQL

Technical requirements   417
Differences between Microsoft SQL
Server and Azure SQL   418
Azure SQL fundamentals   418
Advanced Azure SQL features   421
SQL Server on VMs   422

Creating and configuring an Azure
SQL Database instance   424
Creating an Azure SQL Database instance 424
Azure SQL features in the portal   428

Security features of Azure SQL   432
Firewall   433
Microsoft Defender for SQL   434
Data classification   435

Auditing   437
Dynamic Data Masking   439

Scaling Azure SQL   441
Single database   441
Elastic pool   442
Read scale-out   442
Sharding   443

Monitoring and tuning   444
Monitoring   444
Tuning   445

Summary   446
Questions   447
Further reading   447

18

Big Data Storage – Azure Data Lake

Technical requirements   449
Understanding ADLS   450
ADLS fundamentals   450
Creating an ADLS instance   452

Storing data in ADLS Gen2   454
Using the Azure portal for navigation 454
Using SDKs   457

Security features of ADLS Gen2   460
Authentication and authorization   460
Network isolation   463

Best practices for working with ADLS 464
Performance   464
Security   464
Resiliency   465
Data structure   465

Summary   466
Questions   466
Further reading   466

Part 4: Performance, Scalability, and Maintainability

19

Scaling Azure Applications

Technical requirements	471	Azure Functions scaling behavior	481
Autoscaling, scaling up, scaling out	471	Scaling Azure Cosmos DB	484
Autoscaling	472	Autoscaling for provisioned throughput	484
Scaling up and scaling out	473	Scaling Azure Event Hubs	486
Scaling Azure App Service	475	Summary	487
Manual scaling	475	Questions	487
Autoscaling	477	Further reading	488
Scaling Azure Functions	481		
Scaling serverless applications	481		

20

Serving Static Content Using Azure CDN

Technical requirements	489	Developing applications using Azure CDN	499
Azure CDN fundamentals	490		
Working with CDNs	490	Configuring Azure App Service with Azure CDN	500
Creating an Azure CDN in the portal	492		
Optimization and caching	496	Summary	502
Configuring an endpoint	496	Questions	503
		Further reading	503

21

Managing APIs with Azure API Management   505

Technical requirements	505	Policy schema	509
The main concepts of Azure API Management	506	Provisioning the Azure API Management service	511
API gateway	506	Automated management of the service	516
Management plane	507	Summary	518
Developer portal	507	Questions	518
Guidelines for designing APIs	507	Further reading	519
Basics of Azure API Management policies with examples	509		

22

Building a Scalable Entry Point for Your Service with Azure Front Door

Technical requirements	521	Implementing URL rewrites and redirects	532
When to use Azure Front Door	522	Summary	535
Load balancing with Azure Front Door	524	Questions	535
		Further reading	535

23

Azure Application Gateway as a Web Traffic Load Balancer   537

Technical requirements	537	Configuring routing	540
Azure Application Gateway features	538	Integrating with web applications	547
WAF	539	URL rewriting and redirects	548
Load balancing	539	Summary	553
Multiple-site hosting	540	Questions	553
Rewriting URLs and headers	540	Further reading	553

24

Distributing Load with Azure Traffic Manager

Technical requirements	555	Endpoint monitoring	569
Using Azure Traffic Manager	555	nslookup	570
Functions of Azure Traffic Manager	556	Traffic view	571
Creating Azure Traffic Manager in the Azure portal	558	Summary	572
		Questions	572
Working with Azure Traffic Manager in the Azure portal	564	Further reading	572

25

Tips and Tricks in Azure

Technical requirements	573	A word from the reviewer	580
Using the Azure CLI	573	Using continuous deployment for automated deployments to Azure	583
Using Cloud Shell	578		
Automating infrastructure deployments with ARM templates and Azure Bicep	580	Summary	584
		Questions	585
		Further reading	585

Index	587
Other Books You May Enjoy	604

Preface

Microsoft Azure is one of the most popular cloud computing platforms that are available publicly. As more and more companies decide to migrate their on-premises workloads and modernize them, expertise in at least one cloud vendor becomes critical when planning your next career steps.

The goal of this book is to help you to understand how Microsoft Azure works and what can be achieved when choosing cloud products over a traditional model of hosting. It focuses on presenting managed services such as Azure App Service, Azure SQL Database, and Azure Container Registry, addressing the current direction of modern architectures and the plans of many companies.

Who this book is for

This book is targeted at developers who are familiar with concepts of programming, architecture, and deployment to a desired hosting environment. As Microsoft Azure is a technology closely related to the .NET platform, prior knowledge of that technology stack will help you get the most out of this book.

However, as the cloud is a technology-agnostic platform, there are also examples addressing other programming languages that are supported.

What this book covers

Chapter 1, Web Applications in Azure – Azure App Service, shows you how to build and host web apps in Azure.

Chapter 2, Using Azure Container Registry for Storing and Managing Images, discusses building and hosting Docker images with application code and dependencies.

Chapter 3, Deploying Web Applications as Containers, examines using Docker images as artifacts and running them using Azure services.

Chapter 4, Using Azure Container Instances for Ad Hoc Application Hosting, covers running containers in Azure without provisioning additional infrastructure.

Chapter 5, Building a Search Engine with Azure Cognitive Search, delves into using Azure Search as a managed search engine.

Chapter 6, Mobile Notifications with Notification Hub, discusses enriching applications with notifications.

Chapter 7, Serverless and Azure Functions, shows you how to build serverless applications with a function-as-a-service approach.

Chapter 8, Durable Functions, examines enhancing serverless architecture with a controlled model of data processing.

Chapter 9, Integrating Different Components with Logic Apps, delves into using Azure Logic Apps as a managed service for building low-code solutions.

Chapter 10, Swiss Army Knife – Azure CosmosDB, provides an introduction to Azure Cosmos DB.

Chapter 11, Reactive Architecture with Event Grid, examines using Azure Event Grid with topics and subscriptions.

Chapter 12, Using Azure Storage – Tables, Queues, Files, and Blobs, discusses leveraging the Azure Storage service as a flexible solution for storing data.

Chapter 13, Big Data Pipeline – Azure Event Hubs, explores implementing a streaming solution for events.

Chapter 14, Real-Time Data Analysis – Azure Stream Analytics, covers the analysis of data streams with the in-built functionalities of Azure Stream Analytics.

Chapter 15, Enterprise Integration – Azure Service Bus, focuses on advanced messaging scenarios based on Azure Service Bus.

Chapter 16, Using Application Insights to Monitor Your Applications, delves into a managed monitoring solution based on Azure Application Insights.

Chapter 17, SQL in Azure – Azure SQL, covers hosting SQL Server in Azure.

Chapter 18, Big Data Storage – Azure Data Lake, examines building a data lake in Azure.

Chapter 19, Scaling Azure Applications, discusses how to scale Azure services depending on the requirements and available features.

Chapter 20, Serving Static Content Using Azure CDN, delves into using Azure CDN for integration with applications and improving performance.

Chapter 21, Managing APIs with Azure API Management, focuses on managing APIs and their schemas.

Chapter 22, Building a Scalable Entry Point for Your Service with Azure Front Door, covers load balancing using a global Azure service.

Chapter 23, Azure Application Gateway as a Web Traffic Load Balancer, delves into controlling traffic in your system using a managed load balancer.

Chapter 24, Distributing Load with Azure Traffic Manager, explores implementing DNS-based load balancing.

Chapter 25, Tips and Tricks in Azure, examines various tricks to improve your Azure skills.

To get the most out of this book

Depending on the technology stack you're using, the required software will be different. As most of the examples are presented using .NET 6, basic knowledge of that technology will help you to quickly understand the details of the described topics. There are also multiple samples presented in other technologies such as Java or JavaScript to give you a better perspective of the differences between available runtimes.

Software/Hardware covered in the book	OS requirements
.NET 6	*Windows, macOS, or Linux
Docker	*Windows, macOS, or Linux
VS Code	*Windows, macOS, or Linux
Visual Studio 2022 Community edition	Windows

All the exercises and examples assume that you're able to install VS Code as an IDE. You may work with other IDEs as well, although the book won't address them directly.

Some exercises describe a development process with Visual Studio. It's perfectly fine to use the free Community edition if you don't have access to the commercial license.

Download the example code files

You can download the example code files for this book from GitHub at `https://github.com/PacktPublishing/Azure-for-Developers-Second-Edition`. If there's an update to the code, it will be updated on the existing GitHub repository.

We also have other code bundles from our rich catalog of books and videos available at `https://github.com/PacktPublishing/`. Check them out!

Download the color images

We also provide a PDF file that has color images of the screenshots/diagrams used in this book. You can download it here: `https://packt.link/IPgBV`.

Conventions used

There are a number of text conventions used throughout this book.

`Code in text`: Indicates code words in text, database table names, folder names, filenames, file extensions, pathnames, dummy URLs, user input, and Twitter handles. Here is an example: "If your input contains a property named `Date`, you can use `SELECT date` to push it to your output."

A block of code is set as follows:

```
SELECT
    COUNT(DISTINCT Column1) AS Count_column1,
    System.TIMESTAMP() AS Time
FROM Input TIMESTAMP BY TIME
GROUP BY
    TumblingWindow(second, 2)
```

Code output or a command-line entry is set as follows:

```
npm install applicationinsights
```

Bold: Indicates a new term, an important word, or words that you see onscreen. For example, words in menus or dialog boxes appear in the text like this. Here is an example: "When you click the **Review + create** button and confirm creation, an alert rule will be created."

> **Tips or Important Notes**
> Appear like this.

Get in touch

Feedback from our readers is always welcome.

General feedback: If you have questions about any aspect of this book, mention the book title in the subject of your message and email us at `customercare@packtpub.com`.

Errata: Although we have taken every care to ensure the accuracy of our content, mistakes do happen. If you have found a mistake in this book, we would be grateful if you would report this to us. Please visit `www.packtpub.com/support/errata`, selecting your book, clicking on the Errata Submission Form link, and entering the details.

Piracy: If you come across any illegal copies of our works in any form on the Internet, we would be grateful if you would provide us with the location address or website name. Please contact us at copyright@packt.com with a link to the material.

If you are interested in becoming an author: If there is a topic that you have expertise in and you are interested in either writing or contributing to a book, please visit authors.packtpub.com.

Share Your Thoughts

Once you've read *Azure for Developers*, we'd love to hear your thoughts! Scan the QR code below to go straight to the Amazon review page for this book and share your feedback.

https://packt.link/r/1803240091

Your review is important to us and the tech community and will help us make sure we're delivering excellent quality content.

Part 1: PaaS and Containers

The objective of *Part 1* is to present the most common Azure services. Components such as Azure App Service, WebJobs, and Azure Search are widely used and offer a great number of different features, starting from different deployment options, runtimes, and even slots for multiple application versions. With different containers also available, the whole journey can start to get complicated – we're here to help you understand PaaS and the flexibility it offers.

This part of the book comprises the following chapters:

- *Chapter 1, Web Applications in Azure – Azure App Service*
- *Chapter 2, Using Azure Container Registry for Storing and Managing Images*
- *Chapter 3, Deploying Web Applications as Containers*
- *Chapter 4, Using Azure Container Instances for Ad Hoc Application Hosting*
- *Chapter 5, Building a Search Engine with Azure Cognitive Search*
- *Chapter 6, Mobile Notifications with Notification Hubs*

1
Web Applications in Azure – Azure App Service

Azure App Service is one of the biggest and most used services available in the Azure cloud. It allows the easy development of web applications with multiple features available (such as support for different platforms, including .NET, **PHP:** Hypertext Preprocessor (PHP), and Java), manual and automated scaling, and different performance options. It's a general platform and runtime that fuels other services, such as WebJobs and Azure Functions. This chapter is designed to get you familiar with the basics of web development in Microsoft Azure.

In this chapter, you will learn about the following topics:

- Creating and deploying an Azure App Service resource
- Working with different operating systems and platforms
- Choosing the right App Service plan and exploring what its features are
- Securing App Service resources using different security providers
- Configuring networking for Azure App Service

Technical requirements

To perform the exercises in this chapter, you will need the following:

- Access to an Azure subscription.
- Visual Studio 2022 with the Azure development workload installed. All editions would suffice (Community/Professional/Enterprise).

- **Visual Studio Code (VS Code)** installed (available at `https://code.visualstudio.com/`).

- The **Azure command-line interface (Azure CLI)** (`https://docs.microsoft.com/en-us/cli/azure/`).

Creating and deploying an Azure App Service resource

To get started with Azure App Service, you must learn how to create that service and deploy your code. Throughout the chapter, you will see how many ways Azure provides for doing so. Depending on your current needs and the specification of your application, each path can be easier or harder; still, the strength of a cloud and **Platform-as-a-Service (PaaS)** offering lies in the straightforward and intuitive process of provisioning new components of your system.

> **Note**
>
> PaaS is one of the several cloud infrastructure models available. In general, it stands between **Infrastructure-as-a-Service (IaaS)** and **Software-as-a-Service (SaaS)**, offering a balance between the ability to manage underlying infrastructure and abstraction over used components.

Let's now check the different ways to deploy your very first Azure App Service resource.

Creating an Azure App Service resource using the Azure portal

To begin, you will deploy your service using the Azure portal. All you will need is a browser with access to the internet. Enter `https://portal.azure.com` to get started.

Selecting Azure Web Apps from the available services

To create an Azure App Service resource in the Azure portal, you must first find the option to do so in the list of available services. The easiest way to do so is to click on the **+ Create a resource** button and then click on **Web App**, as shown in the following screenshot:

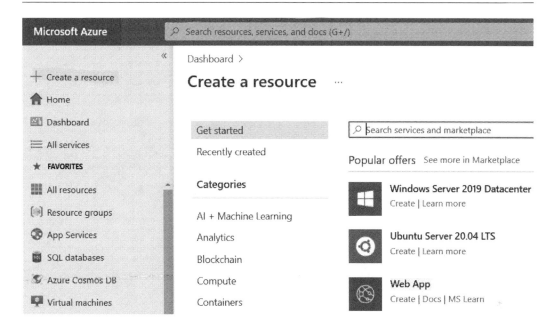

Figure 1.1 – Create a resource screen

Alternatively, you can utilize the search box at the top of the screen to quickly access any service, as shown in the following screenshot:

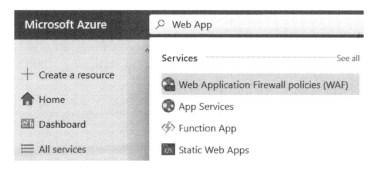

Figure 1.2 – Searching for a resource via the search box

As you can see, the Azure portal already displays the most popular services. If for some reason the **Web App/App Service** resource is not displayed, use the search box by entering the name of a service you are looking for.

When you click on the **Web App** item, you will see the first step of a resource creator, which will guide you through the process of provisioning your application. Now, we will go through all the steps and describe in detail the different parameters that are available to you.

> **Tip**
>
> Here, we are using the *raw* version of Azure App Service, which comes without any additional tools installed. When you gain more experience and become more familiar with the available services, you will see that Azure offers many useful preconfigured setups (such as an integrated Web Apps and **Structured Query Language** (**SQL**) Database instance), which can be used to shorten development and configure all services in one place.

Configuring an Azure web app

Provisioning any Azure service requires going through creators consisting of different steps. In general, not all fields will be required. It is worth remembering that all the mandatory parameters are marked with an * (asterisk) symbol.

The first tab available is the **Basics** tab, which is divided into three different sections: **Project Details**, **Instance Details**, and **App Service Plan**. The very first thing is entering a combination of **Subscription** and **Resource Group** details. Remember that in Azure, resources cannot exist in a vacuum—they require a container for logical separation. Here, you can use any combination you have access to (or you were asked to choose). The process is illustrated in the following screenshot:

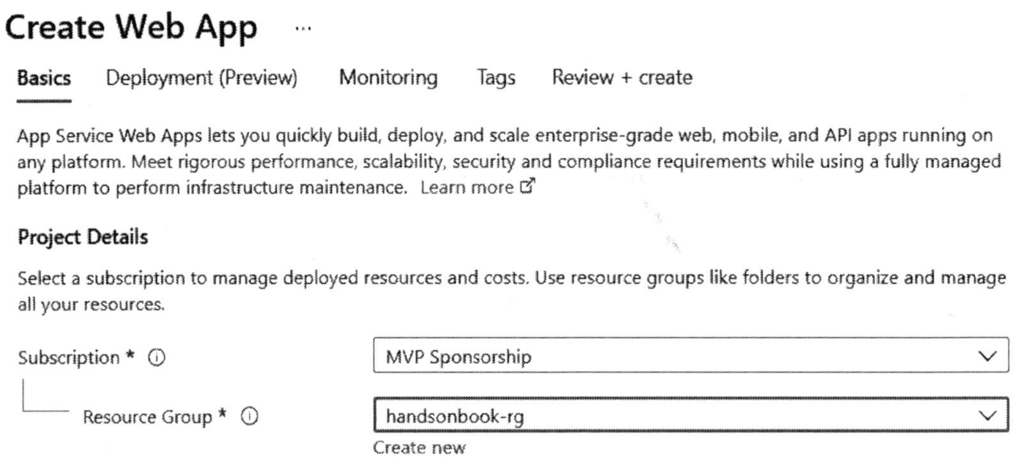

Create Web App   ...

Basics   Deployment (Preview)   Monitoring   Tags   Review + create

App Service Web Apps lets you quickly build, deploy, and scale enterprise-grade web, mobile, and API apps running on any platform. Meet rigorous performance, scalability, security and compliance requirements while using a fully managed platform to perform infrastructure maintenance. Learn more ☐

Project Details

Select a subscription to manage deployed resources and costs. Use resource groups like folders to organize and manage all your resources.

| Subscription * ⓘ | MVP Sponsorship ⌄ |
| Resource Group * ⓘ | handsonbook-rg ⌄ |

Create new

Figure 1.3 – Project Details section

Next, we have the **Instance Details** section, which requires a few more details to be provided. Here, we need to enter the name of our web application (it has to be globally unique), the method used to publish it (**Code** versus **Docker Container**), and **Runtime stack**, **Operating System**, and **Region** details, as illustrated in the following screenshot. While the **Publish/Runtime stack/Operating System** parameters seem self-explanatory and depend on your technology stack, let's talk a little bit about regions next:

Instance Details

Need a database? Try the new Web + Database experience. ☑

Name *	handsonbook ✓
	.azurewebsites.net
Publish *	◉ Code ◯ Docker Container
Runtime stack *	.NET 5 ⌄
Operating System *	◉ Linux ◯ Windows
Region *	West Europe ⌄
	❶ Not finding your App Service Plan? Try a different region.

Figure 1.4 – Instance details section

In Azure, each region represents a co-located set of data centers and directly affects the geographic location of your cloud resources. That also has some legal implications (if you are about to process users' data, it is often forbidden to store it outside the user's origin). Each instance of an Azure service must be deployed to one of the available regions.

> **Tip**
> One of Azure's best practices is to deploy resources to the same region as the resource group they are in. This allows for the best performance and reliability.

The last section of the **Basics** tab is **App Service Plan**. Since you are just starting with Azure, you probably do not have any App Service plans created. As we cannot create an App Service resource without an App Service plan, we will sort this now. Note that if you have an existing App Service plan, the Azure portal may automatically choose it here based on the chosen region. It will also generate a random name if there is no App Service plan available.

Creating an App Service plan

When you click on **Create new**, you will see a popup allowing you to enter the plan name. Click on it, enter the name of your new plan, and then click the **OK** button. It should look like this:

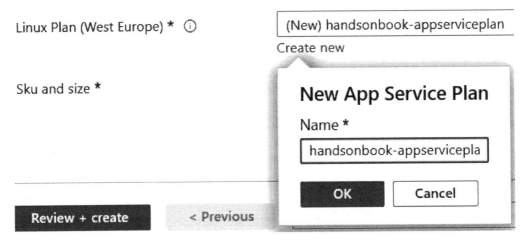

Figure 1.5 – Configuring an App Service plan

The last thing required here is to select the **Sku and size** option. This parameter will directly affect the features available for your web application, its performance, and finally, the price. To make a choice, click on **Change size**. Now, the **Spec Picker** screen should appear, presenting you with the options available, as illustrated in the following screenshot:

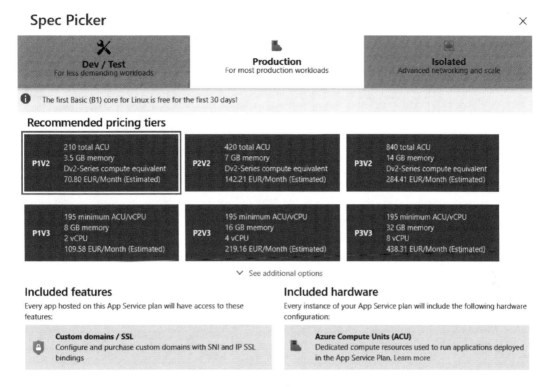

Figure 1.6 – Spec Picker for App Service plan

As you can see in the preceding screenshot, we have three categories of App Service plans, as follows:

- **Dev / Test**: This contains F, D, and B tiers (which stand for free, shared, and basic). They are designed for simple **development/test** (**dev/test**) scenarios and lightweight web applications that do not need features such as autoscaling or backups. Note that the shared tier is unavailable for Linux.

- **Production**: This offers powerful machines and advanced features that are useful in many day-to-day scenarios, such as **application programming interfaces** (**APIs**), e-commerce, and popular portals.

- **Isolated**: This uses the same hardware as the **Production** tier, but with even more features and possibilities to isolate your web apps on the hardware level. This is the most expensive category but can be helpful when creating systems that cannot be made available publicly.

> **Tip**
>
> It is important to remember that tiers F and D have a limited amount of computing time per day. That means that once you exceed the limit (60 minutes for the F tier, and 240 minutes for the D tier) of your processing time, your application will become unavailable and be suspended until the next day.

For this exercise, let's select any tier from the **Dev / Test** category. Once you are satisfied with the option you've selected, you can click the **Apply** button. My configuration, for example, looks like this:

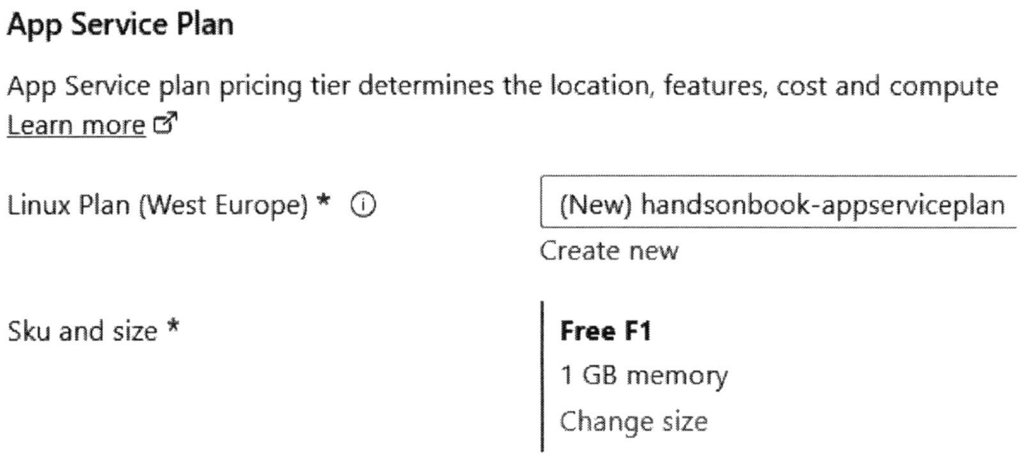

App Service Plan

App Service plan pricing tier determines the location, features, cost and compute
Learn more ☐

Linux Plan (West Europe) * ⓘ   (New) handsonbook-appserviceplan
                                        Create new

Sku and size *   **Free F1**
                                        1 GB memory
                                        Change size

Figure 1.7 – Configure App Service plan with a free tier

> **Tip**
>
> Remember that you can always upgrade (or scale up) the instance of your App Service plan. For example, if you need a specific feature, or the popularity of your application has grown, revisit the **Spec Picker** screen and choose the options that suit you the most. This is one of the biggest advantages of cloud over on-premises, where you would have to buy and set up new machines on your own.

Now, you can click **Next: Deployment (Preview)**, which will bring us to the next tab in our creator, as follows:

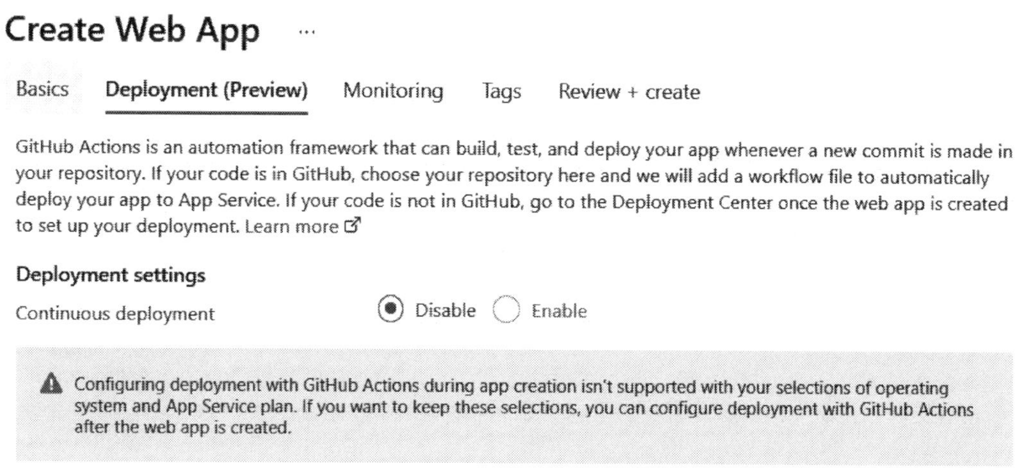

Create Web App ···

Basics   **Deployment (Preview)**   Monitoring   Tags   Review + create

GitHub Actions is an automation framework that can build, test, and deploy your app whenever a new commit is made in your repository. If your code is in GitHub, choose your repository here and we will add a workflow file to automatically deploy your app to App Service. If your code is not in GitHub, go to the Deployment Center once the web app is created to set up your deployment. Learn more ☐

Deployment settings

Continuous deployment   ◉ Disable   ◯ Enable

> ⚠ Configuring deployment with GitHub Actions during app creation isn't supported with your selections of operating system and App Service plan. If you want to keep these selections, you can configure deployment with GitHub Actions after the web app is created.

Figure 1.8 – Deployment tab

This tab allows us to configure the **Continuous deployment** setting for our application using GitHub Actions. Unfortunately, that kind of automated deployment is beyond the scope of this book. If you want to learn more, you can read about it here: `https://docs.microsoft.com/en-us/azure/app-service/deploy-github-actions?tabs=applevel`. For now, we can skip this and click the **Next: Monitoring** button to enable monitoring of our Web Apps resource using Azure Application Insights, as illustrated in the following screenshot:

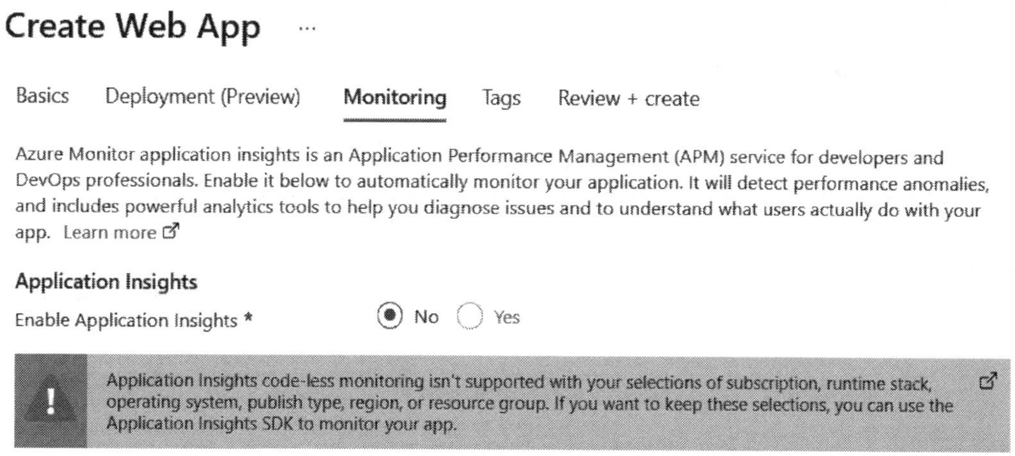

Create Web App ···

Basics   Deployment (Preview)   **Monitoring**   Tags   Review + create

Azure Monitor application insights is an Application Performance Management (APM) service for developers and DevOps professionals. Enable it below to automatically monitor your application. It will detect performance anomalies, and includes powerful analytics tools to help you diagnose issues and to understand what users actually do with your app.   Learn more ☐

Application Insights

Enable Application Insights *   ◉ No   ◯ Yes

> ⚠ Application Insights code-less monitoring isn't supported with your selections of subscription, runtime stack, operating system, publish type, region, or resource group. If you want to keep these selections, you can use the Application Insights SDK to monitor your app.

Figure 1.9 – Monitoring tab

Here, depending on the platform we chose, we can decide whether we want to enable monitoring by choosing the **Yes** option. Unfortunately, because my choice was Linux, the creator disables that for me (although it will be available to you if you selected Windows). Azure Application Insights will be described in detail further in this book, so to keep things simple, let's choose **No**.

We will skip the last tab, **Tags**, for now, so the only thing left is to click on the **Review + create** button and, after confirming all the details are correct, click on **Create**. If Azure detects that something is wrong with your input, it will highlight all the invalid fields and block the process of provisioning a resource.

Now, wait several seconds for the creation of a new resource. During this time, Azure will validate the template and parameters, and orchestrate multiple underlying controllers to create a service. Once a new resource is created, you should see a notification and be able to see your resources. To quickly validate this, click on the **All resources** button on the left and filter all of them using, for example, the name of the App Service resource you have created. The process is illustrated in the following screenshot:

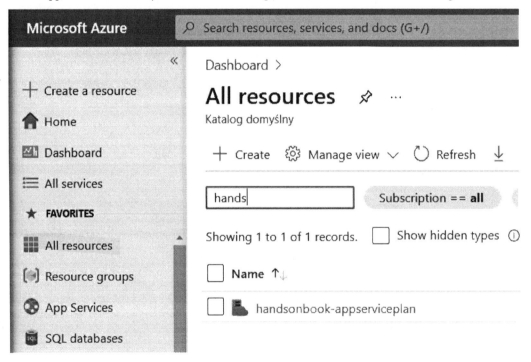

Figure 1.10 – Created App Service plan visible in the Azure portal

Let's now switch our focus to creating an Azure App Service resource using a different toolset.

Creating an Azure App Service resource using Visual Studio

If you do not want to create your web apps using the Azure portal, you can use Microsoft Visual Studio, which has built-in integration for many different Azure services. As Visual Studio is an **integrated development environment** (**IDE**) designed mostly for .NET application development, all the exercises will use .NET as a development platform. For a more generic approach, please look at the next section, where we will describe working with VS Code as an alternative.

> **Note**
>
> This exercise was created using Microsoft Visual Studio Community 2019 (16.8.4) with Azure workloads installed. If you want to configure your instance and ensure everything is set up correctly, please follow the short tutorial available at `https://docs.microsoft.com/en-us/dotnet/azure/configure-visual-studio`.

In Visual Studio, click on **File | New | Project**. This will display a **Create a new project** window, where you can find plenty of different templates for starting with a new application. Because we are aiming at deploying a web application, let's choose a template for **ASP.NET Core Web Application**, as illustrated in the following screenshot:

Figure 1.11 – Creating a new project in Visual Studio

When a template is selected, click on the **Next** button in the bottom-right corner of the window. All that's left to do now is enter a project name and its location on our hard drive, as follows:

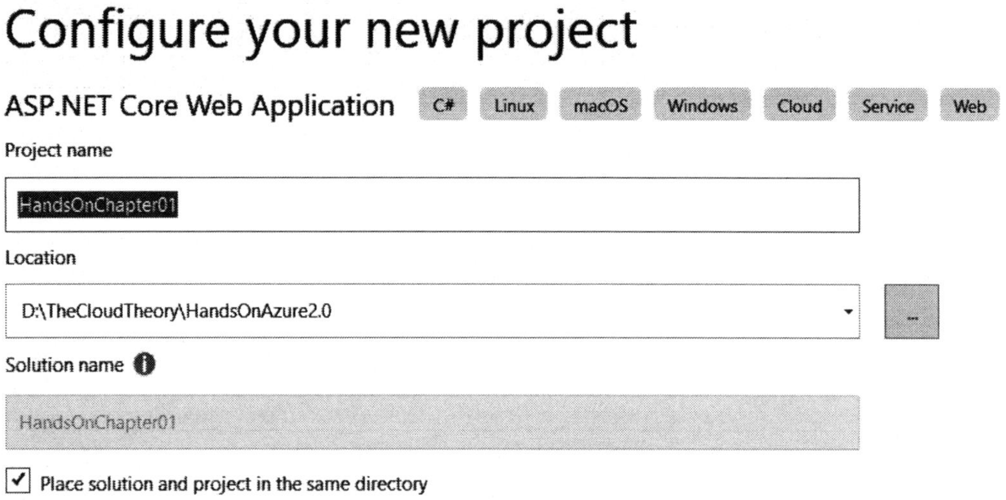

Configure your new project

ASP.NET Core Web Application   C#   Linux   macOS   Windows   Cloud   Service   Web

Project name

HandsOnChapter01

Location

D:\TheCloudTheory\HandsOnAzure2.0

Solution name ⓘ

HandsOnChapter01

☑ Place solution and project in the same directory

Figure 1.12 – Configuring a new project

Enter any name you feel works for you and select a location where the files will be created. When everything is ready, click the **Create** button. The last step is choosing a template for this application. To make things easier, we will go for **Web Application** as this will give us some content to work with. You can see the available templates in the following screenshot:

Create a new ASP.NET Core web application

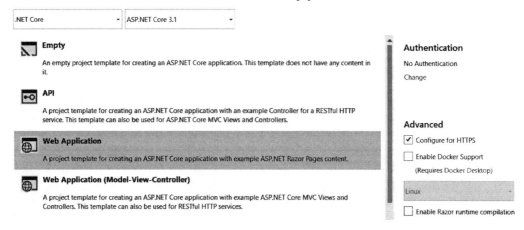

Figure 1.13 – Creating an ASP.NET application

> **Tip**
>
> You have probably noticed an **Authentication** section, which I have not described. It allows you to select the method used for authenticating access to your web application. We will cover that feature in the *Securing App Service resources using different security providers* section.

Let's leave all other options with their default values and click **Create**. After several seconds, Visual Studio should generate your new application, which is ready to work. To ensure that everything is correct, press the *F5* button to run your website locally. After a few seconds, you should see a screen like mine here:

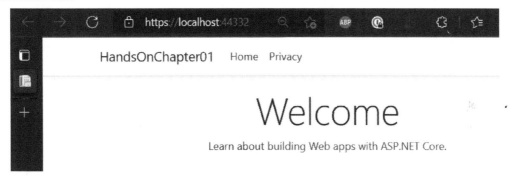

Figure 1.14 – Locally working application

If everything works as expected, there is one question remaining: how can we deploy it to Azure to have our website working in the cloud? Let's go back to Visual Studio for a moment and close the debugger. When you right-click on a project in **Solution Explorer**, you will see a context menu. There, between various menu options, click on **Publish…**, as illustrated in the following screenshot:

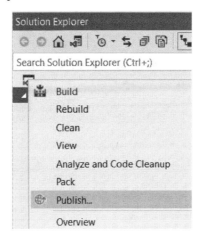

Figure 1.15 – Context menu of a project

As we are building a web application hosted in a cloud environment, our choice for the publish location will be **Azure**, as illustrated in the following screenshot:

Figure 1.16 – Selecting a publish target

Now, click the **Next** button to select a particular Azure service used for our deployment. Currently, we are getting started with Azure App Service, so options for containerization will be a no-go. You will learn more about them in the next chapters. However, depending on your desired platform, you can choose between Linux and Windows machines. If you do not have specific requirements related to your hosting environment, I recommend using Linux for our deployment. The Linux service is shown in the following screenshot:

Figure 1.17 – Publish

Let's click **Next** one more time. The last step is selecting an actual Azure App Service resource for the application. If you do not have one, look at the beginning of this chapter, where we went through the process of creating one in detail. After selecting the desired instance, use the **Finish** button to complete deployment. The process is illustrated in the following screenshot:

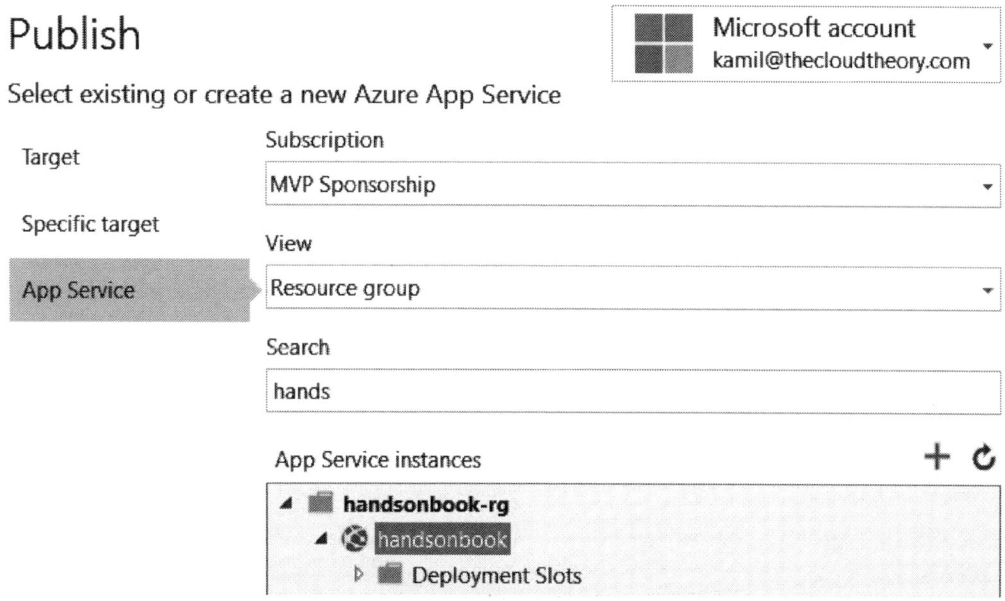

Publish

Microsoft account
kamil@thecloudtheory.com

Select existing or create a new Azure App Service

Target	Subscription
	MVP Sponsorship
Specific target	View
App Service	Resource group
	Search
	hands

App Service instances   + ↻

▲ ▪ **handsonbook-rg**
  ▲ ◉ handsonbook
    ▷ ▪ Deployment Slots

Figure 1.18 – Specifying a publish target

> **Note**
>
> If you do not see any Azure subscription, you may need to authenticate first to your cloud environment. Use the dropdown in the top right of the **Publish** window to select an alternative account or sign in to a new one.

Before Visual Studio sends our files, it will display a summary of the whole process. This is the last moment to reconfigure things such as target framework, deployment mode, or runtime. If everything seems fine, use the **Publish** button, as illustrated in the following screenshot, to publish the site to the selected Azure App Service resource:

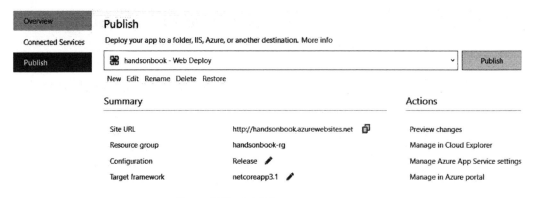

Figure 1.19 – Publish screen summary

Once deployment is completed, you should see your web application open automatically on your default browser, as follows:

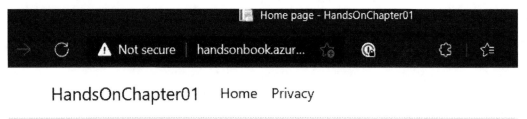

Figure 1.20 – Working application in Microsoft Azure

Congratulations! You have just created and deployed your very first App Service resource. If you look at the **Uniform Resource Locator** (**URL**), you'll see that it contains the name you set in the Visual Studio wizard. All web apps in Azure can be accessed using the following URL format: `http(s)://{appservicename}.azurewebsites.net`.

This also explains why a name must be unique: since, by default, all web applications hosted as Azure Web Apps resources are available publicly, you must select a name that is not already in use in another URL. In the next section, we will use the Azure CLI to deploy our application, as an alternative to using Visual Studio.

Deploying Azure App Service resources using the Azure CLI

Using Visual Studio for deployments is a good idea for testing things and for development, but for sure, it cannot be used for deploying production environments. An alternative, which can be also used on our build agents (if you are using a **continuous integration/continuous deployment (CI/CD)** approach), is to leverage the Azure CLI. As you will see, it allows for a variety of different deployment options that should satisfy most setups.

Deploying Azure App Service resources with a ZIP file

One of the easiest options for deployment is archiving your application package as a ZIP file and sending it to Azure. To use it, you will have to prepare your application using the following structure (this is just an example; in reality, your structure will be more specific to your project):

```
Root
|---- Dir1
|---- Dir2
|  entry_file (index.html / index.php / app.js / …)
|  package_management_file (project.json / bower.json / package.
json / …)
```

> **Tip**
> Consider using build automation instead of packaging all the dependencies into an archive. This will save both time and bandwidth when deploying an application and will make the process much safer. See the rest of this section for more details.

Once you have described the structure, you can package it using any kind of archiving tool (this can be a desktop application or a CLI command)—the important thing is to have a `<filename>.zip` archive that we can send using the Azure CLI. To do so, we will need to execute the following command:

```
az webapp deployment source config-zip --resource-group <group-name> --name <app-name> --src <filename>.zip
```

You will have to provide the name of your Azure App Service resource, its resource group, and the path to the archive you created. The following screenshot shows the result of running that command:

```
D:\TheCloudTheory\HandsOnAzure2.0\Chapter01\bin\Debug\net5.0\publish>az webapp deployment
src Chapter01.zip
Getting scm site credentials for zip deployment
Starting zip deployment. This operation can take a while to complete ...
Deployment endpoint responded with status code 202
{
  "active": true,
  "author": "N/A",
  "author_email": "N/A",
  "complete": true,
  "deployer": "Push-Deployer",
  "end_time": "2021-08-04T13:12:05.2636585Z",
  "id": "6d609790-fc25-42fa-9aae-a35b65e56352",
  "is_readonly": true,
  "is_temp": false,
  "last_success_end_time": "2021-08-04T13:12:05.2636585Z",
  "log_url": "https://handsonbook.scm.azurewebsites.net/api/deployments/latest/log",
  "message": "Created via a push deployment",
  "progress": "",
  "received_time": "2021-08-04T13:12:00.7216981Z",
  "site_name": "handsonbook",
  "start_time": "2021-08-04T13:12:02.1029746Z",
  "status": 4,
  "status_text": "",
  "url": "https://handsonbook.scm.azurewebsites.net/api/deployments/latest"
}
```

Figure 1.21 – Result of publishing a web app via Azure CLI

Once your code is pushed and extracted, a new version of your application should be available and ready to serve the newest content.

Enabling build automation

A caveat of the preceding method of deployment is the need to prepare all the build artifacts upfront and send them to Azure. There are pros and cons to that approach, as outlined here:

- You are sending the final structure of your application and there are no additional steps needed, so any kind of process debugging should be minimal.

- Your application artifacts may be big, which can make the whole process slower as you need to pass all the files and wait until they are uploaded.

As an alternative, you can enable a feature called build automation. This instructs Azure to use your project/package files and run commands such as `npm install` or `dotnet build` before running an application. To enable automation, use the following command:

```
az webapp config appsettings set --resource-group <group-
name> --name <app-name> --settings SCM_DO_BUILD_DURING_
DEPLOYMENT=true
```

If you enable automation, remember not to build your application on your side to avoid duplicated work.

Running from the package

There are some caveats of deploying your application as a ZIP file and then extracting files. As it is running, the extraction and overwriting of files may cause some undesired side effects such as locking or partial updates of the content. To avoid such artifacts, you can use a feature called **Run from Package**. First, you will have to enable the feature using the Azure CLI, like this:

```
az webapp config appsettings set --resource-group <group-name>
--name <app-name> --settings WEBSITE_RUN_FROM_PACKAGE="1"
```

Then, we can once again use the command you are already familiar with, as shown here:

```
az webapp deployment source config-zip --resource-group <group-
name> --name <app-name> --src <filename>.zip
```

Because **Run from Package** is enabled, instead of extracting your files, Azure App Service will mount the whole package as a read-only directory and run your application from it. As the application will be restarted, all the side effects should be mitigated.

Creating Azure App Service resources using VS Code

Microsoft Visual Studio is not the only available IDE that allows you to work with Azure App Service resources. Because this Azure service supports different technology stacks, including .NET, **JavaScript** (**JS**), PHP, Java, and so on, you can easily leverage its capabilities to host different websites using different runtimes. For instance, let's assume that we have the following PHP code that displays a Hello World message:

```php
<?php
echo('Hello world from Azure App Service - PHP here!');
?>
```

Such a simple PHP application can be easily created in any available IDE that supports the PHP language. For this exercise, I chose VS Code, an open source editor, as it can easily be extended using many different plugins. As you can see in the following screenshot, all you need is a single file within your project directory:

Figure 1.22 – PHP project structure

To make things easier, you can install the following extensions:

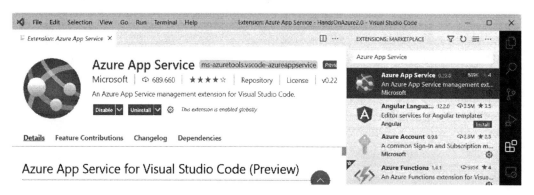

Figure 1.23 – Extensions screen in VS Code

With the **Azure App Service** plugin installed, you will be able to easily deploy your applications from within the IDE, without the need to go to the portal or use other methods.

> **Note**
>
> Before the first use of these extensions, you may need to authenticate them. Follow the displayed instructions, and VS Code will connect to your subscriptions.

Before we deploy our simple PHP application, we must create an Azure App Service resource. Go to the **AZURE** tab (you can also use the *Ctrl + Shift + A* shortcut) and find the **APP SERVICE** section. After that, click on the **Create New Web App...** button, as illustrated in the following screenshot:

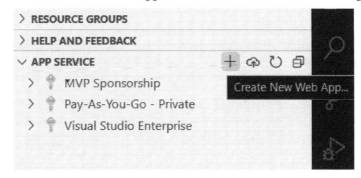

Figure 1.24 – AZURE extension tab with app services

The wizard is a little bit different than in Microsoft Visual Studio, as it acts similarly to a command line, where you provide all fields and information one after another. In VS Code, you will have to enter the following:

- Subscription where an app should be deployed
- The Azure App Service resource name
- Runtime stack (.NET/Node.js/Python/PHP/Ruby/Java)
- App Service plan tier

> **Note**
>
> Using the creator described previously will not give the option to select a resource group and other, more advanced settings. If you want to have full control over the provisioning process, use **Command Palette** (*Ctrl + Shift + P*) and search for the **Azure App Service: Create New Web App (advanced)** option.

In this example, I specified the following:

- Name: `handsonchapter01-code`

- PHP 8.0

- Free tier

Once the provisioning is complete, VS Code will ask you whether to deploy the application. Select **Deploy**, and then choose a folder to deploy from, as illustrated in the following screenshot:

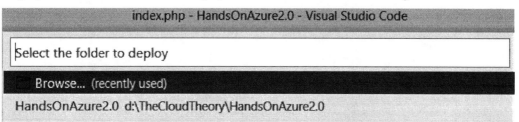

Figure 1.25 – Selecting a folder to deploy from

Next, you will have to select a subscription and the exact instance of the web application in Azure (VS Code may not ask you for that input if it saved your previous choices). The following screenshot illustrates this:

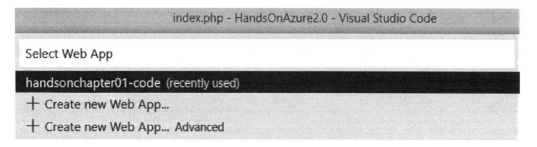

Figure 1.26 – Selecting a web app as a deployment target

Select the instance and confirm the new deployment. Once everything is set and ready, you will see a notification informing you that you are now able to browse the website, as illustrated in the following screenshot:

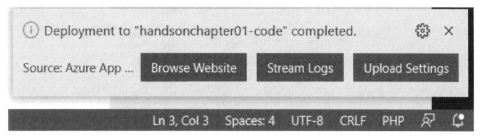

Figure 1.27 – Deployment confirmation

When you click on the **Browse Website** button, you will be forwarded to the web application you have just deployed. Here, you can see a working example:

Figure 1.28 – Working application in Azure

Note that this extension allows you to directly manage the service from within the IDE and gives you access to different features, including application settings, deployment slots, and even streaming logs.

The important thing here is that by using the same path, you will be able to host a variety of different runtimes inside different Azure App Service resources. It doesn't matter whether it is a Java application, a Python script, or a Node.js backend—they are all supported and can be easily developed using IDEs such as VS Code.

Working with different operating systems and platforms

Currently, App Service supports a couple of different configurations when it comes to selecting the operating system, runtime, and platform. Here are some of the possible options for running your website using App Service:

- .NET Core 2/3
- .NET 5/6
- ASP.NET 3.5/4.8
- Node.js 12/14
- PHP 7/8
- Java 8/11
- Python 3
- Static **HyperText Markup Language** (**HTML**) website

Additionally, you can select a platform (32-bit or 64-bit), the **HyperText Transfer Protocol** (**HTTP**) version (1.1 or 2.0), an underlying operating system (Windows, Linux, or container), or even a Java web server powering your website. Let's start by selecting a proper operating system for our application.

Selecting an operating system

To select an operating system to run your web app, we must create a new application in Azure. Currently, there is no possibility to change this setting after an App Service resource is created.

> **Note**
> Be careful when planning to deploy web applications using different operating systems to the same resource group because of some hardware limitations—for example, once a Linux Azure App Service plan is deployed, you cannot create a Windows one next to it. You will need an additional resource group for that.

To create a new website, go to the beginning of this chapter, where we discussed the way to deploy a web application using the Azure portal. Once you see the creator, look at the **Basics** tab. The **Instance Details** section presents the information we are interested in, as follows:

- **Publish**: This offers a way to deploy code or a Docker container. Choosing the **Docker Container** option will hide the **Runtime stack** parameter as it is no longer valid.

- **Operating System**: You can select either **Windows** (which is the most common option for .NET applications, suitable for running .NET Framework, Java, Node.js, or PHP sites) or **Linux**, which can be used for running an application written in .NET Core. Additionally, you can run Java, Node.js, PHP, and Python applications as well.

- **Runtime stack**: Depending on your technology stack, here, you can select exactly what you need to get started with your application.

The choice is yours. Each operating system has different characteristics: Linux is perfect for running Python applications, as Windows has some performance issues regarding this language; on the other hand, you may have many websites written in .NET Framework, which is optimized for Windows systems. Each of the operating system options also has different pricing. Let's compare Windows and Linux here, assuming the **West Europe** region is chosen:

	BASIC	STANDARD	PREMIUM	ISOLATED
Price per hour (Linux)	United States dollars (USD) $0.018	$0.095	$0.115	$0.285
Price per hour (Windows)	$0.075	$0.10	$0.20	$0.30

Figure 1.29 – App Service plan pricing comparison

As you can see, there are some differences between these two operating systems. More importantly, Linux does not currently support the **Shared** tier. The **Isolated** tier is something you should consider if in need of hardware isolation or strict network connectivity requirements. When you have considered all the pros and cons, you can create an App Service resource powered by the operating system of your choice.

Selecting different platforms

In the previous section, you learned how to choose a proper operating system for your application. This is, of course, not everything needed to run a website—you must also enable a specific language if you want to deploy (for example, PHP code). To do so, go to your App Service resource (you have many options by which to do this: either choose **App Service** from the Azure portal menu on the left and select your **Web App** resource or go to the resource group you created by choosing it from the **Resource Groups** blade) and then select the **Configuration** blade, as illustrated in the following screenshot:

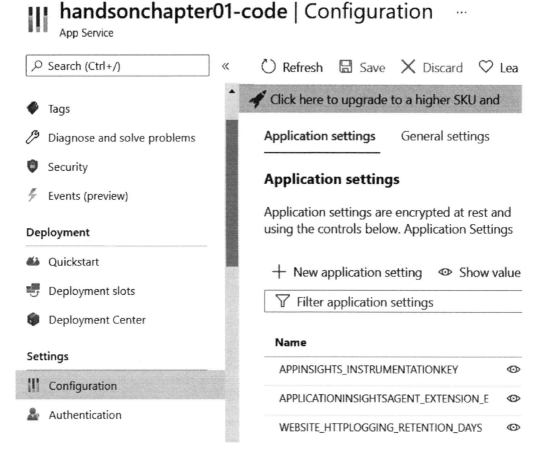

Figure 1.30 – Configuration blade

Initially, you could feel a bit overwhelmed by all those options available, but soon, as you gain more and more experience, all will become clear. You might have noticed the **Click here to upgrade...** notification here—some features, such as **Scaling out** or **Always on**, are only available from the **B1** tier upward.

> **Tip**
>
> Remember that the **Always on** feature could become crucial in some specific scenarios, as it defines whether your application is always running or not (so it can become idle when no one uses it). As you will learn in the coming sections, enabling **Always on** is recommended when running, for example, continuous WebJobs or Azure Functions.

Currently, we are interested in all options mentioning a programming language. These options are available in the **General settings** tab and include the following:

- **.NET version**
- **PHP version**
- **Python version**
- **Java version**
- **Node version**
- **Ruby version**

As opposed to selecting the operating system, which cannot be changed later, you are free to change the stack powering your website anytime. This is unlikely in most cases, but if you ever need to do that, you will not have to recreate the whole App Service instance.

> **Tip**
>
> As mentioned earlier, always select the correct operating system powering your App Service instance, depending on the language that you chose for your application. While it is possible to run PHP or Python on Windows, selecting Linux is recommended as many libraries and packages can run only under this particular operating system.

Let's now check how we can work with web application settings.

Working with application settings

The **Configuration** blade offers more than simply enabling or disabling available features. As you can see, you have three different tabs giving access to various features, as follows:

- **Application settings**: This tab contains settings used by your application while running. It allows you to set parameters available as environment variables and connection strings transmitted over an encrypted channel.
- **General settings**: This tab contains settings for controlling technology stack and platform settings such as WebSocket, HTTP version, or **File Transfer Protocol** (**FTP**) access.
- **Path mapping**: This is used so you can mount Azure files/blobs and access them from within your application without additional configuration.

> **Tip**
>
> Remember that **Application settings** features for .NET applications are injected at runtime and will override existing settings stored in your `web.config` file. When it comes to other platforms (.NET, Java, Node.js), settings from this section will be injected as environment variables to which you can refer. This is also true for **Connection strings** features.

Application settings features in Azure are always hidden when stored. What is more, you can easily secure them by disallowing all users from accessing them or even integrating them with Azure Key Vault for further protection.

> **Tip**
>
> **Connection strings** features for platforms other than .NET are always prefixed with the appropriate connection type. There are four possibilities: `SQLCONNSTR_`, `MYSQLCONNSTR_`, `SQLAZURECONNSTR_`, and `CUSTOMCONNSTR_`.

Now, as we learned a bit about various configuration settings, we can focus our attention on additional basic functionalities App Service offers.

Choosing the right App Service plan and exploring what its features are

We touched on this topic at the beginning of this chapter, so you should have an idea of what we are going to cover now. As you remember, when an App Service resource is created, you must select (or create) an App Service plan, which defines both available performance and additional features. Let's cover all three categories, this time focusing on the differences between each tier. To see your options without going to an Azure App Service creation screen, go to the **Scale up (App Service plan)** blade, as illustrated in the following screenshot:

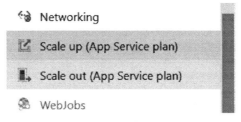

Figure 1.31 – Scale up blade

You will see a screen where all available tiers for the App Service plan will be displayed.

Dev / Test App Service plans

App Service plans designed for development and testing environments can be found in the **Dev / Test** category, as illustrated in the following screenshot:

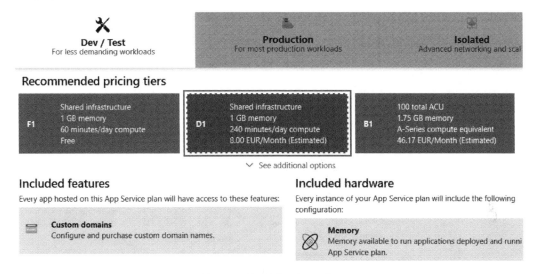

Figure 1.32 – Selecting a tier

We have three different tiers available, as follows:

- **Free (F1)**: The most basic option, with shared infrastructure, 1 **gigabyte (GB)** of memory available, and 60 minutes of compute per day. When using shared tiers, some features of App Service are unavailable (such as **Always on**). **F1** is perfect for quick-testing or deploying an application for a presentation or demonstration. You will not be charged for using this App Service plan.

- **Shared (D1)**: Like **F1**, but this also allows for setting a custom domain for your App Service resource. What is more, you can run your application four times longer than when using the **Free** tier. Still, this is a shared infrastructure, so some features cannot be used, and there will be other Azure customers on the same machine. Unfortunately, it's not available for Linux.

- **Basic (B1)**: This is the first tier that can be considered for running production workloads. It guarantees dedicated A-series machines, and more memory and storage. It is also the first tier that you can scale—though only manually. The **Basic** tier comes with additional versions (**B2** and **B3**), which provide more compute power.

> **Note**
>
> If you are obligated to run your application in Azure in services defined by a **service-level agreement (SLA)**, remember that you cannot use the **Free** or **Shared** tiers, as they do not support this.

Production App Service plans

In this category, there are many more options when it comes to choosing different features available. Remember that, in terms of hardware, the **Basic** tier offers the very same performance as the **Standard** tier. You can see a list of the **Production** category tiers here:

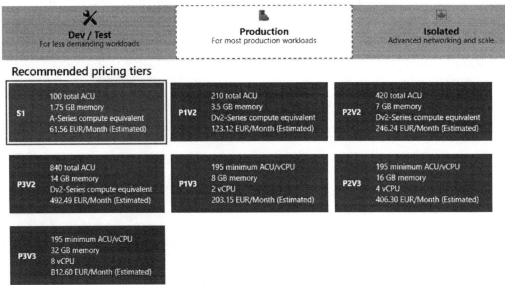

Figure 1.33 – List of production tiers

Here, we can choose between the following:

- **Standard (S1)**: The same A-series as **B1**. What we are getting here is autoscaling, staging slots, backups, and the possibility to use **Traffic Manager** (which will be described in the coming chapters). This used to be the best tier for most production applications, as it supports blue-green deployment scenarios and can handle a bigger load (thanks to integration with **Traffic Manager**). Currently, the price/value ratio is in favor of **Premium** tiers.

- **Premium (P1v2)**: Offers better performance and higher limits when it comes to scaling (a maximum of 20 instances, compared to 10 in **Standard**) and staging slots. You also have the option to choose **P2** or **P3**. If you need the best price/value ratio, this is the tier you are looking for.

> **Tip**
>
> Remember that the maximum number of instances when scaling out in particular tiers is subject to availability. In most cases, these are only soft limits that can be raised after contacting support.

In general, **Standard** should meet most requirements when it comes to performance, reliability, and automation possibilities. However, if you are going to run a very popular website in Azure, you may need **Premium**, as this offers more flexibility and better scalability.

> **Note**
>
> One of the most important things to remember is how scaling affects pricing. In general, you have two options: either you scale up (changing tier to a higher one) or scale out (by deploying multiple instances of the same application). If you are paying, for example, $40 for an **S1** instance, when you scale out to 10 instances, you will pay $400 in total—$40 for each instance running.

Isolated App Service plans

Sometimes, you need even more than the **Premium** tier has to offer. Maybe you must isolate your application from an external network. Maybe you would like to isolate it on a hardware level. Maybe 20 instances are still not enough. Therefore, Microsoft introduced the **Isolated** category, which is a slightly different tier as it requires you to deploy the Azure App Service environment first and then provision isolated instances that will use it. This category is shown in the following screenshot:

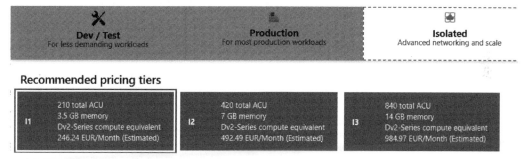

Figure 1.34 – Isolated tiers for App Service plan

In this category, we have only one tier divided into three versions, as follows:

- **Isolated (I1V2/I2V2/I3V2)**: It has the same **virtual machines** (**VMs**) as in the **Premium** tier (**DV2**). It also includes huge storage to store your files (1 **terabyte** (**TB**)), private app access, an integrated virtual network (so that you can access, for example, internal applications), and a more stable environment. This is the most expensive tier but offers the most when it comes to functionality and the range of features provided.

> **Tip**
>
> In general, the **Isolated** tier is the most stable one when it comes to handling a huge load. While **Standard** or **Premium** tiers become unresponsive quickly when utilization hits 100%, **Isolated** App Service resources need more time to return the `HTTP 503 Service Unavailable` response. Take this into account if you need a reliable service that cannot be broken easily.

However, there is one thing worth remembering here—besides paying for each isolated instance, purchasing an **Isolated** plan will also require paying a stamp fee. A stamp fee is a price for isolating your hardware from other Azure customers. As of now, the cost is ~$1,071/month.

Isolated V2 plan

To avoid paying the stamp fee, you can buy an upgraded **Isolated** V2 plan. This eliminates additional costs due to the redesign of the underlying infrastructure. As for now, the cost for an **I1** instance of the upgraded plan is ~$412.45/month.

After describing details of different tiers of Azure App Service plans, we can now switch our attention to security providers that web apps offer and how they can integrate with your application.

Securing App Service resources using different security providers

Most web applications must be secured in some way, either by using your own security system or third-party **identity providers** (**IdPs**), such as Facebook, Google, or Twitter. While working with the traditional application hosted on-premises, you often must configure everything on your own. PaaS solutions, such as Azure App Service, already possess this functionality and make it easily accessible, thanks to the **Authentication** feature. In this section, you will learn how to set this up so that users will be prompted to log in.

Configuring authentication in the Azure portal

As with most PaaS services, you can configure the features of App Service directly from the portal. Thanks to such an approach, you have all options in one place and can easily switch between them.

Using Azure Active Directory to secure App Service resources

Go to your App Service resource and then find the **Authentication** blade on the left, next to **Configuration**, as mentioned previously. When you click on it, you will see a screen for configuration, as illustrated here:

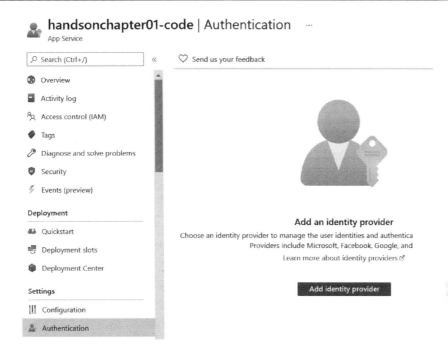

Figure 1.35 – Authentication blade

As you can see, it is currently disabled. When you click the **Add identity provider** button, you will see new options available, as illustrated in the following screenshot. We will use them to configure how authentication is performed for our application:

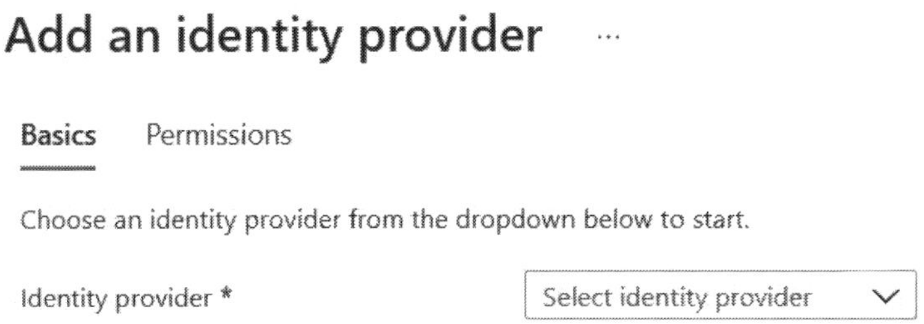

Add an identity provider   ...

Basics   Permissions

Choose an identity provider from the dropdown below to start.

Identity provider * | Select identity provider   ∨ |

Figure 1.36 – Adding an IdP

Change the **Identity provider** setting to **Microsoft**. The screen will change its appearance and display additional options, as illustrated here:

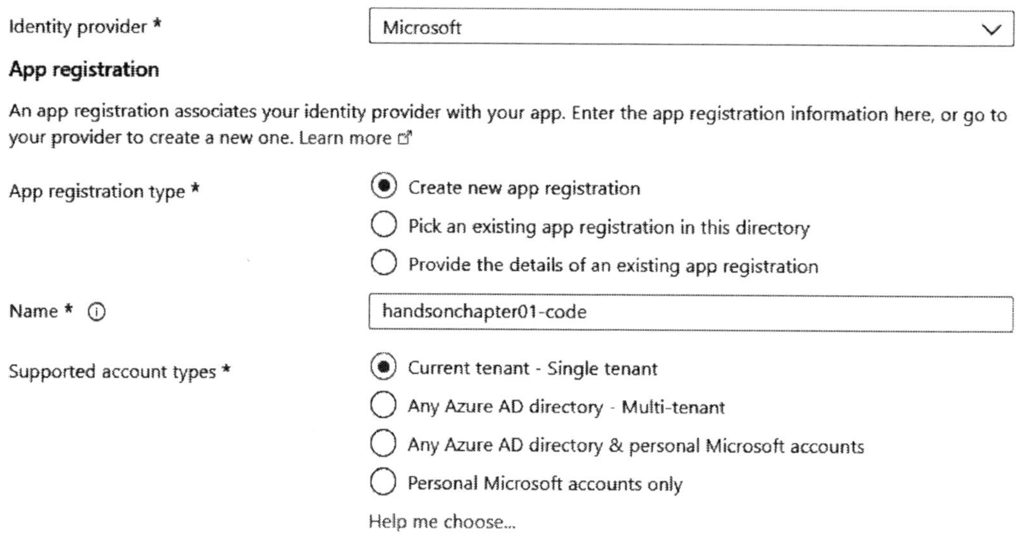

Identity provider *	Microsoft ⌄

App registration

An app registration associates your identity provider with your app. Enter the app registration information here, or go to your provider to create a new one. Learn more ⌐

App registration type *	⦿ Create new app registration
	◯ Pick an existing app registration in this directory
	◯ Provide the details of an existing app registration
Name * ⓘ	handsonchapter01-code
Supported account types *	⦿ Current tenant - Single tenant
	◯ Any Azure AD directory - Multi-tenant
	◯ Any Azure AD directory & personal Microsoft accounts
	◯ Personal Microsoft accounts only
	Help me choose...

Figure 1.37 – Microsoft IdP configuration

> **Note**
> You do not have to be an expert in **Azure Active Directory** (**Azure AD**) to use it with App Service, especially now that there is the possibility to let the Azure portal configure it for you. However, if you would like to learn more about this service, the best place to start is its documentation: `https://docs.microsoft.com/en-us/azure/active-directory/active-directory-whatis`.

To avoid going into unnecessary details, we will use a shortcut and let Azure configure everything for us. Let's leave the default options provided by the wizard (as you can see in *Figure 1.38*) and verify the authentication settings, as illustrated here:

App Service authentication settings

Requiring authentication ensures all users of your app will need to authenticate. If you allow unauthenticated requests, you'll need your own code for specific authentication requirements. Learn more ⬀

Authentication *	◉ Require authentication
	○ Allow unauthenticated access
Unauthenticated requests *	◉ HTTP 302 Found redirect: recommended for websites
	○ HTTP 401 Unauthorized: recommended for APIs
	○ HTTP 403 Forbidden
Redirect to	Microsoft ⌄
Token store ⓘ	☑

Add   < Previous   Next: Permissions >

Figure 1.38 – Default authentication settings

As you can see, once we enable authentication, unauthenticated access will be disallowed, and such requests will receive HTTP 302 as a response. You can go for any option you like.

Now, let's click the **Add** button. After a moment, everything should be set, and you can now access your application to see whether securing it works. Go to the **Overview** blade and click on the URL link or enter it directly in your browser. When a default page is loaded, you will not see it, but rather will be redirected to the login page and asked to give the application permissions, as illustrated in the following screenshot:

Figure 1.39 – Requesting permissions screen

> **Note**
>
> For this exercise, I have assumed that you have your application already deployed. If you did not, please go back to the previous sections and deploy your code with one of the described deployment methods.

Since we configured Azure AD as our authentication provider, a user will be asked to give this application consent to access their information.

> **Note**
>
> We will not cover in this book how to create an application in other authentication providers. However, proper instructions can be found at `https://developers.facebook.com/docs/apps/register/`, `https://developers.google.com/identity/sign-in/web/sign-in`, and `https://developer.twitter.com/en/docs/basics/authentication/guides/access-tokens.html`.

The last topic in this chapter will give you some insights related to networking in Azure App Service.

Configuring networking for Azure App Service

Web applications must often connect with various services. Those can be other apps, databases, container registries, and many more. Some of them will not be available publicly, hence you will have to find a way to reach them. Remember that Azure App Service is a public service and if you are not using an App Service environment, by default it will not be integrated with your networks. Let's verify what options we have to overcome that problem.

The Networking blade

The very first thing you will need to do is go to the **Networking** blade of your App Service resource, as illustrated in the following screenshot:

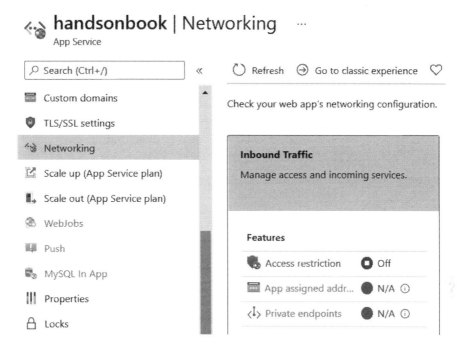

Figure 1.40 – Networking blade

This will provide all the necessary information about your app networking stack, as follows:

- Inbound/outbound addresses

- Access restrictions

- Private endpoints

- **Virtual network** (**VNet**) integrations

- Hybrid connections

Note

To have access to all networking features, you will need to scale up your application to at least the **P1V2** tier.

Access Restrictions

Let's consider a scenario—you want your application to respond only to a single **Internet Protocol** (**IP**) address. If a user reaches it using a different one, they should not have access. This feature is especially useful if you allow users to access your web APIs via API managers (such as Azure API Management). As such, a manager usually offers a static IP, and you normally blacklist all the IPs but this one. This can be done using the **Access Restrictions** feature, as illustrated in the following screenshot:

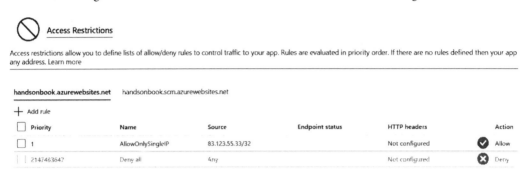

Figure 1.41 - Enabling Access Restrictions

Once such a rule is set, and if I try to access my website and my IP is not whitelisted, I will get an `HTTP 403 Forbidden` response, as follows:

Figure 1.42 – Effect of enabling Access Restrictions

As you can see, with only a few simple clicks, you can block access to your application and whitelist only a specific set of IP addresses.

Private endpoints

Private endpoints are an advanced networking feature of Azure. They are used to ensure that all the traffic stays within the Azure backbone network and never reaches the public internet. They usually work in connection with Azure Private Link to secure a connection between different networks and act as an entry point for communication. We will not go into details of these advanced concepts, but if you are interested in learning more, see an overview of the service here: `https://docs.microsoft.com/en-us/azure/private-link/private-endpoint-overview`.

VNet integration

This feature is an interesting capability of Azure App Service and allows you to reach services enclosed in a VNet while preserving the public availability of your web application. It is worth remembering that even if VNet integration is enabled and you can fetch data, for example, from a database, the database will not be able to call your application. If in the integrated VNet you have a service, it will not be able to communicate with App Service, though opposite communication is possible.

VNet integration is enabled via the **Add VNet** button, as illustrated in the following screenshot:

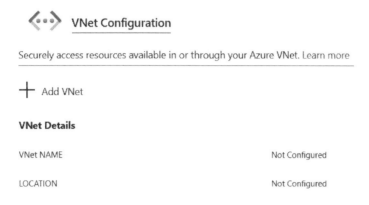

Figure 1.43 – VNet configuration

You will be able to choose a network and subnet that you would like to use for the integration. Remember, though, that you will be able to see networks that are in the same region as your Azure App Service resource. Once a connection is established, the **VNet Configuration** view will change its appearance so that it looks like this:

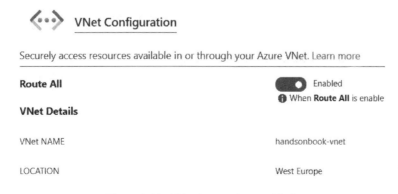

Figure 1.44 – VNet integration enabled

However, take into consideration that VNet integration is not that simple—you will have to consider additional scenarios, such as these:

- Connectivity with service endpoints, which will require connecting to a specific subnet and configuring those endpoints against the selected subnet.

- Connectivity with private endpoints, for which you will have to ensure that **Domain Name System** (**DNS**) lookups resolve to them. This implies integrating a DNS server with your VNet and managing it.

- Using **network security groups** (**NSGs**) for control over outbound traffic.

If you find those scenarios interesting, check out the following link to learn more: `https://docs.microsoft.com/en-us/azure/app-service/web-sites-integrate-with-vnet`.

Summary

In this chapter, you have learned what App Service is, and how to build and deploy a simple application that can easily be pushed to Azure. Learning the basics of this service is crucial for understanding other topics mentioned in this book, such as Azure Functions. Always remember that you can initially use the **Free** tier to avoid paying for an application when testing or developing, and then scale up when you need to do so. I strongly recommend you play around a little bit with Web Apps, as the cloud component has a lot more to it, and some other features are not that obvious initially. We will cover more advanced features such as integration with **Traffic Manager**, Azure SQL Database, and scaling scenarios in the next chapters, but you can now continue your journey and learn something about **Azure Container Registry** (**ACR**) in *Chapter 2*, *Using Azure Container Registry for Storing and Managing Resources*.

Questions

The following are some of the key questions to summarize the chapter:

1. Do the terms *App Service* and *Web Apps* refer to the same Azure service?

2. How many categories of App Service plans are there currently in Azure?

3. Why should **Free** and **Shared** tiers not be used for running production workloads?

4. How many authentication providers can you set up in App Service?

5. Is there any difference in hardware between the **Basic**, **Standard**, and **Premium** tiers?

6. Can you attach a custom domain to each tier available in App Service?

7. Can you attach more than one App Service resource to an App Service plan?

8. Which operating systems are available for App Service?

9. Can you change the operating system after App Service resource creation?

10. What is the difference between scaling up and scaling out?

11. Let's say that you pay $50 for one instance of App Service per month. How much will you pay if you scale up to 10 instances?

12. What is the purpose of using the **Isolated** tier in App Service?

13. Is it possible to run a Go application in App Service?

Further reading

For more information, refer to the following resources:

- Azure App Service documentation: `https://docs.microsoft.com/en-us/azure/app-service/`

- Best practices for Azure App Service: `https://docs.microsoft.com/en-us/azure/app-service/app-service-best-practices`

- Reference architectures for Web Apps: `https://docs.microsoft.com/en-us/azure/architecture/reference-architectures/app-service-web-app/basic-web-app?tabs=cli`

- Deployment slots: `https://docs.microsoft.com/en-us/azure/app-service/web-sites-staged-publishing`

- Azure App Service pricing: `https://azure.microsoft.com/en-gb/pricing/calculator/`

- Azure App Service networking: `https://docs.microsoft.com/en-us/azure/app-service/networking-features`

2

Using Azure Container Registry for Storing and Managing Images

Containerization has become more and more popular with both legacy and greenfield projects. It is not a surprise – being able to run an application using a statically defined runtime environment helps in both development and operations. It also saves time and resources. However, before you run a container, you need to define its image description and store it somewhere so that both developers and applications can fetch and run a container from it. This chapter should help you to find the proper solution for your case using Microsoft Azure.

In this chapter, you will learn about the following:

- How to run and deploy your own image registry using Azure Container Registry
- How to tag and version your images
- What can be done to improve the reliability of your registry?
- How to automate the most common tasks related to images

Technical requirements

To perform the exercises in this chapter, you will need the following:

- Access to an Azure subscription
- Visual Studio Code installed (available at `https://code.visualstudio.com/`)
- The Azure CLI (`https://docs.microsoft.com/en-us/cli/azure/`)
- Docker (`https://www.docker.com/get-started`)

Different hosting options for Azure Container Registry

In Azure, the recommended way of hosting a container image is using a service called **Azure Container Registry (ACR)**. It is a **Platform as a service (PaaS)**, which allows you to focus on uploading and managing images instead of configuring and maintaining a registry infrastructure.

> **Important Note**
>
> If you're looking for an alternative solution or Azure Container Registry doesn't satisfy your requirements, there are many different options available. You can, for example, use Project Quay or host your own Docker registry. Deployment details and configuration will be different for each of those solutions but ultimately give you the same result – your very own image registry that can be customized and modified as you wish. The downside is the need to manage all aspects of the solution – from infrastructure to authentication and updates.

Before we describe the hosting options for ACR, let's quickly answer a question – why do we need a private image registry instead of using a public one such as Docker Hub?

In the enterprise world (or companies, which require more strict privacy policies), using a public registry may be disallowed for a number of reasons:

- You do not manage the infrastructure (even indirectly); thus, it may be difficult or even impossible to reach performance expectations.

- Very often, you do not have any kind of confirmation that you are not using a shared infrastructure with other clients.

- If the public service provider goes down, you lose access to your images (which may render your deployments impossible to finish).

- Public vendors are much more vulnerable to generic cyberattacks than most companies (due to the fact that an attacker may gain access to multiple companies' data).

- Sometimes, it is difficult to integrate a public vendor registry with your networking stack.

For all those reasons, you will be often encouraged to use a solution that somehow addresses the listed issues. This is where ACR comes in – while it is a service built by a cloud vendor and offered as part of their marketplace products, it can still be owned by your company.

Deploying ACR with the Azure portal

To deploy ACR using the Azure portal, we will need to click on the **+ Create a resource** button and search for `Container Registry`:

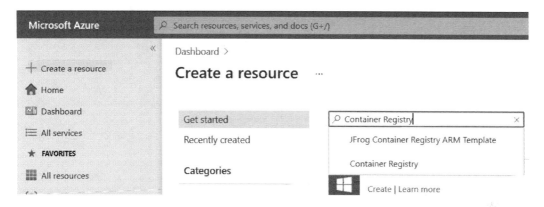

Figure 2.1 – Creating a resource

Then, click the **Create** button, which will forward us to the ACR creation wizard. As per the current portal's **User Interface** (**UI**), the process of provisioning a service is divided into multiple steps (tabs). For ACR, we have three different steps:

- Basics
- Networking
- Encryption

> **Important Note**
> Each service wizard contains two additional tabs, **Tags** and **Review + create**. They are common for all Azure services and do not provide any kind of real value besides tag creation and displaying a summary. In most cases, we will skip their description and go straight to a service instance creation.

The **Basics** tab, as the name suggests, contains most of the initial information related to the service. In our case, it will allow us to provide things such as subscription and resource group configuration, instance name and location, and SKU:

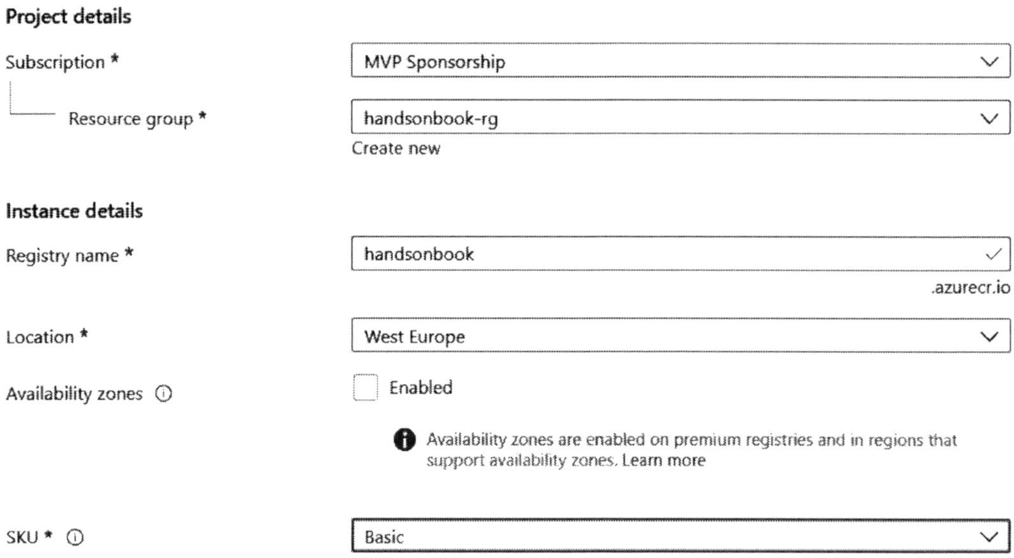

Project details

Subscription *	MVP Sponsorship
Resource group *	handsonbook-rg
	Create new

Instance details

Registry name *	handsonbook
	.azurecr.io
Location *	West Europe
Availability zones ⓘ	☐ Enabled
	ⓘ Availability zones are enabled on premium registries and in regions that support availability zones. Learn more
SKU * ⓘ	Basic

Figure 2.2 – The Basics tab

Let's focus a bit on the most important fields. **Registry name** directly identifies your registry instance and is part of the registry DNS address. That means that it must be globally unique (such records are registered in Azure DNS servers) and cannot contain any special characters. **Location** describes the Azure region in which your registry will be deployed. **Availability zones** affects your service availability, but for now, let's leave it unchecked, as we will come back to that parameter later. The last field is **SKU**; here, we have three different options available:

- **Basic**
- **Standard**
- **Premium**

Each SKU has a different price and offers a different set of features. If we consider a monthly charge, the cost of each SKU will look like this (West Europe – 30 days):

- Basic – $5.01
- Standard – $20.01
- Premium – $50.01

As you can see, the difference is not that big when compared to the overall cost of most IT projects.

> **Tip**
>
> You can always start with the Basic tier and then scale up to more expensive ones. As with most Azure services, ACR supports scaling up and down, so it can be extended in parallel with your application.

When you have entered all the required information, click the **Review + create** button (we will cover the **Networking** and **Encryption** tabs later in this chapter). Once validation passes, click **Create** and wait a moment – after a few seconds, a new ACR instance should be created and ready to work:

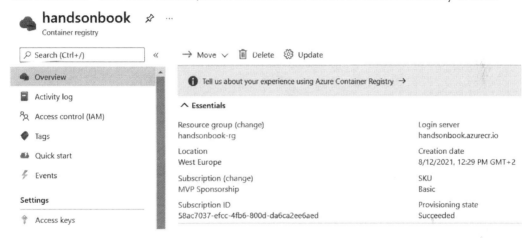

Figure 2.3 – The Overview screen of ACR

We will describe the various features of ACR later in the chapter.

Deploying ACR using the Azure CLI

As a developer, you may want to work with your Azure resources using a **Command-Line Interface** (**CLI**). It may look difficult at first glance, but you will soon realize that it will make things easier on several occasions (especially if you want to do things quicker; going through all the screens in the Azure portal can be cumbersome, especially if you have hundreds of them). To use the Azure CLI for our deployment, open any kind of terminal (it can be **Command Prompt** (**CMD**) in Windows, Bash/Shell in Linux, or even custom terminals such as ConEmu) and ensure that you are signed in by using the following command:

```
az login
```

You should see an output like this:

```
D:\TheCloudTheory\HandsOnAzure2.0>az login
You have logged in. Now let us find all the subscriptions to which you have access...
```

Figure 2.4 – The az login output

Now, the Azure CLI will gather information about all the subscriptions you have access to (it can take a while if there are a lot of them) and display the metadata of all the connections.

> **Important Note**
>
> If you are not signed in, the Azure CLI will open a browser where you can enter your credentials.

To create a new instance of ACR, we will use the following command:

```
az acr create
```

To understand it better, let's see what can be used as a parameter and which one will be required:

```
Command
    az acr create : Create an Azure Container Registry.

Arguments
    --name -n           [Required] : The name of the container registry. You can configure the
                                     default registry name using `az configure --defaults
                                     acr=<registry name>`.
    --resource-group -g [Required] : Name of resource group. You can configure the default group
                                     using `az configure --defaults group=<name>`.
    --sku               [Required] : The SKU of the container registry.  Allowed values: Basic,
                                     Classic, Premium, Standard.
    --admin-enabled                : Indicates whether the admin user is enabled.  Allowed values:
                                     false, true.
    --location -l                  : Location. Values from: `az account list-locations`. You can
                                     configure the default location using `az configure --defaults
                                     location=<location>`.
    --tags                         : Space-separated tags: key[=value] [key[=value] ...]. Use "" to
                                     clear existing tags.
    --workspace         [Preview]  : Name or ID of the Log Analytics workspace to send
                                     registry diagnostic logs to. All events will be enabled. You
                                     can use "az monitor log-analytics workspace create" to create
                                     one. Extra billing may apply.
        Argument '--workspace' is in preview. It may be changed/removed in a future
        release.
```

Figure 2.5 – The az acr create parameters description

As you can see, we will need three parameters (or rather four to be precise, as `location` may not be required; yet it is still worth setting it up explicitly). Let's run it and see the results:

```
D:\TheCloudTheory\HandsOnAzure2.0>az acr create --name handonbookacr --resource-group handsonbook-rg --sku Basic --location westeurope
{
  "adminUserEnabled": false,
  "creationDate": "2021-08-13T08:16:28.201152+00:00",
  "dataEndpointEnabled": false,
  "dataEndpointHostNames": [],
  "encryption": {
    "keyVaultProperties": null,
    "status": "disabled"
  },
  "id": "/subscriptions/          b6-800d-da6ca2ee6aed/resourceGroups/handsonbook-rg/providers/Microsoft.ContainerRegistry/regis
  "identity": null,
  "location": "westeurope",
  "loginServer": "handonbookacr.azurecr.io",
```

Figure 2.6 – The Azure CLI output for creating an ACR

If everything is correct, you will see the command's output describing the created resource.

> **Tip**
> If you do not know the possible location values for your resources, use the following command: `az provider show –namespace Microsoft.ContainerRegistry`.

Congratulations! You have just deployed your own ACR instance using one of the described methods. Now, we will switch our focus to particular features to learn more about the service.

Registries, repositories, and images

In the previous steps, we managed to deploy our own instance of ACR. What we have currently is a private registry that will allow us to push container images for later use. In this section, we will cover two additional topics – repositories and images. Let's briefly describe them:

- A **registry** is an instance of ACR. It is the main layer of the service, which acts as a control plane and gives us the possibility to configure things such as encryption, identity, and networking.

- A **repository** is a logical container for your images. Each registry can have multiple repositories. You can think of them as categories of images or projects – once a repository is created, you can start pushing your images there.

- An **image** is a blueprint for each container. Images can be pulled onto a machine and then used to create an instance of it called a container. In ACR, images must be pushed into repositories.

If you want to remember the main difference between repositories and images, look at the following example:

- `my-image:v1`

- `my-image:v2`

- `my-image:latest`

All those images have the same name; the only difference is the tags. This is exactly what tells you which thing is a repository and which is an image. In ACR, each repository will have images with the same name but a different tag.

> **Tip**
>
> Think about repositories as a collection of container images. If you want to differentiate them further, include a namespace so that you can have setups such as `my-app/my-feature1:v1` and `my-app/my-feature2:v1`.

Let's now see how we can work with repositories and images.

Working with repositories and images

In ACR, there is no direct way to create a repository. Instead, a repository is created once the first image is pushed to a registry. To push anything to an ACR instance, we will need a Docker image locally. To have a Docker image, we need to prepare a Dockerfile, build it, and then upload it using, for example, the Azure CLI. To do so, create a file called `Dockerfile` on your computer and enter the following code:

```
FROM mcr.microsoft.com/hello-world
```

That single command will tell Docker that our base image will be `hello-world`. Now, there are two ways to continue:

- You can use the Docker CLI to build an image and then the Azure CLI to push it.

- You can use the Azure CLI to push your image with the files associated with it to build it in Azure and then automatically push it to ACR.

We will focus on the latter, as it will save us some time. One of the additional ACR features is the ability to build Docker images based on the files sent to it. It is a great feature, which works even if you do not have Docker on your machine. To leverage that, use the following command:

```
az acr build --image handsonbook/hello-world:v1 --registry
handsonbook --file Dockerfile .
```

First, we need to set the `image` parameter, which describes the name of an image. Note that, in my example, it combines two values – `handsonbook` and `hello-world`, with a `v1` tag. The first value is a repository (it will be visible once we push the image). The second describes the name of an image. Then, we need to enter our repository's name and, finally, the `Dockerfile` location with a path to it.

> **Important Note**
>
> The little dot at the end of the command is the location of `Dockerfile`. If used like this, it expects it in the same directory as the working directory of your terminal. It is important to make sure the location is passed along with the command, as failing to do so results in an error.

Here, you can see the result of running the command:

```
D:\TheCloudTheory\HandsOnAzure2.0\Chapter01-code>az acr build --image handsonbook/hello-world:v1 --regist
e .
Packing source code into tar to upload...
Uploading archived source code from 'C:\Users\kamil\AppData\Local\Temp\build_archive_7d98c962eda04b3f80e3
Sending context (354.000 Bytes) to registry: handsonbook...
Queued a build with ID: cb1
Waiting for an agent...
2021/08/16 09:44:46 Downloading source code...
2021/08/16 09:44:48 Finished downloading source code
2021/08/16 09:44:48 Using acb_vol_9bd76cd8-bb76-4b11-a40b-f055392822f2 as the home volume
2021/08/16 09:44:48 Setting up Docker configuration...
2021/08/16 09:44:49 Successfully set up Docker configuration
2021/08/16 09:44:49 Logging in to registry: handsonbook.azurecr.io
2021/08/16 09:44:51 Successfully logged into handsonbook.azurecr.io
2021/08/16 09:44:51 Executing step ID: build. Timeout(sec): 28800, Working directory: '', Network: ''
2021/08/16 09:44:51 Scanning for dependencies...
2021/08/16 09:44:51 Successfully scanned dependencies
2021/08/16 09:44:51 Launching container with name: build
Sending build context to Docker daemon  4.096kB
Step 1/1 : FROM mcr.microsoft.com/hello-world
```

Figure 2.7 – The az acr build command output

Now, if we go back to the Azure portal, we should be able to see our image pushed there:

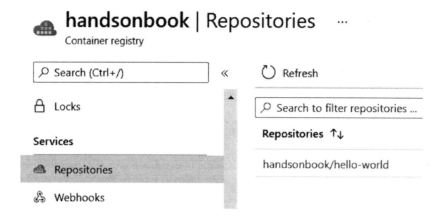

Figure 2.8 – The Repositories blade in ACR

The same result should be returned from the Azure CLI if we use the `az acr repository` command:

```
D:\TheCloudTheory\HandsOnAzure2.0\Chapter01-code>az acr repository show --repository handsonbook/hello-world --name handsonbook
{
  "changeableAttributes": {
    "deleteEnabled": true,
    "listEnabled": true,
    "readEnabled": true,
    "teleportEnabled": false,
    "writeEnabled": true
  },
  "createdTime": "2021-08-16T09:44:55.4441134Z",
  "imageName": "handsonbook/hello-world",
  "lastUpdateTime": "2021-08-16T09:44:55.5479526Z",
  "manifestCount": 1,
  "registry": "handsonbook.azurecr.io",
  "tagCount": 1
}
```

Figure 2.9 – az acr repository showing output

Note that if I use `handsonbook/hello-world` as my image name, the repository's name will be the same.

Granting permissions for pulling/pushing images

In many scenarios, we will be the owners of Azure resources. This gives us almost infinite possibilities when managing them – we can change the configuration, scale up and down, disable encryption, and many other things. However, when applying real-world use cases, we will quickly face problems such as failed authorization. For ACR, if we want, for instance, to push images from our **Continuous Integration/ Continuous Delivery (CI/CD)** pipelines, we need to learn what permissions are required to be able to do so.

There are two special roles in Azure that can be assigned to a particular identity to grant it the ability to pull or push images:

- AcrPull
- AcrPush

To go more into details, let's check the definition of an AcrPush role and see what actions are allowed:

- `Microsoft.ContainerRegistry/registries/pull/read`
- `Microsoft.ContainerRegistry/registries/push/write`

As you can see, if you assign somebody (or something) the AcrPush role, you will grant them the ability to read pushed images and push new ones.

> **Important Note**
>
> Both the AcrPush and AcrPull roles limit the permissions to those two actions listed previously. This is why they are an excellent choice if you do not want a user to be able to do anything else but this.

To grant the described roles, use the **Access control (IAM)** blade in the Azure portal:

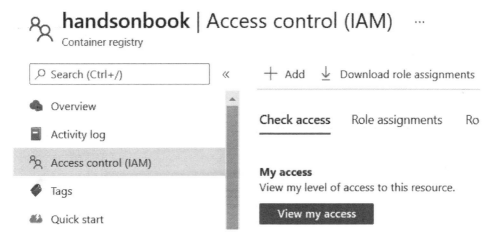

Figure 2.10 – The Access control (IAM) blade

From there, you can use the + **Add** button and click on **Add role assignment**. This will display a new screen, where you can select the desired role and a principal that a role should be assigned to:

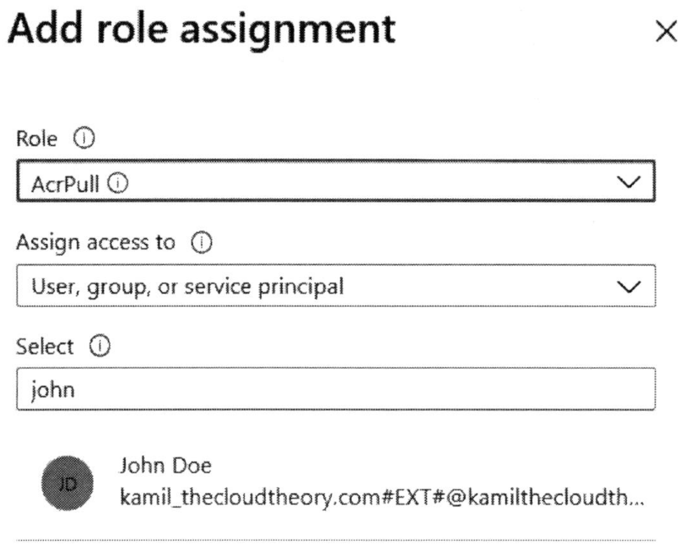

Add role assignment   ✕

Role ⓘ

| AcrPull ⓘ | ∨ |

Assign access to ⓘ

| User, group, or service principal | ∨ |

Select ⓘ

| john |

JD   John Doe
      kamil_thecloudtheory.com#EXT#@kamilthecloudth...

Figure 2.11 – Assigning an AcrPull role for a user

After clicking the **Save** button, a new role for this particular resource will be assigned with the appropriate permissions.

Tagging and versioning

All images in ACR must have a tag associated with them. You can think about it as a way to version your images. Let's consider the following convention:

- `my-image:v1`
- `my-image:v2`
- `my-image:latest`

Here, we follow two paths:

- Each new image is tagged with the `latest` tag.
- We are incrementing the `index` value of our images so that the registry contains all the versions of our application.

It is important to remember that ACR does not change the default value of many tools, which allows you to fetch container images. For most cases, if you omit the `tag` value when downloading an image, you will get the latest version (the one with the `latest` tag).

When building a tagging strategy for ACR, you should follow the same set of rules you would normally follow when using any other kind of image registry:

- *Leverage stable tags*, which do not guarantee content stability but rather allow your automation to fetch a specific image version without changes (for example, `latest` can be used to automatically run tests on the newest application version without a need to introduce changes to the process).

- *Use unique tags*, which can be used as direct links between the application version and deployment. Unique tags can be generated based on things such as timestamps, a `git` commit SHA value, and your build identifier. In contrast to stable tags, unique tags are considered good practice when releasing a new version of your application – most of the time, they will change with each deployment, so you know there is a new version without digging into code. Stable tags do not grant you that certainty – they never change, so it is impossible to tell whether they contain new artifacts or not.

Additionally, each image can be locked, so you can cover yourself in case of an accidental update or image deletion.

> **Important Note**
> The image lock is not the same as the resource lock available on the Azure resource level. They also work differently – resource locking prevents changes and `delete` operations made via Azure Resource Manager; image locking secures an image from deletion and makes it read-only for all registry users (but if you delete your instance of ACR, locked images can still be deleted).

There are two levels of registry locks in ACR:

- An image lock
- A repository lock

What is more, you can use locks in different ways:

- A full-delete/read-only lock
- A delete lock only
- A disabled reading of an image/repository

To lock an image, you can use `az acr repository update` with the `--write-enabled` parameter set to `false`:

```
az acr repository update --name handsonbook --image
handsonbook/hello-world:v1 --write-enabled false
```

As a result, you should get JSON like mine:

```
{
  "changeableAttributes": {
    "deleteEnabled": true,
    "listEnabled": true,
    "readEnabled": true,
    "writeEnabled": false
  },
  "createdTime": "2021-08-16T09:44:55.591151Z",
  "digest": "sha256:92c7f9c92844bbbb5d0a101b22f7c2a7949e
  "lastUpdateTime": "2021-08-16T09:44:55.591151Z",
  "name": "v1",
  "signed": false
}
```

Figure 2.12 – The result of disabling writing on a repository level

As you can see, the command I run disabled writes permission but still preserved deletion and reads permission of the image.

> **Tip**
> If you omit the `tag` name in the `-image` parameter, a lock will be applied on a repository level instead.

Here is a list of the available parameters to disable reads, writes, and deletions:

- `--write-enabled` true/false
- `--delete-enabled` true/false
- `--read-enabled` true/false

A rule of thumb is to use those parameters along with your process – for example, once an application is released, you disable both writes and deletions to secure it from modifications. If you have outdated images, which you cannot delete due to legal requirements and yet people should not be allowed to do anything with them, you can disable writes, deletions, and reads.

Zone redundancy and geo-replication

At the beginning of this chapter, when we were creating our instance of ACR, you probably noted the **Availability zones** option:

Instance details

Registry name *	Enter the name
	.azurecr.io
Location *	West Europe ⌄
Availability zones ⓘ	☑ Enabled
	⚠ During preview, availability zone enablement can not be changed.
SKU * ⓘ	Premium ⌄

Figure 2.13 – Availability zones enabled when creating the ACR instance

To enable it, you must change the **SKU** parameter to **Premium**, as this feature is available only for the highest tier. You can do so via the **Overview** blade and by clicking on the **Update** button.

> **Important Note**
> Availability zones are available only for a subset of Azure resources. If you cannot select that option, make sure your location has them available. A full list of regions with zones is available here: `https://docs.microsoft.com/en-us/azure/availability-zones/az-region`.

Once your instance of ACR is deployed, it will have a feature called zone redundancy enabled without the need for any additional steps. When an Azure service is deployed across availability zones, it offers a much higher availability standard than services, which do not (or cannot) leverage zones.

The concept of availability zones is quite simple – when a service itself supports zone redundancy and is deployed to a region, where zones are available, it is provisioned across multiple physical locations. You can treat them as regions inside regions – each zone has its own physical infrastructure, including power, an internet connection, and cooling. They are also positioned in a way that limits the risk of an outage affecting all of them at once.

Tip

Zone redundancy in Azure is one of the easiest ways to improve the reliability of your application. They cost nothing and the only limitation is region and service support. However, remember that availability zones do not secure you from region-wide disasters. If a whole region goes down, zones cannot do anything to prevent your system from collapsing.

At the time of writing, you cannot enable or disable availability zones once your ACR is created. That feature will be enabled in the future, but for now, the only option is to recreate your instance.

In addition to zone redundancy (which introduces local replication across the region), ACR supports a feature called geo-replication. As the name suggests, it allows us to replicate our instance across multiple Azure locations around the world. Geo-replication in ACR requires Premium SKU, but if your ACR was deployed as a Basic or Standard tier, do not worry – you still can upgrade it to the Premium version. When you access the **Replications** blade in your ACR, you will see a warning telling you that you need to upgrade to Premium SKU to enable that feature:

handsonbook | Replications
Container registry
Search (Ctrl+/)
Add
Refresh
Repositories
Webhooks
Replications
Upgrade to Premium SKU to enable replications.

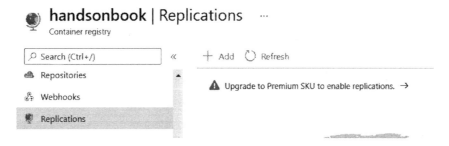

Figure 2.14 – A non-premium ACR notification

Click on that text and change the **SKU** parameter to **Premium**. After clicking the **Save** button, replication should be enabled on your instance:

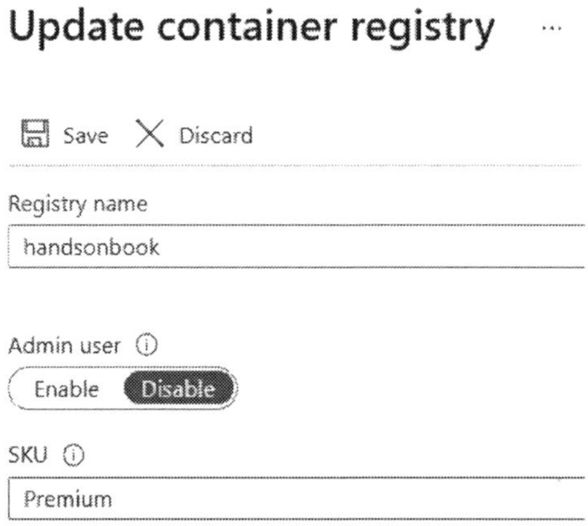

Update container registry
Save
Discard
Registry name
handsonbook
Admin user
Enable
Disable
SKU
Premium

Figure 2.15 – Updating ACR with a new tier

Now, the **Replications** blade should look a little bit different, with Azure locations available to interact:

Figure 2.16 – Replications screen

If you want to configure geo-replication for your ACR, you have two options:

- Click the + **Add** button.
- Click on any of the available regions.

Both methods will display a replication screen, where you can select the desired location and enable zone redundancy for it:

Figure 2.17 – Creating a replication target for ACR

Clicking on the **Create** button below will start the process of replication. Once it is completed, you should be able to see new region availability on your map:

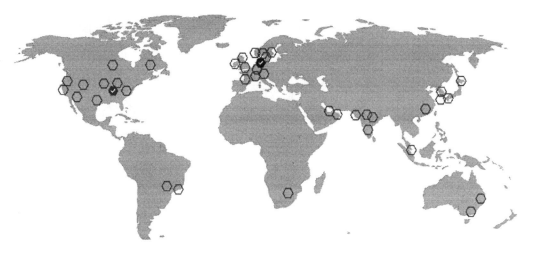

Figure 2.18 – Two replication targets enabled

As with everything, consider the following points when working with geo-replication:

- ACR is responsible for replicating images you are pushing to it, but it will take some time to do that. This is especially true if your ACR is already filled with images. Do not expect immediate replication of images.

- Each location you will choose is an individual Premium SKU ACR, meaning the total cost of your infrastructure will be $N \times$ the Premium SKU charge, where N is the number of regions.

- Azure Traffic Manager is responsible for routing push and pull requests, so they are directed to the closest location. The management of Traffic Manager is ACR's responsibility.

For production environments, using geo-replication in ACR is often a must – it will guarantee that if some regions are unable to serve a request, it is still possible to perform deployment or run an application.

ACR Tasks

The last topic of this chapter is about an additional feature of ACR called **Tasks**. Up until now, we were using ACR as a simple registry of container images that can be tagged and managed. However, there are some additional scenarios that are not covered by the basic ACR functionality:

- Automated image builds

- Base image patching
- Security updates

To address those points, ACR Tasks was created. In general, each task is a file written with YAML following a predefined schema. They consist of steps that dictate what operations should be performed now. An example task may look like this:

```
version: v1.1.0
steps:
  - build: -t $Registry/hello-world -f hello-world.dockerfile .
```

As you can see, it consists of a single step that will build a container image. In ACR Tasks, you have access to three different step types:

- `build`, which is like using `docker build`
- `push`, for pushing a built image to a registry
- `cmd`, to run a command in a similar fashion to `docker run`

Each task file can contain a single step or several (which we call a multi-step task). Task files are then sent to your ACR instance, where all the steps are analyzed and performed.

> **Tip**
> ACR Tasks offers quite a verbose syntax suitable for multiple scenarios and involving various tools (such as Helm, the Azure CLI, or curl). You can learn the whole schema here: https://docs.microsoft.com/en-us/azure/container-registry/container-registry-tasks-reference-yaml.

To run a task, you will need the Azure CLI and the `az acr run` command:

```
az acr run -r MyRegistry -f MyTaskFile.yaml ./<local-context>
```

The same command can be used with the Git repository instead of using a local context:

```
az acr run -r MyRegistry <my-repo>.git -f MyTaskFile.yaml
```

The result for both commands will be the same – a task file will be sent to your instance of ACR and all the steps will be executed there. Here, you can see where the result of running the task is available in the Azure portal:

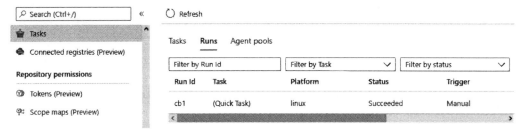

Figure 2.19 – The Tasks blade in ACR

Using tasks may simplify your workloads and pipelines – instead of multiple commands for building a container image, pushing it and testing, and setting up an agent with Docker installed, you can just prepare a task file with all the steps and let ACR do the job.

ACR Tasks has one additional feature – base image updates. Before we dive into that, let's describe what a base image is. In most cases, when you are defining your image using `Dockerfile`, you are using a baseline coming from another container image. Such a link is built using the FROM command in `Dockerfile`:

```
FROM mcr.microsoft.com/hello-world
```

The preceding definition will imply that when an image is built, it should be based on a `hello-world` image available in the `mcr.microsoft.com` registry. Now, base images can (and will) be updated. This is caused by various things:

- New features
- Security patches
- Hotfixes

Normally, you are responsible for monitoring new releases and applying them to your container images. As that kind of activity is rarely considered valuable (it is a repeatable and easy-to-automate task), it is always worth leveraging a solution that can take care of that. This is where base image patches come in handy. To enable that feature in ACR, use the following command:

```
az acr task update --registry myregistry --name mytask --base-
image-trigger-enabled True
```

There are also some additional considerations when using this functionality:

- If you are using multi-stage `Dockerfile` files, updates are only applied for final images.

- Updates work for stable tags only. An update will not be triggered by new tags.

- When creating an ACR using the Azure CLI, the base image trigger is enabled by default. The preceding command should be run only if you created the ACR from the portal or disabled that feature explicitly.

A base image update is a very useful feature of ACR; however, you should consider using it only if base image patches will not trigger any kind of manual process. Many business domains require that artifacts that have reached production environments cannot be mutated. That means that a base image update may render your application noncompliant and enforce starting a release process from the start. If this is not the case for you, you can consider automated patches safe for your process.

Summary

As you can see, Azure Container Registry is a simple service that greatly simplifies the management process of container images and helps store them with ease. In this chapter, you have had a chance to deploy your very own registry and learn something about the main components – repositories and images. We also discussed topics related to the availability of your registry and reliability – zone redundancy and geo-replication. These are the things you should look out for when making your solution production-ready. The next chapter will continue topics related to containers, as we will discuss containerization in web applications.

Questions

1. What is the difference between a registry, a repository, and a tag?
2. Which SKU is required for enabling geo-replication?
3. If ACR is replicated across three different regions, how many instances will you be charged for monthly?
4. Can you build your container image using ACR?
5. What kind of locks are available for container images in ACR?
6. If ACR is removed, will it also delete locked images?
7. What does ACR Tasks do?
8. What is a base image and how can ACR help you keep it updated?

Further reading

- *Azure Container Registry documentation*: `https://docs.microsoft.com/en-us/azure/container-registry/container-registry-intro`

- ACR Tasks documentation: `https://docs.microsoft.com/en-us/azure/container-registry/container-registry-tasks-overview`

- ACR Tasks examples: `https://docs.microsoft.com/en-us/azure/container-registry/container-registry-tasks-samples`

3

Deploying Web Applications as Containers

Containers arc one of *the* hottest topics in the IT industry. They allow for deploying an application in *a box*, so you don't have to worry about the OS your application will run on or the installed services that are required for it. While containers are sometimes criticized for redundant abstraction over underlying resources, they guarantee a stabilized environment for both developing and hosting applications.

In this chapter, we will cover the following topics:

- Different ways of hosting containerized applications

- Azure App Service – a web app for containers

- Azure Kubernetes Service – a managed Kubernetes service

- An introduction to Azure Kubernetes Service, which is a managed Kubernetes service designed to host your applications in a structured way

Technical requirements

To start working with containers in Azure, you will need the following:

- A basic understanding of Docker concepts: `https://docs.docker.com/get-started/`

- A Docker development environment: depending on the OS you are using – `https://docs.docker.com/docker-for-mac/`, `https://docs.docker.com/docker-for-windows/`, or `https://docs.docker.com/install/`

- A Docker Hub account

- The Azure CLI: `https://docs.microsoft.com/en-us/cli/azure/install-azure-cli?view=azure-cli-latest`

- A basic understanding of Kubernetes: `https://kubernetes.io/docs/home/`
- The Kubernetes CLI: `https://kubernetes.io/docs/tasks/tools/install-kubectl/`

Different ways of hosting containerized applications

As already mentioned in the previous chapter, to host a containerized application using any kind of service provider, you will need a container registry. Once a registry is deployed, you can push your images there. This process can be easily visualized with the help of the following diagram:

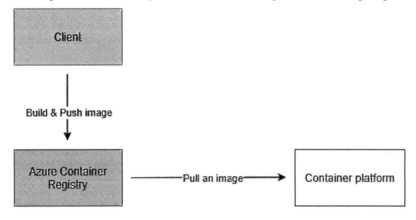

Figure 3.1 – A high-level diagram of a container image life cycle

Once an image is available inside your registry, it can be used by any kind of container platform available on the market, assuming it can authenticate with **Authentication Context Class Reference** (**ACR**). If we consider Azure only, there are several ways to run an application using its container image:

- Using ACR Tasks
- Running an image using Azure Container Instances (to be discussed in *Chapter 4*, *Using Azure Container Instances for Ad Hoc Application Hosting*)
- Deploying a virtual machine with support for running containers and running a container with one of the available options:
  - Installing Docker and pulling images from ACR
  - Pushing your application data along with a Dockerfile to the machine and just using the Docker CLI to run it

- Installing any kind of container platform/orchestrator on a machine and using it to run the application (for example, Kubernetes)

- Using Azure Kubernetes Service

- Using Azure App Service, which can run an application using an image instead of its code

Each of these methods has some pros and cons. We can summarize them using the following table (where green represents the best option, yellow introduces some minor issues, and red constitutes major problems or a lack of key features):

Method	Native	Difficulty	Scalability	Initial cost	Flexibility
ACR Task					
Azure Container Instances					
VM with Docker and ACR					
VM with Docker and code					
VM with container platform					
Azure Kubernetes Service					
Azure App Service					

Figure 3.2 – Different features of various container hosting methods

As you can see, there is not a single method that does not have any kind of flaw. Some of these are bigger (such as the scalability of a virtual machine with code that is way beyond the capabilities of Azure Kubernetes Service) and some are smaller (the flexibility of Azure App Service depends solely on your requirements and often can be addressed by a slightly different application design or the support of an additional Azure service), but ultimately, the choice is yours. You must always apply your business and technical requirements to each of the mentioned services and see what suits you the most.

There are three important factors when hosting web applications using containers:

- What is your scalability target – is this application going to serve tens, hundreds, or thousands of requests in a unit of time?

- What is your deployment method of choice? Are you going to use CI/CD for each of the deployments? How often will deployments be made? Do you need additional checks while deploying code?

- What kind of application do you have? Is it a typical API-like service, a continuously running web job, or a static website?

Now, if you aim for specific characteristics, you must consider how each of the possible solutions will behave when the targeted traffic hits:

- ACR Tasks needs additional orchestration to be able to run multiple containers and, in fact, is not designed to answer any kind of web requests (rendering the whole solution unusable in a web application scenario that needs user/application interaction).

- Azure container instances are mostly used for fire-and-forget scenarios such as performing analysis, data generation, and background tasks. They can easily scale to the desired size though.

- Using a VM gives you the best flexibility (as you govern most of the OS aspects) but it can be cumbersome as it requires infrastructure knowledge (including networking, disks, and firewalls) and often generates lots of technical debt, which is hard to deal with.

- Setting up a container platform can address most of the issues, but it is one of the most difficult tasks to be done properly and is rarely a good solution unless you can really leverage the benefits of that approach.

- Deploying your web application using a managed container platform such as Azure Kubernetes Service is something that is gaining more and more popularity and helps to build a whole ecosystem rapidly and in a business-focused manner. Still, it is not the easiest task as, in most real-world scenarios, you will have to deal with abstraction layers for the underlying infrastructure that have to be understood and applied with care.

- Azure App Service is a safe choice and offers a good balance between flexibility, cost, and required technical knowledge. If you are familiar with web apps in Azure (see *Chapter 1, Web Applications in Azure – Azure App Service*, for more information), there is a huge chance the whole transition will be seamless.

There are also additional options to consider when using Microsoft Azure, but they are mostly connected to virtual machines and often are just an additional layer over currently described solutions. You've probably heard about platforms called service meshes. If you do not know what a service mesh is, here is a short explanation.

Many developed applications consist of multiple services, which communicate with each other. This is often a result of moving from a monolith architecture, where all the parts of the application were the same code base. That kind of fragmented architecture is often called a microservice architecture and can be visualized as follows:

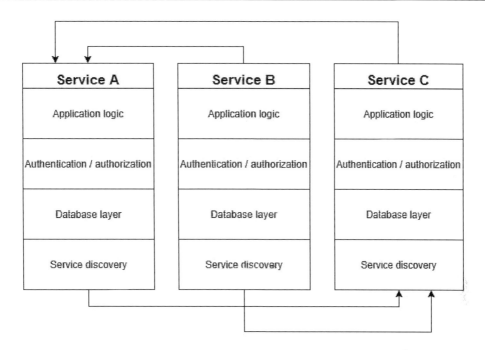

Figure 3.3 – Simple microservices architecture

As you can see, each service can communicate with the others. What's more, each service is built using the same layers, including database access, service discovery, and authentication/authorization logic. For obvious reasons, that method of building an application can become problematic at some point in time:

- Logic duplication forces developers to start building common packages, which quickly become outdated and differ between services.

- Each application implements additional layers for performing common operations, which should be implemented in dedicated services (why does an application perform authorization when its purpose is to push an order into a database?).

- Communication becomes hard to monitor as more and more services are added and they connect with each other chaotically.

Now, let's imagine that each service is a separate container image pushed to our ACR. Containers will help in making hosting much easier as they encapsulate a service ecosystem and can be easily moved between different hosting options. What none of the described solutions solve is the mentioned fragmentation of responsibilities and logic. If your application is already containerized, you can try to leverage the benefits of using service meshes, which will simplify the diagram from *Figure 3.3* to something like this:

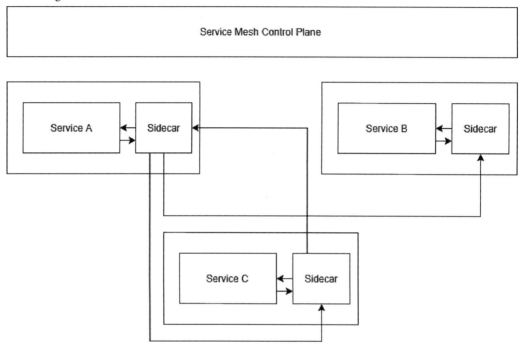

Figure 3.4 – A simple service mesh architecture

To cut a long story short, service meshes change the way services communicate by hosting a thing called a sidecar along with each of the services. Each service has its own sidecar running on the very same host and communicates only with it. Sidecars and service mesh control planes take care of implementing common application logic such as routing, authentication, service discovery, and many, many more. They play very well with containerized applications as most service mesh implementations use either virtual machines or Kubernetes as their host. As Microsoft Azure currently does not offer any kind of managed service mesh, if you want to use it, you will have to install it on your own. There are many different mesh implementations available, but if you want to give it a try, here is a list of the most popular ones:

- Linkerd – `https://linkerd.io/`
- Istio – `https://istio.io/`

- Consul – `https://www.consul.io/`
- Kuma – `https://kuma.io/`

Each of the implementations offers detailed instructions on how to set it up and configure it. If you liked this topic, I encourage you to at least demo one of them. It will give you a better understanding of how service meshes work and what they can offer you.

Azure App Service – a web app for containers

In *Chapter 1*, *Web Applications in Azure – Azure App Services*, we went through the basic configuration of web applications in Azure and discussed ways to deploy them. What we used there was deployment via code – we prepared our application's structure, packaged it, and sent it to Azure App Service. Depending on the deployment choice (whether you are using a simple file deployment or running your application from a package), Azure App Service either just uploaded files to the appropriate directory or used an archive as the source. In this chapter, we will take a little bit of a different approach and deploy our application using a container image.

> **Note**
>
> A prerequisite for this exercise is having an Azure Container Registry deployed. If you do not know how to do that, look at *Chapter 2*, *Using Azure Container Registry for Storing and Managing Images*, where we discussed the process in detail.

Now, let's prepare a simple application for deployment.

Preparing an application

If you are familiar with Docker and any kind of application platform (such as .NET, Java, or Python), you can prepare your very own application and you do not have to follow instructions from this section. I, to keep things simple, will reuse a simple PHP application from *Chapter 1*, *Web Applications in Azure – Azure App Services*, so we can keep track of the important aspects of this exercise.

The first thing we need here is our application code. My application will display a short message once it is run successfully. Its code looks like this and is saved as an `index.php` file:

```php
<?php
echo('Hello world from Azure App Service - PHP here!');
?>
```

As I want to run my application using a container, I will need a Dockerfile, which will containerize it and allow it to be run using any kind of container platform (or in this case, Azure App Service). To run a PHP application inside a container, we will need a PHP base image. You can see it configured in the following Dockerfile:

```
FROM php:8.0-apache
WORKDIR /var/www/html
COPY index.php index.php
EXPOSE 80
```

The above instructions tell Docker to fetch the base PHP image, copy all the files from my working directory to the /usr/src/myapp catalog, and then run PHP from the CLI and pass the index. php file as an argument. You can check whether your Dockerfile is valid by running the docker build command like this:

```
> docker build -t <image-tag> .
```

Depending on your internet connection and the availability of the base image locally, the process may take either several seconds or a few minutes. Be patient – Docker will inform you about all the intermediary steps:

```
D:\TheCloudTheory\HandsOnAzure2.0\Chapter03-code>docker build -t handsonbook-php .
[+] Building 73.7s (8/8) FINISHED
 => [internal] load build definition from Dockerfile                                          0.2s
 => => transferring dockerfile: 129B                                                          0.0s
 => [internal] load .dockerignore                                                             0.2s
 => => transferring context: 2B                                                               0.0s
 => [internal] load metadata for docker.io/library/php:7.4-cli                                3.1s
 => [internal] load build context                                                             0.1s
 => => transferring context: 233B                                                             0.0s
 => [1/3] FROM docker.io/library/php:7.4-cli@sha256:996584aab9a84e53a108d07b183337e0fc50db0beeccca4d41861c5808245223   68.9s
 => => resolve docker.io/library/php:7.4-cli@sha256:996584aab9a84e53a108d07b183337e0fc50db0beeccca4d41861c5808245223   0.0s
 => => sha256:996584aab9a84e53a108d07b183337e0fc50db0beeccca4d41861c5808245223 1.86kB / 1.86kB   0.0s
 => => sha256:52f72d0d748e15d7ababd74a7f35c125fa3aeb8643999bc2849f7b47ef98bae2 2.20kB / 2.20kB   0.0s
 => => sha256:3e0132e4596301353d36b3152d4ba951febddd6b81f1a49c9e0bb621c133a31c 9.81kB / 9.81kB   0.0s
 => => sha256:99046ad9247f8a1cbd1048d9099d026191ad9cda63c08aadeb704b7000a51717 31.36MB / 31.36MB   21.4s
 => => sha256:3875fa64ab1e7ef45b19c31db513b33dd704aead9360fc096cbf4831311233d8 229B / 229B       0.7s
 => => sha256:e9329a8f553a5ecad9cc838034.7dffa88323f980abc0b3698b7ab3ccf1f8c0dc 91.61MB / 91.61MB   58.1s
 => => sha256:9bb327f9b0a4fafe951989e97bdefa22796c2829e0f0d668ff0638958d826f47 270B / 270B       1.5s
```

Figure 3.5 – Building a Docker image locally

You can also use the docker run command to check how a container behaves:

```
> docker run -it --rm --name <container-name> <image-tag>
```

If everything is correct, you should see a result similar to mine:

```
D:\TheCloudTheory\HandsOnAzure2.0\Chapter03-code>docker run -it --rm --name my-running-app handsonbook-php
AH00558: apache2: Could not reliably determine the server's fully qualified domain name, using 172.17.0.2. Set the
 'ServerName' directive globally to suppress this message
AH00558: apache2: Could not reliably determine the server's fully qualified domain name, using 172.17.0.2. Set the
 'ServerName' directive globally to suppress this message
[Fri Dec 10 11:08:34.036935 2021] [mpm_prefork:notice] [pid 1] AH00163: Apache/2.4.51 (Debian) PHP/8.0.13 configur
ed -- resuming normal operations
[Fri Dec 10 11:08:34.036987 2021] [core:notice] [pid 1] AH00094: Command line: 'apache2 -D FOREGROUND'
```

Figure 3.6 – Running a container locally

Now, as everything seems to work locally, we need to prepare our image to be pushed to ACR. To do that, we will need to make an alias for our image. That can be done easily with the docker tag command:

```
> docker tag <current-tag> <login-server><target-tag>
```

In my case, as I named my image handsonbook-php, the command will look like this:

```
> docker tag handsonbook-php handsonbookacr.azurecr.io/
handsonbook-php
```

Note the prefix I added to the target image name – it is a parameter called login server, which can be found in your ACR. To get it, go to the Azure portal and find your ACR instance. **Login server** will be available on the **Overview** blade:

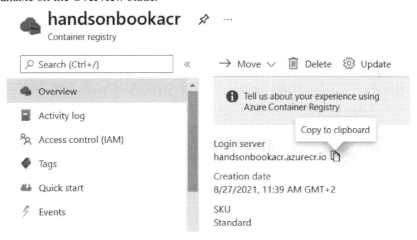

Figure 3.7 – Login server parameter

It can be also fetched using the Azure CLI:

```
> az acr show -g <resource-group> -n <acr-name>
```

Once you run the command, search for the `loginServer` parameter:

```
D:\TheCloudTheory\HandsOnAzure2.0\Chapter03-code>az acr show -g handsonbook-rg -n handsonbookacr
{
  "adminUserEnabled": false,
  "creationDate": "2021-08-27T09:39:17.405716+00:00",
  "dataEndpointEnabled": false,
  "dataEndpointHostNames": [],
  "encryption": {
    "keyVaultProperties": null,
    "status": "disabled"
  },
  "id": "/subscriptions/58ac7037-efcc-4fb6-800d-da6ca2ee6aed/resourceGroups/handsonbook-rg/providers/Microsoft.
es/handsonbookacr",
  "identity": null,
  "location": "westeurope",
  "loginServer": "handsonbookacr.azurecr.io",
  "name": "handsonbookacr",
  "networkRuleSet": null,
```

Figure 3.8 – Finding the loginServer name parameter with the Azure CLI

Let's now create an alias. Prepending the local tag with the name of your login server is required for Docker, so it knows to which server to push an image:

```
D:\TheCloudTheory\HandsOnAzure2.0\Chapter03-code>docker tag handsonbook-php handsonbookacr.azurecr.io/handsonbook-php

D:\TheCloudTheory\HandsOnAzure2.0\Chapter03-code>docker images
REPOSITORY                                    TAG       IMAGE ID       CREATED         SIZE
handsonbook-php                               latest    912d9a50fd35   16 minutes ago  482MB
handsonbookacr.azurecr.io/handsonbook-php     latest    912d9a50fd35   16 minutes ago  482MB
```

Figure 3.9 – Creating an alias for an image and verification

As you can see, immediately after creating an alias, I used the `docker images` command to verify whether a new alias was created. Now we can finally push our image to ACR. To do that, we will simply use the `docker push` command:

```
D:\TheCloudTheory\HandsOnAzure2.0\Chapter03-code>docker push handsonbookacr.azurecr.io/handsonbook-php
Using default tag: latest
The push refers to repository [handsonbookacr.azurecr.io/handsonbook-php]
5f70bf18a086: Preparing
616349049988: Preparing
ce206ca58caa: Preparing
14ce15acd3bf: Preparing
dce8e16cae11: Preparing
e4026e55b209: Waiting
4abcc40aac09: Waiting
6a1a85624e65: Waiting
17f7b8d2829b: Waiting
6e857a211875: Waiting
300b011056d9: Waiting
unauthorized: authentication required, visit https://aka.ms/acr/authorization for more information.
```

Figure 3.10 – Pushing an image to ACR if not authenticated

Unfortunately, the whole process finished with an error – it seems we are not authenticated and ACR rejects such a request. To authenticate, we can use one of the following methods:

- Use `az acr login`
- Use `docker login`

The commands look like this – this is the first one:

```
> az acr login --name <acr-name>
```

And this is the Docker one:

```
> docker login <acr-name>
```

Both will give you the same result, so it is up to you which one to choose. Personally, I always go for the first one using the Azure CLI:

```
D:\TheCloudTheory\HandsOnAzure2.0\Chapter03-code>az acr login --name handsonbookacr
Login Succeeded
```

Figure 3.11 – Successful ACR login

Now, let's try to run `docker push` once again. With ACR authenticated, we should be able to finally push our image:

```
D:\TheCloudTheory\HandsOnAzure2.0\Chapter03-code>docker push handsonbookacr.azurecr.io/handsonbook-php
Using default tag: latest
The push refers to repository [handsonbookacr.azurecr.io/handsonbook-php]
5f70bf18a086: Pushed
616349049988: Pushed
ce206ca58caa: Pushed
14ce15acd3bf: Pushed
dce8e16cae11: Pushed
e4026e55b209: Pushed
4abcc40aac09: Pushed
6a1a85624e65: Pushed
17f7b8d2829b: Pushed
6e857a211875: Pushed
300b011056d9: Pushed
latest: digest: sha256:d87cc5ec0cf7941405ef4617448d5f676566f4899b64866db86d07230ff29e3c size: 2614
```

Figure 3.12 – Container image successfully pushed to ACR

With a container image pushed, we can now create an Azure app service, which will use that image as the application source.

Using a container image in an Azure App Service plan

Go to the Azure portal and click the + **Create a resource** button, and then go and find **Web App** in the marketplace:

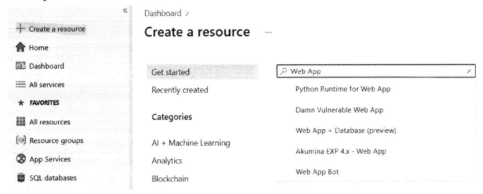

Figure 3.13 – Searching for Web App in Azure Marketplace

Fill in the **Project Details** section as described in *Chapter 1, Web Applications in Azure – Azure App Services*, and then go to the **Instance Details** section. There, set the **Publish** parameter to **Docker Container**:

Instance Details

Need a database? Try the new Web + Database experience. ☐

Name *	handsonbook-docker ✓
	.azurewebsites.net
Publish *	○ Code ⦿ Docker Container
Operating System *	⦿ Linux ○ Windows
Region *	West Europe ∨
	❶ Not finding your App Service Plan? Try a different region.

Figure 3.14 – Configuring Web App to run from a container

The rest of the parameters can be configured as you want as they do not affect how a container is run.

> **Tip**
>
> If you need help configuring the rest of the parameters on the **Basics** tab, refer to *Chapter 1, Web Applications in Azure – Azure App Services*. There, you have all the parameters explained in detail.

Note that once you have selected **Docker Container**, there is a new tab available named **Docker**. Once everything from the **Basics** tab is ready, click the **Next : Docker** button:

Review + create   < Previous   Next : Docker >

Figure 3.15 – Docker tab button

From the **Docker** tab, you will gain access to the Web App configuration related to running an application using a container image. Change the image source to **Azure Container Registry** and select the registry where your image is stored.

> **Tip**
>
> Accessing ACR from Azure App Service requires an admin account enabled for ACR, which is disabled by default. To enable it, see the following article from the documentation: https://docs.microsoft.com/en-us/azure/container-registry/container-registry-authentication?tabs=azure-cli#admin-account. If your Azure Container Registry does not have this option enabled, you need to follow the previous link and restart the creation wizard.

The default parameters for the **Docker** tab should suffice. The final configuration on your side should look like mine:

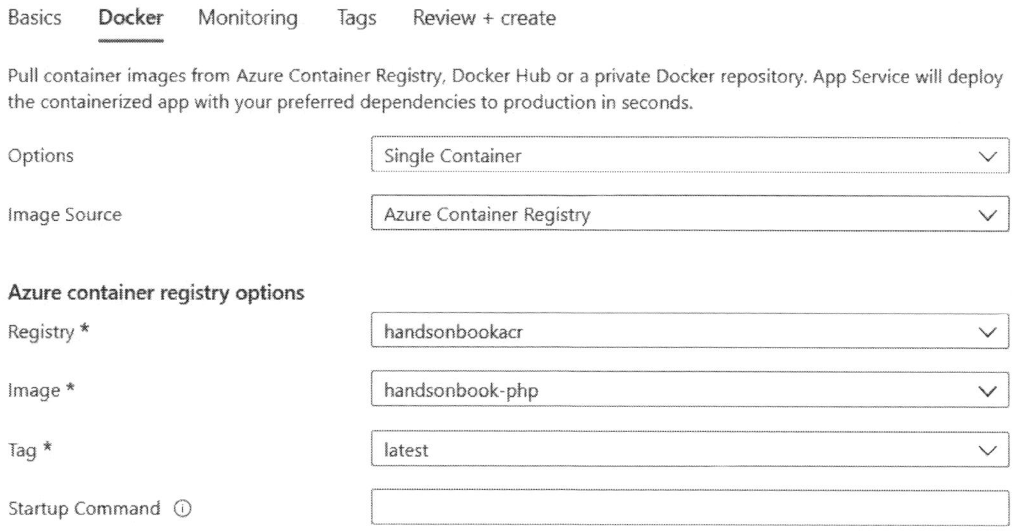

Basics   **Docker**   Monitoring   Tags   Review + create

Pull container images from Azure Container Registry, Docker Hub or a private Docker repository. App Service will deploy the containerized app with your preferred dependencies to production in seconds.

Options	Single Container	⌄
Image Source	Azure Container Registry	⌄

Azure container registry options

Registry *	handsonbookacr	⌄
Image *	handsonbook-php	⌄
Tag *	latest	⌄
Startup Command ⓘ		

Figure 3.16 – Docker configuration for Azure App Service

Now you can click the **Review + create** button and run the final validation and then click on **Create**. The process of provisioning your application will begin and you will have to wait a moment for it to finish. Once it is completed, you can go and try to access your website to see whether it works.

When running a containerized application, you can find Azure App Service in the portal and access the **Deployment Center** blade and then the **Logs** tab:

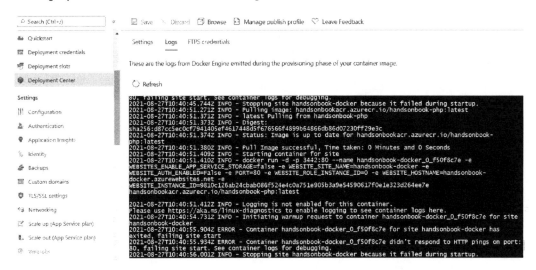

Figure 3.17 – Logs from a container run by Azure App Service

The first run can take some time as Azure App Service needs to download and run a container based on the image fetched from ACR. In this section, we prepared an application that uses Apache as a web server for handling requests. This is a case for languages such as PHP, while other platforms, such as .NET or Java, do not have such a problem with running from Docker images as they often bundle a server with the framework code and allow you to run an application directly from the CLI. The only thing needed here is to provide the link to your application code.

In the last part of this chapter, we will talk a little about Azure Kubernetes Service and how it can be used to run a web application in a container.

Azure Kubernetes Service – a managed Kubernetes service

So far, we have discussed different ways of hosting containerized applications, such as Azure Virtual Machines and Azure App Service. While they provide a set of functionalities that should address most requirements, they lack one key feature, which is important in a real-world scenario – orchestration. It is difficult to orchestrate the deployment of multiple services and arrange communication between them. They also rarely offer optimal hosting density – using virtual machines allows you to utilize their capacity in a way you expect, but this requires custom code and lots of expertise. Azure App Services is designed to host a monolith rather than a set of interconnected services. This is where platforms such as Kubernetes come in handy – they cover all the underlying layers responsible for common tasks such as ingress, partitioning, and intra-service communication, and allow you to focus on building your ecosystem in line with your business requirements. In this section, you will learn about basic Kubernetes concepts and the features of managed clusters.

Kubernetes and managed cluster basics

Kubernetes itself is a cloud-agnostic tool, which can also be run using an on-premises infrastructure. So, if you have access to a set of virtual or physical machines, you can use them to run a Kubernetes cluster. The high-level architecture of such a cluster may look like this:

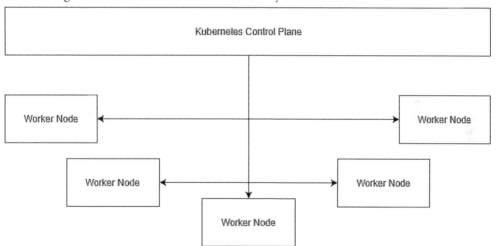

Figure 3.18 – High-level Kubernetes architecture

A standard Kubernetes installation consists of a control plane and a set of worker nodes. The control plane is responsible for controlling the whole cluster – the availability and connectivity of worker nodes, scaling the cluster up and down, and the management tasks. Worker nodes are the actual workers in your cluster – they run your application code and scale services as per their definitions. This setup comes with a few things to consider:

- If you want to have a highly available cluster, you must replicate your control plane. Worker nodes do not have to be replicated as they are only used to run application code and it is up to the application's definition to decide how many copies of it should be available.

- Control plane configuration and management operations are critical for the stability of your cluster. If you do not have experience with that, you may easily render the whole cluster unavailable.

- The security of the control plane is crucial so that all applications can run in a safe environment. Again, this requires prior knowledge and experience and it is better if it is done by Kubernetes experts.

Because of all the things mentioned, it is easier (and safer) to use a managed installation of Kubernetes such as Azure Kubernetes Service.

> **Note**
> Bare metal and unmanaged installations of Kubernetes are still viable for all applications, which require a higher level of security, isolation, or very strict networking policies. If you do not want to use managed Kubernetes in Azure, you can use a fully customized installation on Azure Virtual Machines or aks-engine as a way to provision a self-managed cluster.

In Azure Kubernetes Service, responsibility for the control plane is moved to your cloud provider:

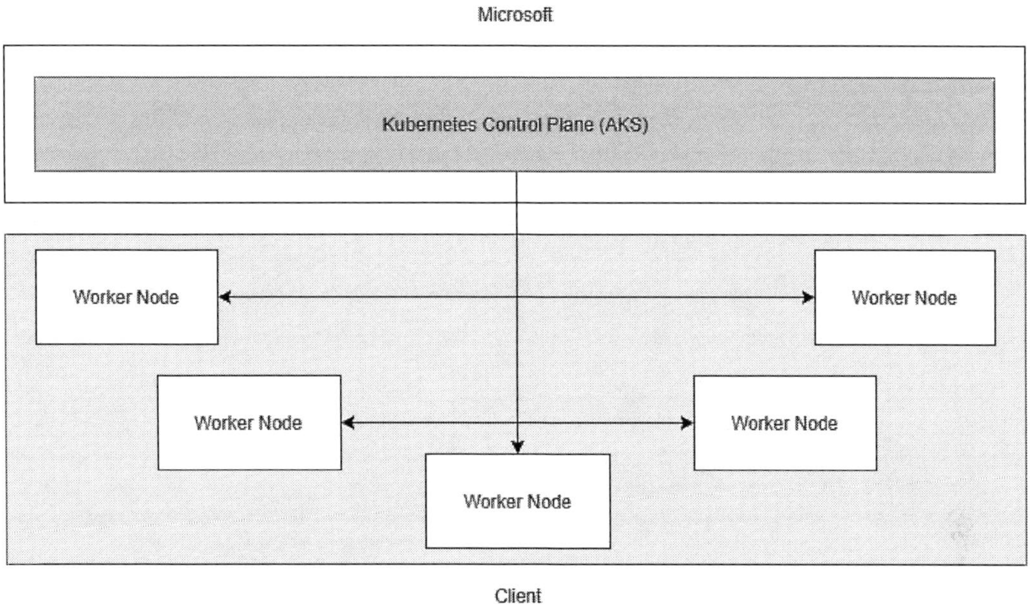

Microsoft

Client

Figure 3.19 – Azure Kubernetes Service responsibilities

Your responsibility will be the management of worker nodes. The control plane will still be available to you, but not physically – you can manage it via tools such as kubectl, but cannot alter anything regarding its infrastructure. Also, the only way of scaling your cluster will be adding or removing worker nodes – you do not have access to change the number of nodes used by the control plane.

> **Note**
>
> In Azure Kubernetes Service, you pay only for your worker nodes – the pricing for that service does not include the cost of the control plane, which is free of charge.

Let's now see how to set up your first cluster and deploy an application to it.

Azure Kubernetes Service deployment

To deploy a cluster, we will use the Azure portal to describe all the steps in detail. In the portal, click the **+ Create a resource** button and search for `Kubernetes service`, as shown in the following screenshot:

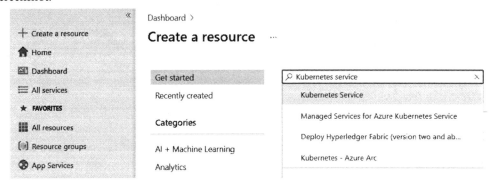

Figure 3.20 – Searching for Kubernetes service in Azure Marketplace

Click on the highlighted position and then proceed to the resource creation wizard. You will see a common resource creation layout, where we can enter all the required parameters. In the **Project details** section, enter the subscription and resource group, which will be used as the landing zone for our Kubernetes cluster:

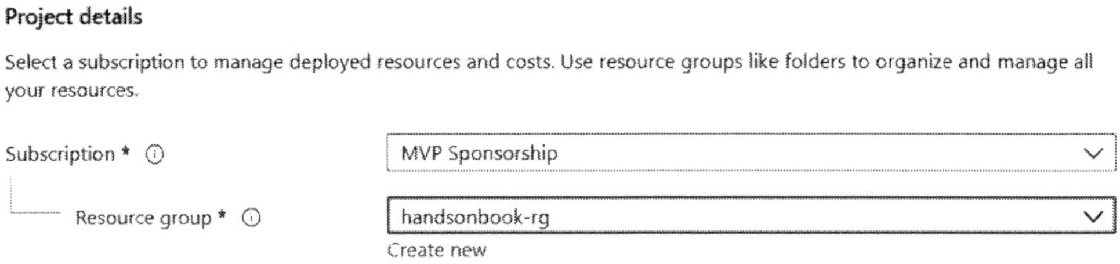

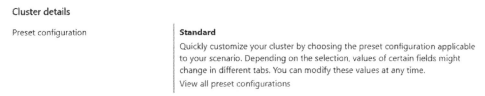

Figure 3.21 – Project details

Now, in the **Cluster details** section, click on **View all preset configurations**. This will display a screen that can be used to quickly configure the most common settings:

Cluster details

Preset configuration

Standard

Quickly customize your cluster by choosing the preset configuration applicable to your scenario. Depending on the selection, values of certain fields might change in different tabs. You can modify these values at any time.

View all preset configurations

Figure 3.22 – Preset configurations

From the displayed list, select **Dev/Test** and click the **Apply** button. We do not need additional features of the rest of the available presets for now – you can learn more about them later by reading the Azure Kubernetes Service documentation:

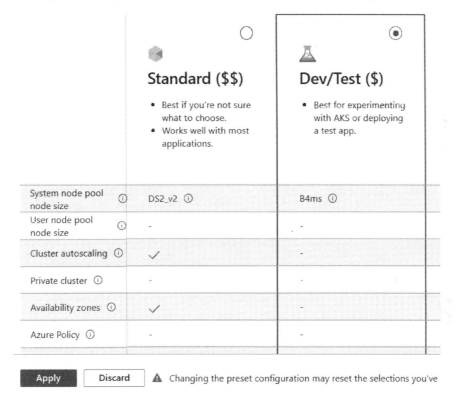

Create Kubernetes cluster   ...

Choose your scenario to view and apply the recommended configurations suited to your needs. The se will be updated to the specified values based on your selection. All other cluster settings will remain un

	Standard ($$) · Best if you're not sure what to choose. · Works well with most applications.	Dev/Test ($) · Best for experimenting with AKS or deploying a test app.
System node pool node size	DS2_v2	B4ms
User node pool node size	-	-
Cluster autoscaling	✓	-
Private cluster	-	-
Availability zones	✓	-
Azure Policy	-	-

Apply   **Discard**   ⚠ Changing the preset configuration may reset the selections you've

Figure 3.23 – Selecting the Dev/Test preset

Selecting a preset will set most of the parameters to some default values. The only thing left here is entering our cluster's location and its name. Here you can find my configurations:

Cluster details

Preset configuration	**Dev/test**
	Quickly customize your cluster by choosing the preset configuration applicable to your scenario. Depending on the selection, values of certain fields might change in different tabs. You can modify these values at any time.
	View all preset configurations

Kubernetes cluster name * ⓘ	handsonbook-aks ✓
Region * ⓘ	(Europe) West Europe ⌄
Availability zones ⓘ	None ⌄
Kubernetes version * ⓘ	1.20.7 (default) ⌄

Figure 3.24 – Cluster configuration

Now go and click the **Review + create** button for the final confirmation and complete it by clicking on **Create**. This will initialize the process of cluster creation, which may take a few minutes.

> **Note**
> To keep things simple, we are not diving into the more advanced configuration parameters of Azure Kubernetes Service and are skipping most of the non-default settings. To learn more about those service capabilities, look at the *Further reading* section at the end of this chapter.

Once our cluster is provisioned, we can prepare our application for deployment.

Application deployment

To deploy an application to the Kubernetes cluster, we will need a bunch of things:

- Application code
- Dockerfile
- Azure Container Registry (or any other kind of registry that can be integrated with Kubernetes)
- Application definition for Kubernetes

For the sake of this chapter, we will focus on describing the steps required to build your application configuration and all the deployment components. We will use a simple static HTML page to display hello text for a user.

Here is the code for our static HTML page:

```
<!DOCTYPE html>
<head>
    <title>HandsOnBook 2.0</title>
</head>
<body>
    Hello from AKS!
</body>
```

As you can see, once deployed, it should display **Hello from AKS!** as our welcome text. Save it as `index.html` for further use. To host such a static website, we will need a web server. There are plenty of different options available (which one you choose depends on your technology stack, experience, and technical requirements) and in fact, most of them can handle our page. To keep things simple, we will go for NGINX.

As Azure Kubernetes Service hosts containerized applications, we will prepare a Dockerfile, which should allow us to build an image running the NGINX server with our static HTML file attached to it. Our Dockerfile will be as simple as this:

```
FROM nginx:alpine
COPY . /usr/share/nginx/html
```

As you can see, it will perform two steps:

- Build an image from a base NGINX image
- Copy all the files from the working directory to the appropriate NGINX directory

Now, let me remind you how to utilize such an image and push it to Azure Container Registry. To do that, we need a compiled image prefixed with our Azure Container Registry login server.

> **Tip**
> If you do not remember how to find your login server, take a look at the *Azure App Service – a web app for containers* section earlier in this chapter.

Let's use the Docker CLI to build a Docker image using a tag, which will allow us to push it to our registry:

```
D:\TheCloudTheory\HandsOnAzure2.0\Chapter03-code\aks>docker build -t handsonbookacr.azurecr.io/handsonhtml .
[+] Building 12.4s (7/7) FINISHED
 => [internal] load build definition from Dockerfile
 => => transferring dockerfile: 84B
 => [internal] load .dockerignore
 => => transferring context: 2B
 => [internal] load metadata for docker.io/library/nginx:alpine
 => [internal] load build context
```

Figure 3.25 – Building a Docker image with a prefixed login server

Now, we can use the following command to test our web server locally:

```
> docker run -d -p 80:80 <your-tag>
```

With the preceding command executed, you should be able to access the local server using the `http://localhost:80` address in your internet browser. Note that, here, we have two ports – one is for the machine where a container is run, while the other is for the container itself. In other words, the command tells Docker to expose container port `80` using port `80` on the local machine (the first port is related to the container). Once you access the link, seeing our welcome text means everything is correct:

Figure 3.26 – NGINX working locally

Let's finish our container image setup by pushing it to our Azure Container Registry instance:

```
> docker push <your-tag>
```

After a moment, your image should be pushed to your registry and be available for further use:

```
D:\TheCloudTheory\HandsOnAzure2.0\Chapter03-code\aks>docker push handsonbookacr.azurecr.io/handsonhtml
Using default tag: latest
The push refers to repository [handsonbookacr.azurecr.io/handsonhtml]
b24bd2b8a0ec: Pushed
45d993692050: Pushed
1ea998b95474: Pushed
95b99a5c3767: Pushed
fc03e3cb8568: Pushed
24934e5e6c61: Pushed
e2eb06d8af82: Pushed
latest: digest: sha256:5216c6d49d36814042eb567c9b2ff048230fcbb574b11f5059d74e22956ccfb6 size: 1775
```

Figure 3.27 – A successfully pushed container image

> **Note**
>
> While pushing, if you get an authentication required error, ensure you are logged in to your registry by using the `az acr login` command.

The last step before pushing our application to Azure Kubernetes Service is to build its Kubernetes definition. We will need two components here:

- Deployment, describing what we are trying to host
- Service, which will expose our application to public access

We will combine the whole definition in a single file called `aks.yaml`. Here you can find how it should look:

```yaml
apiVersion: apps/v1
kind: Deployment
metadata:
  name: handsonazure-html
spec:
  replicas: 1
  selector:
    matchLabels:
      app: handsonazure-html
  strategy:
    rollingUpdate:
      maxSurge: 1
      maxUnavailable: 1
  minReadySeconds: 5
```

```
    template:
      metadata:
        labels:
          app: handsonazure-html
      spec:
        nodeSelector:
          "beta.kubernetes.io/os": linux
        containers:
        - name: handsonazure-html
          image: handsonbookacr.azurecr.io/handsonhtml
          ports:
          - containerPort: 80
          resources:
            requests:
              cpu: 250m
            limits:
              cpu: 500m
---
apiVersion: v1
kind: Service
metadata:
  name: handsonazure-html
spec:
  type: LoadBalancer
  ports:
  - port: 80
  selector:
    app: handsonazure-html
```

To deploy it, we will use the kubectl tool, but there is one additional step required here to finish our exercise. kubectl is based on a cluster context to authenticate with a control plane – unfortunately, we do not have any context yet for our Azure Kubernetes Service cluster. To get it, use the following command:

```
> az aks get-credentials -g <resource-group> -n <aks-cluster-
name>
```

The result of running it will look like this:

```
D:\TheCloudTheory\HandsOnAzure2.0\Chapter03-code\aks>az aks get-credentials -g handsonbook-rg -n handsonbook-aks
Merged "handsonbook-aks" as current context in C:\Users\kamil\.kube\config
```

Figure 3.28 – Getting a cluster context

Now let's use kubectl to deploy our application:

```
D:\TheCloudTheory\HandsOnAzure2.0\Chapter03-code\aks>kubectl apply -f aks.yaml
deployment.apps/handsonazure-html created
service/handsonazure-html created
```

Figure 3.29 – Deploying the definition using kubectl

While the deployment is orchestrated right away, getting a public IP address for your service may take a while. To see its configuration, use the following command:

```
D:\TheCloudTheory\HandsOnAzure2.0\Chapter03-code\aks>kubectl get service handsonazure-html --watch
NAME                 TYPE           CLUSTER-IP     EXTERNAL-IP    PORT(S)        AGE
handsonazure-html    LoadBalancer   10.0.166.47    20.101.14.78   80:31839/TCP   51s
```

Figure 3.30 – Getting a Kubernetes service using the –watch switch

Using –watch will give you updates each time a new value is added to the service. Wait until the EXTERNAL-IP column shows a value. Once you get it, you can use it to access your application. However, it is quite possible that you may get no response from those addresses. This is caused by the fact that Azure Kubernetes Service is unable to authenticate to Azure Container Registry. The easiest way to fix that is by updating your cluster with your registry name:

```
az aks update --name <your-aks-name> --resource-group
<resource-group> --attach-acr <acr-name>
```

Running it will add a new role to your registry level for your cluster so it is able to pull images from it.

> **Note**
>
> You may face some issues when using the above command related to your Azure permissions. If you lack authorization for managing roles, the command will probably end with an error. In that scenario, either elevate your permissions or ask your Azure administrator for help.

Once the update is ready, run your deployment once again to restart your Pod. Now you should be able to access your application:

Figure 3.31 – Static HTML site with NGINX running on Kubernetes

As you can see, deploying and running a simple web application is a piece of cake in Azure when using a managed Kubernetes cluster. Of course, it was just a demo – Kubernetes was made to run much more advanced workloads and we just scratched the surface of that service. There are many additional objects to learn about and configurations to do if you want to have a cluster that is production-ready. To learn more about all the other features of Azure Kubernetes Service, look at the *Further reading* section.

Summary

As you saw, when working with containers in Azure, you can focus on the delivery and shape of your application rather than the configuration or maintenance. Of course, available features are not limited to those we covered in this chapter—you can also leverage functionalities such as continuous deployment, networking, or data volumes. Nonetheless, containers are one of the most popular topics of recent months and it is quite possible that building and evolving that skill will help you in your future projects.

In the next chapter, you will learn a bit about another service that allows you to build your very own search engine – Azure Cognitive Search.

Questions

1.   What are the options for hosting containerized applications in Azure?

2.   Can you run your own Kubernetes cluster in Azure?

3.   Are you paying for the control plane in Azure Kubernetes Service?

4.   How can you push an image to Azure Container Registry from your computer?

5.   What do you have to do if AKS cannot authenticate to your instance of Azure Container Registry?

Further reading

- Azure Kubernetes Service documentation: `https://docs.microsoft.com/en-us/azure/aks/`.

- Configuring a custom container in Azure App Service: `https://docs.microsoft.com/en-us/azure/app-service/configure-custom-container?pivots=container-linux`.

- Kubernetes documentation: `https://kubernetes.io/`.

4

Using Azure Container Instances for Ad Hoc Application Hosting

Let's assume your application is containerized. You are looking for hosting options and see that in Microsoft Azure you can use a managed Kubernetes cluster, an App Service plan, or a **virtual machine** (**VM**). All these options will serve your needs; still, they may be too complicated for your case. What if you need a simple service that would take your container, run it, and charge you only for the time it was used? Fortunately, we have **Azure Container Instances** – a simple solution for hosting and running containers only if you need them.

In this chapter, you will learn about the following:

- Provisioning and configuring a service
- Container groups as the main unit of work
- Security baseline and considerations

Technical requirements

To perform the exercises in this chapter, you will need the following:

- Access to an Azure subscription
- Visual Studio Code installed (available at `https://code.visualstudio.com/`)
- Azure CLI (`https://docs.microsoft.com/en-us/cli/azure/`)
- Docker (`https://www.docker.com/get-started`)

Provisioning and configuring a service

As you saw in the previous chapters, provisioning a service in Azure is a matter of choosing the right method. The easiest path is using the Azure portal, which has a graphical interface and various guidelines. You could also use a **command-line interface (CLI)** (the Azure CLI and Azure PowerShell are good choices) or deploy via an **Infrastructure-as-Code (IaC)** solution – it depends on your experience and current need. To deploy Azure Container Instances, we will initially use the Azure portal and, in further exercises, switch to the Azure CLI.

In the Azure portal, locate the + **Create a resource** button, click on it to access the marketplace, and search for `container instances`:

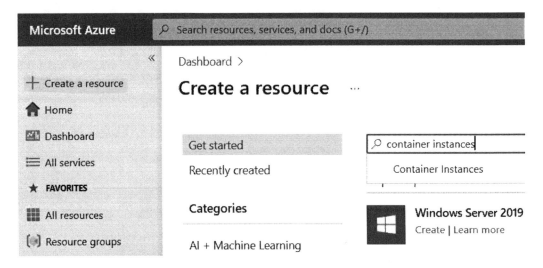

Figure 4.1 – Searching for Azure Container Instances in Azure Marketplace

Select the displayed position (**Container Instances**) and then click on **Create**. You will see a wizard for service creation in which you will be able to enter all the details. You should already be familiar with the **Project details** section; therefore, we will not cover it here (if you want the details, see *Chapter 1, Web Applications in Azure – Azure App Service*). As of now, we are interested in the **Container details** section. We will have to provide the following information:

- **Container name**: The name of our Azure Container Instance
- **Region**: Where the service will be deployed
- **Image source**: Where our image is stored (you may find that option just like hosting a container using Azure App Service)
- **Image**: The image that will be used in our container instance
- **Size**: The compute resources our container is expected to consume

In the following screenshot, you can see the values I used for this exercise:

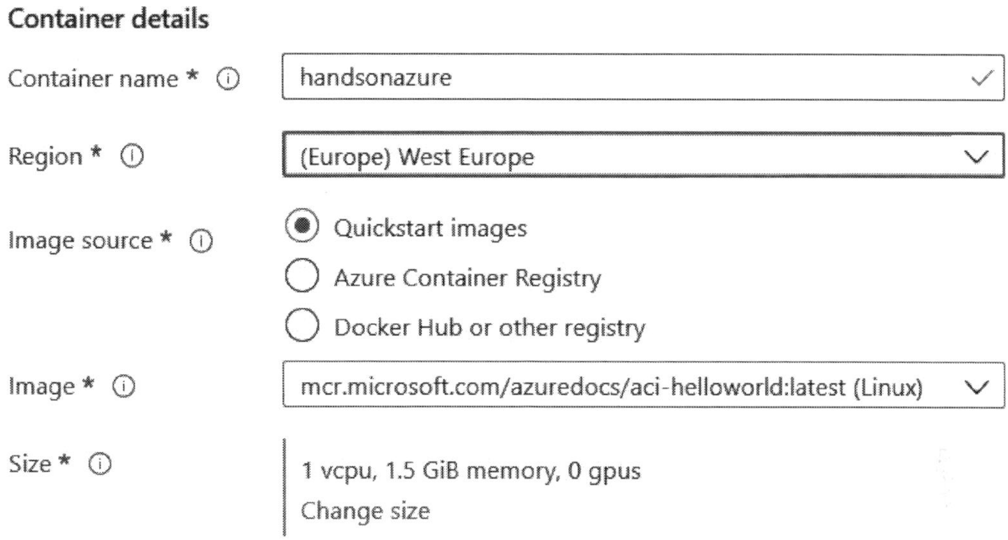

Container details

Container name * ⓘ   handsonazure ✓

Region * ⓘ   (Europe) West Europe ⌄

Image source * ⓘ
  ⦿ Quickstart images
  ○ Azure Container Registry
  ○ Docker Hub or other registry

Image * ⓘ   mcr.microsoft.com/azuredocs/aci-helloworld:latest (Linux) ⌄

Size * ⓘ   1 vcpu, 1.5 GiB memory, 0 gpus
         Change size

Figure 4.2 – Example container details

As you can see, my example uses a Quickstart image (currently, you have three different images to choose from). However, switching to other source options will render new fields in the creator. For example, if you use **Azure Container Registry**, you will have the option to select a registry to fetch an image from:

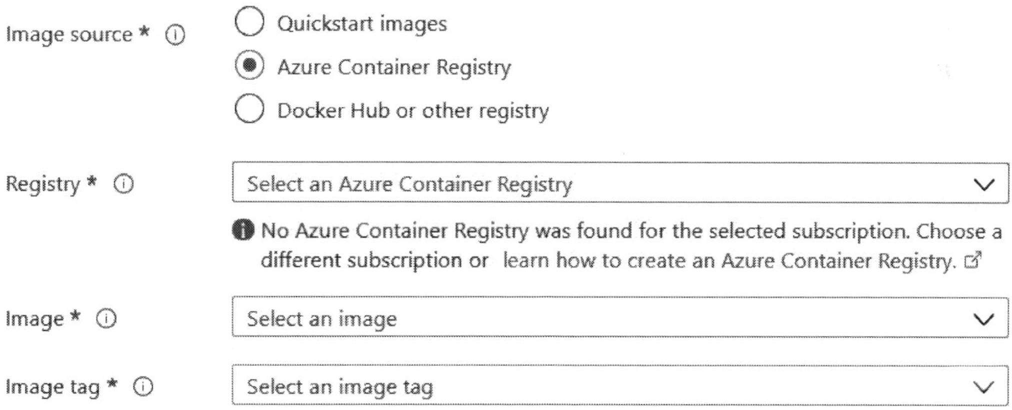

Image source * ⓘ
  ○ Quickstart images
  ⦿ Azure Container Registry
  ○ Docker Hub or other registry

Registry * ⓘ   Select an Azure Container Registry ⌄

ⓘ No Azure Container Registry was found for the selected subscription. Choose a different subscription or learn how to create an Azure Container Registry. ☐

Image * ⓘ   Select an image ⌄

Image tag * ⓘ   Select an image tag ⌄

Figure 4.3 – Different creator view when Azure Container Registry is selected

If your image has additional tags, you will also be able to select the appropriate image. The same situation happens if the **Docker Hub** option is selected:

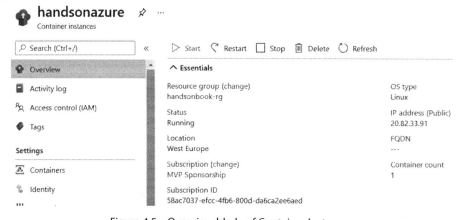

Image source *   ⓘ
- ◯ Quickstart images
- ◯ Azure Container Registry
- ⦿ Docker Hub or other registry

Image type *   ⓘ
- ⦿ Public   ◯ Private

Image *   ⓘ

> Example: mydockerregistry/hello-world

> ❶ If not specified, Docker Hub will be used for the container registry and the latest version of the image will be pulled.

OS type *
- ⦿ Linux   ◯ Windows

> ❶ This selection must match the OS of the image chosen above.

Figure 4.4 – The options when Docker Hub (or another registry) is selected

Depending on the **Image type** option selected, you may need to enter additional details required for authentication. Once you have filled in all the details, click the **Review + create** button at the bottom of the page. After confirming all the details, you can go to your service.

Let's describe the **Overview** blade of the **Container instances** instance. As you can see, it gives you information about things such as the operating system used for your container, the public IP address, the number of containers, and its **Fully Qualified Domain Name (FQDN)**. If you have running containers, you will also see updated metrics telling you the current CPU and memory usage.

Figure 4.5 – Overview blade of Container Instances

However, service usage may be empty as our container is just starting. To check if everything is up and running, go to the **Containers** blade:

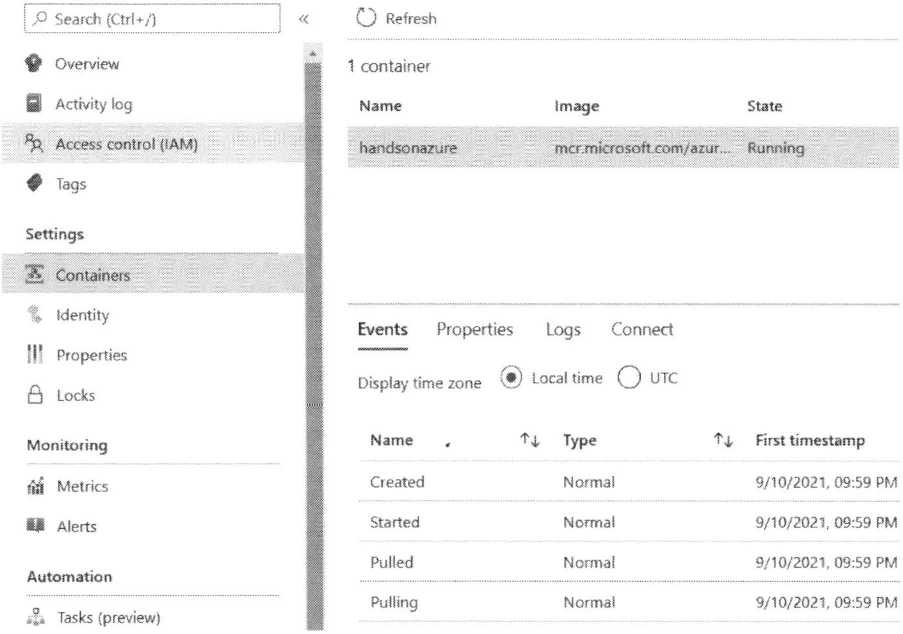

Figure 4.6 – Containers blade

As you can see, the Azure portal displays the full lifetime of our container. Container Instances automatically pull an image and then attempt to start it.

> **Note**
> *Figure 4.6* shows you events that occurred while running a Quickstart image. You might have noticed that the **Started** event happened before the **Created** event. It is a small bug in the Azure portal, which sorts events by timestamp and then by name. If the timestamp is the same, then the order of events may be wrong.

It is worth mentioning that once you have configured Container Instances to run a container from a selected image, you will not be able to change it. Any changes required to the container image force you to recreate the whole instance and start from the beginning. This is a downside of running containers using this service – it is a one-way ticket and if you make a mistake (for example, provision Container Instances to run an outdated image tag), you must start from the beginning. However, remember that this setup is made by design – Container Instances cover *fire-and-forget* scenarios where you just want to execute a container, gather results (if any), and then destroy the provisioned infrastructure. As everything happens behind the scenes, you can focus on more important tasks and let Azure do the work.

Let's now learn something about container groups, which are the main unit of work in Container Instances.

Container groups as the main unit of work

When running containers in Container Instances, you always have two options:

- Run a single container for one job.
- Deploy a group of containers, which are specialized in more complex tasks and allow you to partition your work.

The group of containers in Container Instances is called a **container group**. You may think about it as a single unit of work – all the containers in a group share CPU, memory, network, and storage. They work as a single unit and are destroyed in the same moment as each other. There are two ways to deploy a container group:

- Deploy your IaC (using, for example, **Azure Resource Manager** templates or Bicep files) and include a container group there.
- Use a YAML file that contains the definition of your container group.

In this chapter, we will focus on using YAML as this is a more concise and native way of deploying containers (which, in fact, is very similar to Kubernetes deployments). Deploying a container group is extremely simple – you just need a single Azure CLI command, which takes the YAML file as the parameter:

```
> az container create --resource-group <resource-group> --file
<yaml-file>
```

> **Note**
>
> Remember that at any time, you can create a resource group either in the portal or by using the `az group create -n <resource-group> -l <region>` command.

Still, before we deploy the file, we need to create it. The following snippet is an example of such a file with all the parameters, and its features are described in the following section:

```
apiVersion: 2019-12-01
location: eastus
name: handsonazuregroup
properties:
  containers:
  - name: helloworld
```

```
      properties:
        image: mcr.microsoft.com/azuredocs/aci-helloworld:latest
        resources:
          requests:
            cpu: 1
            memoryInGb: 1.5
        ports:
        - port: 80
        - port: 8080
    - name: sidecar
      properties:
        image: mcr.microsoft.com/azuredocs/aci-tutorial-sidecar
        resources:
          requests:
            cpu: 1
            memoryInGb: 1.5
    osType: Linux
    ipAddress:
      type: Public
      ports:
      - protocol: tcp
        port: 80
      - protocol: tcp
        port: 8080
  tags: {exampleTag: handsonazure}
  type: Microsoft.ContainerInstance/containerGroups
```

The first thing is the definition of the container group. We need to enter the location of deployment and its name. Remember that in almost all Azure cases, you want all components that are integrated and communicate with each other to be in the same region. Then we have the properties of our container group – we must define each container that is part of the whole group.

As you can see, we define the following parameters:

- image, which will be used as the base of our containers
- resources utilized by this container
- ports used by it

There are also some additional settings that you may find helpful:

- The operating system used to run containers

- The IP address configuration, which states whether the whole group is accessible from the internet or stays private

You may also enter tags, which will decorate the whole group. As we have the whole configuration, we can start the deployment:

```
PS D:\TheCloudTheory\HandsOnAzure2.0\Chapter04> az container create --resource-group handsonbook-rg --file aci.yaml
{
  "id": "/subscriptions/58ac7037-efcc-4fb6-800d-da6ca2ee6aed/resourceGroups/handsonbook-rg/providers/Microsoft.Conta
  "identity": null,
  "kind": null,
  "location": "westeurope",
  "managedBy": null,
  "name": "handsonazuregroup",
  "plan": null,
  "properties": {
    "containers": [
      {
        "name": "helloworld",
        "properties": {
          "environmentVariables": [],
          "image": "mcr.microsoft.com/azuredocs/aci-helloworld:latest",
          "instanceView": {
            "currentState": {
              "detailStatus": "",
              "startTime": "2021-10-02T15:28:05Z",
              "state": "Running"
            },
```

Figure 4.7 – Starting the deployment

If the process of provisioning of your group is successfully completed, you will get a long JSON response containing the containers' metadata. The whole group will be also available in the Azure portal and via Azure CLI commands, allowing you to query resources, as shown in the following screenshot:

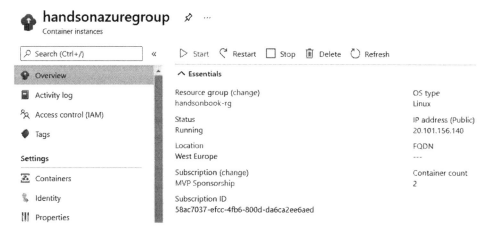

Figure 4.8 – Container group deployed and visible in the Azure portal

If you go to the **Containers** blade, you will see that we have now two containers running on a single Container Instances instance:

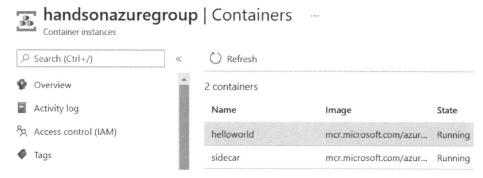

Figure 4.9 – Two containers running on the single instance of Azure Container Instances

The last thing we need to check is access to the running container. Let's go back to the **Overview** blade and search for the IP address parameter. If you copy it and paste it in your browser, you should be able to access a web page running inside your service:

Figure 4.10 – A running web page inside Azure Container Instances

As you can see, deploying multiple containers is still amazingly simple when using Container Instances. All you need is to write your YAML file and deploy it using, for example, the Azure CLI. All the work (infrastructure provisioning, pulling images, and creating containers) is the responsibility of Azure.

In the next section, we will talk about security basics for Container Instances.

Security baseline and considerations

All cloud resources should consider security to be their priority. That said, you should always ensure that your service uses all the security features that are required for your business case. In Container Instances, you have access to the following security areas:

- Networking
- Monitoring and logging
- Access control

There are, of course, even more areas to consider here:

- Web access security
- Data protection
- Incident management
- Pen testing

When creating a Container Instance service, you can configure network access and ports that are open in your instance of the service, as shown in the screenshot:

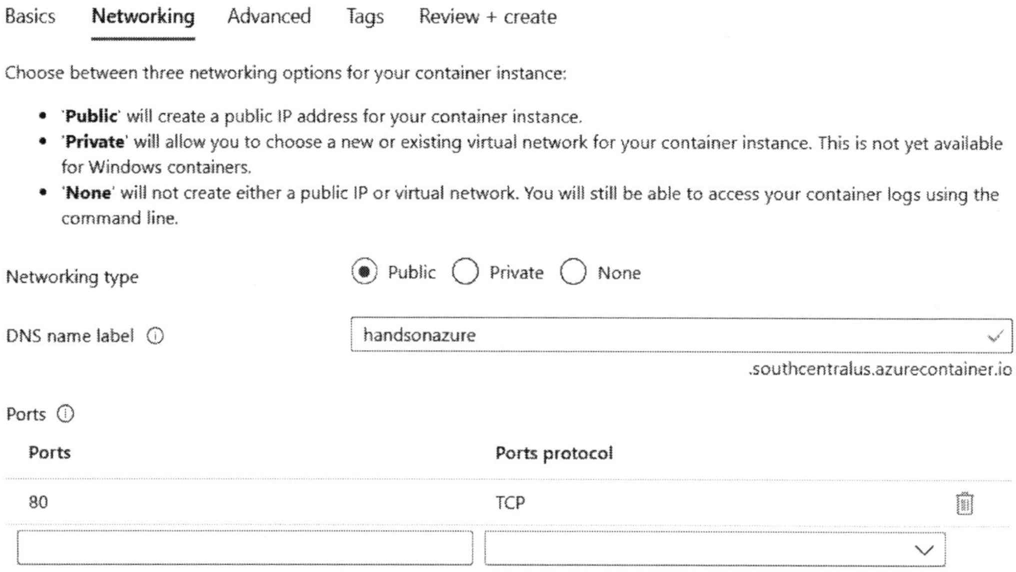

Basics   **Networking**   Advanced   Tags   Review + create

Choose between three networking options for your container instance:

- `Public` will create a public IP address for your container instance.
- `Private` will allow you to choose a new or existing virtual network for your container instance. This is not yet available for Windows containers.
- `None` will not create either a public IP or virtual network. You will still be able to access your container logs using the command line.

Networking type   ◉ Public   ○ Private   ○ None

DNS name label ⓘ   handsonazure   ✓

                                                        .southcentralus.azurecontainer.io

Ports ⓘ

Ports	Ports protocol	
80	TCP	🗑
	⌄	

Figure 4.11 – Networking configuration

As you can see, there are three different types of networking available:

- **Public**, which allows connections from everywhere
- **Private**, which can integrate Container Instances with a network of your choice
- **None**, which completely seals your containers but still allows you to browse logs via the CLI

The rule of thumb is that you should only deploy Container Instances to a virtual network and select **Public** access if you really need it. Connection via a virtual network will require a more advanced setup (you must use a VM deployed to Azure or set up integration between an Azure network and your computer), but it is always the best choice if you design your application with security in mind.

Selecting **None** as your networking type may look like an interesting choice, but it has limited usage. That option is useful only if your container is supposed to perform operations that have no artifacts and does not have to connect to external services. As you mostly run containers for a specific purpose (such as generating output from an operation), the lack of any integration renders that option useless in many real-world scenarios.

Each instance of Container Instances allows you to browse logs and metrics. Logs are available via the **Containers** blade and will give you insights into what is really happening inside a container:

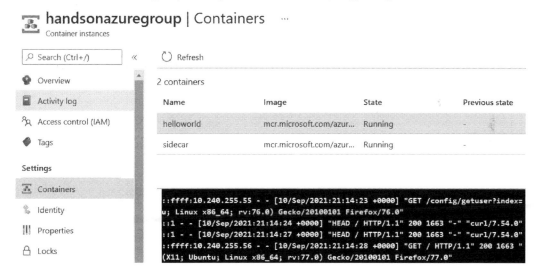

Figure 4.12 – The logs of a helloworld container from a container group

Always make sure you are not logging anything important from the security point of view when your container is running. Examples of such data include the following:

- Connection string

- Authorization keys

- Authorization tokens

- Passwords and logins

- SSH keys

It is a common practice for developers to put some of that data into code when developing as it helps them understand the current behavior of an application. Always perform a detailed review of the application's code and the image definition to avoid surprises.

Access control in Container Instances is performed using the same component as in other Azure services. There is an **Access control (IAM)** blade available, where you can configure who has access to the service and with what permissions:

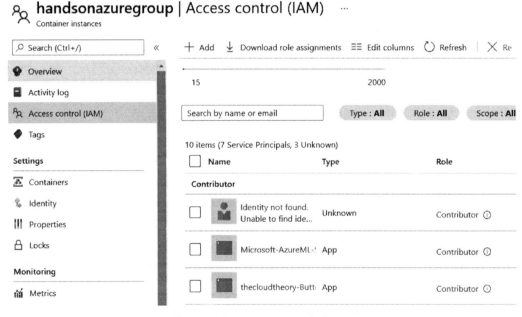

Figure 4.13 – Access control in Azure

It is always a good practice to avoid assigning roles granting full access to a service and following the **Least Privilege** principle.

Container Instances also allow you to set up a **Managed Identity** using the **Identity** blade. It is the very same feature as available in, for example, Azure App Service – you can decide whether you are assigning a unique identity for a particular instance of Container Instances (so it is available only for a single service) or using a user assigned identity, which can be shared by multiple services, allowing centralized access management.

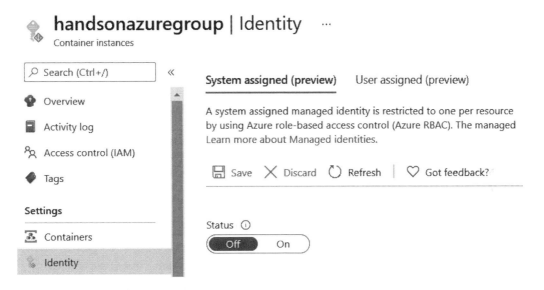

Figure 4.14 – Identity configuration in Container Instances

Using Managed Identity is also one of the security baselines – you can avoid putting secrets into your containers as they can use the identity assigned to Container Instances. Using this feature also allows us to control access to other services using the **Access control (IAM)** capability – a service with Managed Identity assigned is considered a principal in the whole Azure ecosystem, allowing for proper access management.

Summary

Container Instances is a simple yet robust solution for running your containers in a managed environment. It simplifies things such as infrastructure provisioning, authentication to registries, and hosting multiple containers in a single place. Of course, there is a cost of such simplicity – you cannot control the operating system's features and the environment in which a container runs. Still, if your goal is to run a container quickly, get the job done, and move ahead with the process, this looks like the service for you. In the next chapter, we will change the topic a little bit, as we will switch our focus to search engines and build a custom one using **Azure Cognitive Search**.

Questions

Following are some key questions to summarize the chapter:

1. Can Container Instances integrate with virtual networks in Azure?

2. What are the ways to deploy container groups?

3. Can you select a virtual machine used for running containers in Container Instances?

4. What are the networking types in Container Instances?

5. Can Container Instances leverage Managed Identity?

Further reading

For more information, refer to the following resources:

- Azure Container Instances documentation: `https://docs.microsoft.com/en-us/azure/container-instances/container-instances-overview`

- Azure Container Instances security baseline: `https://docs.microsoft.com/en-us/security/benchmark/azure/baselines/container-instances-security-baseline`

5

Building a Search Engine with Azure Cognitive Search

When in need of a search engine, it's always a good idea to use tested and well-known solutions that have been available on the market for a while. One of those solutions is **Azure Cognitive Search** (formerly known as Azure Search), which offers a search-as-a-service cloud solution with an API for developers, so users can focus on developing a working solution without the need to manage infrastructure or configuration.

The following topics will be covered in this chapter:

- Creating an Azure Cognitive Search instance
- A full-text search in Azure Cognitive Search
- Linguistic analysis in full-text search
- Indexing in Azure Cognitive Search
- Cognitive search – adding AI to the indexing workloads

Technical requirements

To perform the exercises in this chapter, you will need the following:

- Access to an Azure subscription
- A tool for sending HTTP requests (such as *curl* or *Postman*)

Creating an Azure Cognitive Search instance

Creating an Azure Cognitive Search instance is an easy task and should not take more than a few minutes. The important thing to remember here is that if you must recreate a service, there is no way to back up and restore data – if you make mistakes here, everything must be done again from scratch.

The reason for recreating a service is if you needed to change the datatypes or other search attributes of the search index columns. While it will not be a problem during this exercise, keep that in mind when creating a production workload.

Using the Azure portal

As with most services in Azure, we will start our journey by creating an Azure Cognitive Search instance in the portal. To do so, click on + **Create a resource** and search for Azure Cognitive Search. On the introduction screen, click on the **Create** button, which will take you to the configuration of this service:

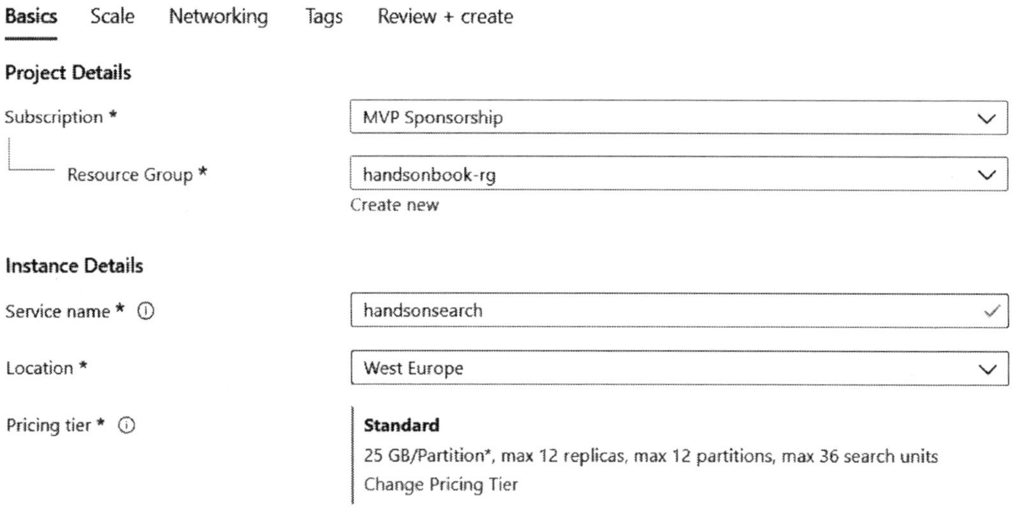

Basics   Scale   Networking   Tags   Review + create

Project Details

Subscription *   MVP Sponsorship   ⌄

     Resource Group *   handsonbook-rg   ⌄
                 Create new

Instance Details

Service name * ⓘ   handsonsearch   ✓

Location *   West Europe   ⌄

Pricing tier * ⓘ   **Standard**
                          25 GB/Partition*, max 12 replicas, max 12 partitions, max 36 search units
                          Change Pricing Tier

Figure 5.1 – The Basics tab in the creation wizard

As you can see, the **Basics** tab does not contain any surprising options and should be clear to you at this point. There is, however, an option to select **Pricing tier**, where currently there are different options to choose from:

- **Free**: This is the most basic one without replicas and shared resources available.
- **Basic**: This comes with load balancing, scaling, and dedicated resources available.
- **Standard**: This has three different tiers with more compute power and partitions available.
- **High-density**: The same as **Standard** but with more indexes available (and fewer partitions). This tier is designed for **Software as a Service (SaaS)** developers specifically.
- **Storage Optimized**: This offers similar capabilities as the **High-density** tier but comes with fewer indexes in favor of making huge storage available.

Before we proceed, we need to understand what all these concepts are:

- **Replica**: This is an individual instance of your search service, which hosts one copy of an index. If you have more than one replica, you can load-balance your queries.
- **Index**: You can think of this as a table that contains multiple rows (or, in other words, documents) with additional metadata used by a service.
- **Search Unit (SU)**: This is a billing unit for Azure Cognitive Search, which is a composition of the number of replicas and partitions ($SU = replicas \times partitions$).
- **Partition**: Each partition provides storage and **Input/Output (I/O)** for your instance of Azure Search, so scaling this unit will provide more of those.

The main difference between replicas and partitions is that if you need more computational resources, you can increase partitions, while for larger query volumes, you need more replicas (so that a query can be load-balanced).

Once you have filled all the fields from the **Basics** tab, select the **Scale** tab. You will see a new screen, where you can see the scaling options for your search engine instance:

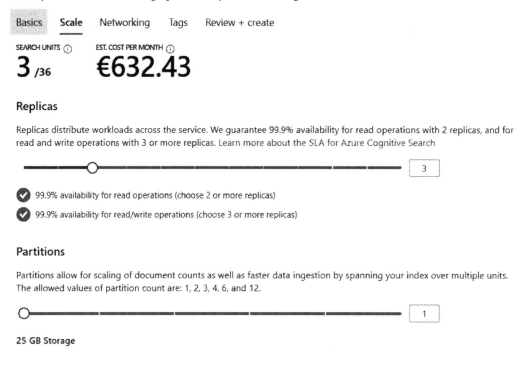

Figure 5.2 – The Scale tab for Azure Cognitive Search

As with many cloud services, at some point in time, you will have to consider the availability of your solution. For non-production workloads, that parameter is negligible, but production environments, in most cases, must work as consistently as possible. For Azure Cognitive Search, you will need at least the **Basic** tier to achieve 99.9% availability for both read and write operations. The reason for that is the requirement of having at least three replicas in your service to get a proper replication setup.

> **Important Note**
> If you need availability only for reads, you can stay with two replicas. Also, remember that each additional replica increases the overall cost of the solution.

We will skip the **Networking** tab for now, so you can go to the **Review + create** tab and click on the **Create** button to initialize the provisioning of your service. Wait for a moment for service creation, and once it is created, go to the **Overview** blade. Once there, select **Import data** so that we can start with some samples before diving deeper into Azure Cognitive Search:

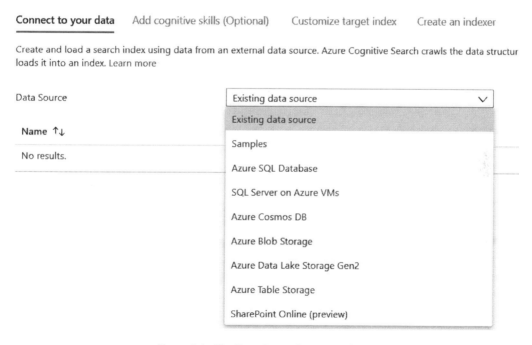

Figure 5.3 – Import data on the Overview blade

On the next screen, you will see multiple options for importing records – you will be able to select the data source and index, and enable **Cognitive Search**, which we will cover in the next sections:

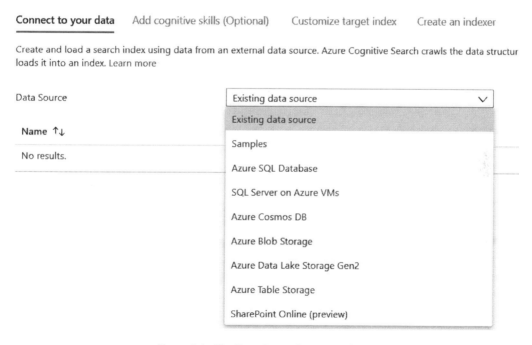

Figure 5.4 – The Data Source import options

Remember that it is possible to delete or change the fields used for indexing data, but such operations require re-indexing all documents. By re-indexing, I mean that you must delete and then recreate the index. However, it is possible to add new fields without re-indexing the documents – in that case, the values for the new columns will be null.

For now, let's select the **Samples** option, which you can see in *Figure 5.5*, to ease things a bit. It will give us an option to select a source database for our exercise. Select the **SQL** database and proceed to the next tab:

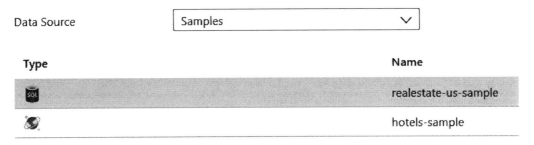

Figure 5.5 – Two samples available in a training data source

We will skip adding cognitive skills for now, as they are part of the latter exercises. Let's go directly to the **Customize target index** tab, where we can configure the search engine index:

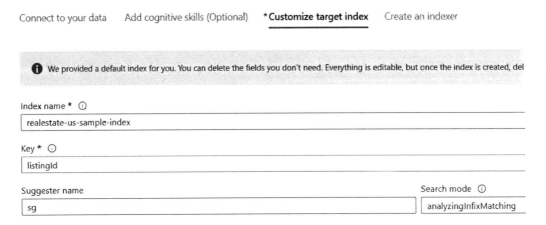

Figure 5.5 – The preconfigured index

As you can see, **Index name** is already filled with some default values. Normally, you would adjust them according to your needs, but for now, we should be good with the default values. Now, you can proceed to the next tab, where we can create an indexer. You may wonder what an indexer is exactly. Its definition is quite simple – it is a crawler that looks at your data source and extracts everything from it, based on the mapping between an index and stored information. For example, if you selected a field named `Status` as a part of your index, the indexer will search for all records containing it and push them to your index.

Indexers can be configured either to fetch data once or on schedule. We will cover scheduled indexers in the section regarding indexes and indexing documents:

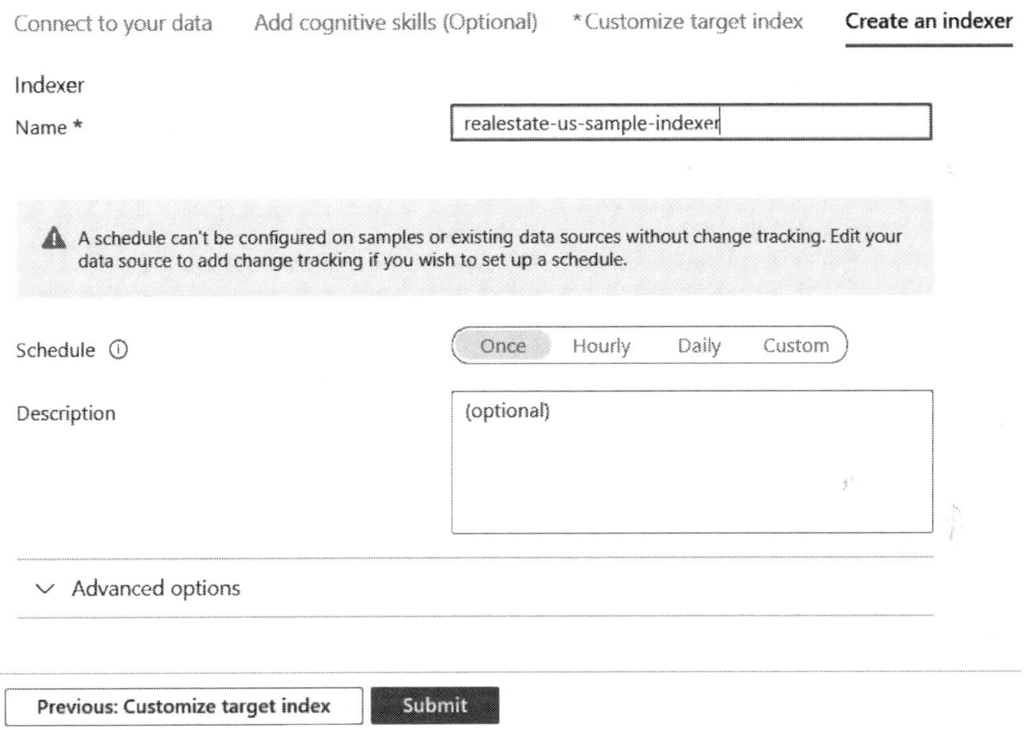

Figure 5.6 – The configuration of an indexer

If you are satisfied with the import configuration, click on the **Submit** button and wait a moment until the data is imported and indexed. Now, we can test how our service works – on the **Overview** blade, you will find the **Search explorer** button. When you click on it, you will see a new screen, where you can enter your **Query string** and **Request URL** details, which can be used in your application to get results:

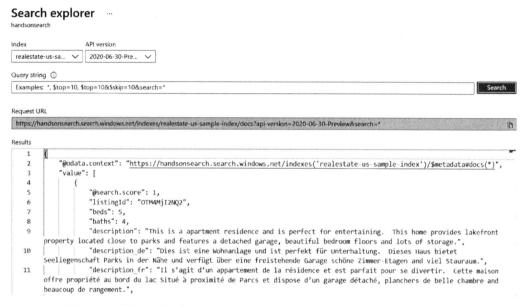

Figure 5.7 – The result of sending a query to an instance of Azure Cognitive Search

In the next section, we will learn what a full-text search is and how it can be performed in Azure.

A full-text search in Azure Cognitive Search

The power of Azure Cognitive Search comes when you need to perform a full-text search to find relevant documents that will satisfy your query. This Azure service uses **Apache Lucene** under the hood, which is a well-known high-performance search engine written in Java. In many cases, common text queries should be covered by the basic capabilities of search engines built with the help of Azure Cognitive Services. For more sophisticated scenarios, a full-text search can help in getting the desired results.

You can find more information about Lucene here: `https://lucene.apache.org/core/`. It is an open source project that everyone can download.

In this chapter, you will learn how to perform a full-text search, what the syntax is, and how to recognize potential issues.

Sending a request

In the first section of this chapter, you created your Azure Search instance and saw **Search explorer**, which enables you to send simple queries. Now, we will extend our requests so that you can select which fields should be used for query analysis to filter results and to order by a particular property. Here is the basic URL, which you can use for all your requests:

```
https://[service name].search.windows.net/indexes/[index name]/
docs/search?api-version=2016-09-01
```

However, before we proceed, we need to do one more thing – as with most APIs, Azure Cognitive Search is secured and requires a key to authorize a request. If you do not send it, you will get an HTTP 403 response error message. To obtain a key, go to the Azure portal and select the **Keys** blade:

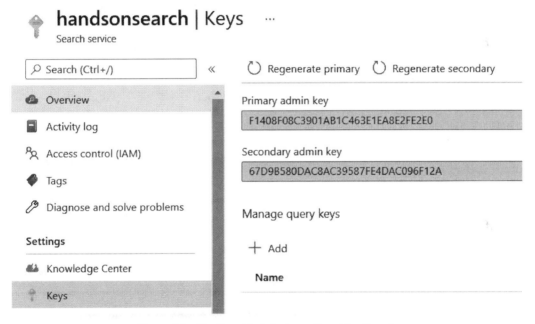

Figure 5.8 – The Keys blade in Azure Cognitive Search

Now, with each request to your API, you will have to use the api-key header with the appropriate value. Here, you can find an example:

```
GET /indexes/realestate-us-sample/docs?api-version=2016-09-
01&search=* HTTP/1.1
Host: handsonazuresearch.search.windows.net
api-key: 38B4F66ACD480406328C62273C056CA4
Cache-Control: no-cache
```

Nonetheless, in most cases, we are not interested in literally all documents available – we have specific parameters that we would like to use. Let's assume that you would like to search for a specific city. In such a case, we must use another endpoint and pass a valid payload, which will be used to build a query:

```
POST /indexes/realestate-us-sample/docs/search?api-
version=2020-06-30 HTTP/1.1
Host: handsonazuresearch.search.windows.net
api-key: {API_KEY}
Content-Type: application/json
Cache-Control: no-cache


{
    "search": "Sammamish",
    "searchFields": "city"
}
```

The most important thing, however, is the body – for now, we'll use two fields:

- search: This is our query string, which we are using to tell Azure Search what we are interested in.

- searchFields: Here, we are passing fields, which should contain our query string.

Please remember that the fields passed in the request body are case-sensitive, and you should follow camel case if there are multiple words.

If you run the preceding query on the sample index, you should see some results returned. If you search for a city that is not in the indexed documents, you will see an empty result:

```
{
    "@odata.context": "https://handsonazuresearch.search.
windows.net/indexes('realestate-us-sample')/$metadata#docs",
    "value": []
}
```

You may ask what the rules are for choosing a search field – the only requirement is that it must be marked as `Searchable`, which can be defined during index creation. Let's see what will happen if I use `beds` to search for records with a specific number:

```
{
    "error": {
        "code": "",
        "message": "The field 'beds' in the search field list
is not searchable.\r\nParameter name: searchFields"
    }
}
```

It seems we cannot use any field we would like to. You can check which fields can be used for searching on the index screen. To do so, go to the **Overview** blade and search for the **Indexes** tab:

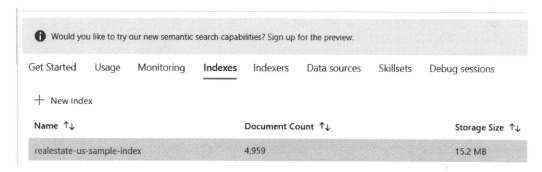

Figure 5.9 – The Indexes tab

Now, click on the name of your index and proceed to the **Fields** tab. You should be able to see a field that we are trying to use at the very beginning of the screen:

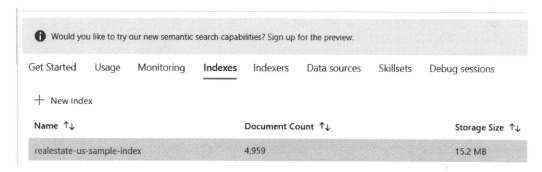

Figure 5.10 – Fields inside an index

As you can see, the beds field is here, but we are unable to check it. In fact, you cannot use any field of the Edm.Int32 type as Searchable. There are some other types that are also not supported (for example, Edm.GeographyPoint) – you can find more information about them when building or modifying fields used in an index.

To overcome the problem, you can use filters – these are expressions based on the OData syntax, which you can leverage to search for the entities you are interested in. The only requirement is to make a field that you want to use as a filter using filterable. Here, you can find all the possible fields, which you can use in such an HTTP request:

```
{
    "count": true | false(default),
    "facets": ["facet_expression_1", "facet_expression_2", ...],
    "filter": "odata_filter_expression",
    "highlight": "highlight_field_1, highlight_field_2, ...",
    "highlightPreTag": "pre_tag",
    "highlightPostTag": "post_tag",
    "minimumCoverage": #( % of index that must be covered to
declare query successful; default 100),
    "orderby": "orderby_expression",
    "scoringParameters": ["scoring_parameter_1", "scoring_
parameter_2", ...],
    "scoringProfile": "scoring_profile_name",
    "search": "simple_query_expression",
    "searchFields": "field_name_1, field_name_2, ...",
    "searchMode": "any" (default) | "all",
    "select": "field_name_1, field_name_2, ...",
    "skip": #(default 0),
    "top": #
}
```

Not all of the fields are shown in the preceding snippet.

> **Important Note**
> For full reference of the fields, you can check the following link: https://docs.
> microsoft.com/rest/api/searchservice/preview-api/search-
> documents#request-body.

We will not cover them all, as this would take the whole chapter; however, we will focus a little more on the actual syntax of queries sent to Azure Cognitive Search. As you probably remember, this service uses the Lucene search engine to index data and handle requests. Lucene supports a variety of different query types, such as fuzzy search and wildcard search. You can decide which parser should be used by sending the `queryType` parameter with one of the available values – `simple` or `full` (Lucene).

You can find the query operations supported by Lucene by reading the following page: `https://docs.microsoft.com/azure/search/query-lucene-syntax`.

Linguistic analysis in a full-text search

When doing a full-text search, you have to understand what the rules are for performing such an operation. Search engines must analyze search queries lexically to be able to extract important information and pass it to a query tree. In this section, we will cover the most common lexical analysis, which is linguistic analysis, to help you understand how Azure Search works and how to perform correct queries.

Analyzers in Azure Cognitive Search

To perform linguistic analysis, Azure Search supports a variety of different analyzers, which can be specified in the index definition. However, before we start defining one of those, we need a brief overview of what we are talking about. When creating an index, each search service must analyze all input documents and decide what will be important when performing a search procedure.

Additionally, each search query should be adjusted to some common rules so that the search engine can understand it. The necessary operations can be described as follows:

- All non-essential words should be removed (such as *the* in English).
- All words should be lowercase.
- If a word contains multiple words (such as "upfront"), it should be divided into atomic ones.

Now, let's assume that you are searching for an apartment using the following search query – `Spacious apartment with 4 and the Red Kitchen`. Your analyzer will have to perform all the preceding operations before passing the query to a search engine, and in fact, you can find the result of this analysis here:

```
{
    "@odata.context": "https://handsonazuresearch.search.
windows.net/$metadata#Microsoft.Azure.Search.V2016_09_01.
AnalyzeResult",
    "tokens": [
        {
            "token": "spacious",
            "startOffset": 0,
            "endOffset": 8,
            "position": 0
        },
        {
            "token": "apartment",
            "startOffset": 9,
            "endOffset": 18,
            "position": 1
        },
        {
            "token": "with",
            "startOffset": 19,
            "endOffset": 23,
            "position": 2
        },
        {
            "token": "4",
            "startOffset": 24,
            "endOffset": 25,
            "position": 3
        },
        {
            "token": "and",
            "startOffset": 26,
            "endOffset": 29,
```

```
                  "position": 4
        },
        {

            "token": "the",
            "startOffset": 30,
            "endOffset": 33,
            "position": 5
        },
        {

            "token": "red",
            "startOffset": 34,
            "endOffset": 37,
            "position": 6
        },
        {

            "token": "kitchen",
            "startOffset": 38,
            "endOffset": 45,
            "position": 7
        }
    ]
}
```

As you can see, each word has its position and offset. To get a result like the previous one, you can send the following query:

```
POST /indexes/[index name]/analyze?api-version=2016-09-01
HTTP/1.1
Host: [service name].search.windows.net
api-key: [api key]
Content-Type: application/json
Cache-Control: no-cache

{
  "text": "Spacious apartment with 4 and the Red Kitchen",
  "analyzer": "standard"
}
```

In the request's body, you must provide both texts to use the analyzer. Note that I used `standard` here, which means that the standard Lucene analyzer is used here.

Azure Cognitive Search supports several different analyzers for different languages – what's more, both Microsoft and Lucene versions are available. To get the full list, go to the documentation page: `https://docs.microsoft.com/pl-pl/rest/api/searchservice/language-support`.

If you are proficient in language analysis and syntax, you can create a custom analyzer that can be used for text analysis. Such analyzers can be defined during index creation; however, we will not cover that topic in this book, as it is an advanced exercise and is out of our present scope. You will find a link to the tutorial in the *Further reading* section of this chapter.

Analyzer selection

You can select an analyzer for a specific field either during the creation of an index or while editing it. If you go to the Azure portal and your Azure Cognitive Search instance, you can click on an index and select the **Fields** section. It should display a list of all the fields used in that index:

Field name	Type	Retrievable ☐	Filterable ☐	Sortable ☐	Facetable ☐	Searchable ☐	Analyzer	Suggester ☐	
🔑 listingId	Edm.String	✓	☐	☐	☐	☐			...
beds	Edm.Int32	✓	✓	✓	✓				...
baths	Edm.Int32	✓	✓	✓	✓				...
description	Edm.String	✓	☐	☐	☐	✓	English - Micro... ∨		...
description_de	Edm.String	✓	☐	☐	☐	✓	German - Micr... ∨		...
description_fr	Edm.String	✓	☐	☐	☐	✓	French - Micros... ∨		...
description_it	Edm.String	✓	☐	☐	☐	✓	Italian - Micros... ∨		...
description_es	Edm.String	✓	☐	☐	☐	✓	Spanish - Micro... ∨		...
description_pl	Edm.String	✓	☐	☐	☐	✓	Polish - Micros... ∨		...
description_nl	Edm.String	✓	☐	☐	☐	✓	Dutch - Micros... ∨		...
sqft	Edm.Int32	✓	✓	✓	✓				...
daysOnMarket	Edm.Int32	✓	✓	✓	✓				...
status	Edm.String	✓	✓	☐	✓	☐			...
source	Edm.String	✓	☐	☐	☐	✓	English - Micro... ∨		...

Figure 5.11 – The fields available inside an index

In the preceding listed fields, you will see the + **Add field** button, which enables you to add a new field. If you would like to select an analyzer, you will need to mark a field as **Searchable**. Doing so will allow you to select an analyzer for that field:

Figure 5.12 – Adding a new field to an index with the analyzer selected

Note that selecting a different analyzer than the custom one is crucial when you have fields containing multiple languages. In such a scenario, you should select an analyzer appropriate for the language used.

Indexing in Azure Cognitive Search

An index is one of the most important constructs in Azure Search. We defined it as a table that contains all imported documents with searchable data defined in it. At the beginning of this chapter, we learned how to create it and add or edit fields. In this section, we will learn a bit more about modifying it, as an index is not a fixed being and can be altered and adjusted to your needs.

Importing more data

There is always a need to push more data to your index – your application grows, the storage of your documents becomes bigger and bigger, especially if you are creating a document repository, and you would like to be able to find what you are searching for even in the most recent documents. However, there are two options to add data to your index:

- The push model
- The pull model

We will cover both these models in the following sections.

The push model

The push model is the best solution for applications that have low-latency requirements. As opposed to the pull model, using this model indexes your document immediately after pushing it using a RESTful API.

Currently, there is no other option to use a push model besides using a RESTful API or the .NET SDK to perform an operation. In the pull model, it is also possible to get data using the Azure portal. Here, you can find an example request for pushing a document:

```
POST /indexes/realestate-us-sample/docs/index?api-
version=2016-09-01 HTTP/1.1
Host: [service name].search.windows.net
api-key: [api key]
 Content-Type: application/json
Cache-Control: no-cache

{
   "value": [
     {
       "listingId": "12344234",
       "@search.action": "upload",
       "price": 250.0,
       "description": "The very apartment in Warsaw",
       "city": "Warsaw",
       "tags": ["pool", "view", "wifi", "gym"],
       "beds": 4,
       "location": { "type": "Point", "coordinates": [52.237049,
21.017532] }
     }
   ]
}
```

If everything is correct, you should see a successful result:

```
{
    "@odata.context": "https://handsonazuresearch.search.
windows.net/indexes('realestate-us-sample')/$metadata#Collectio
n(Microsoft.Azure.Search.V2016_09_01.IndexResult)",
    "value": [
        {
            "key": "12344234",
            "status": true,
```

```
            "errorMessage": null,
            "statusCode": 201
        }
    ]
}
```

Now, let's check whether the document is already indexed and available:

```
POST /indexes/realestate-us-sample/docs/search?api-
version=2016-09-01 HTTP/1.1
Host: [service name].search.windows.net
api-key: [api key]
 Content-Type: application/json
Cache-Control: no-cache


{
    "search": "Warsaw",
    "searchFields": "city"
}
```

The result should be a document that contains all the fields we passed in the push request.

The pull model

A pull model is a bit different than a push model, as it uses indexers to fetch the data. When using it, you are configuring both a data source and deciding how frequently data should be pulled. As opposed to the push model, it can be configured and accessed when using the Azure portal.

Please note one important difference between push and pull – when using push, you can use any data source you want. When using the pull model, you are limited to Blob storage, Table storage, CosmosDB, and SQL Database (both on Azure and **Virtual Machines** (**VMs**).

Here, you can find an indexer configuration for pulling data when using Table Storage as a source:

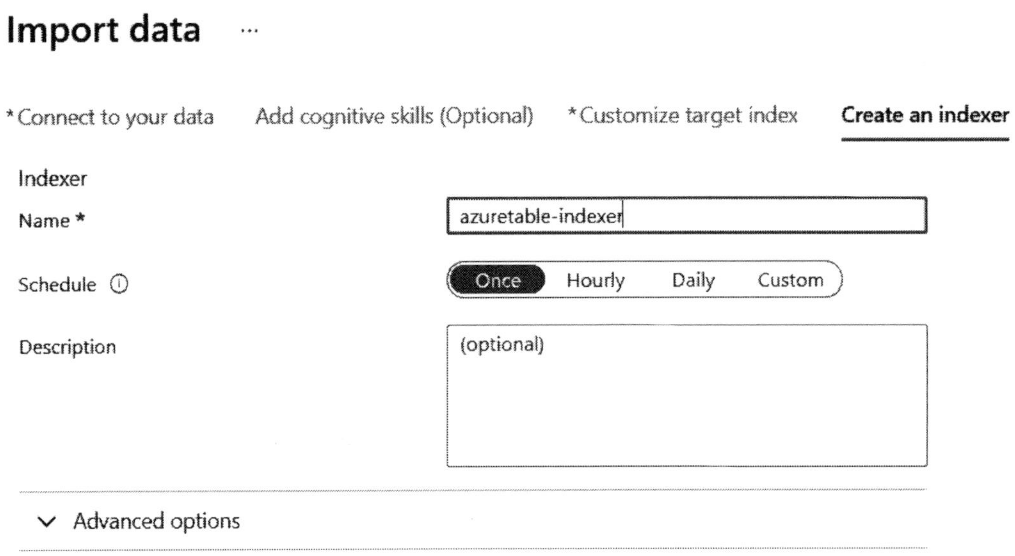

Import data ···

| *Connect to your data | Add cognitive skills (Optional) | *Customize target index | **Create an indexer** |

Indexer
Name *

azuretable-indexer

Schedule ⓘ

Once   Hourly   Daily   Custom

Description

(optional)

∨ Advanced options

Figure 5.13 – The indexer configuration when importing data from Table Storage

In the next section of this chapter, we will cover one of the most interesting capabilities of Azure Cognitive Search – an ability to add AI to enrich indexing and enhance the functionalities of your search engine.

Cognitive Search – adding AI to the indexing workload

When creating and managing an index, you must always make sure that you have selected all the required fields and marked them as searchable where needed. Additionally, we are limited to the current service functionalities, so we cannot use things such as image or natural language processing. Fortunately, Azure Cognitive Search now supports AI enrichment of your indexing operations, allowing for richer analysis using more vectors. In this chapter, you will learn how to configure it so that you can start using it from the very beginning.

Configuring cognitive skills

Cognitive Search can be configured when importing data for your service. When you click on the **Import data** button, you will see that one of the available tabs gives you the possibility to add AI through cognitive skills:

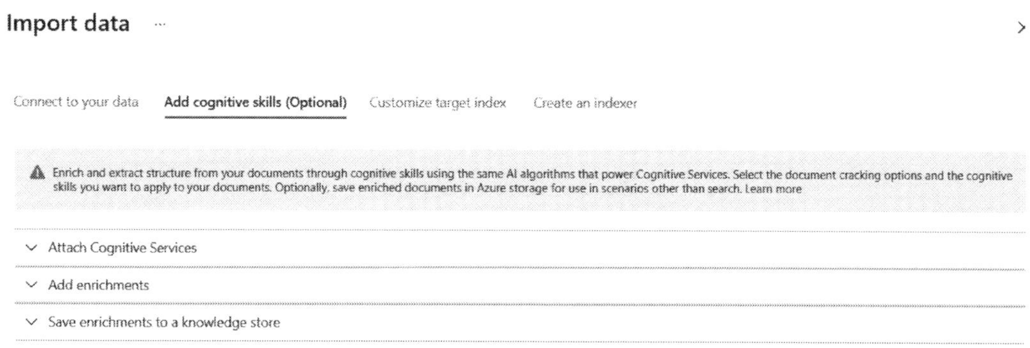

Import data   ...   >

Connect to your data   **Add cognitive skills (Optional)**   Customize target index   Create an indexer

> ⚠ Enrich and extract structure from your documents through cognitive skills using the same AI algorithms that power Cognitive Services. Select the document cracking options and the cognitive
> skills you want to apply to your documents. Optionally, save enriched documents in Azure storage for use in scenarios other than search. Learn more

∨ Attach Cognitive Services

∨ Add enrichments

∨ Save enrichments to a knowledge store

Figure 5.14 – Cognitive skills screen

There is a list of cognitive skills (called **enrichments**) that can be used for indexing your data. Whether you use one or not depends on your actual requirements – for the purpose of this exercise, I selected **Detect language**. You can customize the name of a field also; this can be crucial if your index contains another field with the same name, as it will be added to the result of a query:

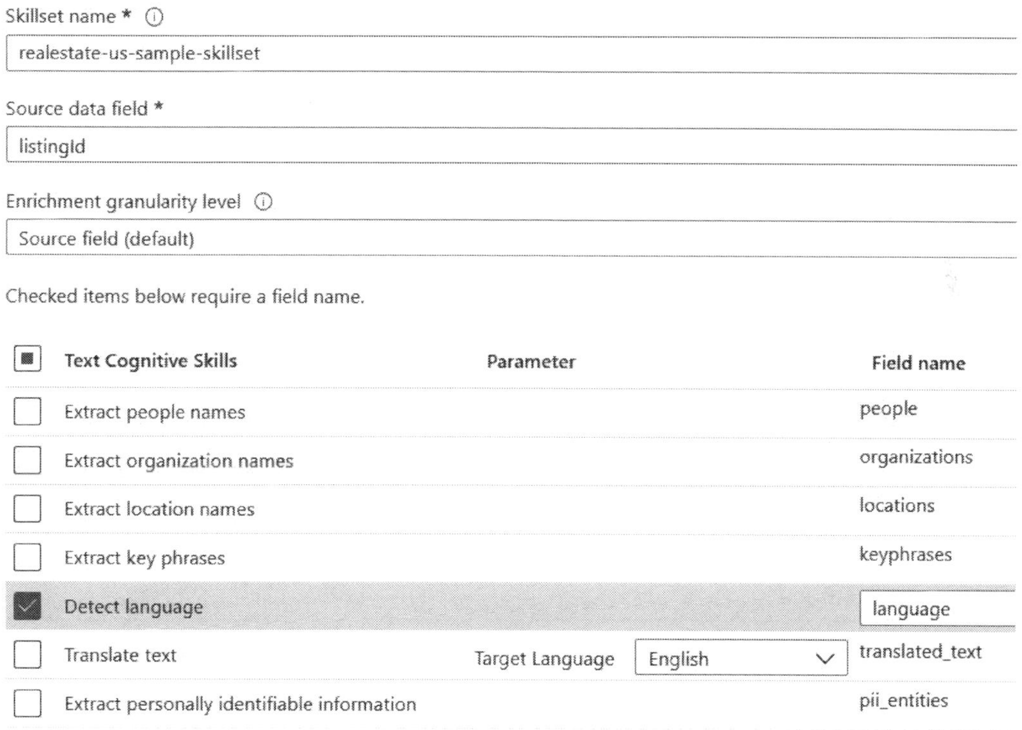

Skillset name * ⓘ

| realestate-us-sample-skillset |

Source data field *

| listingId |

Enrichment granularity level ⓘ

| Source field (default) |

Checked items below require a field name.

■ Text Cognitive Skills	Parameter		Field name
☐ Extract people names			people
☐ Extract organization names			organizations
☐ Extract location names			locations
☐ Extract key phrases			keyphrases
☑ Detect language			language
☐ Translate text	Target Language	English ∨	translated_text
☐ Extract personally identifiable information			pii_entities

If a cognitive skill is added to your index, you should be able to see it on the fields list. As the **detect language** option adds a **language** column, we now can see that it is available among the other fields in our index:

price	Edm.Int64	☑	☑	☑	☑				•••
thumbnail	Edm.String	☑	☐	☐	☐	☐		☐	•••
tags	Collection(E...	☑	☑		☑	☑	English - Micro... ⌄	☑	•••
language	Edm.String	☑	☐	☐	☐	☑	Standard - Luce... ⌄	☐	•••

[Previous: Add cognitive skills (Optional)] [Next: Create an indexer]

Additionally, when I query a service using a newer index, I get a result containing the **language** field:

```
{
  (...)
"location": {
  "type": "Point",
  "coordinates": [
    -122.388,
    47.576
  ],
  "crs": {
    "type": "name",
    "properties": {
      "name": "EPSG:4326"
    }
  }
},
"price": 762048,
"thumbnail": "https://searchdatasets.blob.core.windows.net/
images/bd2bt2apt.jpg",
"tags": [
  "condominium",
  "dream home",
  "lake access",
  "no outlet",
```

```
    "miele appliances",
    "wall of windows",
    "guest room"
  ],
  "language": "en"
  }
```

As you can see, the use of cognitive skills can quickly enhance your search results and can simplify the development of more advanced search engines. This gives you more time for focusing on actual business requirements and lowers the chances of errors on your side.

Summary

Azure Cognitive Search is a great service if you want to have your very own search solution and do not plan to maintain its infrastructure and configuration. With its flexibility and intuitiveness, you can quickly develop your application, leveraging features such as the push/pull model, scheduled indexing, and support for different kinds of data sources. Additionally, with the option to start from the free tier, even for production workloads, you can gradually progress and scale your solution up, adjusting costs based on real requirements. This chapter has given you your first steps in developing search engines in the cloud and should help you as an entry point for further exploration of the service.

In *Chapter 6, Mobile Notifications with Notification Hubs*, we will cover topics related to handling mobile applications and push notifications using Azure Notification Hubs.

Questions

As we conclude, here is a list of questions for you to test your knowledge regarding this chapter's material. You will find the answers in the Assessments section of the Appendix:

1. What is an index?

2. What is the difference between the push and pull models?

3. Can an indexer be scheduled using a custom interval?

4. What analyzer does Azure Cognitive Search use by default?

5. Can you implement a custom analyzer and use it in Azure Cognitive Search?

6. What is the difference between a partition and a replica?

7. What is the name of a header used for authorizing requests to Azure Cognitive Search?

Further reading

To learn more on the topics covered in this chapter, please visit the following links:

- Azure Cognitive Search documentation:

  ```
  https://docs.microsoft.com/en-us/azure/search/
  ```

- Cognitive skills for Azure Cognitive Search:

  ```
  https://docs.microsoft.com/en-us/azure/search/cognitive-
  search-predefined-skills
  ```

- Apache Lucene documentation:

  ```
  https://lucene.apache.org/core/
  ```

- Filters in Azure Cognitive Search:

  ```
  https://docs.microsoft.com/en-us/rest/api/searchservice/
  odata-expression-syntax-for-azure-search
  ```

6

Mobile Notifications with Notification Hubs

Push notifications are one of the main features of mobile phones and desktop applications. They facilitate informing a user about new messages, features, or even a temporary discount that is available only for a few minutes within an application. While each vendor has its own service for such notifications, it's always nice to configure such a feature in one place so that we don't have to worry about changes in the underlying **application programming interface** (**API**) or the parameters required. Azure Notification Hubs simplifies things greatly by providing a single service that acts as a single endpoint for our mobile applications, easing both development and testing.

The following topics will be covered in this chapter:

- Reasons to use Notification Hubs
- Push notification architecture
- Registering a device within Notification Hubs
- Sending notifications to multiple vendors
- Sending a rich content notification through Notification Hubs

Technical requirements

To perform the exercises in this chapter, you will need the following:

- An active Azure subscription
- Visual Studio with the Azure **software development kit** (**SDK**) installed

Reasons to use Notification Hubs

If you have ever had a chance to develop an application that was integrated with any notification system, you probably know the challenges that are faced when creating such a product. In this chapter, I will try to introduce you to some basic concepts such as **platform notification services** (**PNSes**), push notifications, and device registrations. This will ensure that we can easily start developing applications leveraging Notification Hubs features and focus on learning details and hidden functionalities.

The exercises from this chapter are prepared using the .NET platform, but the core concepts, methods, and design are the same as others such as Java or Node.js.

Challenges for application design

Let's assume you have the following architecture:

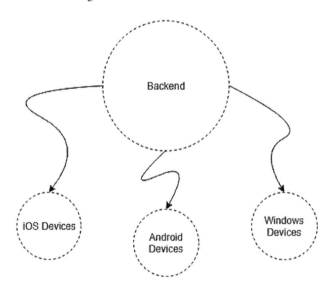

Figure 6.1 – Simple application multiplatform ecosystem

Here, we have a backend that sends some messages to the following three different platforms:

- iOS
- Android
- Windows

Now, if these messages are push notifications, our backend will have to communicate with the following three different services:

- **Apple Push Notification Service (APNS)**
- **Firebase Cloud Messaging (FCM)**
- **Windows Notification Service (WNS)**

Each of these services is called a PNS. Their responsibility is to accept a request to send a notification and send it to the appropriate device. They also handle the registration of the devices that want to accept notifications (for instance, by tokens in APNS). The downside of such a solution is that none of these services has a common interface—we cannot introduce a simple wrapper in our backend to handle each request in the same fashion. The solution for that kind of trouble would be to alter our architecture a little bit so that it contains a service that aggregates the logic for each PNS and is able to communicate with them, as illustrated in the following diagram:

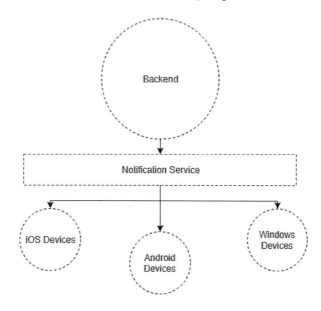

Figure 6.2 – High-level design for PNSes

Notification Hubs is such a service; it's an abstraction over different PNSes and can handle different device registration. We can consider two more problems—scaling and routing. It is important to know that, according to the PNSes' guide, the device token must be refreshed with each app launch. Now, if it is your backend responsibility, you may end up with a solution that tries to handle refresh requests instead of focusing on your business logic.

Additionally, if you want to send a notification to a particular device, you must store its **identifier** (**ID**) somewhere so that you are able to route a message to it. All these responsibilities can be moved to a notification service, so this whole overhead can be taken from the backend.

After briefly covering the main reasons for using Azure Notification Hubs, let's move on to a more technical explanation by describing the overall solution architecture.

Push notification architecture

Creating a whole system that relies on push notifications is not a trivial task. Besides ensuring that you are not focusing on handling each PNS logic individually and providing reliable device registration and routing systems, you must introduce a pipeline for passing messages from one part of your system to the end device. In this section, we will focus on incorporating Notification Hubs into a few reference architectures, which will help you understand its role and the connections between different cloud services.

Direct connection

The simplest architecture we could think of would be a direct connection between a backend and notification service, as illustrated in the following diagram:

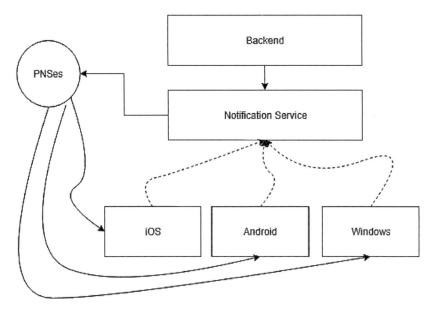

Figure 6.3 – Architecture for handling multiplatform push notifications

In such a scenario, each sent notification request is handled by **notification services**, which communicate with different **PNSes**. Each PNS individually handles a request and sends a notification to a registered device. Device registration is handled by the notification service—each device must register in it to be able to receive a notification. Note that, even in that simple scenario, the notification service (in our case, Notification Hubs) takes responsibility for two important things, as outlined here:

- Providing a common interface for different PNSes

- Handling device registration and routing

Devices never communicate directly with the PNS itself—they only receive push notifications because of sending a request to the notification service.

Queued communication

Sometimes, exposing a notification service to the backend is not the way to go—it could become unresponsive, have some performance issues, or just be overloaded. In such a situation, it is always good to have something that can cache messages and store them until all issues are resolved. Let's modify the previous architecture with one more service, as illustrated here:

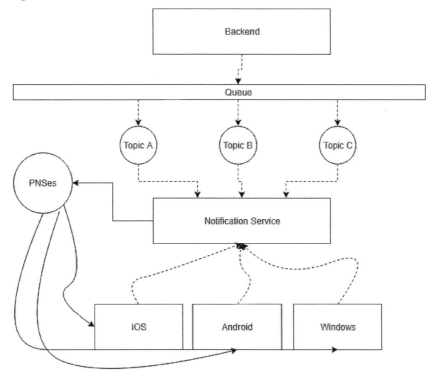

Figure 6.4 – Push notification for multiplatform service with queue

By introducing a **queue** with readers, you can absolve the backend from handling communication with the notification service and move the responsibility for delivering a message to it (the queue). Now, the **backend** does not have to know how to handle undelivered messages and will not be aware of a storage solution for storing them. This solution can be also scaled much more easily than the previous one, as you do not have to worry about losing a message—a queue should be able to cache messages if needed.

Make sure that your caching mechanism makes sense in the business domain you are working with. Caching a notification request for a day, for example, and sending a notification after that time may not make any sense in scenarios such as *geolocalization*, a specific time, or a short-lived discount.

Triggered communication

Sometimes, you might wish to send a notification based on some specific set of parameters or by raising an event. Let's assume you would like to send it whenever a photo is uploaded to storage, as illustrated in the following diagram:

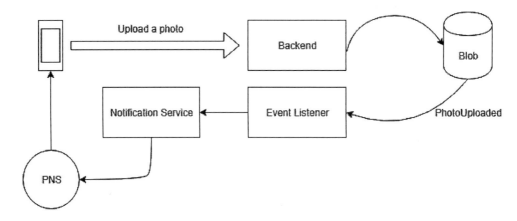

Figure 6.5 – Triggered communication for push notifications

In this asynchronous scenario, you have an **event listener** that listens to an event publication and performs an action based on the passed metadata. It sends a request to a **notification service**, which communicates with **PNS** to send a notification with the appropriate content (probable information regarding an upload status). Once more, we see the advantages of having a service acting as a proxy to PNSes—the whole communication can be made asynchronous, and each component has its own responsibility.

Let's now see how you can register a device in Azure Notification Hubs and start working with the service.

Registering a device within Notification Hubs

To be able to send a notification, you have to register a device in the PNS. Without using a service such as Notification Hubs, you would have to know the individual logic of each PNS and store device data somewhere. Such a challenge would be problematic in most cases, as you usually do not want to handle external dependencies by yourself; rather, your aim is to simplify the overall system logic. In this section, you will learn how device registration is handled in Notification Hubs and how to monitor it.

Notification Hubs device registration

When you register a device in Notification Hubs, you are associating it with a template of a notification and tag. To create such a link, you need a PNS handle, which can be understood as an ID of a specific vendor (such as a token or a **Google Cloud Messaging** (**GCM**) registration ID). In fact, there are two ways to register a device, as outlined here:

- **Use registration**: Where you pass an ID, tag, and template
- **Use installation**: An enhanced registration with an additional set of push-related properties

> **Note**
>
> Please note that currently, if you want to use installation, there is no possibility to use the .NET SDK—you are limited to using the **REpresentational State Transfer** (**REST**) API of a service.

We must also describe what tags and templates are to fully understand the process. Here's an overview of this:

- **Tag**: This is a way to route a notification to a particular set of (or all) registered devices. It allows you to segment users so that you can easily decide who is an addressee of a message; you can use, for example, `version_Beta` to send a notification to a limited group of devices using a preview version of your application.

- **Template**: This is a particular schema of data designed to be sent to a client application. It differs depending on the PNS used and varies from **JavaScript Object Notation** (**JSON**) data to **Extensible Markup Language** (**XML**) documents. By using Notification Hubs, you can create a platform-agnostic template that can be reused between different platforms.

Now, we will try registering a device using both methods and understand the differences between them.

Creating a notification hub

Before we start sending notifications, we must have a notification service provisioned and working. To create a notification hub instance, go to the portal and click on the **+ Create a resource** button. Search for `Notification Hub` and click **Create**. Here, you can see a completed configuration:

*Basics   Tags   Review + Create

Basic Details

Details of the subscription and the resource group to use.

Subscription *	MVP Sponsorship ⌄
└── Resource group *	handsonbook-rg ⌄
	Create new

Namespace Details

Details of the notification hub namespace.

Notification Hub Namespace *	handsonns ✓

◉ Create new   ◯ Select existing

Notification Hub Details

Details of the notification hub.

Notification Hub *	handsonhub ✓
Location *	West Europe ⌄
Select pricing tier	**Free**
	Change tier

Figure 6.6 – Creation of Azure notification hub

As you can see, the process of provisioning an Azure notification hub is really simple—the only things that need clarification are **Namespace Details** and **Select pricing tier**, which we will explain in more detail here:

- **Namespace Details**: You can have multiple Notification Hubs inside the same namespace. A namespace is a logical container for your hubs and holds the limit of available pushes for them.

- **Select pricing tier**: Depending on the selected tier (**Free**, **Basic**, or **Standard**), you will have different features available and a different number of available pushes for your hubs. Additionally, it defines the price of extra pushes and the number of active devices. What's more, the **Standard** tier comes with handy enterprise features such as multi-tenancy or scheduled pushes.

For this exercise, the **Free** tier will be more than enough. Once you are satisfied with your configuration, click on the **Create** button and wait for a second for service creation. When the service is created, you can go to its page where you will see an **Overview** blade, as illustrated in the following screenshot:

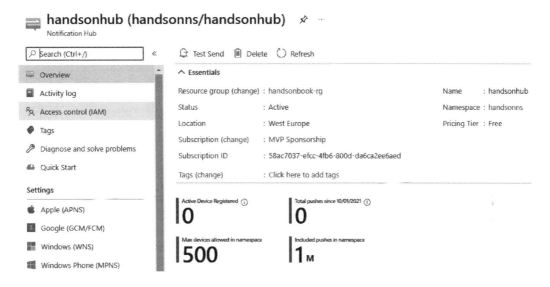

Figure 6.7 – Overview blade in Azure Notification Hub

There, you can click on the hub you created to see its features. We will cover them later in this chapter.

Creating a registration

In this section, I will show you which methods from the SDK you should use to be able to perform registration. As mentioned at the beginning of this chapter, examples will be performed with the use of the .NET SDK, but I will also point you to appropriate places in other platforms' SDKs.

> **Note**
>
> All the SDKs can be found at the following link:
>
> ```
> https://docs.microsoft.com/en-us/azure/notification-hubs/
> notification-hubs-sdks
> ```

Each operation performed at a Notification Hubs level needs a Notification Hubs client in your code. To create it, you can use the following method:

```
// using Microsoft.Azure.NotificationHubs
NotificationHubClient hub = NotificationHubClient.
CreateClientFromConnectionString(connectionString, hubName);
```

As you can see, there are two parameters required here, as follows:

- `connectionString`—A connection string to your namespace containing credentials to your notification hub

- `hubName`—The actual name of the hub you are connecting to

A connection string can be obtained for using the Azure portal, for example—when you access the **Access Policies** blade, you will see the default policies that define permissions and generate full credentials for your connection, as illustrated in the following screenshot:

Figure 6.8 – Access Policies blade with two policies generated

If you want, you can generate a new policy that will grant a different set of permissions (for instance, you need a policy that will be passed to clients with a send-only permission). For our purpose, we will use the listen-only policy.

> **Tip**
> Using a common, full-access policy in production environments is generally discouraged and considered a bad practice. You not only expose yourself to a greater risk of breaking your security and increasing the blast radius but also make it difficult to manage different clients independently.

The name of your hub is available on the **Overview** blade (see *Figure 6.7*). Once you have two required parameters prepared, we can try to create a registration description. Such an object is a direct definition of a registration, which contains various data such as this:

- Platform

- Notification channel **Uniform Resource Identifier (URI)**

- Device token

- Platform-oriented metadata

In code, all registrations share a common interface—what is different is their interface. Therefore, you can create multiple registrations, as shown in the following code snippet, and use the same method to process them:

```
var winReg = new WindowsRegistrationDescription(channelUri,
tags);
var appleReg = new AppleRegistrationDescription(deviceToken,
tags)

await hub.CreateRegistrationAsync(winReg);
await hub.CreateRegistrationAsync(appleReg);
```

> **Note**
>
> When using Android notifications, you will need slightly different method to create a registration—`hub.CreateFcmNativeRegistrationAsync(fcmRegistrationId)`.

This short code block is everything you need to register a device in Azure Notification Hubs. It performs several additional tasks under the hood to make sure connectivity is maintained and registration is completed. As you can see, it greatly simplifies the development of an application—you can focus on your business logic while keeping external dependencies easy to maintain and understand.

Checking available registrations

There are cases where you may want to check whether a particular registration is available in Notification Hubs. Of course, you will get an error if you try to access a non-existing one, but the rule of thumb tells us that you should always be prepared for errors and handle them if possible. For that purpose, the following method is available in the SDKs:

```
// .NET
GetAllRegistrationsAsync(string continuationToken, int top,
CancellationToken cancellationToken)

// Java
getRegistrations() throws NotificationHubsException;

// All above methods are part of NotificationHubClient
```

If you do not want to check all the existing registrations, you can always search for a single one, as shown in the following code snippet:

```
var registration = await hub.GetRegistrationAsync<RegistrationD
escription>("<registration-id>");
```

This is a better method if you know the registration ID you are looking for and do not want to browse all the registrations available.

Using installations

Installations is a newer feature that allows you to handle each device registration using slightly different syntax and tools. It has a few important advantages over registrations, as follows:

- While it is possible to duplicate registrations (by registering the same device twice), installations are idempotent. This means that sending the same installation multiple times will not result in the creation of more than one registration record.

- By using HTTP PATCH, you can update a specific parameter in an installation.

- It is easier to perform individual pushes since each installation is automatically tagged using an installation ID. In registrations, you would have to create such a tag yourself and maintain it somehow to get the same functionality.

As I said in a previous part of this book, it is not currently possible to use installations with the .NET SDK on the client side—to check this functionality, we will have to use the Notification Hubs RESTful API or use the SDK for the backend. Here, you can find an example request for calling an API method:

```
PUT /{hub}/installations/{id}?api-version=2015-01 HTTP/1.1
Host: <namespace>.servicebus.windows.net
Authorization: <authorization token>
Content-Type: application/json
Cache-Control: no-cache


{
```

```
    "installationId": "{id}",
    "platform": "wns",
    "pushChannel": "{push channel}",
    "templates": {
        "myTemplate" : {
            "body" : '<toast><visual lang="en-US"><binding
template="ToastTest01"><text id="1">$myTextProp1</text></
binding></visual></toast>',
            "headers": { "X-WNS-Type": "wns/toast" },
            "tags": ["foo", "bar"]
            }
        }
}
```

To generate an authorization token, you will need to generate a **shared access signature** (**SAS**) token. You can find a guide on how to generate one here: `https://msdn.microsoft.com/library/azure/dn495627.aspx`.

Let's now see what you must do to send a notification using Azure Notification Hubs.

Sending notifications to multiple vendors

The main functionality of Notification Hubs is to send a notification to a set of registered devices. You will see that, using its SDK and portal, you can easily start using this feature without knowing the internal logic of different PNSes. After this section, you should be able to use Notification Hubs without problems and incorporate it into your applications.

Sending a test notification

While developing your application, you always need a way to test it. When using Notification Hubs, you have two options when it comes to sending a test notification—either use the portal or its SDK. Both possibilities allow for similar results; however, using the SDK is a bit more flexible as it is easier to find all the devices to which you would like to send a notification or add any kind of logic.

Test notifications in the Azure portal

When you go to the hub you created, you will see that, at the top of the page, there is a **Test Send** button, as illustrated in the following screenshot:

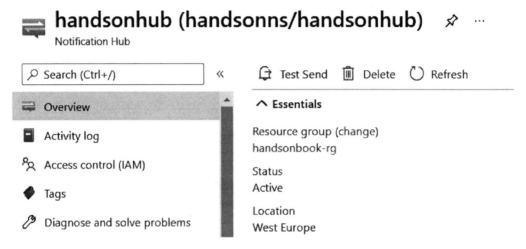

Figure 6.9 – Test Send button on the Overview blade

When you click on it, you will see a screen for the **Test Send** functionality. There are a few fields available, and they all depend on the platform selected. In the following screenshot, you can find a sample request for the Windows platform:

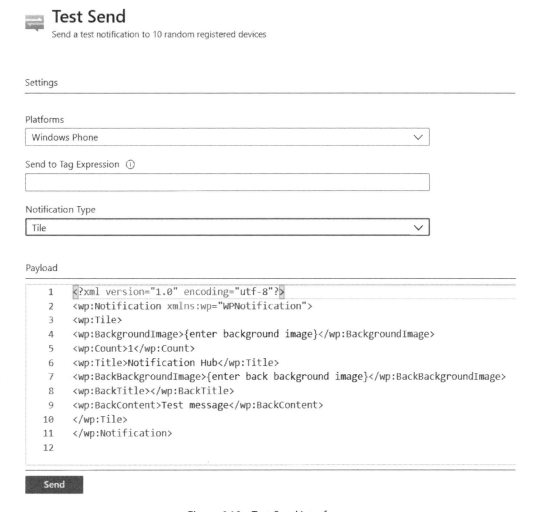

Test Send

Send a test notification to 10 random registered devices

Settings

Platforms

Windows Phone   ∨

Send to Tag Expression ⓘ

Notification Type

Tile   ∨

Payload

```
 1   <?xml version="1.0" encoding="utf-8"?>
 2   <wp:Notification xmlns:wp="WPNotification">
 3   <wp:Tile>
 4   <wp:BackgroundImage>{enter background image}</wp:BackgroundImage>
 5   <wp:Count>1</wp:Count>
 6   <wp:Title>Notification Hub</wp:Title>
 7   <wp:BackBackgroundImage>{enter back background image}</wp:BackBackgroundImage>
 8   <wp:BackTitle></wp:BackTitle>
 9   <wp:BackContent>Test message</wp:BackContent>
10   </wp:Tile>
11   </wp:Notification>
12
```

Send

Figure 6.10 – Test Send interface

Now, if you click the **Send** button, Notification Hubs will select 10 different registered devices that will receive a notification. If you want, you can change both the type and the payload sent. What's more, you can send a message to a specific set of devices by specifying the **Send to Tag Expression** option.

Test notifications in the SDK

It is also possible to send a test notification using the Notification Hubs SDK. Consider the following example:

```
var hub = NotificationHubClient.
CreateClientFromConnectionString(
                "{connection string}",
                "{hub}", true);
```

The last parameter enables sending a test notification. That means that each time you send a notification using the SDK, it will be sent to a maximum of 10 registered devices. Additionally, you will get the outcome of each operation (whether it succeeded or failed).

Remember that when test mode is enabled, each request to Notification Hubs is throttled. That means that you will not be able to overload your communication channel, as send operations will be queued and executed in a controlled manner.

You can check whether **Test Send** is enabled by checking a property on the NotificationHubClient object, as follows:

```
var hub = NotificationHubClient.
CreateClientFromConnectionString(
                "{connection string}",
                "{hub}", true);

if (hub.EnableTestSend)
{
    // Do something....
}
```

This simple conditional statement is everything you need to implement an alternative route in your code and use it—for example, in your tests. To learn more about sending a notification in general, let's continue this topic in the next section.

Using the SDK to send a notification

The Notification Hubs SDK brings with it many different methods for sending notifications, depending on the configuration and expected output. Here, you can find all the methods available in the SDK:

```
hub.SendAdmNativeNotificationAsync();
hub.SendAppleNativeNotificationAsync();
hub.SendBaiduNativeNotificationAsync();
hub.SendDirectNotificationAsync();
hub.SendNotificationAsync();
hub.SendTemplateNotificationAsync();
hub.SendGcmNativeNotificationAsync();
hub.SendWindowsNativeNotificationAsync();
```

As you can see, we have two different categories, as follows:

- **Native notifications**: Methods for sending a notification to a specific platform only

- **Generic notifications**: A set of methods for sending a notification to a specific tag

I strongly encourage you to experiment and test different possibilities, as each method is a bit different. Here, you can find the result of calling `SendAppleNativeNotificationAsync()` and serializing the output:

```
var hub = NotificationHubClient.
CreateClientFromConnectionString(
                "<connection string>",
                "<hub>", true);
await hub.
SendAppleNativeNotificationAsync("{\"aps\":{\"alert\":
\"Notification Hub test notification\"}}");
```

The result will look like this in my case:

```
{

  "Result": {
    "Success": 8,
    "Failure": 0,
    "Results": [{
      "ApplicationPlatform": "apple",
      "PnsHandle": "<pns handle>",
```

```
        "RegistrationId": "1013412858828458675-
3388525925469165319-3",
        "Outcome": "The Notification was successfully sent to the
Push Notification System"
      },
      ...]

    },
    "Id": 9,
    "Exception": null,
    "Status": 5,
    "IsCanceled": false,
    "IsCompleted": true,
    "CreationOptions": 0,
    "AsyncState": null,
    "IsFaulted": false
}
```

As you can see, we get the complete result of sending a notification to a set of registered devices. You can leverage that output to work with your application and, for instance, display the appropriate status or report.

The last topic of this chapter covers an advanced concept called rich content notifications. If you are searching for a solution that will allow you to send messages with a customized appearance, this subject is for you.

Sending a rich content notification through Notification Hubs

In the last section of this chapter, we will talk a bit about another type of notification that is called a **rich content notification**. Sometimes, you may wish to send something more than plain text. In Notification Hubs, it is possible to send—for example—an image to enhance the look and feel of an application.

Please note that receiving rich content notifications requires making changes on the client side. We will not cover that in this chapter but, at the end of it, you will find a link where such an operation is described in detail.

Creating and sending a rich content notification

To create and send a rich content notification, you will need the following two things:

- A model of a notification
- The notification payload and content

The idea is to send it in a way that will enable a client application to fetch rich content and handle it on its side. In fact, the simplest way to do so would be to have an API that provides two operations, as follows:

- Sends a notification
- Fetches notification data

In the following snippet, you can find example code for both actions:

```
[ApiController]
public class HubController :  ControllerBase
{
  public static Lazy<NotificationHubClient> Hub = new
Lazy<NotificationHubClient>(() =>
NotificationHubClient.
CreateClientFromConnectionString("<connection string>",
"<hub>"));

  [HttpPost]
  public async Task<IActionResult> Send()
  {
    var notification = new Notification("Hey, check this
out!");
    var fullNotification = "{\"aps\": {\"content-available\":
1, \"sound\":\"\"}, \"richId\": \"" + notification.Id +
            "\", \"richMessage\": \"" + notification.Message +
"\", \"richType\": \"" +
            notification.RichType + "\"}";
    await Hub.Value.
SendAppleNativeNotificationAsync(fullNotification, "<tag>");

    return Ok();
```

```
  }

  public IActionResultGet(string id)
  {
    var image = Notification.ReadImage(id);
    var result = new HttpResponseMessage(HttpStatusCode.OK)
{Content = new StreamContent(image)};

    result.Content.Headers.ContentType = new System.Net.Http.
Headers.MediaTypeHeaderValue("image/{png}");
    return Ok(result);
  }
}
```

As you can see, the only thing we must do is to keep the correct schema for sending a notification to a particular PNS. In the previous example, I used APNS but, of course, it is possible to use other vendors (if their software supports receiving images or audio through push notifications). You can find an example in the source code for this chapter.

Summary

In this chapter, you have learned what Notification Hubs is and how you can use it to incorporate push notifications into your applications. We covered some reference architectures and possible scenarios that should help you understand what the purpose of this service is and how it solves problems when sending notifications to multiple PNSes and devices.

This chapter ends the first part of this book. In the next one, we will focus on serverless components and architectures.

Questions

Here are some questions to test your knowledge of the important topics in this chapter:

1. What is a PNS?
2. Do multiple platforms (iOS, Android, and Windows) have different PNSes?
3. What is the difference between registration and installation?
4. Can you register the same number of devices in the **Free** and **Basic** tiers?

5. What is the easiest way to check registered devices in Notification Hubs?

6. How can you send a test notification?

7. What are rich content notifications?

Further reading

For more information refer to the following sources:

- Azure Notification Hubs documentation: `https://docs.microsoft.com/en-us/azure/notification-hubs/`

- **Universal Windows Platform** (**UWP**) apps notifications: `https://docs.microsoft.com/azure/notification-hubs/notification-hubs-windows-store-dotnet-get-started-wns-push-notification`

- iOS push notifications: `https://docs.microsoft.com/en-us/azure/notification-hubs/notification-hubs-aspnet-backend-ios-apple-push-notification-service-apns-rich`

- Registration management in Azure Notification Hubs: `https://docs.microsoft.com/en-us/azure/notification-hubs/notification-hubs-push-notification-registration-management`

Part 2: Serverless and Reactive Architecture

Serverless is often a misleading term having different meanings, but we can't deny that it's here to stay and is becoming one of the foundations of cloud architectures. Thanks to the different pricing models and simplified development, it adds even more *sugar* to Azure, allowing a faster time to market and complete focus on delivering business goals.

This part of the book comprises the following chapters:

- *Chapter 7, Serverless and Azure Functions*
- *Chapter 8, Durable Functions*
- *Chapter 9, Integrating Different Components with Logic Apps*
- *Chapter 10, Swiss Army Knife – Azure Cosmos DB*
- *Chapter 11, Reactive Architecture with Event Grid*

7
Serverless and Azure Functions

Azure Functions is the main product of serverless architecture in Azure. It allows the execution of small pieces of code within a fully managed runtime, so we don't have to worry about performance and scalability. It is open source, open for extensions, and built on top of App Services, so it provides an experience that is similar to **Azure WebJobs**. Microsoft pays a lot of attention to the development of new features for Azure Functions, and with great support from the community, it's one of the best tools for quickly developing both simple and complex applications.

In this chapter, the following topics will be covered:

- Understanding Azure Functions
- Configuring the local environment for developing Azure Functions
- Creating a function
- The features of Azure Functions
- Integrating functions with other services

Technical requirements

To begin using Azure Functions and to perform the exercises in this chapter, you will need *Visual Studio Code* with Azure and the Azure Functions extensions installed.

Understanding Azure Functions

Azure Functions is a part of the so-called serverless components that are available in the Azure cloud. Before you start learning about this service, you will have to understand what serverless really means. Initially, you might think that this concept implies no servers at all, but you will quickly reevaluate your way of thinking (as we are still quite far away from not using any kind of machine for our applications and workloads).

Being "serverless"

You can easily find many different articles describing the term "serverless"—to be honest, I would like to avoid promoting a single correct definition. That's because this topic is currently so fuzzy that it is hard to find the best description. However, my goal is to give you some hints and best practices that will enable you to understand this term in a way that makes the most sense to you.

Note that this chapter refers to serverless as a **Function-as-a-Service** (**FaaS**) service. Later in this book, we will cover other Azure components that are also considered serverless, but not FaaS.

The responsibilities of cloud vendors

Let's start with the following screenshot:

Model	IaaS	PaaS	Serverless
Data center	√	√	√
Network security	√	√	√
Operating systems	×	√	√
Dev tools	×	√	√
Application Host	×	×	√

Figure 7.1 – A responsibilities matrix

In the preceding screenshot, you can see a comparison of two of the most popular cloud models with serverless architecture regarding vendor responsibility. I have compared them using five different fields:

- **Data center**: This includes the **data center** (**DC**) infrastructure, security, maintenance, and staff.

- **Network security**: This involves implementing correct and secure solutions regarding the network (such as firewalls, pen tests, and anti-DDoS solutions).

- **Operating systems**: This includes updates, maintenance, and configuration.

- **Dev tools**: This involves developing and delivering multiple features for programmers and administrators (such as extensions to the IDE, management portals, and appropriate tools for managing services).

- **Application host**: This refers to the specific runtime that hosts and runs our application (such as the App Service Plan model).

As you can see, the only difference (at least when using the described characteristics) is the application host. When it comes to serverless components, the only thing that you deliver to your solution is your code (or the configuration that is needed to set up the service)—the rest is delivered and handled by your cloud vendor. Of course, this is not the only way to define this concept.

The pricing model

One of the most popular features of serverless services and architectures is the option to pay for the number of executions and amount of computing power used. This pricing model is the exact opposite of the most common prepaid models, where you pay a fixed price depending on a set of configured fields, such as the number of VMs used or the size of a cluster. Here, you can find a table describing the pricing for Azure Functions (in the West Europe region):

Meter	Price	Free grant (per month)
Execution time	$0.000016/GB/s	400 GB/s
Total executions	$0.2 per million executions	1 million executions

Now, you might be wondering how to decipher this correctly so that you can calculate the estimated cost of your solution. There are two things you need to understand to make your calculation correct:

- **Execution**: This is a single function execution, which lasts N seconds.
- **Consumption**: This defines how many resources (CPU and memory) your function consumes within a fixed time.

Now, if you compare the preceding terms with the table, you will see that they differ slightly. This is because, in Azure Functions, pricing does not directly define the price of consumption, but rather it uses the execution time.

You have probably noticed the **Free grant** column in the pricing table. Remember that this only applies to the Consumption model—it will not work for the prepaid one.

Now, let's assume that you have estimated the following:

- You will need 10 million executions of your function per month.
- Each execution lasts ~80 ms.
- You are using 145 MB of memory per execution.

To calculate the whole price of using Azure Functions, you can use the following formula:

$$(Rx \cdot \$0.000016/GB - s) + (Te \cdot \$0.2)$$

In the previous formula, the following is applicable:

- **Rx**: Here, resource consumption is defined as a product of memory consumed and execution time (in GB/s).

- **Te**: The total number of executions (in millions).

Now, if you enter the correct values and calculate the formula, you will get the following result:

$$((\frac{256}{1024}GB \cdot 1Ms) \cdot 0.000016/GB - s) + 10 \cdot 0.2)$$

This will give you the following cost: 6 USD. However, you might find the previous formula a bit confusing—for instance, why did I use *256* (instead of 128) as the amount of memory consumed and *1 ms* (instead of 800 Ks) as the execution time? Well, there is one important thing to remember when using the Consumption plan: the minimum execution time is 100 ms. Additionally, when it comes to resource consumption, this is always **rounded up** to the nearest 128 MBs.

In fact, when it comes to function execution, you cannot go under 100 ms and 128 MBs of used memory. This is very important when calculating the possible cost of optimization, as often, you should not aim at optimizing functions and, instead, focus on the overall algorithm changes (such as batching or better serialization methods).

The concepts of Azure Functions

Now that you are slightly more familiar with what serverless architecture is, we can start learning about something else to do with Azure Functions. To proceed, you will need to have a clear understanding of the differences between the following topics:

- Function apps
- Functions
- Triggers and bindings

Function apps

The logical container for multiple functions is called a function app. A function app can host one or more functions that will share the configuration, settings, and runtime version. It is possible to run functions using multiple languages in the same function app.

Here, you can see what a single-function app looks like, with a few individual functions hosted within it:

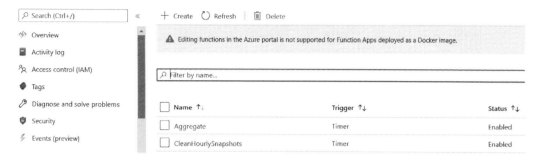

Figure 7.2 – A working function app

If you are required to use both pricing plans (that is, Consumption and App Service), you will need two different function apps, as one on its own does not support such a scenario.

Functions

A single executable part of Azure Functions that hosts your code is called a **function**. Each function can execute code written in different supported languages (for instance, one function can use C#, while another function can leverage Python features). The currently supported languages are as follows:

- C#
- Java
- JavaScript
- PowerShell
- Python
- TypeScript
- Go
- Rust

Here, you can find an example function with some boilerplate code written in C#:

```csharp
namespace Company.Function
{
    public static class HttpTrigger1
    {
        [Function("HttpTrigger1")]
        public static HttpResponseData Run([HttpTrigger(AuthorizationLevel.Function, "get", "post")] HttpRequestData req,
            FunctionContext executionContext)
        {
            var logger = executionContext.GetLogger("HttpTrigger1");
            logger.LogInformation("C# HTTP trigger function processed a request.");

            var response = req.CreateResponse(HttpStatusCode.OK);
            response.Headers.Add("Content-Type", "text/plain; charset=utf-8");

            response.WriteString("Welcome to Azure Functions!");

            return response;
        }
    }
}
```

Figure 7.3 – The boilerplate Azure function triggered by an HTTP request

As you can see, a function consists of the following components:

- **Function decorator**: For example, [Function], which allows the runtime to find a function and delivers the required metadata.

- **Trigger**: For example, [HttpTrigger] —each function requires a trigger to be configured correctly.

- **Trigger data**: For example, HttpRequestData, which will be passed for each function invocation individually.

- **Function code**: This is the actual logic that will be executed each time the function is called.

Of course, some parts of a function will differ depending on the features you use. In the previous example, we used a trigger for a common HTTP call, but there are also other possibilities (such as Azure Storage Queue, Azure Service Bus, or Azure CosmosDB). Additionally, you can use other bindings and provide custom code each time. We will cover all of these topics in the upcoming sections of this chapter.

Triggers and bindings

The power of Azure Functions becomes evident when you consider all possible integrations that can be used seamlessly and without much additional effort. In fact, the list of available triggers and bindings is quite impressive:

- Blob storage
- Azure CosmosDB

- Dapr
- Azure Event Grid
- Azure Event Hub
- HTTP
- IoT Hub
- Microsoft Graph
- Azure Mobile Apps
- Azure Notification Hub
- Azure Service Bus
- Timer
- Twilio
- SendGrid
- SignalR
- Table storage

Additionally, you have access to some experimental triggers and bindings that might not be officially supported, but they can be used in your application if you decide to do so (such as external files and external tables). Remember that some experimental triggers and bindings will never reach **General Availability** (**GA**) status as there are specific recommendations that, in most cases, should be followed.

Of course, it is possible to introduce custom triggers and bindings since Azure Functions provides a full SDK that can be used to extend runtime. However, this is an advanced topic that will be not covered in this book—you can find a reference to the appropriate tutorials in the *Further reading* section. Custom solutions are especially helpful if you feel as though some native features lack the functionalities you expect, or for instance, you require better performance.

Pricing models

In Azure Functions, there are three pricing models available:

- **The Consumption model**: This was described in the earlier sections. Here, you pay for the number of executions of your functions and the computing power used.

- **The App Service plan model**: This is where you select an App Service plan version, which has a fixed price no matter how many times you execute your functions.

- **The Premium plan**: If you feel that the Consumption model for Azure Functions has many downsides (such as cold starts, a lack of VNet access, or not-so-great performance), you could leverage the Premium plan, where you can allocate CPU and memory specifically for your application.

All of these options serve a different purpose and offer a different experience when hosting your application. We will discuss them in more detail throughout this chapter.

Scaling

One of the most important features of serverless components and architectures is their ability to scale out as they are loaded more and more. While in traditional **Platform-as-a-Service (PaaS)** services, you often have to worry about available instances or scaling configuration, serverless allows for the seamless handling of incoming requests, even if a service is hit by unexpectedly high traffic. In this section, we will talk about the scaling capabilities of Azure Functions, with a focus on the differences between the Consumption and App Service models.

Scaling in the Consumption model

When you use the Consumption model in Azure Functions, you are not defining any available instances for your service and are unable to configure the autoscaling settings. In fact, in this model, you are completely unaware of the number of machines running your workloads (however, if you integrate your functions with Azure Application Insights, you will be able to see how many instances have been created by looking at the **Live Stream** blade).

In the Consumption model, you have a fixed limit when it comes to the amount of memory available for each execution of your function—this is 1.536 MB. Whether your functions will scale or not depends on the current utilization of both memory and CPU.

The advantage of this plan is the ability to easily scale to hundreds of functions while running the same code concurrently. Of course, this all depends on the actual trigger used in a function—while, with the HTTP trigger, you must scale out to be able to handle multiple requests at once, using the event hub trigger, for instance, will automatically increase the number of working instances for each partition used. On the other hand, you cannot always rely on the Consumption plan to ensure there are no expected delays in responses or temporary unavailability—immediate scaling out is not guaranteed by any means, so this pricing plan is not always the best solution when your application needs to be able to face quick peaks of traffic.

Remember that the current maximum for scaling a function app is limited to 200. It is also worth noting that the runtime will allocate new instances no more than every 10 seconds.

Scaling in the App Service model

Using the App Service model has its benefits, especially when it comes to covering some cases of scaling that are not covered in the Consumption plan. As mentioned in the previous section, if you need to be sure that you can handle the incoming load, it is often a better idea to use this particular model. This is because it ensures that some fixed resources will be available for your function app. Additionally, you can be 100% sure that the provided hardware is provisioned for your application—this is not always the case in the Consumption model since you have no guarantees when it comes to delivered machines and their characteristics. What's more, you can ensure that your runtime is always running since, in the consumption model, when a function is not used, its resources will be deallocated, so you can face quite common issues such as cold starts.

Scaling in the Premium plan

Premium plan scaling works in a similar way to the Consumption plan. Here, the difference is in how quickly a new instance can be made usable for your application. When configuring your Premium plan parameters, you can enter how many pre-warmed instances should be made available for your service. While the default value is 1, you can decide whether that is insufficient. Azure will take care of provisioning any additional compute power for you and keep it ready for the scaling operations. In contrast to the Consumption plan, the Premium functions do not charge you for execution. Instead, you are billed for the time the whole compute power was allocated to you. Therefore, the Premium plan is an optimal solution for these scenarios, whereas the Consumption plan seems like a wrong choice—a huge number of small executions, requiring a stable environment and good performance.

Now that we have covered the high-level details of Azure Functions, let's switch our focus to local development and more technical stuff.

Configuring the local environment for developing Azure Functions

Before we get started with Azure Functions, we will need an environment that will allow us to test our functions and start developing them quickly and seamlessly. Fortunately, this Azure service comes with multiple tools that help us during the programming and running of them locally. Additionally, I will describe some extra applications that should help you to analyze and debug possible problems and test triggers before deploying them to the cloud.

Starting with Azure Functions locally

If you have installed all of the required software mentioned at the beginning of this chapter, you should be able to start developing them without any additional configuration. To begin, we will create a simple function that we will try to run to ensure that everything is set up and ready.

When you open your Visual Studio Code instance, use the *Ctrl + Shift + P* keyboard combination to open the command palette. Search for `Azure Functions: Create new project` to start a creator. This will guide you through the process of creating a function app:

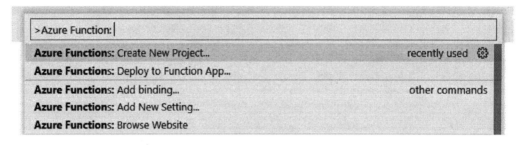

Figure 7.4 – The Azure Functions command in Visual Studio Code

Here, the first step that is needed will be the selection of a directory, where a new project will be created. It can be any folder you have access to, but make sure it is inside the working directory you have currently opened:

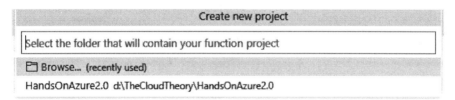

Figure 7.5 – Selecting a project directory

Next, select a language for your functions. Note, that the available options might rely on the version of the Azure Functions extension you have installed:

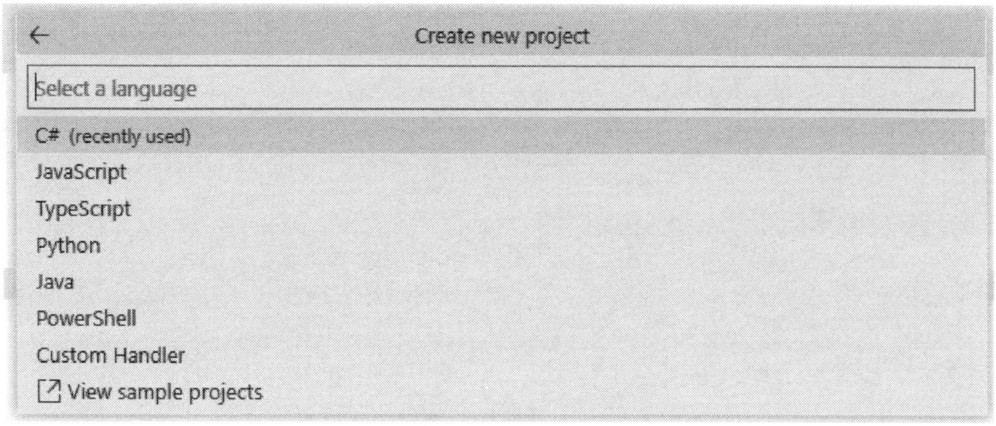

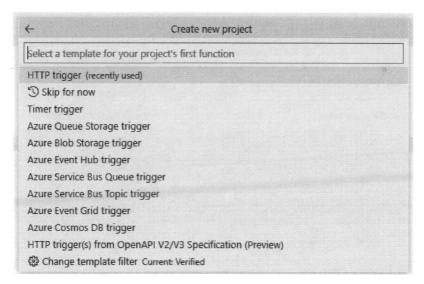

Figure 7.6 – Language selection

Additionally, depending on the language of your choice, it might be necessary to select the version that will be used to create your functions. The options that are available will solely depend on the platform you have selected. In my example, I chose the **.NET 5** (isolated) option, as it offers better control over my environment compared to previous versions of the framework. The last step is to tell the creator what trigger should be used for the first function:

Figure 7.7 – The trigger selection

For the sake of this exercise, I have selected the HTTP trigger, as it does not require additional knowledge related to the Azure services. After providing the name of a function (and, optionally, its namespace), you will be probably asked for the method of authorization when calling the function:

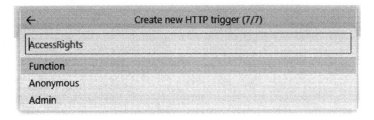

Figure 7.8 – Selecting the authorization method

Authorization methods are only available for triggers, which allows for interaction with a user. If you decide that you would like to go for a timer trigger or a queue trigger, you will not be asked for authorization as there is no such concept, at least from an Azure Functions point of view.

> **Note**
> Authorization does not affect your functions when you are working with them using a local environment. In other words, it does not matter what method is chosen for a function called locally—you will be able to call it anonymously nonetheless.

After completing the wizard, wait a few seconds for the files to be created. Once the creator has finished, you will see a project generated, with all the files ready:

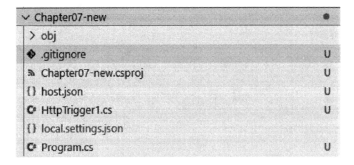

Figure 7.9 – The structure of the Azure Functions project in C#

Of course, the files created will be different for each platform you selected (for instance, there will be different elements for Java and different elements for Python). However, the overall structure should be the same. For now, look at the `local.settings.json` file—as you can see, it is ignored in Git by default because it will only contain the settings that have been designed on your machine. Let's open it and check one important setting.

The general structure of the local settings file will appear, more or less, as follows:

```
{
  "IsEncrypted": false,
  "Values": {
    "AzureWebJobsStorage": "",
    "FUNCTIONS_WORKER_RUNTIME": "dotnet-isolated"
  }
}
```

Here, in the `Values` object, you can enter any value in a key-value fashion. The important thing here is the `AzureWebJobsStorage` key. Apparently, it is empty — for now. This setting is one of the fundamental parameters required to run most Azure Functions triggers. The empty value is the outcome of us selecting an HTTP trigger for the first function. When deployed to Azure, it will be replaced with an Azure Storage connection string (or Managed Identity if you decide to work with the newer versions of the extensions). However, to run the functions in your own isolated environment, you can replace them with `UseDevelopmentStorage=true`, as follows:

```
{
  "IsEncrypted": false,
  "Values": {
    "AzureWebJobsStorage": "UseDevelopmentStorage=true",
    "FUNCTIONS_WORKER_RUNTIME": "dotnet-isolated"
  }
}
```

The preceding snippet will tell your local runtime to connect to **Storage Emulator** instead of a real cloud service.

> **Note**
>
> A new version of SDK for Azure should install **Storage Emulator** automatically. If, for some reason, you are missing it, navigate to `https://docs.microsoft.com/en-us/azure/storage/common/storage-use-emulator#get-the-storage-emulator` and install the missing component. Also, make sure it is running before starting your functions locally.

To ensure that everything is working correctly, press *F5* and wait until the project has been compiled. In the terminal window, you should see how the project is initialized and how the runtime starts all the functions it could find:

```
> Executing task: func host start <


Azure Functions Core Tools
Core Tools Version:      3.0.3568 Commit hash: e30a0ede85fd498199c28ad699ab2548593f759b  (64-bit)
Function Runtime Version: 3.0.15828.0


Functions:

        HttpTrigger1: [GET,POST] http://localhost:7071/api/HttpTrigger1

For detailed output, run func with --verbose flag.
[2021-10-17T15:28:00.440Z] Worker process started and initialized.
[2021-10-17T15:28:04.945Z] Host lock lease acquired by instance ID '000000000000000000000000FEAC3730'.
```

Figure 7.10 – The boilerplate project has been initialized and is running

As we are using an HTTP trigger, our function is exposed as a simple HTTP endpoint, which can be called by any client that knows it. In addition to the URL used, you can see that your endpoint has been exposed with an `/api` prefix, port `7071` will be used for connections, and both the **GET** and **POST** methods have been accepted.

Now, we will try to call it to see whether it works by simply going to any browser and accessing the endpoint:

```
Welcome to Azure Functions!
```

Figure 7.11 – Working with the Azure Functions endpoint

As you can see, it returns a welcome message, which is a part of our recently created function. If you send the same request, you should be able to see the same result. If, for some reason, you are unable to do so, perform the following checks:

- Make sure that your function's host is still working and that it displays no error.

- Make sure that the port under which the runtime listens for incoming requests is open.

- Make sure that the Azure Functions CLI is not blocked by your firewall.

- Make sure that you are calling the correct endpoint.

In the next section, I will describe the function's structure in detail so that you will be able to proceed with more advanced scenarios and features.

Creating a function

We discussed the overall serverless approach and went through local configuration to make sure that we have some basic understandings of what Azure Functions is and how we can start working with it. In the remainder of this chapter, I will show you what exactly this service offers and how to work with it on daily basis. This will enable you to start developing full projects with Azure Functions—from the simplest to the most advanced ones.

Using Visual Studio Code

In the previous section, you created a function using a wizard in Visual Studio. If you go back to this project and open its file, you will see some common code, which is always created with this template:

```
using System.Collections.Generic;
using System.Net;
using Microsoft.Azure.Functions.Worker;
using Microsoft.Azure.Functions.Worker.Http;
using Microsoft.Extensions.Logging;


namespace Company.Function
{
    public static class HttpTrigger1
    {
        [Function("HttpTrigger1")]
        public static HttpResponseData
Run([HttpTrigger(AuthorizationLevel.Function, "get", "post")]
HttpRequestData req,
```

```
                FunctionContext executionContext)
        {
            // Here goes your function code…
        }
    }
}
```

Here, we can see some attributes that decorate both a C# method and its parameters—they all are a part of the runtime that runs your functions. Let's compare it with a function that is triggered by Azure Storage Queue:

```
using System;
using Microsoft.Azure.Functions.Worker;
using Microsoft.Extensions.Logging;

namespace Company.Function
{
    public static class QueueTrigger1
    {
        [Function("QueueTrigger1")]
        public static void Run([QueueTrigger("myqueue-items",
Connection = "AzureWebJobsStorage")] string myQueueItem,
            FunctionContext context)
        {
        }
    }
}
```

Here, you can see that we still have the `[FunctionName]` attribute and the trigger attribute. What differs between those two functions is, in fact, the type of trigger parameter—in HTTP, we had `HttpRequestData`, while in Queue, we have a simple `string` parameter. This parameter (and its type) directly defines the type of message delivered to a function. In general, each HTTP request is deserialized and delivered as `HttpRequestData`, while each message in a queue is a string.

> **Note**
>
> Static types and attributes are only usable in languages that support them. If you go for a platform that is not typed (such as JavaScript), the function structure will be slightly different and will mostly rely on convention.

However, input parameter binding is not limited to a single type only. Depending on the trigger type, we might add additional parameters that are passed as a part of a trigger:

```
using System.Collections.Generic;
using System.Net;
using Microsoft.Azure.Functions.Worker;
using Microsoft.Azure.Functions.Worker.Http;
using Microsoft.Extensions.Logging;


namespace Company.Function
{
    public static class HttpTrigger1
    {
        [Function("HttpTrigger3")]
        public static HttpResponseData
Run([HttpTrigger(AuthorizationLevel.Function, "get", "post",
Route = "Function3/name/{name}")] HttpRequestData req, string
name,
            FunctionContext executionContext)
        {
        }
    }
}
```

As you can see, the preceding example introduced one more parameter—name. This is a string, though the whole function is triggered by an HTTP request. This parameter will be used during the binding procedure. During this procedure, you will find that this function's route contains it in its URL template. This is the very same model that is used in traditional MVC/Web API frameworks, which provide the same feature.

The binding procedure itself is quite complicated and mostly depends on the type of trigger used. Unfortunately, this is beyond the scope of this book, so I will not cover it in detail—fortunately, Azure Functions are OSS, so you can check how the host works directly in the code.

If you want to quickly add a new function to your project, perform the following steps:

1. Use *Ctrl + Shift + P* to open the command palette.

2. Search for the Azure Functions: Create function menu item.

3. Select a function template and follow the creation wizard.

This whole procedure is very similar to the creation of an Azure Functions project. Depending on the function template, you might need to answer slightly different questions. However, in the end, a function is added to the project you selected.

Using the Azure portal

As with all other Azure services, it is also possible to create a function app instance by creating it directly in the Azure portal:

1. When you log in, click on + **Create a resource** and search for Function App.

2. When you click on **Create**, you will see a common screen, which will guide you through the process of creating a new function app resource:

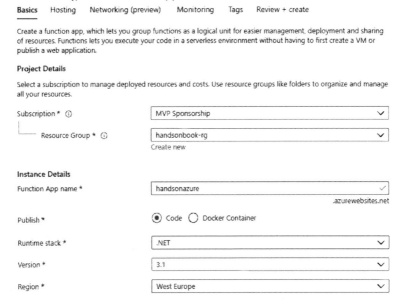

Figure 7.12 – The Azure Functions resource creation wizard

As you can see, the preceding form is familiar to the one we used when creating an App Service instance. This is because, under the hood, Azure Functions is powered by these services, and multiple available features are shared between them. In the **Hosting** tab, you can select whether you want to use the **Consumption Plan**, **Premium Plan**, or **App Service** models for pricing. What is more, you will have the ability to select the OS that is used and the storage account required to power up your functions (remember the **AzureWebJobsStorage** setting?):

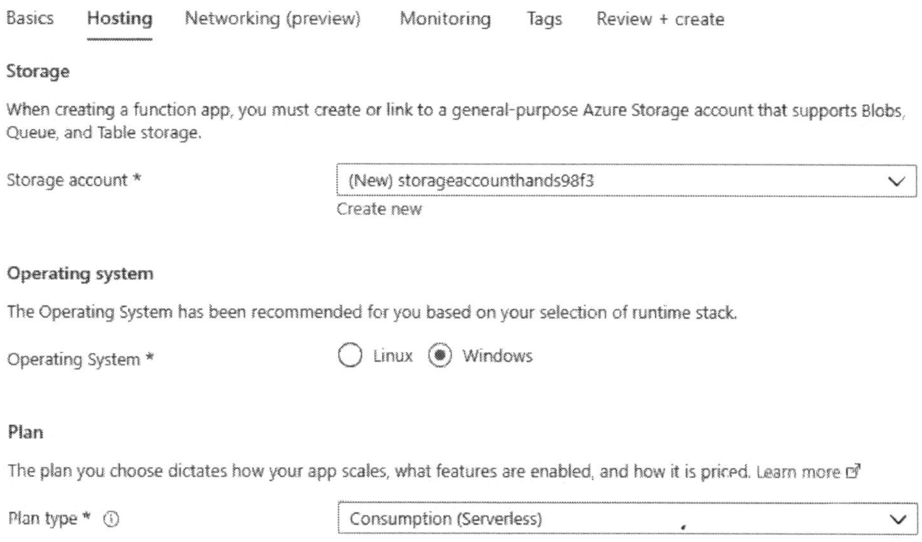

Basics   **Hosting**   Networking (preview)   Monitoring   Tags   Review + create

Storage

When creating a function app, you must create or link to a general-purpose Azure Storage account that supports Blobs, Queue, and Table storage.

Storage account *   (New) storageaccounthands98f3   ⌄
                            Create new

Operating system

The Operating System has been recommended for you based on your selection of runtime stack.

Operating System *   ◯ Linux   ⦿ Windows

Plan

The plan you choose dictates how your app scales, what features are enabled, and how it is priced. Learn more ◨

Plan type * ⓘ   Consumption (Serverless)   ⌄

Figure 7.13 – The Hosting tab

We discussed the differences between these models earlier in the chapter, so you should be able to decide which one to use by yourself. This wizard also gives you the option to enable the **Application Insights** integration. Since we have not discussed this service yet, I will skip it in this chapter. However, if you are interested in monitoring your functions, note that it is a much better option than the integrated **Monitor** feature—it gives you much more detail and is far more intuitive in daily work.

Enabling **Application Insights** for your function app can drastically change the overall price of the whole service, as initially, each function produces many different traces and logs. For production, it is always a good idea to lower the severity of logged messages—you can find more information about this configuration at `https://docs.microsoft.com/en-us/azure/azure-functions/functions-monitoring`.

When you are satisfied with your settings, you can click on **Create**. The Azure portal will validate all the fields and initiate the service provisioning procedure. After several seconds, your function app should be ready for work. When you navigate to it, you will see the dashboard, which is the starting point for accessing all the features of Azure Functions:

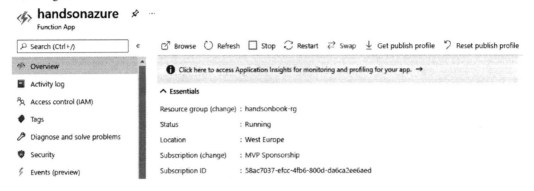

Figure 7.14 – The overview tab of Azure Functions

Now, if you want to create a function, navigate to the **Functions** blade. From there, you will be able to access the **Create** button to get started with a new template:

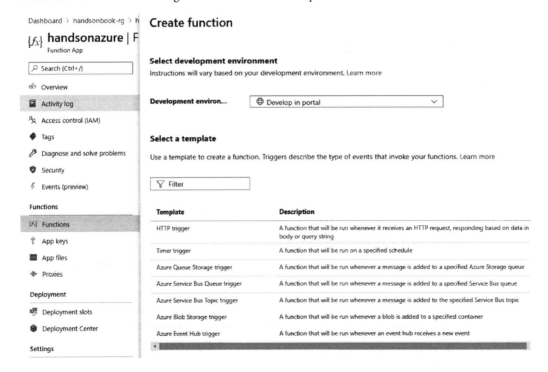

Figure 7.15 – Creating a function from the Azure portal

As you can see, from there, we can select our development environment (this depends on whether you would like to use the portal or one of the supported IDEs). For this exercise, I decided to go for the timer function:

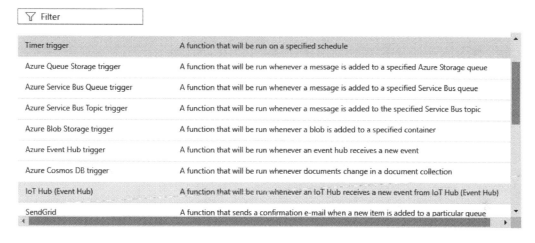

Figure 7.16 – Configuring a function triggered by a timer

> **Note**
>
> In the previous versions of Azure Functions, you could host multiple runtimes using the same function app. In that scenario, it was possible to start with a Java function and then add a JavaScript function to the same function app. Unfortunately, that is no longer possible.

After clicking on the **Create** button, you will see that a function code has been generated and can be altered directly in the portal. The portal also allows you to edit a function directly in your browser window, so if you want to try out some custom code, there is nothing preventing you from doing so:

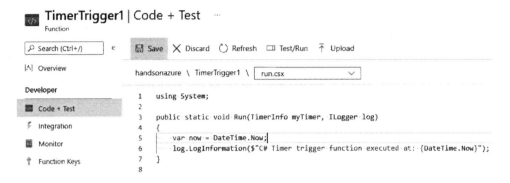

Figure 7.17 – A function generated inside the portal

Additionally, you can click on **Test/Run**—this is the so-called **manual trigger** and enables you to start a function immediately. The result of running a function will be visible in the **Logs** window:

```
Connected!
2021-10-18T07:11:49Z    [Information]    Executing 'Functions.
TimerTrigger1' (Reason='This function was programmatically
called via the host APIs.', Id=7b4b5a29-e3fb-4d58-b668-
2444c2210f72)
```

Congratulations—you have learned how to create a function using both Visual Studio Code and the Azure portal. In the next section, I will describe more advanced scenarios and focus on understanding the features of Azure Functions further.

The features of Azure Functions

Azure Functions is not only about providing executable code that can be handled by the runtime. It allows for even more advanced scenarios, which make this service an excellent choice when you want to start developing quickly and with minimal configuration required. In this section, I will show you how to leverage more advanced features of functions and how to enhance your skill in using this Azure component.

Platform features

As you might recall, Azure Functions is built on top of App Service, which allows you to use multiple features that you already know, such as **Custom domains**, **Application settings**, and **Authentication/Authorization**. To check what is available, navigate to your function app in the Azure portal and search for the **Settings** section:

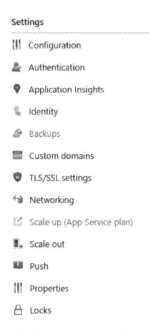

Figure 7.18 – The Settings section of Azure Functions

As you can see, we have a variety of different features available—what you are interested in depends solely on your specific requirements. However, there is one function-specific feature that I would like to describe: **Configuration**. This is where your **Function App** settings are stored and can be changed. Navigate to this blade to access the parameters:

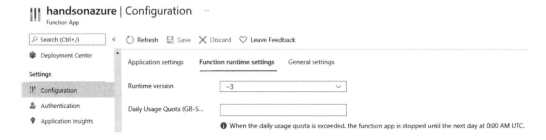

Figure 7.19 – Function runtime settings

The way that the function app configuration works is that it combines with **Application settings**, which is available in Azure App Services with some additional layers introduced by it. As you can see in *Figure 7.19*, you can change the runtime version of your functions' host and decide how much memory they can use on a daily basis. Here, you can find more details about those capabilities:

- **Daily Usage Quota (GB-Sec)**: If you want to set a hard limit for function app usage, you can set it here. Thanks to this, you can ensure that it will not exceed the predefined quota you are aiming for.

- **Runtime version**: This setting defines the current runtime version that your function app uses. Note that it is not possible to change v1 to beta (in this case, v2), as it is possible that the newer version introduces some changes that could break your application.

While the Azure portal allows you to change the mentioned parameters, in most cases, you will rarely use them directly. In general, they should be managed via automation scripts and never modified manually, as they can easily break a running function.

Security

We have not covered another important topic yet—Azure Functions security. While it is possible to use, for example, Azure Active Directory or other social providers as identity sources (and, as a result, add authentication to a function app), by default, functions are secured by their keys. You can check the available keys when you click on the **App keys** blade in the portal:

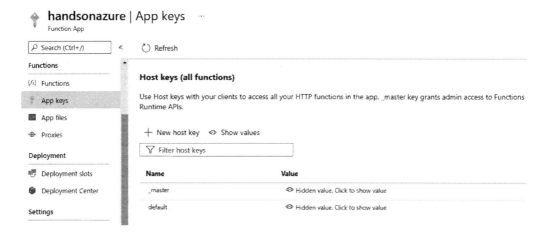

Figure 7.20 – The App keys blade containing host keys for the functions

However, we previously talked about different authorization levels. In *Figure 7.20*, you can see host keys, which give you *admin* access – if a user has them, they can call any function (which is, of course, callable). As this is not something you would like to use constantly, different options are available. To access function keys, go to your function and search for the **Function Keys** tab:

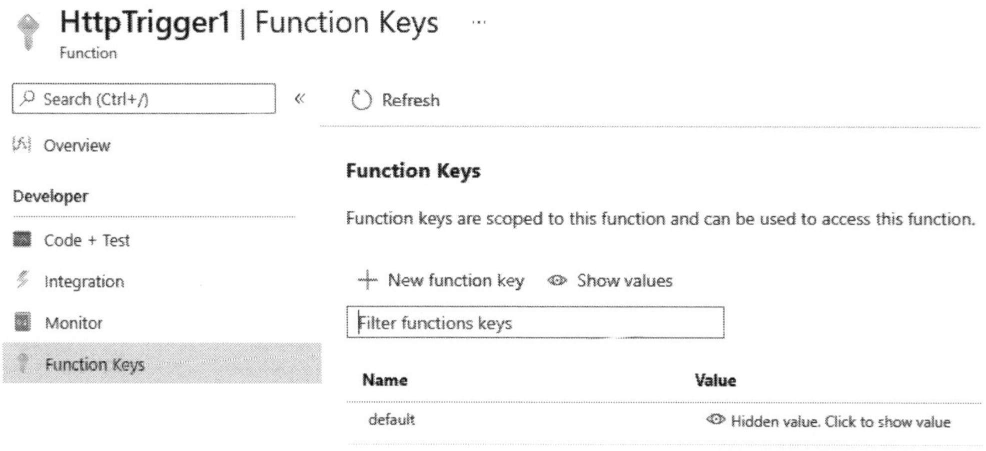

Figure 7.21 – Function Keys available for a function

In general, you can use keys as an easy way to implement authorization in your function app. You can generate a new one for each client, revoke them, and set a particular value.

Note that function keys are designed for functions that are triggered by HTTP requests—there is no possibility to use them for other kinds of triggers.

There are two ways of using function keys to authorize a request. First, you can put them inside the query string:

```
https://handsonazurefunctionapp.azurewebsites.net/api/HttpTrig-
gerJS1?code=awKhkdPqyQvYUwzn6zle6V4hqk460YwOBs9RyaQUthX/AWGBM-
jtRIA==
```

Second, you can use headers and introduce the `x-functions-key` header, which will contain a key inside it:

```
GET /api/HttpTriggerJS1 HTTP/1.1
Host: handsonazurefunctionapp.azurewebsites.ne
Content-Type: application/json
x-functions-key: awKhkdPqyQvYUwzn6zle6V4hqk460YwOBs9RyaQUthX/
AWGBMjtRIA==
Cache-Control: no-cache
```

The choice is yours here – both options offer the same functionality, and the only difference is whether you prefer passing a key over the URL or using headers.

Monitor

Each call and execution of a function is monitored and saved. When you click on the **Monitor** tab, you will see a screen that contains the next execution with some diagnostics data. Here, you can see the log of executions for my function, triggered by a timer:

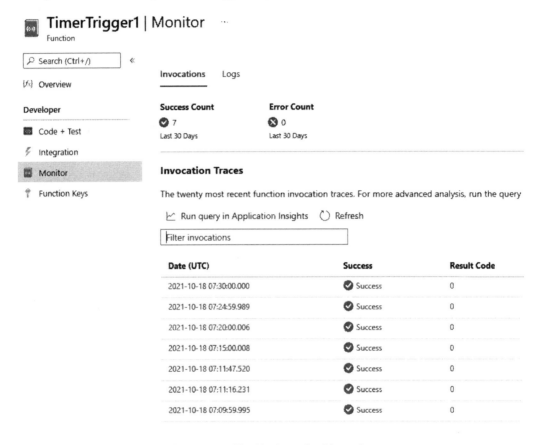

Figure 7.22 – The Monitor tab with results

As you can see, it contains information about each execution, the success and error count, and the invocation details. When you select a specific item, you will also see all the logs from a function. The **Monitor** feature is quite useful for quickly analyzing issues and seamlessly integrates with **Application Insights** for more advanced queries and filters. We will talk about that service in more detail later in the book.

host.json

When you create a function, you will see that a `host.json` file is automatically created. While initially empty, it is a global configuration file that defines how the triggers and functions will behave. Here, you can find an example file with most features, such as binding configurations and generic features, available:

```json
{
    "version": "2.0",
    "aggregator": {
        "batchSize": 1000,
        "flushTimeout": "00:00:30"
    },
    "extensions": {
        "blobs": {},
        "cosmosDb": {},
        "durableTask": {},
        "eventHubs": {},
        "http": {},
        "queues": {},
        "sendGrid": {},
        "serviceBus": {}
    },
    "extensionBundle": {
        "id": "Microsoft.Azure.Functions.ExtensionBundle",
        "version": "[1.*, 2.0.0)"
    },
    "functions": [ "QueueProcessor", "GitHubWebHook" ],
    "functionTimeout": "00:05:00",
    "healthMonitor": {
        "enabled": true,
        "healthCheckInterval": "00:00:10",
        "healthCheckWindow": "00:02:00",
        "healthCheckThreshold": 6,
        "counterThreshold": 0.80
    },

    "managedDependency": {
```

```
        "enabled": true
    },
    "retry": {
      "strategy": "fixedDelay",
      "maxRetryCount": 5,
      "delayInterval": "00:00:05"
    },
    "singleton": {
      "lockPeriod": "00:00:15",
      "listenerLockPeriod": "00:01:00",
      "listenerLockRecoveryPollingInterval": "00:01:00",
      "lockAcquisitionTimeout": "00:01:00",
      "lockAcquisitionPollingInterval": "00:00:03"
    },
    "watchDirectories": [ "Shared", "Test" ],
    "watchFiles": [ "myFile.txt" ]
}
```

As you can see, it contains things such as the function timeout value and configuration of particular triggers. In the *Further reading* section, you will find a link where each section of the host.json file is described in detail.

Publish

Azure Functions publishes in the same way as App Service since they share many common parts. If you use the *Ctrl + Shift + P* combination in Visual Studio Code and select **Azure Functions: Deploy to Function App option**, you will see a wizard, which will guide you through the process of deployment:

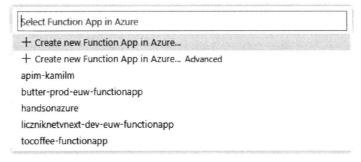

Figure 7.23 – The publish wizard for Azure Functions in Visual Studio Code

Traditionally, you have the option to select whether you want to create a new function app or use an existing one. When you want to use the existing one, just click on it and confirm that you would like to overwrite the previous deployment:

Figure 7.24 – Overwrite confirmation

Now, when you click on **Deploy**, the process of deployment will start and, within a few seconds, a new version of your function app will be available. With the function deployed, let's learn how it can be integrated with different services.

Integrating functions with other services

In the last part of this chapter, we will focus a little bit on understanding how Azure Functions integrates with other Azure services. We will look at the available triggers and bindings and try to figure out the best use cases for them along with how they really work. This section is designed in a way that enables you to explore more by yourself—thanks to a common understanding of how Azure Functions works.

The Function file

The way in which the Azure Functions bindings work is that they are compiled into a metadata file, which is generated when your function app is built. This file can be found among your compilation artifacts (try searching for the `functions.metadata` file). The file structure can be a little bit different depending on the platform used and the actual triggers/outputs, but the generic structure can be presented as follows:

```
[
  {
    "name": "HttpTrigger1",
    "scriptFile": "Chapter07-new.dll",
    "entryPoint": "Company.Function.HttpTrigger1.Run",
    "language": "dotnet-isolated",
    "properties": {
      "IsCodeless": false
    },
```

```json
    "bindings": [
      {
        "name": "req",
        "type": "HttpTrigger",
        "direction": "In",
        "authLevel": "Function",
        "methods": [
          "get",
          "post"
        ],
        "route": "Function3/name/{name}"
      },
      {
        "name": "$return",
        "type": "http",
        "direction": "Out"
      }
    ]
  },
  {
    "name": "QueueTrigger1",
    "scriptFile": "Chapter07-new.dll",
    "entryPoint": "Company.Function.QueueTrigger1.Run",
    "language": "dotnet-isolated",
    "properties": {
      "IsCodeless": false
    },
    "bindings": [
      {
        "name": "myQueueItem",
        "type": "QueueTrigger",
        "direction": "In",
        "dataType": "String",
        "queueName": "myqueue-items",
        "connection": "AzureWebJobsStorage"
      }
```

```
      ]
    }
]
```

As you can see, this contains the definition of each function along with the bindings used there. The schema for the metadata file is primarily designed for the function host to understand, and in general, you should not bother learning it. Of course, if you ever decide you need that kind of functionality, you can generate the metadata file on your own – from my perspective, it is rather a complex task and, in most cases, not worth the time invested.

The information stored in the metadata directly reflects the structure of each function. For example, the metadata stores information related to all the parameters used in a function definition:

```
[Function("HttpTrigger1")]
public static HttpResponseData
Run([HttpTrigger(AuthorizationLevel.Function, "get", "post",
Route = "Function3/name/{name}")] HttpRequestData req,
    FunctionContext executionContext)
{
}
```

When you compile your project, a compiler will add all the functions to the metadata file for each function defined in your code. Here, you can find the output for the event hub trigger:

```
{
    "name": "EventHubTrigger1",
    "scriptFile": "Chapter07-new.dll",
    "entryPoint": "Company.Function.EventHubTrigger1.Run",
    "language": "dotnet-isolated",
    "properties": {
      "IsCodeless": false
    },
    "bindings": [
      {
        "name": "input",
        "type": "EventHubTrigger",
        "direction": "In",
        "eventHubName": "samples-workitems",
        "connection": "AzureWebJobsStorage",
        "cardinality": "Many",
```

```
        "dataType": "String"
    }
  ]
}
```

As you can see, it has the same structure and only the `bindings` field differs, so it reflects another trigger type.

Note that the content and structure of `function.metadata` might differ depending on the SDK version used. Do not use it in your application directly to avoid problems involving a lack of backward compatibility.

Input/output bindings

Some bindings are bidirectional, whereas some can only be used in one direction. What's more, not every binding can be used as a trigger. An example of both a bidirectional binding and a trigger binding is Azure Blob storage. Here, you can find an example of how it works as a trigger (note that this is written in Java):

```java
@FunctionName("handsonblobprocessor")
public void run(
  @BlobTrigger(name = "file",
              dataType = "binary",
              path = "blob/{name}",
              connection = "Connection") byte[] content,
  @BindingName("name") String filename,
  final ExecutionContext context
) {
}
```

Compare this with the example of a function triggered by a queue but accepts a blob as input:

```java
@FunctionName("copyBlobHttp")
  @StorageAccount("Storage_Account_Connection_String")
  public HttpResponseMessage receiveBlob(
    @HttpTrigger(name = "req",
      methods = {HttpMethod.GET},
      authLevel = AuthorizationLevel.ANONYMOUS)
    HttpRequestMessage<Optional<String>> request,
```

```
@BlobOutput(
  name = "target",
  path = "blob/{Query.file} ")
OutputBinding<String> outputItem,
  final ExecutionContext context) {
}
```

As you can see, the syntax is still similar in both cases. However, instead of using `BlobTrigger`, I am using `BlobOutput` in the second example. The overall configuration and the way bindings are configured depend solely on the platform of your choice. While for C# or Java, you define most of the things directly in the code, others such as JavaScript or Python require a slightly more sophisticated approach. For example, if you would like to define a function that accepts a queue message as a trigger and a blob as both an input and an output, the following code can get the job done:

```
def main(msg: func.QueueMessage, input: bytes, output: func.
Out[bytes]):
    logging.info(f'Python Queue trigger function processed
{len(inputblob)} bytes')
    output.set(input)
```

However, in addition to this, you will need to set all the bindings inside a `function.json` file that is available for your function:

```
{
  "bindings": [
    {
      "queueName": "myqueue-items",
      "connection": "QueueConnection",
      "name": "msg",
      "type": "queueTrigger",
      "direction": "in"
    },
    {
      "name": "input",
      "type": "blob",
      "dataType": "binary",
      "path": "files/{queueTrigger}",
      "connection": "StorageConnection",
      "direction": "in"
```

```
    },
    {
      "name": "output",
      "type": "blob",
      "dataType": "binary",
      "path": "files/{queueTrigger}-Copy",
      "connection": "StorageConnection",
      "direction": "out"
    }
  ],
  "disabled": false,
  "scriptFile": "__init__.py"
}
```

This is the main difference when working with Azure Functions using various languages—some might require a little bit more work to achieve the same level of functionality.

Summary

In this chapter, you learned a lot about Azure Functions and how to work with this serverless component. You read about the differences between the pricing models, scalability concerns, and basic triggers and bindings. Additionally, we worked on some simple scenarios regarding monitoring, deploying, and developing this Azure service.

In the upcoming chapters of this book, you will learn even more about serverless services. Following that, we will resume working with functions even more, as this is one of the most popular Azure components that can be easily integrated with other tools and products. In the next chapter, we will learn how Azure Functions can be used for long-running operations. We will discuss Durable Functions, which is an extension to the standard set of functionalities available for Azure Functions.

Questions

1. What is the difference between the App Service, Premium, and the consumption pricing models?
2. What is GB/s?
3. What is the name of the container that's used for functions?
4. What languages can be used in Azure Functions?
5. Can a binding act as both a trigger and an output? Can you provide an example?
6. Can you use the **Application Settings** feature in the same way as in App Services?

Further reading

- An overview of Azure Functions: `https://docs.microsoft.com/en-us/azure/azure-functions/functions-overview`

- A description of the `host.json` file: `https://docs.microsoft.com/en-us/azure/azure-functions/functions-host-json`

- The schema of the `functions.json` file: `http://json.schemastore.org/function`

- Triggers and bindings for Azure Functions: `https://docs.microsoft.com/en-us/azure/azure-functions/functions-triggers-bindings`

- Durable Functions: `https://docs.microsoft.com/en-us/azure/azure-functions/durable-functions-overview`

8

Durable Functions

Azure Functions is a great service for developing a variety of different applications but lacks one key feature when building more complicated workloads – **state management**. To leverage things such as orchestrations, replays, and external events, you will need to use an advanced framework called **Durable Functions**. It is specifically designed to cover all those scenarios where Azure Functions may not be the best choice and excels in bringing stateful services into the Function-as-a-Service model. In this chapter, you will learn about the following things:

- What is Durable Functions?

- Working with orchestrations

- Timers, external events, and error handling

- Eternal and singleton orchestrations, stateful entities, and task hubs

- Advanced features – instance management, versioning, and high availability

Technical requirements

To perform the exercises in this chapter, you will need the following:

- Access to an Azure subscription

- Visual Studio Code installed (available at `https://code.visualstudio.com/`) with the Azure Functions extension

- The Azure CLI (`https://docs.microsoft.com/en-us/cli/azure/`)

What is Durable Functions?

In most cases, the best idea for working with Azure Functions is to keep them stateless. This makes things much easier as you do not have to worry about sharing resources and storing state. However, there are cases where you would like to access it and distribute it between different instances of your functions. In such scenarios (such as orchestrating a workflow or scheduling a task to be done), a better option to start with would be to leverage the capabilities of Durable Functions, an extension to the main runtime, which changes the way you work somewhat.

The Durable Functions framework changes the way Azure Functions works as it lets you resume from where the execution was paused or stopped and introduces the possibility to take the output of one function and pass it as input. To get started, you don't need any extra extensions—the only thing you will need is the very same extension in Visual Studio Code that you used for standard Azure Functions.

> **Note**
>
> Durable Functions is IDE-agnostic. This means that you can use them in any software environment, which supports running Azure Functions. However, as they present a different behavior and are a separate feature of the Azure Functions service, the overall experience in different IDEs besides Visual Studio and Visual Studio Code may be a little bit lacking.

In Visual Studio Code, a Durable Functions template can be selected when creating a new project or when adding a new function to an already existing project.

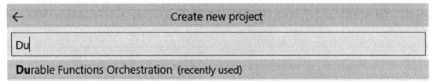

Figure 8.1 – Durable Functions template in Visual Studio Code

However, before acquiring some hands-on experience, let's briefly describe Durable Functions and its main elements.

Orchestrations and activities

The main elements of Durable Functions are orchestrations and activities. There are some significant differences between them:

- **Orchestrations**: These are designed to orchestrate different activities. They should be single-threaded and idempotent, and they can use only a very limited set of asynchronous methods. They are scaled based on the number of internal queues. What's more? They can also control the flow of one or more activities.

- **Activities**: These should contain most of the logic of your application. They work as typical functions (without the limits of orchestrations). They are scaled to multiple VMs.

Here, you can find the code for both types of functions:

```
[FunctionName("Orchestration")]
public static async Task Orchestration_
Start([OrchestrationTrigger] DurableOrchestrationContext
context)
{
  var payload = context.GetInput<string>();
  await context.CallActivityAsync(nameof(Activity), payload);
}

 [FunctionName("Activity")]
public static string Activity([ActivityTrigger]
DurableActivityContext context)
{
  var payload = context.GetInput<string>();
  return $"Current payload is {payload}!";
}
```

As you can see, they are both decorated with the [FunctionName] attribute as a typical function—the difference comes from the trigger that's used.

Orchestration client

To get started with an orchestration, you need a host. In Durable Functions, that host is the orchestration client, which enables you to perform the following actions on an orchestration:

- Start it

- Terminate it

- Get its status

- Raise an event and pass it to an orchestration

The basic code for a client is shown as follows:

```
[FunctionName("Orchestration_Client")]
public static async Task<string> Orchestration_Client(
  [HttpTrigger(AuthorizationLevel.Anonymous, "post", Route =
```

```
"start")] HttpRequestMessage input,
  [OrchestrationClient] DurableOrchestrationClient starter)
{
  return await starter.StartNewAsync("Orchestration", await
input.Content.ReadAsStringAsync());
}
```

As you can see from the preceding code, we started an orchestration by providing its name and passing some payload, which will be deserialized and decoded. Here, you can find an example of a client that has been hosted to terminate an instance by passing its identifier:

```
[FunctionName("Terminate")]
public static async Task Terminate(
  [HttpTrigger(AuthorizationLevel.Anonymous, "post", Route =
"terminate/{id}")] HttpRequestMessage input,
  string id,
  [OrchestrationClient] DurableOrchestrationClient client) {
  var reason = "Manual termination";
  await client.TerminateAsync(id, reason);
}
```

To terminate an instance, you just need its ID and a reason (which, of course, can be empty). Once the function is executed, your orchestration will shut down.

Orchestration history

The way Durable Functions works ensures that there is no duplicated work. In other words, if any activity is replayed, its result will not be evaluated again (hence, orchestrations must be idempotent). Here, you can find a diagram that shows how the framework works in detail:

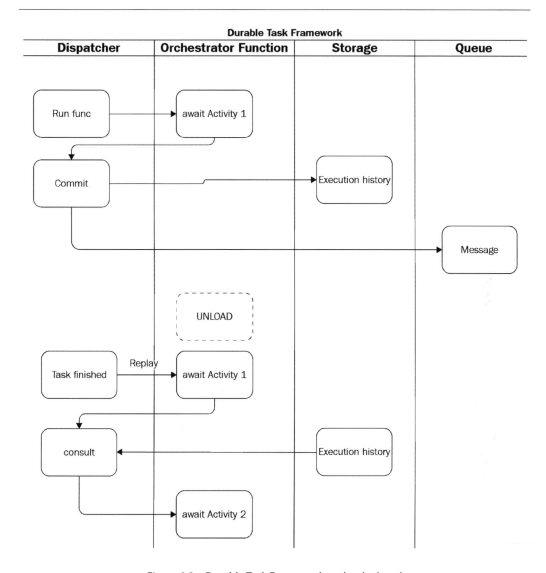

Figure 8.2 – Durable Task Framework under the hood

To cut a long story short, I have divided the process into four parts:

- **Dispatcher**: This is the internal part of the framework, which is responsible for calling orchestrations, performing replays, and saving the state.
- **Orchestrator function**: This is an orchestration that calls activities.
- **Storage**: This is the place where the orchestration history is stored.
- **Queue**: This is an internal queue (implemented using Azure Storage Queues), which is used to control the flow of execution of an orchestration.

The way Durable Functions works is explained as follows:

1. Dispatchers run an orchestration, which calls `Activity1` and awaits its result.
2. The control is returned to a dispatcher, which commits the state in the orchestration history and pushes a message to a queue.
3. In the meantime, orchestration is deallocated, saving memory and processor space.
4. After fetching a message from a queue and finishing a task, the dispatcher recreates an orchestration and replays all activities.
5. If it finds that this activity has been finished, it retrieves the result and proceeds to another activity.

The preceding process lasts until all the activities are processed. Information about execution history can be found in a table called `DurableFunctionsHubHistory`, which you can find inside the Azure Table storage used by your function app.

Let's now learn how we can work with orchestrations and how they can be used for more advanced scenarios.

Working with orchestrations

As described before, orchestrations are the main components of each workflow built with Durable Functions. It is important to remember that orchestrations are responsible for running the process and routing all the requests to appropriate places. In other words, when you implement your orchestration, it becomes the boundary of your process – Durable Functions takes care of creating checkpoints each time you await asynchronous methods.

What is more, remember that you may have several instances of the same orchestration running – in reality, it is only a matter of how long an orchestration takes to complete and how frequently it is run. For example, if your orchestration takes 8 hours to complete but is started every 4 hours, you will always have at least 2 instances of your orchestrations active. The reason I am stating this right now is simple – each orchestration has its own identity. You can treat it as an ID that is assigned to an instance of orchestration so that it can be identified.

> **Tip**
>
> Orchestration's identity can be either autogenerated or user-generated. There are pros and cons of both methods, but in most cases, you should go for autogenerated identities because they are easier to maintain and grant sufficient functionality for the majority of scenarios. If your process involves mapping between external processes and orchestrations in Durable Functions, you may find user-generated identities helpful.

It is important to understand the limits of orchestrations as currently described by the framework:

- Orchestrations cannot perform I/O operations (filesystem read, networking) – instead, you should delegate such operations to activities.

- Dates should be fetched via the Durable Functions API (such as accessing the `CurrentUtcDateStamp` property in your orchestration context) because standard libraries are nondeterministic.

- Random values and numbers should be generated by activities so that they are the same with each replay.

- Asynchronous operations are forbidden unless performed via the `IDurableOrchestrationContext` API.

- Environment variables shouldn't be used.

- Avoid infinite loops so that you will not run out of memory.

As you can see, these are strict requirements for running an orchestration. Personally, I believe that they can be simplified to a single rule – activities should perform all the work, while orchestrations should be used only for their control. To avoid performance or data integrity problems, avoid doing any custom logic in orchestration. Instead, delegate all the operations to activities, especially if you are unsure where that logic belongs.

Sub-orchestrations

When your process keeps getting bigger and bigger, it is difficult to manage it using a single orchestration. Fortunately, Durable Functions offers a feature called **sub-orchestration**, which looks exactly like this:

```
public static async Task ProcessReportOrchestration(
    [OrchestrationTrigger] IDurableOrchestrationContext
context)
{
    var date = context.GetInput<string>();
    Uri blobUrl = await context.
CallActivityAsync<Uri>("SubmitPollingRequest", date);

    await context.CallActivityAsync("DownloadReport",
blobUrl));
}
```

As you can see, it is just a normal orchestration. What is different in sub-orchestration is how they are called. To use the preceding orchestration as part of a bigger process, simply call it using the `CallSubOrchestratorAsync` function:

```
[FunctionName("ProcessCostReport")]
public static async Task ProvisionNewDevices(
    [OrchestrationTrigger] ProcessCostReport context)
{
    string[] dates = await context.
CallActivityAsync<string[]>("Dates");

    var reportingTasks = new List<Task>();
    foreach (string date in dates)
    {
        Task reportingTask = context.
CallSubOrchestratorAsync("ProcessReportOrchestration", date);
        reportingTasks.Add(reportingTask);
    }

    await Task.WhenAll(reportingTasks);
}
```

Without sub-orchestration, you would need to perform all the steps in sequence. When using that feature of Durable Functions, remember that sub-orchestrations must be defined in the same function app. Unfortunately, cross-function calls are not supported and for that kind of functionality, you would need to implement your own consumer pooling pattern (refer to the *Further reading* section for details).

Let's now learn about the additional features of Durable Functions that allow the implementation of timers, handling errors, and events.

Timers, external events, and error handling

As we have already mentioned, Durable Functions are implemented in a way that implies some specific patterns. In this section, we will discuss some proper ways of implementing common scenarios, starting with timers.

Timers

Sometimes, you might want to schedule work following a specific delay. While using traditional functions, you must create a custom solution that will somehow trigger a workflow at a specific time. In Durable Functions, it is as easy as writing one line of code. Consider the following example:

```
[FunctionName("Orchestration_Client")]
public static async Task<string> Orchestration_Client(
    [HttpTrigger(AuthorizationLevel.Anonymous, "post", Route =
"start")] HttpRequestMessage input,
    [OrchestrationClient] DurableOrchestrationClient starter)
{
  return await starter.StartNewAsync("Orchestration", null);
}


[FunctionName("Orchestration")]
public static async Task Orchestration_
Start([OrchestrationTrigger] DurableOrchestrationContext
context, TraceWriter log)
{
  log.Info($"Scheduled at {context.CurrentUtcDateTime}");

  await context.CreateTimer(context.CurrentUtcDateTime.
AddHours(1), CancellationToken.None);
  await context.CallActivityAsync(nameof(Activity), context.
CurrentUtcDateTime);
}
```

```
[FunctionName("Activity")]
public static void Activity([ActivityTrigger]
DurableActivityContext context, TraceWriter log)
{
  var date = context.GetInput<DateTime>();
  log.Info($"Executed at {date}");
}
```

In the preceding example, I used the `context.CreateTimer()` method, which allows for the creation of a delay in function execution. If the previous orchestration is executed, it will return control to the dispatcher after awaiting a timer. Thanks to this, you will not be charged for this function execution as it will be deallocated and recreated later, after waiting for a specific interval.

External events

In Durable Functions, it is possible to wait for an external event before proceeding with a workflow. This is especially helpful if you want to create an interactive flow, where you initiate a process in one place and have to wait for someone's decision (could be a process or a person) indefinitely. To raise an event, you can use the following function:

```
[FunctionName("Orchestration_Raise")]
public static async Task Orchestration_Raise(
   [HttpTrigger(AuthorizationLevel.Anonymous, "post", Route =
"start_raise/{id}/{event}")] HttpRequestMessage input,
   string id,
   string @event,
   [OrchestrationClient] DurableOrchestrationClient starter) {
   await starter.RaiseEventAsync(id, @event, await input.
Content.ReadAsStringAsync());
}
Here, you can find an example of waiting for an event:
[FunctionName("Orchestration")]
public static async Task<string> Orchestration_
Start([OrchestrationTrigger] DurableOrchestrationContext
context)
{
  var @event = await context.
WaitForExternalEvent<int>("Approved");
```

```
   if (@event == 1)
   {
      var result = await context.
CallActivityAsync<string>(nameof(Activity), @event);
      return result;
   }


   return "Not Approved";
}
```

The way this works can be described as follows: the first function allows you to raise a custom event by passing the appropriate parameters. The second function is paused while waiting for the `context.WaitForExternalEvent()` function. If you send an event with the `Approved` type, a function will be resumed and will continue. Additionally, you can pass a payload of an event, which will be passed as a result of `WaitForExternalEvent()`. This method works in the same way as timers and other Durable Functions, which are available in `DurableOrchestrationType`—while waiting, control is returned to the dispatcher and the function itself is deallocated.

Error handling

In Durable Functions, error handling is a straightforward feature, yet the whole behavior can be a little misleading initially. In general, remember, that each error that happens inside an activity function will be thrown as a `FunctionFailedException` error and should be handled inside an orchestration function. Consider the following example:

```
[FunctionName("MoneyTransfer")]
public static async Task Run([OrchestrationTrigger]
IDurableOrchestrationContext context)
{
    await context.CallActivityAsync("Subtract",
        new
        {
            Account = "John Doe",
            Amount = 1000
        });

    try
    {
        await context.CallActivityAsync("Add",
```

```
            new
            {
                Account = "Jane Doe",
                Amount = 1000
            });
    }
    catch (Exception)
    {
        await context.CallActivityAsync("Add",
            new
            {
                Account = "John Doe",
                Amount = 1000
            });
    }
}
```

This simple example presents you with the following logic:

- Subtract a value of 1000 from the first account.

- Add a value of 1000 to the second account.

- If something goes wrong, add a value of 1000 back to the first account.

The presents pattern can be called "compensation" – you are basically creating a special logic inside your code to reset the system's state in case anything goes wrong. In Durable Functions, the only thing worth remembering is handling such cases inside orchestrations – this allows us to use the basic framework components and ensure that the whole history is properly saved.

> **Note**
>
> You may be wondering – what if the activity inside the catch block also throws an exception. Well, if you believe this is feasible, you will need to implement a more sophisticated logic. Maybe multiple try/catch blocks? Maybe you should leverage a thing called a **poison queue** and let a human operator fix those errors case by case? It will depend on the characteristics of your system – the more complex the tasks you are performing, the more safeguards should be inside your code base.

An interesting feature of Durable Functions is the ability to call an activity with a retry using a native API function:

```
[FunctionName("TimerOrchestratorWithRetry")]
public static async Task Run([OrchestrationTrigger]
IDurableOrchestrationContext context)
{
    var retryOptions = new RetryOptions(
        firstRetryInterval: TimeSpan.FromSeconds(5),
        maxNumberOfAttempts: 10);

    await context.
CallActivityWithRetryAsync("ActivityWhichCanBeRetried",
retryOptions, null);
}
```

As you can see, you need to use the `CallActivityWithRetryAsync` function and then pass the `RetryOptions` object containing your retry logic. It is especially helpful in cloud environments, where many services can face transient errors and often are not available with the very first call. Using a retry ensures that your application logic can withstand such scenarios and will not break because of an error, which can be safely ignored.

With the common patterns covered, let's switch our focus to more advanced scenarios available when using Durable Functions.

Eternal and singleton orchestrations, stateful entities, and task hubs

Let's now focus on some more advanced features of Durable Functions. In this section, we will cover things such as infinite orchestrations, entity functions, and aggregating all the components into a single hub.

Eternal orchestrations

By default, in Durable Functions, each orchestration ends at some point. You can think about it as a line from point A to point B – between those points, you will have multiple activities, which can be called and replayed. Once you reach point B, the workflow ends, and you must start from the beginning.

To overcome that problem, you could probably implement an infinite loop. While the idea is correct, you need to take into consideration the history of your orchestration. If you leverage a loop inside your orchestration, the history will grow infinitely. As this is undesirable, eternal orchestrations were introduced to grant you the possibility to run an orchestration, which never ends.

Eternal orchestrations have one additional advantage, As they very often represent fire-and-forget scenarios, you do not need to implement a scheduler to keep the work going. You can simply start your orchestration and then focus on monitoring instead of scheduling. An example of eternal orchestration looks like this:

```
[FunctionName("Infinite_Loop")]
public static async Task Run(
    [OrchestrationTrigger] IDurableOrchestrationContext
context)
{
    await context.CallActivityAsync("DoPeriodicTasks", null);

    DateTime waitTime = context.CurrentUtcDateTime.AddHours(1);
    await context.CreateTimer(waitTime, CancellationToken.
None);

    context.ContinueAsNew(null);
}
```

The preceding example represents a simple orchestration, which performs a task, waits for an hour, and then starts again. There is no need for loops and custom code – it is up to Durable Functions to wait for the timer to fire and then start the process from the beginning.

Singleton orchestrations

I mentioned in this chapter that there are scenarios where multiple orchestrations can run in the same moment. In many cases, this will not be a problem, but you may face requirements that will force you to implement a singleton orchestration to have the process run correctly. Fortunately, Durable Functions offers a pattern that can fix that problem.

As you probably remember, orchestrations in Durable Functions have their IDs assigned. These IDs can be either autogenerated or user-generated. To implement a singleton orchestration, you need to leverage the latter – ask the Durable Functions API for the running orchestrations and search for the ID you assigned previously. The code for that functionality can look like this:

```
[FunctionName("HttpStartSingle")]
public static async Task<HttpResponseMessage> RunSingle(
```

```
    [HttpTrigger(AuthorizationLevel.Function, methods: "post",
HttpRequestMessage req,
    [DurableClient] IDurableOrchestrationClient starter,
    ILogger log)
{
    var existingInstance = await starter.
GetStatusAsync(instanceId);
}
```

Here, we are using the `GetStatusAsync()` method to fetch the status of an orchestration having the given ID. There are multiple ways to obtain the ID of an orchestration:

- It can be passed via a URL if your function is triggered via HTTP requests.
- It can be fetched from a database.
- It can be generated based on the set of coded parameters.

Once the status is downloaded, you can use a simple `if/else` statement to implement your logic:

```
if (existingInstance == null
|| existingInstance.RuntimeStatus ==
OrchestrationRuntimeStatus.Completed
|| existingInstance.RuntimeStatus ==
OrchestrationRuntimeStatus.Failed
|| existingInstance.RuntimeStatus ==
OrchestrationRuntimeStatus.Terminated)
{
    // Start new
}
else
{
    // Orchestration already exists
}
```

Simply put, we are checking whether orchestration has been completed – if not, we are assuming that it is active and skip the creation of a new one.

Stateful entities

As opposite to standard orchestrator functions, which manage state implicitly (via control flow), Durable Functions offer an alternative approach called **entity functions**. They leverage a special kind of trigger called an entity trigger, which looks like this:

```
[FunctionName("Counter")]
public static void Counter([EntityTrigger]
IDurableEntityContext ctx)
{
    // Function code
}
```

The difference between orchestrator and entity functions is the way in which a state is managed – for entity functions, you manage your state explicitly by using the `SetState()` function. The state we are referring to is set for an object, which is called a durable entity. Each durable entity has some important traits worth mentioning:

- Each entity has its own ID, which can be used to find it.

- Entities can be unloaded from memory if not used.

- Each entity is lazily created when needed.

- When operations are performed on an entity, they are called serially.

The operation of setting the state for an entity looks like this:

```
ctx.SetState(<state value>);
```

You can also use the `IDurableEntityClient.SignalEntityAsync()` method for communication from a client (function) to an entity, or `IDurableOrchestrationContext.SignalEntity()` for one-way communication from an orchestration. You can find more information in the *Further reading* section.

Task hubs

A task hub is a logical container used by your orchestrations and activities. Technically, hub implementation relies on your storage provider – if you are using storage accounts, the task hub structure will be different from the one for MSSQL. However, the concept of a hub is always the same – if your function apps share the same storage account, they need to be configured with separate task hubs. The name of your hub can be configured inside the `host.json` file:

```
{
  "version": "2.0",
```

```
  "extensions": {
    "durableTask": {
      "hubName": "MyTaskHub"
    }
  }
}
```

The reason why you need separate task hubs for each function app is related to how Durable Functions are managed under the hood. To cut a long story short, if you fail to give your apps different task hubs, your orchestration may end up corrupted because different functions will try to access the same resources. This may cause distractions in your application or even lead to incorrect results.

As we have discussed most of the low-level functionalities, let's now check how you can work with Durable Functions on an architecture level.

Advanced features – instance management, versioning, and high availability

Besides the purely technical stuff, such as different kinds of orchestrations, handling infinite loops, and managing state, Durable Functions offer a bunch of high-level capabilities that can help you manage your services according to more advanced business requirements. In the final section of this chapter, we will cover some additional topics that you may find interesting, such as managing different instances of orchestrations, versioning your orchestrations, and achieving high availability.

Instance management

We talked about unique IDs in this chapter, which are assigned to each instance of your orchestration. Those IDs can be used for various functionalities, including singleton orchestrations, monitoring, and inter-orchestration communication. Additionally, Durable Functions offer a dedicated API, which can be used to manage different instances of orchestration functions. This API is accessible via the IDurableOrchestrationClient object, which is available in your trigger function:

```
[FunctionName("HelloWorldQueueTrigger")]
public static async Task Run(
    [QueueTrigger("queue")] string input,
    [DurableClient] IDurableOrchestrationClient starter,
    ILogger log)
{
}
```

Now, when we have access to the object, we can perform many different operations by accessing its methods. For example, if you would like to start an orchestration, you simply need to call the `StartNewAsync()` method like this:

```
string instanceId = await starter.StartNewAsync("HelloWorld",
input);
```

The preceding method will start a new instance of `"HelloWorld"` orchestration and return its `instanceId` string, which can be used for further management. Optionally, you could specify your own ID for an instance – in that scenario, you would receive the same `instanceId` string as the one you set.

When talking about singleton orchestrations, we discovered that there is a method called `GetStatusAsync()`, which allows us to fetch an orchestration status. Let's recall its syntax:

```
DurableOrchestrationStatus status = await client.
GetStatusAsync(instanceId);
```

All we need is to use the previously obtained `instanceId` string of our orchestration – once we have the status returned, we can perform additional actions based on the value:

- Let the process continue and check the status later.
- Terminate the orchestration if it takes too long to complete.
- Notify operators regarding the current state of an orchestration.

Additionally, if you wish to just load all the instances and query on your own, you can simply use the `ListInstancesAsync()` method to get them and iterate through the returned collection.

> **Tip**
> Listing all the instances of orchestrations can be achieved with or without a filter. To introduce a filter, use the `OrchestrationStatusQueryCondition` class and pass it as the first parameter of the `ListInstancesAsync()` method.

In Durable Functions, orchestration can also be terminated. Termination is achieved via `TerminateAsync()` like this:

```
client.TerminateAsync(instanceId, reason);
```

As you can see, to terminate an orchestration, you will need both its ID and a reason, which will be saved to the orchestration history. A reason can be by any string you wish – it is only important to pass a self-explanatory value in case you ever had to come back to the orchestration.

To check even more functionalities related to instance management, check the *Further reading* section. Durable Functions documentation presents additional scenarios that you may find helpful, such as sending an event to an instance of orchestration, purging history, or even deleting a task hub. In the meantime, let's check how we can implement versioning for the orchestrations to prevent problems when updating our system.

Versioning

The idea of versioning is important in many computer systems and its proper implementation is often a prerequisite to building a well-maintained system. In Durable Functions, this concept is also present – when developing orchestrations, sooner or later you will face a need to change something while preserving backward compatibility (at least for some time).

You may wonder why you need to preserve compatibility. Well, let's consider the following scenario – you have a working process, which is constantly scheduled with new instances. At the same moment, you need to introduce new functionality or a new element, which affects how your orchestrations handle part of the results. To help us visualize the scenario, let's use the following code snippet:

```
int result = await context.CallActivityAsync<int>("Foo");
```

Our orchestration can call the "Foo" activity at any moment and, if it is currently running, it will expect an integer value as the result.

> **Note**
> Remember that orchestrations call activities by using their name – this is a dynamic dependency, and it cannot be guaranteed at compilation time.

Now, let's assume we are introducing the following change – the "Foo" activity will start returning a Boolean value instead:

```
bool result = await context.CallActivityAsync<bool>("Foo");
```

If we have running orchestrations at this moment, they will probably fail as they will expect an integer instead of a true/false value (remember that even though the code base changed, an orchestration that is already active will use the old one until unloaded). The same problematic scenario can arise if you change the logic inside your orchestration or reorder activities inside it. As orchestrations can be resumed and replayed, changing the order of activities can render an orchestration inconsistent. In that scenario, Durable Functions will report a `NonDeterministicOrchestrationException` error and the whole workflow will stop.

To avoid that kind of error, some strategy for versioning must be implemented. While it is possible to just do nothing (and to be honest, this is a viable strategy for all those cases where you see no value in implementing more sophisticated approaches for your functions), in general, it is not advised as it can even lower the performance of your functions. Instead, you can leverage two alternative approaches:

- Wait for all the orchestrations to stop.
- Deploy new code as separate orchestrations/activities.

Both strategies have their pros and cons, but ultimately lead to a much better experience than the "do nothing" strategy. The first one can be implemented with proper instance management – you need to pause the creation of new orchestrations and wait until existing instances are finished. Then you can restart the process (for example, using an external event).

Deploying a separate code is straightforward – you just copy some part of your code base as a new orchestration and introduce changes there. This approach can quickly allow you to run your orchestrations, but if applied incorrectly, can lead to increasing your technical debt.

High availability

As with all cloud services, at some point, you will consider increasing the availability of your systems and making sure they can withstand possible errors and outages. By default, Durable Functions uses Storage Account as its storage mechanism and relies on that service when replication is considered. In general, there are three main scenarios for availability when using Durable Functions:

- Shared storage
- Individual storage
- Replicated storage

When using the shared storage approach, you deploy two function apps in two regions, but the storage behind them is deployed only to the single region:

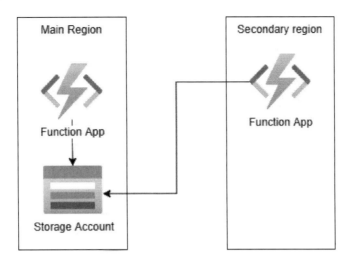

Figure 8.3 – Shared architecture

This approach will allow you to run your functions in an active-passive model, but still, the single point of failure will be the storage account used for your functions. This model, however, will help you in running all the orchestrations, even if the main region fails. An alternative approach to that is deploying a storage individually:

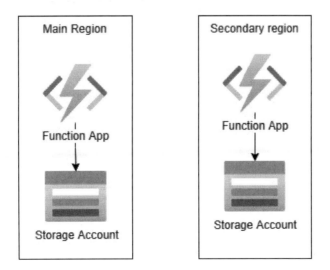

Figure 8.4 – Architecture with individual storage accounts

The difference here is mostly related to the individual storage accounts, which are deployed for each function app. While this will defend you against regional errors, the downside of this approach is being unable to replay all the orchestrations, which are stuck in the region where an outage occurs. In that scenario, you will have to wait until the main region works again. An alternative is to use a storage solution with **Geo-redundant storage (GRS)**

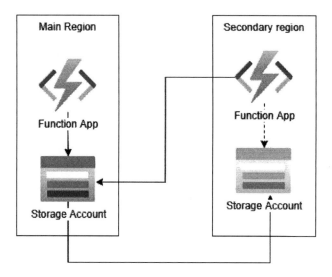

Figure 8.5 – GRS replication

This approach will allow you to combine two previously described patterns. Here you are using the native approach for data replication and if an outage occurs, you are enabling failover in the main region to start running your process from the secondary region. The main downside to this solution is waiting for the failover process to complete.

Those three ideas for high availability should help you in discovering even more ways to implement replication for your Durable Functions. Remember that those concepts may need additional components if, for example, your functions are triggered by an HTTP request. If that is the case, you will need to add a load-balancing component to distribute the traffic properly.

That is all as regards the topic of Durable Functions for this book. I hope you liked it and remember that the *Further reading* section offers some additional information about different aspects of working with those functions.

Summary

In this chapter, you learned about Durable Functions, including implementing your own workflows and using both basic and advanced features. This knowledge should help you when designing and developing your own solutions based on serverless/Function-as-a-Service components.

In the next chapter, you will learn about Azure Logic Apps, which offers similar functionality to Durable Functions but with a different audience and way of development.

Questions

1. How can you achieve singleton orchestrations in Durable Functions?
2. What is the difference between an orchestrator function and an entity function?
3. Can you set a custom ID for an orchestration instance?
4. Can you use a custom storage provider for Durable Functions?
5. Can you use infinite loops in Durable Functions?
6. What are the differences between orchestrations and activities?

Further reading

- HTTP features – consumer pooling: `https://docs.microsoft.com/en-us/azure/azure-functions/durable/durable-functions-http-features?tabs=csharp`
- Entity functions: `https://docs.microsoft.com/en-us/azure/azure-functions/durable/durable-functions-entities?tabs=csharp`
- Instance management: `https://docs.microsoft.com/en-us/azure/azure-functions/durable/durable-functions-instance-management?tabs=csharp`
- Durable Functions repository: `https://github.com/Azure/azure-functions-durable-extension`
- Azure Functions code examples: `https://docs.microsoft.com/en-us/samples/browse/?products=azure-functions`

9

Integrating Different Components with Logic Apps

Azure Logic Apps is a main enterprise-level integration service and lets us automate processes as workflows across the organization. It allows for the simple connection of different services and applications with multiple connectors. Furthermore, by leveraging a serverless model, it reduces costs and shortens the time needed for developing a working solution.

The following topics will be covered in this chapter:

- What Azure Logic Apps is and how it works
- Connectors for logic apps
- Creating a logic app and integrating it with other services
- **Business-to-Business** (**B2B**) integration and how it works
- Virtual network integration

Technical requirements

To perform exercises from this chapter, you will need the following:

- Visual Studio Code
- A Visual Studio Code extension for Azure Logic Apps

What is Azure Logic Apps?

Sometimes, you need to integrate multiple services and automate tasks such as sending an email, creating a file, or generating a report based on some input data (maybe a database table or a social media feed). If you work with a specific cloud vendor (in this case, Microsoft Azure), it can be crucial to be able to rapidly develop workflows that can be versioned and are natively integrated with multiple cloud services, using a tool that does not require learning many different concepts to get started. Such a service is Azure Logic Apps, which you will learn about in this chapter.

Azure logic apps – how they work

In *Chapter 7, Serverless and Azure Functions* and *Chapter 8, Durable Functions*, you learned about Azure Functions, which required a trigger to be executed. The situation is similar with Azure Logic Apps – you need to define specific criteria that tell the runtime when a logic app instance should be executed. During the execution, even more actions are performed:

- Input data is converted so that it meets the initial requirements.
- All conditional flows are executed so one specific execution flow is evaluated.
- Temporary variables are assigned values.

The following shows an example of a flow that is executed daily and sets a variable that is used to remove outdated blobs:

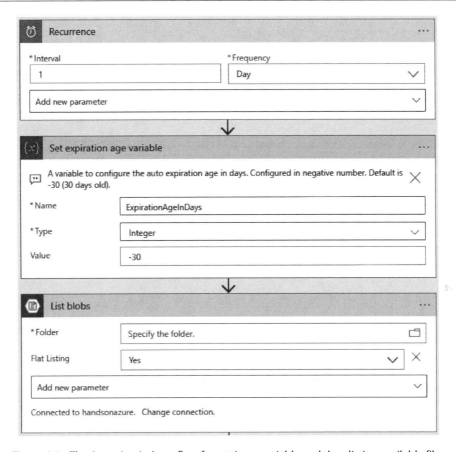

Figure 9.1 – The Azure Logic Apps flow for setting a variable and then listing available files

As you can see, it contains three different blocks, which are the initial part of the flow (in fact, the whole workflow is much bigger, as it contains a loop and different conditions and actions – we will cover all of these later):

- The first one defines how often an instance of a logic app should be executed.

- The second one defines a variable, which is used in the next steps – it specifies the maximum age of a file in Azure Blob storage.

- The third one feeds the next step (a `for each` loop) with a list of available blobs within a specific storage account and container.

You probably noticed one more thing – the workflow is built using graphical blocks, which can be connected by defining multiple relations. While such a solution is a real handful when creating and modifying logic apps, it can be problematic when versioning and developing within a team. Fortunately, each flow is also defined in JSON:

```
1  {
2      "definition": {
3          "$schema": "https://schema.management.azure.com/providers/Microsoft.Logic/schemas/2016-06-01/workflowdefinition.json#",
4          "actions": {
5              "For_each": {
6                  "actions": {
7                      "Condition": {
8                          "actions": {
9                              "Delete_blob": {
10                                 "description": "If blob is older than the expiration age, delete it",
11                                 "inputs": {
12                                     "host": {
13                                         "connection": {
14                                             "name": "@parameters('$connections')['azureblob']['connectionId']"
15                                         }
16                                     },
17                                     "method": "delete",
18                                     "path": "/datasets/default/files/@{encodeURIComponent(encodeURIComponent(items('For_each')?['Id']))}"
19                                 },
20                                 "runAfter": {},
21                                 "type": "ApiConnection"
22                             }
23                         },
24                         "description": "Check LastModified timestamp and whether older than the expiration age variable",
25                         "expression": "@less(ticks(items('For_each')?['LastModified']), ticks(addDays(utcnow(), variables('ExpirationAgeInDays'))))",
26                         "runAfter": {},
27                         "type": "If"
28                     }
29                 },
30                 "description": "Scan all blobs in this folder",
31                 "foreach": "@body('List_blobs')?['value']",
32                 "runAfter": {
33                     "List_blobs": [
34                         "Succeeded"
35                     ]
```

Figure 9.2 – JSON representation of the Azure Logic Apps flow

Thanks to such a representation, you can add your logic apps to any version control system (for example, Git or **Subversion** (**SVN**)) and modify them when you wish. Additionally, you can automate the creation of different logic apps by generating code files on the fly.

Azure Logic Apps – advantages

You may wonder what the real use case for Azure Logic Apps is when you have other possibilities available (Azure Functions and custom workflows). If you take a closer look at its features, you will notice the following:

- You do not have to be a cloud developer to develop workflows – even less advanced users (for example, IT professionals, IT admins, and data scientists) can create the one they need without learning much about this service.

- You do not need to worry about scaling – as Azure logic apps are also a part of serverless services available in Azure, you can focus on delivering business value rather than server configuration and capabilities.

- In general, you do not have to write code – however, you are not limited to a "codeless" environment, as it is possible to host it within Azure Functions and just execute it on demand.

- You can implement B2B integration, which leverages enterprise standards relating to exchanging messages and communication, such as **Applicability Statement 2 (AS2)** or EDIFACT.

The following shows the current pricing for Azure Logic Apps:

- Each action costs $0.000025 per execution.

- Each connector costs $0.000125 per execution.

> **Important Note**
> In Azure Logic Apps, the first 4,000 executions are free if you are using the Consumption plan.

The preceding prices refer to the Consumption plan, which works in a similar way as the Consumption plan for Azure Function – you are paying for your usage. However, there is also a way to use the Standard plan, which is structured almost identically to the Premium plan of Azure Functions:

- You pay $0.1972 for each hour of vCPU.

- You pay $0.0141 for each hour of memory.

However, to fully understand the Consumption plan, we have to describe these two terms:

- **Action**: This is each step executed after a trigger (for example, listing files, calling an API, or setting a variable).

- **Connector**: This is a binding to multiple external services (for example, Azure Service Bus, SFTP, or Twitter) that you will use in your workflows.

Note that Azure Logic Apps can be quite expensive when performing complicated workflows very often. In such scenarios, consider using other services (such as Azure Functions), which, of course, require much more time spent on developing but, on the other hand, offer better pricing.

Connectors for logic apps

The main concept of Azure Logic Apps is connectors. Connectors are both actions and triggers that you can use in your workflows to fetch data, transform it, and extend the current capabilities of your applications. Currently, Azure logic apps have 200 different connectors available, which allow you to integrate with multiple Azure services (such as Azure API Management or Azure Functions), other systems (OneDrive and Salesforce), and even on-premises systems.

Connector types

In Azure Logic Apps, connectors are divided into two categories:

- **Built-in connectors**: These are designed to work with Azure services and create workflows, and are organized around handling application logic and working with data.

- **Managed connectors**: These connectors ease integration with other systems and services.

Managed connectors are divided into even more detailed groups:

- Managed API connectors

- On-premises connectors

- Integration account connectors

- Enterprise connectors

In this section, we will go through multiple examples of different types of connectors so that you will be able to understand their use cases and functionality.

Built-in connectors

The following shows examples of built-in connectors that you can use in your Azure logic apps:

- **Schedule**: For running logic apps on a specific schedule or pausing their executions

- **HTTP**: For communicating with endpoints over the HTTP protocol

- **Request**: For making a logic app callable from other services or sending responses

- **Batch**: For processing messages in batches

- **Azure Functions**: For running custom code snippets

- **Azure API Management**: For integrating triggers and actions defined by other services

- **Azure App Service**: For calling API apps and web apps

- **Azure Logic Apps**: For calling other logic apps

As you can see, we have here more generic connectors (schedule, HTTP, and request) and those specific to a service (such as Azure Functions and Azure App Service). In general, these connectors are the foundation of most Azure logic apps – when it comes to creating workflows, we very often are required to call an API or perform various other HTTP requests.

Note that each connector has detailed documentation available, describing its use cases and how you can develop workflows with it. You can find a link to it in the *Further reading* section in this chapter.

Managed API connectors

When using managed API connectors, you will be able to integrate with services and systems that require configuring a connection; these can be used when executing an instance of a logic app. The following shows an example of a logic app in a resource group with an additional resource defined as the API connection:

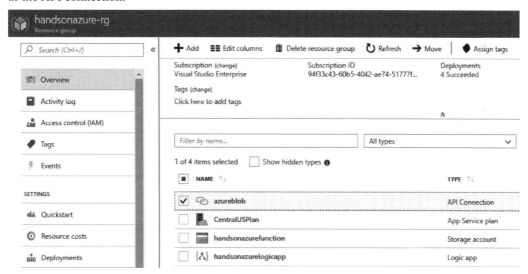

In the documentation, plenty of different API connectors are described – including the following:

- Azure Service Bus
- SQL Server
- Office 365 Outlook
- Azure Blob storage
- **Secure File Transfer Protocol (SFTP)**
- SharePoint Online

As you can see, with these connectors, we have access to a variety of different Azure services and other systems (here, Office 365 and SharePoint), which can be leveraged in your workflows to extend your application's logic.

On-premises connectors

As I described previously, with Azure Logic Apps, you can also integrate with on-premises services such as different database systems (Oracle, MySQL, and SQL Server), business analytics systems (Teradata), or filesystems.

To access on-premises data, you will have to create a resource called an on-premises data gateway. Instructions about how to do so can be found here: `https://docs.microsoft.com/en-us/azure/logic-apps/logic-apps-gateway-connection`.

Integration account connectors and enterprise connectors

Azure Logic Apps also lets you build so-called B2B solutions using integration accounts and leveraging a variety of advanced connectors, such as XML Transforms and X12 encoding/decoding, or even accessing enterprise systems, such as the **Systems Applications and Products in Data Processing** (**SAP**). While, for most users, these capabilities are not that useful (as these are rather advanced topics that most people are not familiar with), being able to build logic apps that allow for seamless communication between partners is an interesting functionality. We will cover more about B2B integration within Azure Logic Apps at the end of this chapter.

Creating logic apps and integrating services

As Azure Logic Apps is also targeted at non-developers, the process of creating instances and working with them is quite straightforward. In this section of this chapter, we will learn how to work with them in the Azure portal and Visual Studio, and how to integrate multiple services and use actions to control a workflow.

Creating logic apps in the Azure portal

To create an instance of a logic app, follow these steps:

1. Click on + **Create a resource** and search for `Logic App`. When you click on the **Create** button, you will see a simple form that allows you to create a new instance of a logic app:

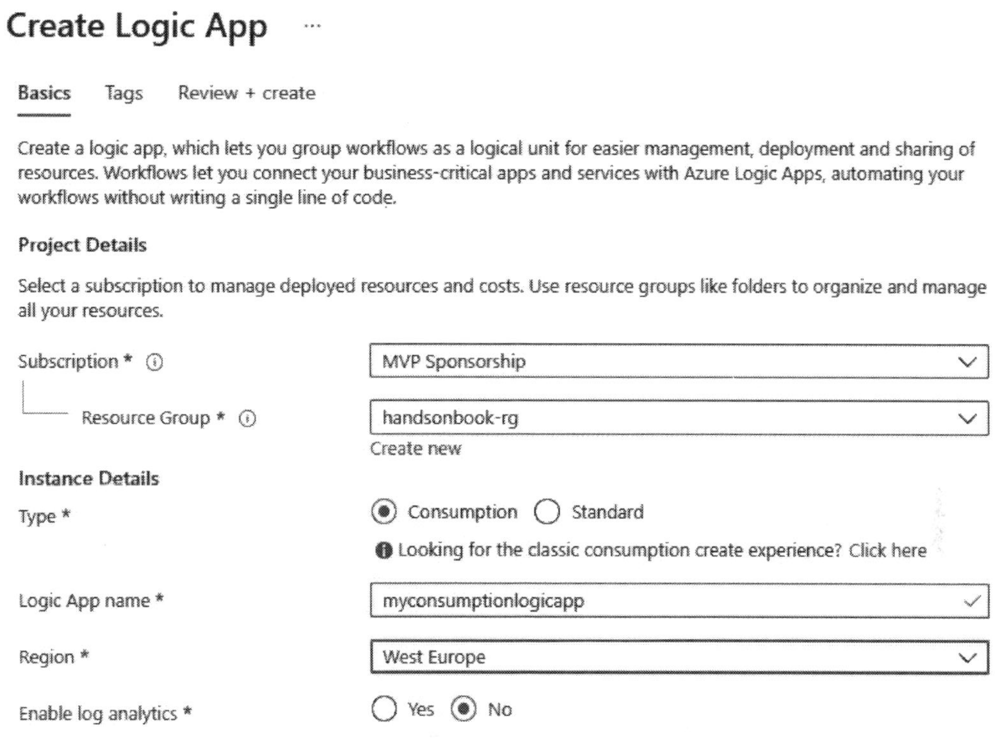

Create Logic App   ...

Basics   Tags   Review + create

Create a logic app, which lets you group workflows as a logical unit for easier management, deployment and sharing of resources. Workflows let you connect your business-critical apps and services with Azure Logic Apps, automating your workflows without writing a single line of code.

Project Details

Select a subscription to manage deployed resources and costs. Use resource groups like folders to organize and manage all your resources.

Subscription * ⓘ   MVP Sponsorship   ⌄

  └── Resource Group * ⓘ   handsonbook-rg   ⌄
                               Create new

Instance Details

Type *   ⦿ Consumption ◯ Standard
                    ❶ Looking for the classic consumption create experience? Click here

Logic App name *   myconsumptionlogicapp   ✓

Region *   West Europe   ⌄

Enable log analytics *   ◯ Yes ⦿ No

Figure 9.3 – The creation of an Azure logic app in the portal

2. In fact, the only extra thing you can configure here is enabling Azure Log Analytics. Since this service will not be covered in this book, I will skip it in this chapter. When you click on the **Review + create** button to confirm your choice, Azure will start the creation of a new logic app.

3.   When the creation is finished, you can go to the service to check what it initially looks like:

Figure 9.4 – The created Azure logic app

4.   Now, you can click on the **Logic app designer** button on the left to access a new blade that enables you to create a brand-new workflow. Initially, you will see plenty of different templates available – it is a great start if you are already familiar with this service, as it displays many different possibilities and configurations that you can achieve using Azure logic apps. To get started, in the **Templates** section, select the **Schedule** option in the **Category** drop-down menu and choose **Scheduler - Add message to queue**:

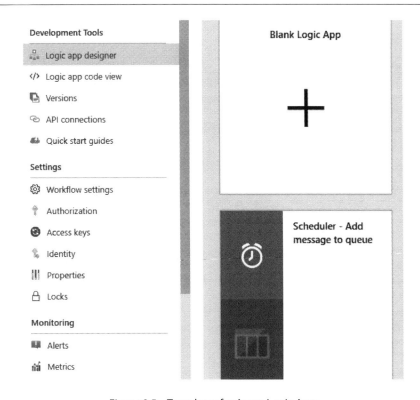

Figure 9.5 – Templates for Azure Logic Apps

5. When you click on the template and then the **Use this template** button, you will see a designer window where you will be able to finish configuring the workflow. However, before we can start developing the individual steps of our app, we need to connect to a storage account (see *Chapter 12, Using Azure Storage – Tables, Queues, Files, and Blobs*, for detailed instructions on working with Azure Storage). In this case, you will need to use the **Sign in** option and enter the connection details for the storage of your choice:

Figure 9.6 – Connecting to Azure Storage

6. With the Azure Storage account connected, we can then proceed to the workflow configuration. As you can see in the following screenshot, we can enter parameters such as the frequency of our process, the exact queue configuration, and the setup for a poison queue. All the fields decorated with an asterisk are required for the flow to work:

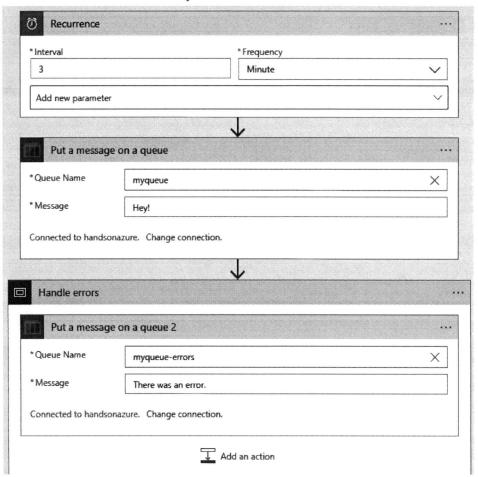

Figure 9.7 – The configuration of the scheduler flow

Note that this connector does not create a queue if it does not exist. Make sure that you have one before starting a logic app instance. If you do not know how to do so, refer to *Chapter 11, Reactive Architecture with Event Grid*, where we will discuss Azure Storage features and queues.

With the workflow configured, click on the **Save** button and then select **Run Trigger**. You will be able to see how the full flow was executed:

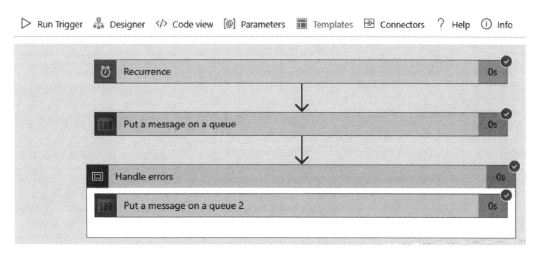

Figure 9.8 – The executed flow

This flow was executed correctly, but what if there is an error? Well, fortunately, Azure Logic Apps offers an option to debug each step and display all the errors that were the cause of a failed flow. When you go to the **Overview** blade in your logic app, you can click on the flow that was not successful:

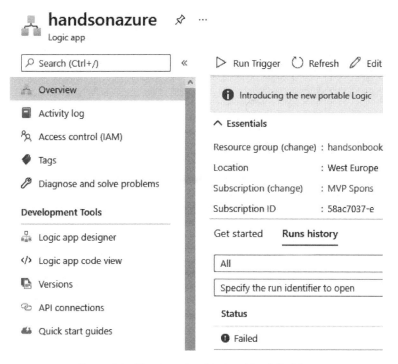

Figure 9.9 – The Overview blade with a failed flow

When you click on it, you will see a new screen containing all the steps executed with their status and errors (if any):

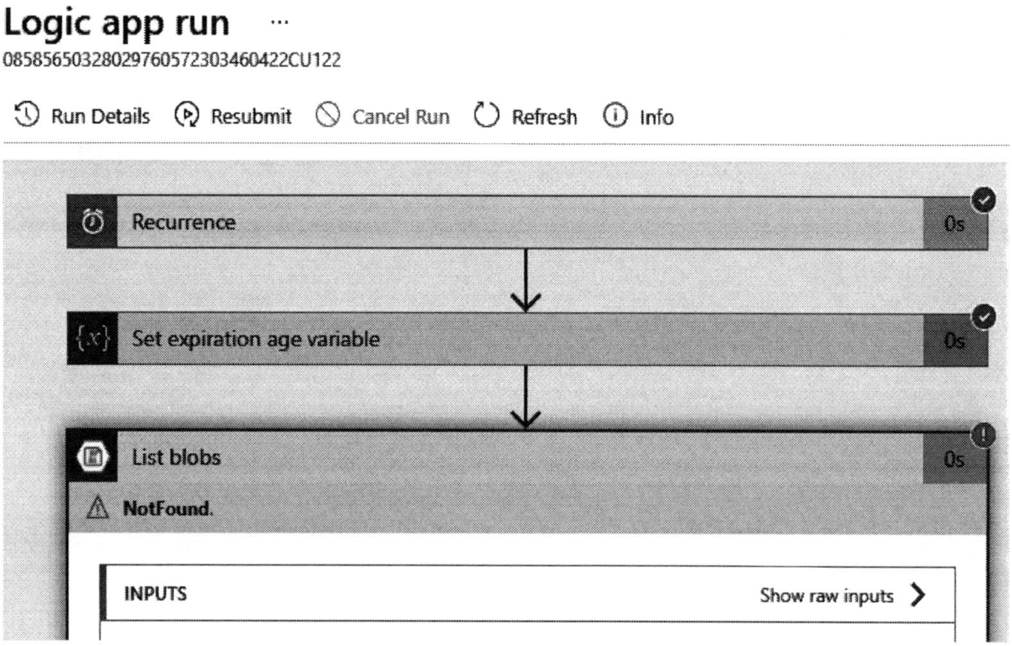
Logic app run
08585650328029760572303460422CU122
Run Details
Resubmit
Cancel Run
Refresh
Info
Recurrence
0s
Set expiration age variable
0s
List blobs
0s
NotFound.
INPUTS
Show raw inputs

Figure 9.10 – The failed flow with an error stating that there was no blob found

Congratulations! You have created your first Azure logic app! In the next section, we will see how we can work with it in Visual Studio.

Working with Azure logic apps in Visual Studio Code

While it is perfectly fine to work with your logic apps using the Azure portal, you do not always want to log in and use its **User Interface** (**UI**). As it is possible to install an extension to Visual Studio Code, which enables you to work with Azure logic apps, we will try this to see how it works:

1. To start working with your logic apps in Visual Studio Code, you need the Azure Logic Apps extension installed. If you do not have it by now, no worries – you can open the **Extensions: MARKETPLACE** tab window and install it in seconds:

Figure 9.11 – The Azure Logic Apps extension

This will add a new section for your **Azure** tab, showing all the logic apps available for the account that you are currently signed in with.

2. In the **AZURE** tab, select **LOGIC APPS (CONSUMPTION)** for a full view of the resources available:

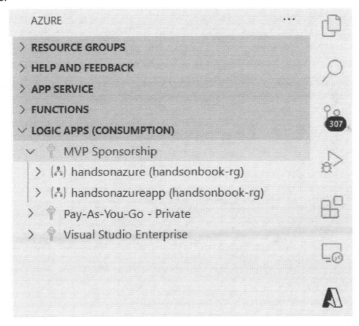

Figure 9.12 – The logic apps available in Visual Studio Code

Remember that the availability of the logic apps depends on the account you used to sign in to Azure in Visual Studio Code. If you are missing some resources, make sure that they are available for your account.

3. When you right-click on a logic app, you will see a menu with additional options to work with this resource. Select **Open in Designer** to see how the Azure logic apps designer looks in Visual Studio Code:

Figure 9.13 – Azure logic apps designed in Visual Studio Code

You can work with your logic app in Visual Studio Code in the same manner as you would work in the Azure portal. Additionally, you can look at its history and disable and delete it. To do so, extend the item in the view presenting your resource:

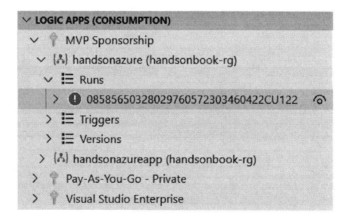

Figure 9.14 – Accessing logic app history

When you double-click on an item in the run history, you will see a JSON representation of your run, where you can debug a particular invocation. This is very helpful, as you can quickly develop and test your logic apps and work on other parts of your application without leaving your IDE.

I strongly encourage you to play a little bit with Azure Logic Apps by yourself in Visual Studio Code, as this is a great addition to the whole service and has the same feeling as the portal.

B2B integration

To a slight extent, we have already covered B2B integration of Azure Logic Apps in this chapter, but I wanted to give you some more information regarding this topic, as this service is not always recognized as an enterprise integration tool. Surprisingly, Azure Logic Apps has many interesting features to offer when it comes to exchanging messages and data between partners, and you'll find the relevant details in this section.

Starting B2B integration in Azure Logic Apps

To get started with B2B integration, you will need an **integration account** – this is a special container for integration artifacts that you will work with. In general, it allows you to store a variety of different items (such as certificates, schemas, and agreements) in one place so that you can work with them in Azure Logic Apps.

To create such an account, click on + **Create a resource** and search for Integration Account:

Create an integration account ...

Basics   Tags   Review + create

Build enterprise integration and B2B/EDI solutions with logic apps. Learn more ☐

Project details

Select the subscription to manage deployed resources and costs. Use resource groups like folders to organize and manage all your resources.

Subscription *	MVP Sponsorship ∨
└─ Resource group *	handsonbook-rg ∨
	Create new

Instance details

Integration account name *	handsonazureaccount ✓
Region *	West Europe ∨
Associate with integration service environment ⓘ	☐
Integration service environment	∨
Pricing Tier *	Free ∨
Enable log analytics ⓘ	☐
Log Analytics workspace	∨

Figure 9.15 – Creating an integration account

As you can see, it offers a simple form where, in fact, the only thing you need to do is select the proper pricing tier. There is also an option to associate it with an **Integration Service Environment** (**ISE**). We will cover ISE in the next section of this chapter.

The selected tier changes the maximum number of stored artifacts. You can, of course, change it later.

Once you have an integration account instance, you will need to link it with your logic app. To do so, go to the **Workflow settings** blade in your instance of Azure Logic Apps and search for the **Integration account** section. Once the integration account is selected, click **Save** to complete the setup:

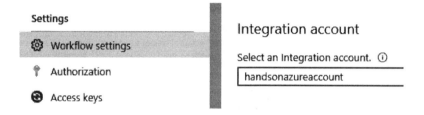

Figure 9.16 – Configuring an integration account

Now, you should be able to use connectors, which require an integration account to work.

Normally, if your logic app has no integration account linked, when you add a step requiring such functionality, you will have to provide a custom name. Once such a connection is available, you will not be asked for additional information again.

In the *Further reading* section of this chapter, you will find additional links that can help you gather more information regarding B2B integration in Azure Logic Apps.

Integrating with virtual networks

As Azure logic apps often work in enterprise environments, establishing secure connectivity is a must. Whether you want to connect to other Azure resources inside virtual networks or use hybrid connectivity to connect to your on-premises services, you need a way to integrate individual components of your system and allow them to talk to each other. The overall setup will depend on the plan used to host your logic apps:

- For the Consumption plan, you will need additional ISE runtime.

- For the Standard plan, you can leverage private endpoints/**Virtual Network** (**VNet**) integration.

When choosing a model that works for you, you need to consider several details. Use of ISE is not free of charge – there are two pricing tiers, which are charged as follows:

- Developer – $1.18 per hour
- Premium – $7.21 per hour

> **Important Note**
> Take into consideration that the Developer tier does not offer an SLA for the service.

As you can see, those charges are high, and when ISE is deployed, it will cost you a considerable amount of money. There are, however, many benefits of that setup:

- In ISE, your logic apps run in a dedicated environment that is isolated from other logic apps.
- Data is always stored in the same region as an ISE, so you will have more confidence in not violating your legal requirements.
- You do not need to deploy and configure additional services for cross-resource connectivity.
- You will have your own static IP address.

You must consider all the pros and cons and decide whether the high price of an ISE is worth it. The alternative of using the Standard plan may be tempting, but remember that it does not come without downsides:

- You lose the pay-per-execution model.
- You must configure private endpoints for inbound and VNet integration for outbound connectivity.
- You will lose the ability to use a Request/Webhook trigger publicly, as that networking model renders your logic app completely private as opposed to using an ISE.

For more information, refer to the *Further reading* section. It contains additional details about networking in Azure Logic Apps and private endpoints.

Summary

In this chapter, you have learned about Azure Logic Apps, a simple yet useful service whose use isn't restricted to Azure ninjas. You read about different connectors and multiple ways of working with your logic apps, using both the Azure portal (both with templates and the code editor) and Visual Studio Code. Additionally, you now know a little about B2B integration in that service and how to start it.

In *Chapter 10, Swiss Army Knife – Azure Cosmos DB*, we cover Azure CosmosDB – a serverless database that enables you to use different data models in the same service.

Questions

As we conclude, here is a list of questions for you to test your knowledge regarding this chapter's material. You will find the answers in the Assessments section of the Appendix:

1. What is the pricing model for Azure Logic Apps?
2. Can we use a loop in a logic app workflow?
3. What is needed to open a logic app in Visual Studio Code?
4. How can we debug a particular logic app execution?
5. Can a logic app push a message directly to a queue, such as Azure Service Bus or Azure Storage Queue?
6. How can we version multiple logic apps?

Further reading

For more information, you can refer to the following links:

*   Azure Logic Apps overview:

    `https://docs.microsoft.com/en-us/azure/logic-apps/logic-apps-overview`

*   Exchanging AS2 messages:

    `https://docs.microsoft.com/en-us/azure/logic-apps/logic-apps-enterprise-integration-as2`

*   Integrating Azure Logic Apps with enterprise solutions: `https://docs.microsoft.com/en-us/azure/logic-apps/logic-apps-enterprise-integration-overview`

- Azure Logic Apps connectors:

  `https://docs.microsoft.com/en-us/connectors/`

- Private endpoints:

  `https://docs.microsoft.com/en-us/azure/private-link/`
  `private-endpoint-overview`

- Networking in Azure Logic Apps:

  `https://docs.microsoft.com/en-us/azure/logic-apps/connect-`
  `virtual-network-vnet-isolated-environment-overview`

10
Swiss Army Knife – Azure Cosmos DB

When it comes to storage, we often need to store multiple schemas of data using multiple databases. Due to the need to use multiple services, managing our solution becomes cumbersome, and it requires a lot of skill to do it in the right fashion. Thanks to Azure Cosmos DB, we can both store records using different database models (such as MongoDB, Table storage, and Gremlin) and pay only for what we agreed on – throughput, latency, availability, and consistency, all thanks to the serverless model.

The following topics will be covered in this chapter:

- What Azure Cosmos DB is and how it compares to other storage systems
- Partitioning, throughput, and consistency
- Different Azure Cosmos DB database models
- Security features
- Autoscaling, different methods of optimization, and managing capacity
- Using change feed to track changes

Technical requirements

To perform the exercises in this chapter, you will need access to an Azure subscription.

Understanding Cosmos DB

When working with storage, you have probably heard about different kinds: relational databases, NoSQL databases, graph databases, and document databases. There are plenty of different models available, with different characteristics when it comes to storing data. If you need to easily maintain relationships between tables, in most cases, you will choose something such as SQL Server. On the other hand, maybe you want to save each record in the JSON file format, where the best solution would be an instance of MongoDB. While the choice is all yours, the biggest problem is that you need to have a different kind of service to serve the same purpose – storing data. This is where Azure Cosmos DB comes into play. With its multi-model capabilities, flexibility, and scalability, it is a great choice for globally distributed and highly responsive applications. In this section, you will learn how to start working with this service and what its main functionalities are.

Creating a Cosmos DB instance in the portal

We will start our journey with Azure Cosmos DB by creating it in the Azure portal.

When you click on + **Create a resource** and search for `Azure Cosmos DB`, you will see a screen that allows you to select the API used for your instance of the database.

Azure Cosmos DB enables you to select a specific API during instance creation. Currently, there are five available APIs: SQL, MongoDB, Cassandra, Azure Table, and Gremlin. Depending on the API selected, you will have different capabilities available (and furthermore, different packages will be required for communicating with your database through the application's code).

> **Note**
>
> Remember that in Cosmos DB, the selected API only impacts the interface for communication with databases. It does not change the underlying infrastructure of the service or generic features.

When you click the **Create** button of a selected API, you will see a wizard, where you need to enter the rest of the service details, starting with some basic information:

Select the subscription to manage deployed resources and costs. Use resource groups like folders to organize and manage all your resources.

Subscription *	Visual Studio Enterprise
└─ Resource Group *	

Create new

Instance Details

Account Name *	Enter account name
Location *	
Capacity mode ⓘ	⦿ Provisioned throughput ◯ Serverless

Learn more about capacity mode

Figure 10.1 – Basic information about Azure Cosmos DB

Besides **Subscription** and **Resource Group**, you need to enter the name of your Cosmos DB account (which, in fact, will be the name of your instance) and its location, and set **Capacity mode**. Currently, you have two options:

- **Provisioned throughput** – Best for workloads that require predictable performance, geo-distribution, and unlimited storage

- **Serverless** – Ideal for not-so-critical databases with lower performance and reliability requirements

When you have made sure that all the information you have entered in the form is correct, click on the **Review + create** button. We will cover the rest of the features later in the chapter. Once your service is created, you can access the **Overview** blade to see how it works initially:

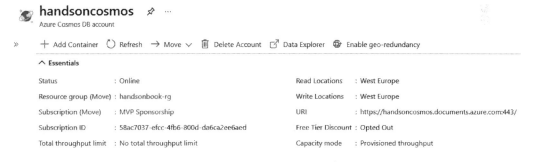

Figure 10.2 – The Overview blade of the Azure Cosmos DB instance

Azure Cosmos DB is different in many ways compared to other database solutions, as it implements some unique features:

- You can have multiple read/write locations, allowing you to improve the performance of your DB operations.

- It can be easily distributed to other regions with a single click or a single command.

- It offers a **Service-Level Agreement (SLA)**, even for request latency.

- It has an autopilot feature implemented, meaning it can automatically tune depending on your traffic.

By clicking on the **Replicate data globally** menu item, you will see the available regions, which can be used for extending your Cosmos DB infrastructure and replicating data to the region of your choice:

Figure 10.3 – The data replication feature in Azure Cosmos DB

> **Note**
>
> Geo-replication is available only for provisioned throughput. If you selected **Serverless** as the provisioning method, the preceding blade will not be available.

Figure 10.4 – Multiple read regions in Azure Cosmos DB

In the current setup, you are unable to add write regions. To be able to do so, you must enable **Multi-region writes**, as shown in *Figure 10.4*.

> **Note**
>
> Remember that enabling writes or reads in multiple regions will deploy additional instances of Azure Cosmos DB. This is not a free feature and will cost you additional money at the end of each month.

Once you save additional regions, both **Manual Failover** and **Automatic Failover** will become active. The concept for failover is simple – if your write region goes down and becomes unavailable, another available read region can take its place. The only difference is whether you want to perform this failover manually or automatically.

If you opt for automatic failover, you can decide on the order of switching between read and write regions. If you want, for example, to switch from **North Europe** to **West Europe** in the first place, **West Europe** must be the first item in the list.

Let's now check the pricing model of Azure Cosmos DB.

Pricing in Azure Cosmos DB

Azure Cosmos DB is part of the serverless services available in Azure, meaning there is no infrastructure to manage. As you have probably noticed, we were not able to define how many instances (or nodes or clusters) of a service we would like to run. Instead, we must define throughput for each collection individually.

You can verify that by using the **Data Explorer** feature in the portal. Go to **Data Explorer** and click on the **New Container** button:

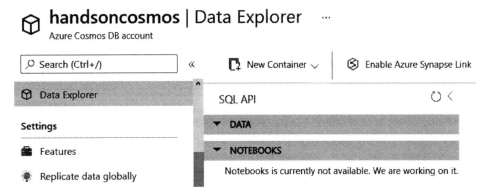

Figure 10.5 – The Data Explorer feature

By clicking on the button, you will open a new window, where you can enter the details of both the database (whether it is created or not) and a container. As you will see later, containers are basically the equivalent of tables in relational databases:

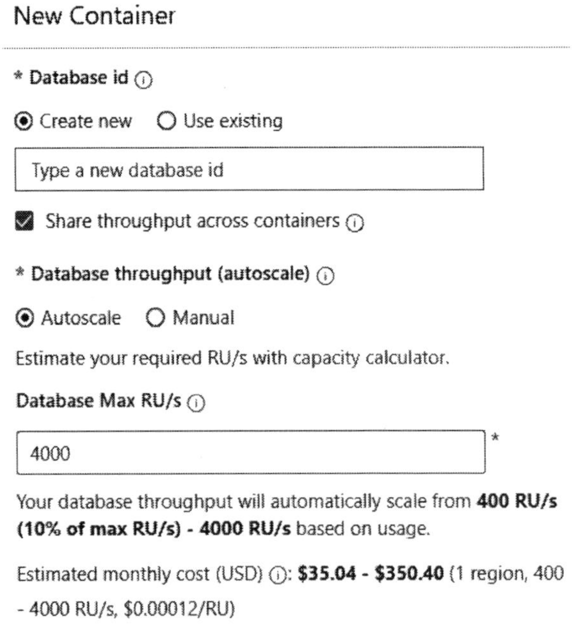

New Container

* Database id ⓘ

⦿ Create new   ◯ Use existing

Type a new database id

☑ Share throughput across containers ⓘ

* Database throughput (autoscale) ⓘ

⦿ Autoscale   ◯ Manual

Estimate your required RU/s with capacity calculator.

Database Max RU/s ⓘ

4000

Your database throughput will automatically scale from **400 RU/s (10% of max RU/s) - 4000 RU/s** based on usage.

Estimated monthly cost (USD) ⓘ: **$35.04 - $350.40** (1 region, 400 - 4000 RU/s, $0.00012/RU)

Figure 10.6 – The configuration of a database and container in Azure Cosmos DB

As you can see, when creating a container, you can decide how many **Request Units** (**RUs**) you want for your database. In general, an RU represents the performance of a Cosmos DB collection and tells you how many operations can be performed in a unit of time.

> **Tip**
>
> An RU can be described as the cost of reading a single collection item and is often defined as 1 RU = the cost of reading a 1 KB collection item. The number of RUs needed for an operation differs, depending on the operation performed.

If you are unsure how many RUs you need, you can use the capacity calculator available directly in the configuration window, which is also available directly from its URL: `https://cosmos.azure.com/capacitycalculator/`.

In Cosmos DB, you are paying for both the amount of data stored ($0.25 GB a month), and reserved RUs ($.008 an hour per every 100 RUs). This means that the smallest bill possible for the service is close to $26. However, there is a very important caveat. You are paying per each collection/table/container. That means that if you have, for example, 20 different tables in your database, you will pay 20 x $26 = $520. In such a scenario, it is sometimes better to model your database in such a way that it will be possible to store all data within a single container.

While Azure Cosmos DB seems like quite an expensive service, please do remember that it does many things for you, such as geo-redundancy, multiple read regions, and multi-master models. You always must calculate the best options for you (and whether you are able to achieve similar results). To do so, look at the capacity planner described in the *Further reading* section.

Now that we have briefly described what Azure Cosmos DB is, let's learn more about its throughput, partitioning, and data consistency models.

Partitioning, throughput, and consistency

Now we have learned something about Azure Cosmos DB – how it works and its most common features – we can focus a little bit on three important topics in this service, namely partitioning, throughput, and consistency. These factors are crucial when selecting a database engine to power your application. They directly tell you how it will be performing, how many requests it will be able to handle, and what guarantees apply when it comes to your data integrity.

Partitions in Azure Cosmos DB

Partitioning is directly connected with scaling in Azure Cosmos DB, as it allows for load-balancing incoming requests. In fact, there are two different types of partition in this service:

- **Physical**: These are a combination of fixed storage and variable amounts of computing resources. This type of partition is fully managed by Cosmos DB – you cannot directly affect how your data is physically partitioned and how a service handles those partitions. In fact, you are also unaware of how many of those partitions are currently in use. Therefore, you should not design your containers based on that specific concept.

- **Logical**: This kind of partition holds data that has the same partition key. Because you can define that key (by specifying it in each entity), you are able to control how your data is partitioned.

Remember that a logical partition has a limit of 10 GB. Additionally, all data for a logical partition must be stored within one physical partition.

Now, you may wonder how partitioning works in Azure Cosmos DB. This can be described in a few steps:

1. Each time a new container is provisioned (and you are providing several RUs), Cosmos DB must provision physical partitions, which will be able to serve the number of requests specified in the number of RUs.

2. It may turn out that the specified number of RUs exceeds the maximum number of requests per second served by a partition. In that case, Cosmos DB will provision the number of partitions it needs to satisfy your requirements.

3. The next thing to do is to allocate space for partition key hashes. All provisioned partitions must have the same space allocated (so it is distributed evenly).

4. Now, if any partition reaches its storage limit after some time, it is split into two new partitions, and data is distributed evenly between them.

Of course, the partition key used for partitioning differs for each database model – for a table, it is a partition key; for SQL, it will be a custom path. In general, this operation is slightly different depending on the database type, yet the overall concept remains the same.

Remember that if your container has only one partition key for all the entities in it, then Cosmos DB will not be able to split a partition. That means that you could hit a maximum of 10 GB per partition and not be able to add any more data.

The best value for the partition key depends solely on your application data specification. In general, you must choose a value that is quite differential (so that partitioning can happen). On the other hand, you should not create a unique partition key for each record (while it is possible, it will be quite expensive). There is no single solution to that problem – you always must analyze each scenario and select what suits you the most.

In most cases, it is worth including a partition key while filtering data, as it allows for high concurrency.

Throughput in Azure Cosmos DB

In the *Further reading* section, you will find a capacity calculator – a tool that enables you to plan your Cosmos DB instance and estimate the required RUs. As mentioned previously, in this service you are not defining the number of instances or clusters. Instead, while creating a container, you must state your expected throughput for that specific collection (or a set of collections). Thanks to an SLA for Azure Cosmos DB, that value will be guaranteed for you. Additionally, even if you replicate a database to another region, you can expect that a problem in one region will not affect others.

There is one important definition of a RU – it is the processing capacity, which enables you to read a 1 KB entity using, for example, a simple `GET` request. The same is not true for operations such as inserting or deleting, as those require more computing power to be performed.

If you would like to know exactly how many RUs a specific operation consumes, you must consult the `x-ms-request-charge` header in a response from a Cosmos DB instance. This will tell you the cost of this operation – of course, you must remember that it can differ depending on the number of records returned. In the documentation, you can find the following table:

Operation	Request unit charge
Create item	~15 RU
Read item	~1 RU
Query item by ID	~2.5 RU

Those are values for executing an operation against an entity 1 KB in size. As you can see, the values are completely different depending on the operation type. You also can see that it is crucial to carefully check all the operations' requirements – if you fail to do so, you may face an `HTTP 429` response, which tells you that you have exceeded the reserved throughput limits. In such a scenario, you should honor the `x-ms-retry-after-ms` header response, which allows for an easy retry policy.

Consistency in Azure Cosmos DB

Besides the different models of a database, Azure Cosmos DB also offers a different level of consistency. You may wonder what consistency is and how it affects your data. In fact, we can define it as follows:

Consistency is a parameter of a database system, which reflects the way a transaction affects data. It defines the rules that are applied when different constraints or/and triggers affect data written to a database.

So, basically, it tells you what the guarantees are that, if your data becomes affected by a set of operations, it will not be malformed, and you will be able to rely on it. The following are the available consistency models in Cosmos DB:

- **STRONG**
- **BOUNDED STATELESS**
- **SESSION**
- **CONSISTENT PREFIX**
- **EVENTUAL**

In the preceding list, each level below **STRONG** gives you less consistency. This is especially true for **EVENTUAL**, which might be familiar to you thanks to a topic known as eventual consistency. In general, Azure Cosmos DB allows you to set the default consistency level for your account – if needed, it is possible to override it per request. If you want to know how exactly each consistency level works, please refer to the *Further reading* section. To set a particular level in your Cosmos DB instance, click on the **Default consistency** blade:

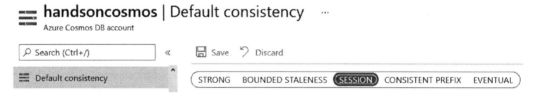

Figure 10.7 – Various consistency models in Azure Cosmos DB

As you can see, it allows you to easily switch to another consistency level depending on your needs. What's more, it displays a nice animation that describes how reads/writes in multiple regions will work for a particular level. The following screenshot shows the animation for **EVENTUAL** consistency:

Figure 10.8 – Eventual consistency data replication

In the preceding screenshot, each individual note represents an individual read or write in a particular region. Note that some consistency models allow you to configure additional parameters, which allow you to adjust the chosen model. For example, selecting **BOUNDED STALENESS** will give you an option to enter a maximum lag time for the data replication operation:

Figure 10.9 – Bounded staleness configuration

Selection of the data replication model is a direct choice of your application – some applications or features (such as tweets on Twitter or likes on Facebook) do not have the requirement of happening immediately – they need to happen eventually; thus, the **EVENTUAL** consistency model would suit in those cases. However, if you need your data to be replicated at once, you should select a more consistent model.

> **Note**
>
> Remember that with multi-region writes selected, you will be unable to select the **Strict** consistency model. Azure Cosmos DB is unable to guarantee that kind of consistency if it needs to geo-replicate each request linearly.

With the basic definitions of imports for Azure Cosmos DB discussed, we will now switch our focus to data models in detail.

Azure Cosmos DB models and APIs

As mentioned earlier, Azure Cosmos DB offers six different database models, all sharing the same infrastructure and concepts. This is a great feature that makes this service flexible and able to serve multiple different purposes. In this section, I will briefly describe each database model so that you will be able to select one that best serves your purposes.

SQL

If you think about SQL, you probably see a relational database with tables, relations, and stored procedures. When working with the **SQL API** in Cosmos DB, in fact, you will work with documents that can be queried using the SQL syntax. Let's assume you want to query documents using the following call:

```
SELECT * FROM dbo.Order O WHERE O.AccountNumber = "0000-12-223-
12"
```

Here, you can find an example of a query written in C#:

```
// using Microsoft.Azure.Documents.Client;
// client is DocumentClient class
var order =
  client.CreateDocumentQuery<Order>(collectionLink)
    .Where(so => so.AccountNumber == "0000-12-223-12")
    .AsEnumerable()
    .FirstOrDefault();
```

As you can see, it is all about a simple LINQ query, which allows you to use a specific property to filter data. Because all records in Cosmos DB are stored as JSON documents, you can easily transform them from table to document representations (and possibly denormalize them).

Using document databases is completely different from storing data in relational databases. Always remember to model your data appropriately in line with database capabilities.

MongoDB

As Cosmos DB implements the MongoDB wire protocol, you can easily use all your applications that currently use that document database with new instances of Azure Cosmos DB, without changing anything (besides the connection string, of course). While it cannot mimic MongoDB completely yet (the full list of supported operations can be found in the *Further reading* section), in most cases, you will be able to use it seamlessly. As Cosmos DB has a strict requirement regarding security, you will have to use **Secure Sockets Layer** (**SSL**) when communicating with it:

```
mongodb://username:password@host:port/[database]?ssl=true
```

Here, you can see a template for a connection string, where `ssl=true` is present – it is required when communicating with this Azure service. What's more, you will not be able to set a communication without authenticating a request.

Graph

Azure Cosmos DB supports Gremlin as a graph database model. If you are not familiar with graph databases, you can think of them as a structure composed of vertices and edges. They can very easily show you relations between different elements of a graph, as you can quickly traverse the connections and see that element *A* knows something about element *B* indirectly, thanks to element *C*. To be more specific, Cosmos DB supports a more specific model of a graph database known as a **property graph**. The following is an example query for Gremlin:

```
:> g.V('thomas.1').out('knows').out('uses').out('runsos').
group().by('name').by(count())
```

The preceding example is taken from the documentation and literally answers the question, what operating systems do relations of the user of the `thomas.1` ID use? Graph databases are great for applications such as social media portals or **Internet of Things** (**IoT**) hubs.

Table

While you can use Azure Table storage for your applications (which will be covered in the upcoming chapters), it is possible to also take advantage of Cosmos DB's Table API and consider more advanced scenarios with that service. There are some differences between both services:

- While the current maximum limit for operations in Azure Table storage is 20,000 operations per second, with Cosmos DB, you can achieve millions of them.

- You cannot initiate failover for Table storage.

- In Cosmos DB, data is indexed on all properties, not only on the partition key and row key.

- Different pricing (storage versus throughput).

- Different consistency levels.

Developing against the Cosmos DB Table API is the same as working with Azure Table storage. The following is an example of code in C# retrieving entities from a table:

```
// NuGet: Microsoft.Azure.Cosmos.Table
CloudStorageAccount storageAccount = CloudStorageAccount.Parse(
    CloudConfigurationManager.
GetSetting("StorageConnectionString"));
CloudTableClient tableClient = storageAccount.
CreateCloudTableClient();
CloudTable table = tableClient.GetTableReference("people");
TableQuery<CustomerEntity> query = new
TableQuery<CustomerEntity>().Where(TableQuery.
GenerateFilterCondition("PartitionKey", QueryComparisons.Equal,
"Smith"));
foreach (CustomerEntity entity in table.ExecuteQuery(query))
{
    Console.WriteLine("{0}, {1}\t{2}\t{3}", entity.
PartitionKey, entity.RowKey,
        entity.Email, entity.PhoneNumber);
}
```

Similar logic will be valid for other supported languages such as Java.

Cassandra

The last available model in Azure Cosmos DB is Cassandra. Cassandra is a scalable, durable, and decentralized database for storing massive amounts of data. Now, if you use it with Cosmos DB, you can focus on development rather than on operations or performance management, and have a choice of consistency. Under the hood, it uses the Cassandra API, so it is possible to use the Cassandra Query Language to communicate and interact with data. This model has the same feel as MongoDB – you can use the same tools that you used for your current Cassandra instances and should not notice any difference.

Capacity, autoscale, and optimization

Azure Cosmos DB has multiple different features that can be used to lower your bills, secure an instance, or integrate with other services. In this section, we will quickly look at most of them so that you will fully understand the basics of this service and will be able to progress on your own.

Container throughput

In Azure Cosmos DB, throughput can be set at multiple levels. One of those levels is the container throughput, which allows us to exclusively reserve capacity for an individual container. It is important to consider it for all cases where reliability is critical – as per the Azure Cosmos DB documentation, this operation is financially backed by the SLA of the service. This means that Microsoft is sure that throughput set at a container level is stable and can be relied on.

Container level throughput can be set using the Azure portal (as mentioned previously in this chapter) or by using one of the **Software Development Kits** (**SDKs**) or the **Command Line Interface** (**CLI**). Here is the example of setting up a container with a fixed throughput using the Azure CLI:

```
az cosmosdb sql container create -a <account-name> -g
<resource-group-name> -d <database-name> -n <container-name> -p
<partition-key> –throughput <throughput-value>
```

The same can be done using, for example, a .NET SDK:

```
// using Microsoft.Azure.Documents
DocumentCollection myCollection = new DocumentCollection();
myCollection.Id = "myContainerName";
myCollection.PartitionKey.Paths.Add("/partitionkey");
// client is DocumentClient class
```

```
await client.CreateDocumentCollectionAsync(
    UriFactory.CreateDatabaseUri("databasename"),
    myCollection,
    new RequestOptions { OfferThroughput = 400 });
```

Specifically, once throughput is defined on a container level, it is distributed evenly amongst its partitions. This requires a good partition key selection – if you fail to select a partition key, which divides your data into similar parts, you may face an issue called a hot partition. More information related to partitioning good practices can be found in the *Further reading* section.

Database level throughput

In Azure Cosmos DB, it is also possible to provision throughput directly on a database. To do so, you need to select the **Provision throughput** checkbox during database creation:

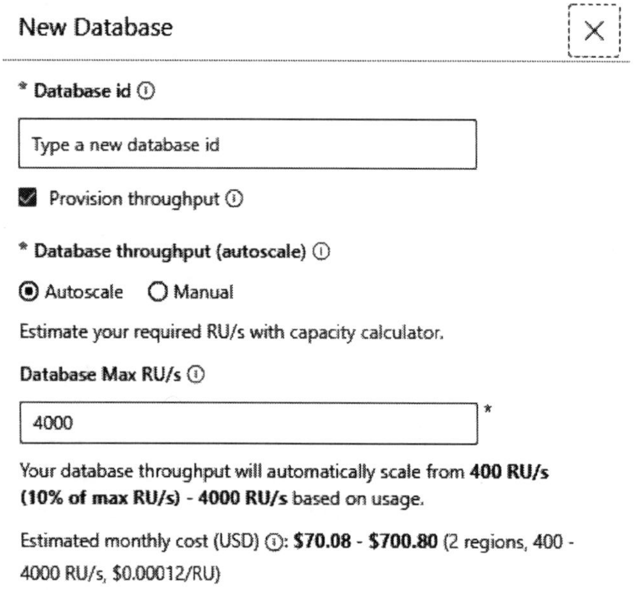

New Database   [×]

* **Database id** ⓘ

Type a new database id

☑ Provision throughput ⓘ

* **Database throughput (autoscale)** ⓘ

◉ Autoscale   ○ Manual

Estimate your required RU/s with capacity calculator.

Database Max RU/s ⓘ

4000   *

Your database throughput will automatically scale from **400 RU/s (10% of max RU/s)** - **4000 RU/s** based on usage.

Estimated monthly cost (USD) ⓘ: **$70.08** - **$700.80** (2 regions, 400 - 4000 RU/s, $0.00012/RU)

Figure 10.10 – Creating a database in the portal

With that feature on, all provisioned RUs will be shared across all the collections available for a database. The same can be done using, for example, a .NET SDK:

```
// Nuget: Microsoft.Azure.Cosmos
var databaseName = "MyDatabaseName";
await this.cosmosClient.CreateDatabaseIfNotExistsAsync(
```

```
        id: databaseName,
        throughput: 4000);
```

There are at least two use cases for the database-level throughput scenario:

- A multitenant application, where you do not wish to configure throughput on each container individually

- Migration scenarios from other NoSQL databases, where throughput was defined at a database level and you want to reuse a similar design in Azure

There is one important detail, however, when using throughput defined at a database level – there is a limitation on how many containers can be created for such a database. The current limit allows you to host only 25 containers inside a single database, which will leverage the shared throughput feature. After reaching that value, you will still be able to add more containers; however, they have to be provisioned with dedicated throughput.

Firewall and virtual networks

At any time, you can access the **Firewall and virtual networks** blade to configure networking features of your Azure Cosmos DB instance. As this database service is offered in a serverless model, your ability to configure low-level features of a virtual network will not be available. However, you can still define which networks can connect with your instance. Here, you can see how the functionality looks in the Azure portal:

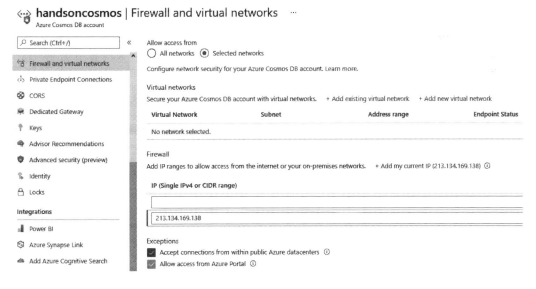

Figure 10.11 – The Firewall and virtual networks feature in Azure Cosmos DB

As you can see, you can additionally configure a firewall, which limits access to Azure Cosmos DB by whitelisting specific IP addresses from the list. Note that both firewall rules and virtual network integration can be enabled on a single Cosmos DB account. What is important to remember though is that they are complementary – a firewall is designed to block public access from static IP addresses while network integration defines which **VoiceNets** (VNETs) and subnets can access the account.

Azure Functions

One of the interesting features of Azure Cosmos DB is the ability to easily integrate with Azure Functions by using the **Add Azure Function** blade:

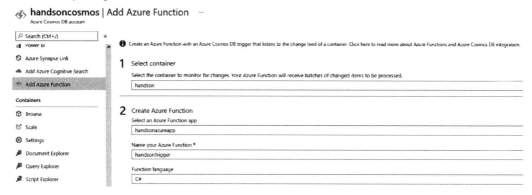

Figure 10.12 – Adding Azure Functions integration

In the **Add Azure Function** blade, you will need to select a container and your Azure function, which will handle incoming triggers. Enabling that feature creates a new function in your function app, which is triggered with each new document added to the container selected in the configuration selection. The created function will look like the following code snippet:

```
#r "Microsoft.Azure.Documents.Client"

using Microsoft.Azure.Documents;

using System.Collections.Generic;
using System;

public static async Task Run(IReadOnlyList<Document> input,
TraceWriter log)
```

```
{
    log.Verbose("Document count " + input.Count);
    log.Verbose("First document Id " + input[0].Id);
}
```

This is CSX code, which we did not cover, and in fact, there was a reason for that – simply put, using CSX is far from an optimal solution. Personally, I recommend using C# or any of the other supported languages in Azure Functions, as they offer more predictable performance and easier management of your code. When using Azure Functions with the Cosmos DB trigger, the concepts of functions that you should already be familiar with are the same – as you can see in the following snippet, we are still using attributes. There are triggers and bindings, and the whole framework does most of the work for us:

```
[FunctionName("DocByIdFromJSON")]
public static void Run(
    [QueueTrigger("inputqueue")] string message,
    [CosmosDB(
        databaseName: "somedb",
        collectionName: "Items",
        ConnectionStringSetting = "CosmosDBConnection",
        Id = "{ItemId}",
        PartitionKey = "{PartitionKeyValue}")] ContainerItem
item,
    ILogger log)
{
    // Your code
}
```

Besides using the Cosmos DB trigger specifically, there is nothing different compared to integrating Azure Functions with other services.

Stored procedures

Azure Cosmos DB allows you to create stored procedures that can be executed individually and can hold extra logic, which you do not want to share.

If you go to your collection in **Data Explorer**, you will see the **New Stored Procedure** tab and the option to create one:

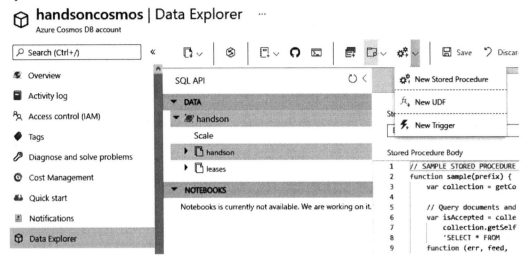

Figure 10.13 – Adding a new stored procedure

Stored procedures are written in JavaScript – this allows you to easily access a document's schema (as they are all JSON). What is more, they are registered per collection. Here, you can find an example of the stored procedure generated in the Azure portal:

```javascript
function sample(prefix) {
    var collection = getContext().getCollection();

    // Query documents and take 1st item.
    var isAccepted = collection.queryDocuments(
        collection.getSelfLink(),
        'SELECT * FROM root r',
    function (err, feed, options) {
        if (err) throw err;

        // Check the feed and if empty, set the body to 'no
docs found',
        // else take 1st element from feed
        if (!feed || !feed.length) {
            var response = getContext().getResponse();
            response.setBody('no docs found');
```

```
        }
        else {
            var response = getContext().getResponse();
            var body = { prefix: prefix, feed: feed[0] };
            response.setBody(JSON.stringify(body));
        }
    });


    if (!isAccepted) throw new Error('The query was not
accepted by the server.');
}
```

Each stored procedure can create, update, delete, and read items when executed. Stored procedures can be executed using one of the supported SDKs (.NET, Java, Python, or JavaScript) by calling it in the context of the collection where the stored procedure is saved:

```
const newItem = [{
    name: "John",
    surname: "Doe
}];
const container = client.database("myDatabase").
container("myContainer");
const sprocId = "spCreatePerson";
const {resource: result} = await container.scripts.
storedProcedure(sprocId).execute(newItem, {partitionKey:
newItem[0].category});
```

The main use case of stored procedures is to encapsulate logic and performance improvement of the database operations.

User-defined functions and triggers

To extend the query language, you can write your own **User-Defined Function** (**UDF**) in your queries. Note that you cannot use these in stored procedures. UDFs are used to extend the SQL query language in Azure Cosmos DB and can be only called from inside queries. Triggers, however, are divided into two categories:

- Pre-triggers
- Post-triggers

Additionally, you can select an operation that this trigger refers to:

- `All`
- `Create`
- `Delete`
- `Replace`

Here, you can find an example of a trigger that updates a timestamp in a document before it is created:

```
var context = getContext();
var request = context.getRequest();
var documentToCreate = request.getBody();

if (!("timestamp" in documentToCreate)) {
  var ts = new Date();
  documentToCreate["my timestamp"] = ts.getTime();
}
request.setBody(documentToCreate);
```

Triggers, of course, are also available from **Data Explorer**:

Figure 10.14 – Creating a trigger

When creating a trigger, you will need to specify its ID, type, and what kind of operations can be performed by it. Each trigger also has a body that defines the logic behind the trigger:

```
function validate () {
    var context = getContext();
    var request = context.getRequest();
    var item = request.getBody();

    if (!("date" in item)) {
```

```
        var ts = new Date();
        item ["date"] = ts.getTime();
    }
    request.setBody(item);
}
```

Depending on the type (pre- or post-), triggers can be used for validation of data, decorating with additional information, or modifying the contents of a record.

Autoscale in Azure Cosmos DB

When creating a database or a container, you can decide whether you want to use a fixed throughput or let Azure Cosmos DB decide how well it should perform at each moment in time. The choice is quite simple:

- If you are searching for predictable performance, **fixed throughput** should address your requirements.

- If you want to have a more cost-effective setup that offers flexible performance aligned with the current utilization of your database, the **autoscale** feature is something for you to consider.

Here, you can see where **Autoscale** is being defined during database creation:

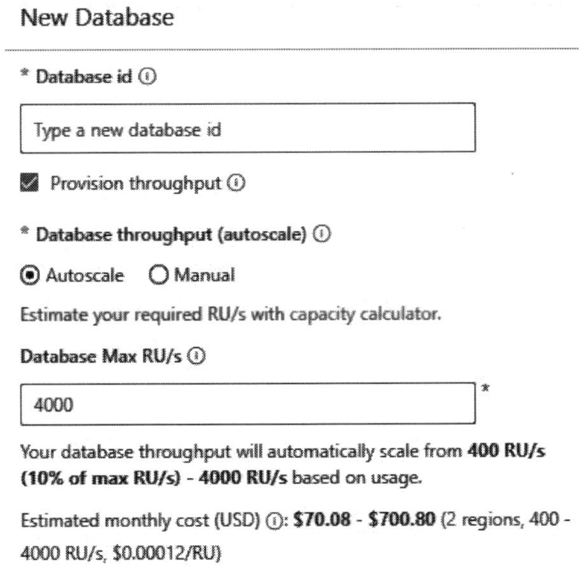

New Database

* **Database id** ⓘ

Type a new database id

☑ Provision throughput ⓘ

* **Database throughput (autoscale)** ⓘ

◉ Autoscale   ○ Manual

Estimate your required RU/s with capacity calculator.

Database Max RU/s ⓘ

4000

Your database throughput will automatically scale from **400 RU/s (10% of max RU/s)** - **4000 RU/s** based on usage.

Estimated monthly cost (USD) ⓘ: **$70.08** - **$700.80** (2 regions, 400 - 4000 RU/s, $0.00012/RU)

Figure 10.15 – Creating a database with Autoscale enabled

While using the autoscale feature can help you in establishing a solution, which can easily scale its cost, it has some drawbacks to consider. Compared to fixed throughput, which will perform at a stable rate, autoscale always needs some time to adjust the capacity of a database or a container. This means that you may experience worse performance of your Cosmos DB collections during a time when autoscaling increments the available RUs.

On the other hand, autoscale will automatically scale down your instance of Cosmos DB if your application does not need as many RUs as currently defined. A similar functionality can be implemented using fixed throughput, but it will require a custom solution developed by you.

With the various features of Azure Cosmos DB described, let's now switch to the last topic of this chapter, where we will discuss a way to track changes that happen to the items stored in Cosmos DB collections.

Using change feed for change tracking

When processing high volumes of data in Azure Cosmos DB, you may want to react to all the documents that are inserted or updated. While it is possible to query each container at a certain time interval, such a solution has many downsides:

- It is difficult to determine the correct interval.
- You can query the data even if there are no changes to the dataset.
- You do not know what record was added or altered, so you often need to query the whole collection.

To address these issues, a feature called **change feed** was introduced to Azure Cosmos DB. It allows for the implementation of various business cases, including the following:

- Calling an HTTP endpoint passing information about an added or updated document
- Processing data in a streaming fashion
- Migrating data with no or limited downtime

Change feed can be easily integrated with multiple real-time processing tools such as *Apache Spark* or *Apache Storm*, giving you a powerful solution for extending the capabilities of your system.

When implementing functionalities based on change feed, you have two options to choose from – you can use the simplest option and leverage the capabilities of Azure Functions, which integrate seamlessly with that feature, or implement your own functionality with the change feed processor library.

> **Note**
>
> At the time of writing, the trigger for change feed can be implemented only for Cosmos DB accounts with the SQL API selected.

A function using change feed can look like this:

```
[FunctionName("CosmosTrigger")]
public static void Run([CosmosDBTrigger(
    databaseName: "MyDatabase",
    collectionName: "Items",
    ConnectionStringSetting = "CosmosDBConnection",
    LeaseCollectionName = "leases",
    CreateLeaseCollectionIfNotExists = true)]
IreadOnlyList<Document> documents,
    Ilogger log)
{
    if (documents != null && documents.Count > 0)
    {
        log.LogInformation($"Documents modified: {documents.
Count}");
        log.LogInformation($"First document Id: {documents[0].
Id}");
    }
}
```

The advantage of this approach is its ability to quickly focus on you implementing your own functionality – you do not need to fully understand the underlying concepts, leaving the implementation details to the trigger implementation. On the other hand, it forces you to use Azure Functions in your architecture, which is not always desired.

The alternative of using the change feed processor library will require a more sophisticated approach, as you will have to host the processor on your own and ensure it works constantly. The first thing needed will be acquiring an SDK that has the processor implemented. Currently, it is available in SDKs for C#, Java, and Python – all you need is to select an appropriate class to implement the necessary logic. For the change feed processor, you will need to divide your code into two sections:

- An entry point, which starts the process

- A handler, which executes the processor logic

In C#, the entry point is implemented using the `ChangeFeedProcessor` class:

```
ChangeFeedProcessor changeFeedProcessor = cosmosClient.
GetContainer(databaseName, sourceContainerName)
.GetChangeFeedProcessorBuilder<YourCollectionClass>
(processorName: "changeFeedProcessorName", onChangesDelegate:
HandleChangesAsync)
          .WithInstanceName("instanceName")
          .WithLeaseContainer(leaseContainer)
          .Build();
```

The handler is passed to the processor by the `onChangesDelegate` parameter, which needs to be implemented as an asynchronous delegate:

```
static async Task HandleChangesAsync(
    ChangeFeedProcessorContext context,
    IreadOnlyCollection<YourCollectionClass> changes,
    CancellationToken cancellationToken)
{
// Processor logic…
}
```

A similar functionality needs to be implemented in each platform you want to use for your application. Here is one additional example covering the implementation in Python:

```
@staticmethod
    def ReadFeed(client):
        print('\nReading Change Feed\n')


        options = {}
        options["startFromBeginning"] = True
```

```
        response = client.QueryItemsChangeFeed(collection_link,
options)
        for doc in response:
            print(doc)
```

In the preceding example, you are just passing an instance of the Azure Cosmos DB client for Python. You will also need a `collection_link` parameter value, which is a Cosmos DB-specific link for your collection and looks like this:

```
dbs/<your-db>/colls/<your-collection>
```

In general, using the change feed processor gives you more control over the process of fetching records delivered by this feature. Still, you will need to take into consideration additional aspects to ensure everything works smoothly:

- You must decide how to run your processor to ensure that the application runs continuously. It can be through a virtual machine, a Kubernetes cluster, an Azure WebJob, or a web service.

- Control RUs utilized on a lease container. A lease container is a special container created for the change feed functionality to allow different processors to work on your collections simultaneously.

- Implement a restart mechanism to start reading your feed from a point in time where processing was stopped previously.

- Implement life cycle notifications, which can help you understand the current state of your processor and decide how to recover from an error in lease operations.

The preceding considerations are the reason why, initially, the Azure Functions trigger was a much better option – it handled all those aspects natively, giving us more time to focus on our business logic. In the *Further reading* section, you will find more information related to the topic, as change feed is one of the most complex features of Azure Cosmos DB.

Summary

In this chapter, you have learned about another serverless Azure component, Azure Cosmos DB. You saw multiple database models that this service supports and different features, such as geo-redundancy and the ability to easily scale up and introduce new read regions, where data will be replicated. What's more, you are now aware of multiple consistency models and how to change them in the Azure portal.

In the next chapter, you will learn about another hot topic – reactive architecture with Azure Event Grid.

Questions

As we conclude, here is a list of questions for you to test your knowledge regarding this chapter's material. You will find the answers in the Assessments section of the Appendix:

1. Which APIs does Azure Cosmos DB support currently?
2. Are there any differences between the capabilities of Azure Table storage and the Table API in Cosmos DB?
3. What are the available consistency models?
4. Which consistency model is more consistent – bounded staleness or eventual?
5. Is it possible to restrict access to Azure Cosmos DB to only a single IP address?
6. Is the SQL API the same as the SQL Server?
7. What is the reason for using stored procedures?
8. Is it possible to provision throughput in Azure Cosmos DB for the whole account instead of per collection?
9. What are the options to run change feed functionality?

Further reading

To learn more on the topics covered in this chapter, please visit the following links:

*   *Partitioning data in Azure Cosmos DB*: `https://docs.microsoft.com/en-us/azure/cosmos-db/partition-data`
*   Capacity planner: `https://www.documentdb.com/capacityplanner`
*   Azure Cosmos DB RUs: `https://docs.microsoft.com/en-us/azure/cosmos-db/request-units`
*   Consistency levels: `https://docs.microsoft.com/en-us/azure/cosmos-db/consistency-levels`
*   Mongo DB support: `https://docs.microsoft.com/en-us/azure/cosmos-db/mongodb-feature-support#mongodb-protocol-support`
*   Graph API and Gremlin: `http://tinkerpop.apache.org/docs/current/reference/#intro`
*   The Azure Cosmos DB change feed: `https://docs.microsoft.com/en-us/azure/cosmos-db/sql/read-change-feed`

11

Reactive Architecture with Event Grid

Azure Event Grid is another cloud component that represents serverless services in Azure. It can be considered an events gateway or a handler. It is able to both make our solution work faster and reverse control, so our services don't have to wait for others, burning available resources just to be idle. Additionally, it's a great routing tool that is able to quickly distribute load and multiply it, allowing jobs to be finished faster.

In this chapter, the following topics will be covered:

- Azure Event Grid and reactive architecture
- Connecting to other services through Azure Event Grid
- The security features of Azure Event Grid
- Using different event schemas
- Receiving and filtering events

Technical requirements

To perform exercises within this chapter, you will need the following:

- An Azure subscription
- Visual Studio Code
- The Azure CLI

Azure Event Grid and reactive architecture

When working with multiple services in the cloud, often, you need to have a centralized service that is responsible for routing events to a different endpoint. This makes the exchange of data a piece of cake—you do not have to maintain different URLs of APIs, as you can leverage a common event schema and custom routing configuration that is based on, for example, the event type. In Azure, such a service is called **Azure Event Grid**—a serverless event gateway, which is one of the newer cloud components available. With a pay-as-you-go pricing model, you can quickly build a reactive architecture that inverts the communication between your services and makes them passive. In this chapter, you will learn how to work with Event Grid and integrate it with other Azure components.

Reactive architecture

To get started, let's consider the architecture shown in the following diagram:

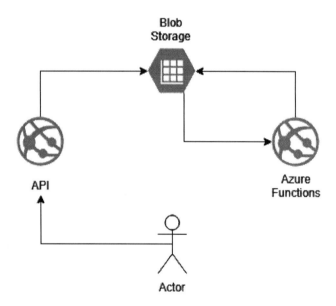

Figure 11.1 – A simple flow of pushing a file from an actor to a blob

In the preceding diagram, you can see an example flow of uploading, for instance, an image for an avatar from a user. A file is transferred through **Azure App Service** and put into **Azure Blob Storage**. Then, it is processed by **Azure Functions**. While such a setup is perfectly fine, consider the following disadvantage—to be able to process the image, Azure Functions must be notified about the fact that a new file was uploaded.

Since Azure Blob Storage is unable to do so (at least with the functionality available publicly), the only way to achieve that is to pool some kind of storage and somehow maintain the processed files. While conceptually, this is not rocket science, you must bear in mind that, in the cloud, when you use a resource, you pay for the time taken. So, essentially, in the preceding scenario, you would be paying even if no file was uploaded to storage, since a trigger in **Azure Functions** (here, a Blob trigger) will have to maintain a state of the available files and check, at intervals, whether something new appeared, so you will often pay for nothing. Now, consider the following change:

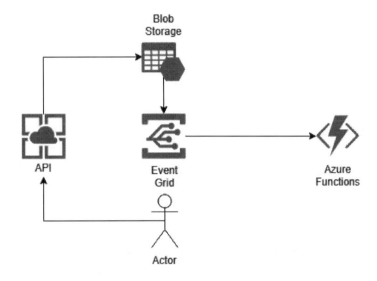

Figure 11.2 – Using Event Grid as an intermediary handler of an event

As you can see, I put **Azure Event Grid** between **Azure Blob Storage** and **Azure Functions**. What has it changed? Well, functions processing a blob do not have to pool storage to get information about the uploaded files. This is possible thanks to version 2 of Azure Storage (you can find a link to a description in the *Further reading* section)—it can publish events to **Azure Event Grid** so that they can then be forwarded to all subscribers of that event type. Thanks to this, Azure Functions can remain passive—they will be called by Azure Event Grid when needed, so if nothing is uploaded, you will pay nothing. Of course, this is an element of serverless architecture—being able to pay for usage makes such a setup possible.

> **Note**
>
> Remember that you will not be charged if you only use the Consumption plan in Azure Functions. If you must use an App Service or Premium Service plan for your functions, you will not be able to save money with the preceding architecture—on the other hand, you will save some compute power, which could be used for other workloads, so reactive architecture concepts will still be valid.

This is what we call **reactive architecture**—a model where your components can remain idle and wait for upcoming requests.

Topics and event subscriptions

There are five main topics when it comes to working with Azure Event Grid:

- Events
- Event handlers
- Event sources
- Topics
- Event subscriptions

In this section, we will go through each of them to gain a better understanding of this service.

Event sources

Currently, Azure Event Grid supports the following event sources:

- Azure App Configuration
- Azure App Service
- Azure API Management
- Azure Blob Storage
- Azure Container Registry
- Azure Machine Learning
- Azure Media Services
- Azure Subscriptions
- Azure Key Vault
- Resource groups
- Azure Event Hubs

- Azure IoT Hub

- Azure Policy

- Azure SignalR

- Azure Maps

- Azure Cache for Redis

- Azure Kubernetes Service (currently in preview)

- Azure Service Bus

- Azure FarmBeats

- Azure Communication Services

- Custom topics

As you can see, there are plenty of different services integrated and available when working with Event Grid. While we know which event sources we can use, we still have not defined what an event source is. Look at the following diagram:

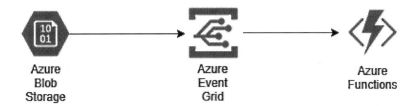

Figure 11.3 – A simple flow of pushing a blob to Azure Functions via Azure Event Grid

In this scenario, a file uploaded to **Azure Blob Storage** triggers an event, which is then fetched by **Azure Event Grid** and passed further to the consumer. The event source is the origin of an event that was then handled by Event Grid. When working with this service, all event sources have a way to publish an event and communicate with Azure Event Grid. There is also one extra event source possible—that is custom topics. It is possible to publish your own custom events directly to an Event Grid endpoint—we will cover that later in this chapter.

Event handlers

In the previous example, we covered event sources. Let's take a similar scenario:

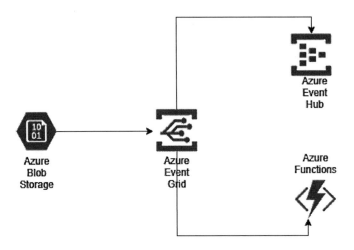

Figure 11.4 – Handling an event in two different Azure services

Once more, we have **Azure Blob Storage** as a publisher. However, this time, events are forwarded to both **Azure Functions** and **Azure Event Hub**. In this architecture, services presented on the right-hand side are event handlers. Here is a list of currently supported services:

- Azure Functions
- Azure Logic Apps
- Azure Automation
- WebHooks
- Azure Queue Storage
- Hybrid Connections
- Azure Event Hubs
- Power Automate
- Azure Service Bus

So, what is an event handler? You can think of it as the processor of an event—based on the configuration, Azure Event Grid will forward events to handlers, where they will be deserialized and analyzed.

> **Note**
>
> In general, Azure Event Grid uses a common event schema when delivering events to handlers. What is more, it can deliver more than just one event at a time—you must be prepared for a possible batch of events.

Topics and subscriptions

A topic is a general messaging concept that allows for one-to-many communication. It works with subscriptions in the following way—you publish a message to a topic in a messaging service and then subscribe to it with your consumers. In Azure Event Grid, you are responsible for creating a topic—that means you must publish a custom application that handles communication between publishers and the Event Grid endpoint. You can have a single application or many of them—this depends on your design and expected throughput. Additionally, you must configure subscriptions—in the next section, you will see how to do that and how to set up proper filtering. The general structure could look like this:

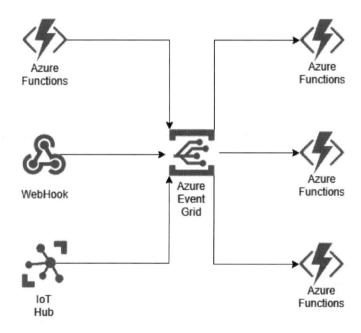

Figure 11.5 – Sending events to multiple event handlers after fetching them from publishers

The left-hand side of the preceding diagram represents publishers and a topic (the line between the publisher and **Azure Event Grid**) and subscriptions with handlers. Each line is a different topic and subscription. The whole configuration and routing reside within the Event Grid endpoint and can be managed there.

> **Note**
> Azure Event Grid takes care of retrying undelivered messages. This can be configured with a custom policy that defines the rules for retrying. Additionally, when a custom topic is used, events must be published in batches to make it work.

To sum up, we can define both a topic and a subscription as follows:

- **Topic**: A channel between a service and Azure Event Grid, which allows the former to push an event to the Azure service
- **Subscription**: A channel between Azure Event Grid and a service, which is used to retrieve events in the former

Now, let's check how we can connect to various services using Azure Event Grid and what the main configuration options are.

Connecting services through Azure Event Grid

Now that you have learned something about what Azure Event Grid is and how it works, we will try to test your knowledge and create a working solution. We will start by creating an instance in the Azure Portal and configuring it to accept and route events. Additionally, you will learn what the schema of an event is and how to leverage it so that you can send custom events that will be handled by Event Grid.

Creating Azure Event Grid in the Azure Portal

To get started with Azure Event Grid, do the following in the Azure Portal:

1. Click on + **Create a resource** and search for Event Grid. From the list, select **Event Grid Topic** and click on **Create**.
2. You will see a simple form, where you must enter the name of the instance of a service. For now, we will skip the rest of the settings:

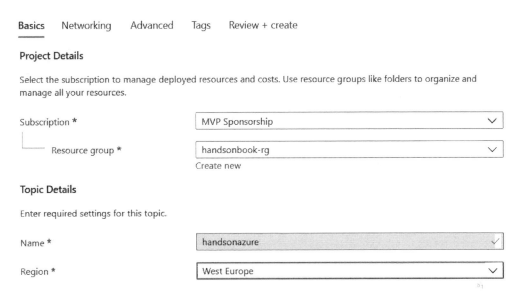

Figure 11.6 – Creating a topic in the Azure Portal

3. When you click on **Review + create** and wait a moment, an instance of a service will be created. Once it is finished, you can go to your resource to see an empty instance:

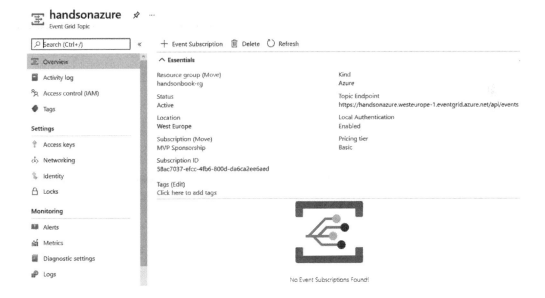

Figure 11.7 – The Overview blade for the Event Grid topic

As you can see, there is no subscription created yet. What is more, there is also no topic, which is what would send events to our instance. Before we proceed, let's look at what we have in the **Overview** blade. Besides the option to create a subscription, there is also one other important thing—**Topic Endpoint**. This can be used to publish events from your custom topics. There is also an important blade—**Access keys**. When you click on it, you will see two keys that can be used to authorize access to Azure Event Grid:

Figure 11.8 – Access keys for an instance of an Event Grid topic

Now, let's try to add a subscription to the topic. To do this, we will use the following code snippet:

```
az eventgrid event-subscription create --name <subscription-
name> --source-resource-id <source-resource-id> --endpoint
<event-receiving-endpoint>
```

Your endpoint should be a generic HTTP endpoint that accepts passing an authorization code from Azure Event Grid, as follows: `https://mywebsite.net/api/eventgrid?code=code`.

Before we proceed, let's explain a little bit about the preceding command. As you can see, there are three parameters required to complete the process:

- `--name`: This represents the custom name of your subscription.
- `--source-resource-id`: This is the fully qualified identifier (resource ID) of your resource from which events will be fetched. You must use a resource that is supported by Event Grid as an event source.
- `--endpoint`: This is an HTTP endpoint called by Event Grid when an event has been sent.

After running the command, Event Grid will start pushing events to an endpoint defined in the `--endpoint` parameter. However, if you execute the code, you might notice the following warning and the process freezes in the `Running` state:

```
If you are creating an event subscription from a topic that has
"Azure" as the value for its "kind" property, you must validate
your webhook endpoint by following the steps described in
https://aka.ms/eg-webhook-endpoint-validation.
```

So, what has happened? Well, it turns out that we cannot create a subscription, because our endpoint is not validated. The **Kind** property can be seen when you access the **Overview** blade of your topic:

Figure 11.9 – The Kind property in the Overview blade

How can we validate our endpoint so that it will be possible to create a subscription? I will explain this shortly.

Azure Event Grid security

Besides access tokens, Azure Event Grid also checks whether an endpoint is valid and secure. This validation will not happen for the following handler types:

- Azure Logic Apps

- Azure Automation

- Azure Functions when `EventGridTrigger` is used

The remaining endpoints (and especially those triggered by an HTTP request) must be validated to be used. Here is how that kind of validation is processed:

1. Firstly, `SubscriptionValidationEvent` is sent to an endpoint containing multiple fields, such as a topic, validation code, and more. Additionally, a special `aeg-event-type: SubscriptionValidation` header is sent.

2. Secondly, Event Grid expects a successful response containing a validation code that was sent in the request.

Here is an example of a validation event:

```
[{
  "id": "3d178aaf-364c-67b-bq0c-e34519da4eww",
=  "topic": "/subscriptions/xxxxxxxx-xxxx-xxxx-xxxx-
xxxxxxxxxxxx",
  "subject": "",
  "data": {
```

```
    "validationCode": "512d38b6-c7b8-40c8-89fe-f46f9e9622b6",
    "validationUrl": "<validation-url>"
  },
  "eventType": "Microsoft.EventGrid.
SubscriptionValidationEvent",
  "eventTime": "2018-08-10T10:20:19.4556811Z",
  "metadataVersion": "1",
  "dataVersion": "1"
}]
```

In this scenario, to validate an endpoint, you would have to return the following response:

```
{
    "validationResponse": "512d38b6-c7b8-40c8-89fe-f46f9e9622b6"
}
```

After that, you should be able to create a subscription.

> **Note**
>
> As you might have noticed, the validation event also contains the `validationUrl` property. This allows you to manually validate a subscription instead of redeploying code with proper application logic.

Creating a subscription

Now that you are familiar with the topic of endpoint validation, we can try to create a subscription once more:

1. To do this, I created a function that is triggered by an HTTP request. It can be a function written in any of the supported languages (the following example has been written in CSX for simplicity):

    ```
    #r "Newtonsoft.Json"
    using System.Net;
    using Newtonsoft.Json;
    public static async Task<HttpResponseMessage>
    Run(HttpRequestMessage req, TraceWriter log)
    {
      var @event = JsonConvert.DeserializeObject(await req.
    Content.ReadAsStringAsync());
      log.Info(@event.ToString());
    ```

```
    return req.CreateResponse(HttpStatusCode.OK);
  }
```

Thanks to the preceding code, I can see that the validation event data was sent to an endpoint. Note the value of `validationUrl` in the payload.

2. Now, when you can see the whole validation event payload, you can use it to prepare validation logic. In the following snippet, you can find the overall concept of such a function:

```
#r "Newtonsoft.Json"
using System.Net;
using Newtonsoft.Json;
public static async Task<HttpResponseMessage>
Run(HttpRequestMessage req, TraceWriter log)
{
  var @event = JsonConvert.
DeserializeObject<ValidationEvent[]>(await req.Content.
ReadAsStringAsync())[0];
  return req.CreateResponse(HttpStatusCode.OK, new
{validationResponse = @event.Data.ValidationCode} );
  }
public class ValidationEvent {
  public ValidationEventData Data {get;set;}
  }
public class ValidationEventData {
  public string ValidationCode {get;set;}
}
```

3. Note that I am deserializing the validation event as `ValidationEvent[]`, so it is actually an array of events. It is important to bear this in mind to avoid any potential issues.

> **Note**
> If events were sent to an endpoint that wasn't validated, the batch would be divided into two parts: one with a single validation event and the second one with the actual events.

4. Now, for example, if you create a resource in the resource group that publishes events to Event Grid, an event similar to the following will occur:

```
{
    "subject": "/subscriptions/.../Microsoft.Storage/
storageAccounts/handsonazure",
```

```
    "eventType": "Microsoft.Resources.
ResourceWriteSuccess",
    "eventTime": "2018-08-10T08:51:32.3888833Z",
    "id": "37f85f91-1af9-4ee3-84a6-ee1955c74edc",
    "data": {
      "authorization": {
        "scope": "/subscriptions/.../handsonazure-rg/
providers/Microsoft.Storage/storageAccounts/
handsonazure",
        "action": "Microsoft.Storage/storageAccounts/
write",
        "evidence": {
          "role": "Subscription Admin"
        }
      },
      "claims": {
        "aud": "https://management.core.windows.net/",
        (...)
      }
    }
  }
}
```

5.   Also, it is possible to create a connection like this without the CLI—if you navigate to your resource group, you will see the **Events** blade:

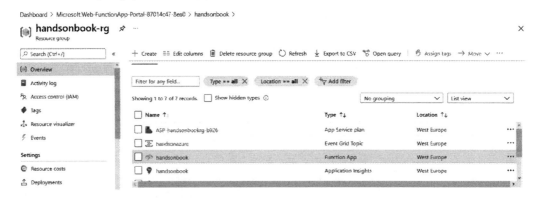

Figure 11.10 – The Events blade in a resource group

6. When you click on the + **Event subscription** button, you will see a form that makes the whole process much easier. You can use this form if you prefer configuring services in the portal, instead of the CLI:

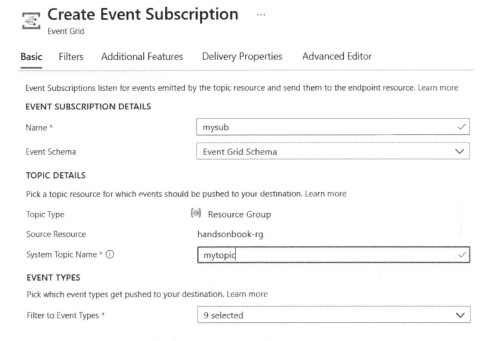

Figure 11.11 – Configuring an event subscription in a resource group

Note that when creating a topic directly on a resource group level, you are asked for a system topic name. In fact, in Azure Event Grid, there are two types of topics:

- System topics, which can be used only by Azure to publish events

- Custom topics, which do not have that limitation

System topics will not be visible to you as they are created in the background. What is more, if you create a system topic and, for example, use Azure Functions with an HTTP trigger, you will not be asked to validate the endpoint as opposed to the custom topic.

Now, let's see how you can work with different event schemas.

Using different schemas in Event Grid

When creating an Event Grid instance, you have the option to choose which event schema will be used for your system:

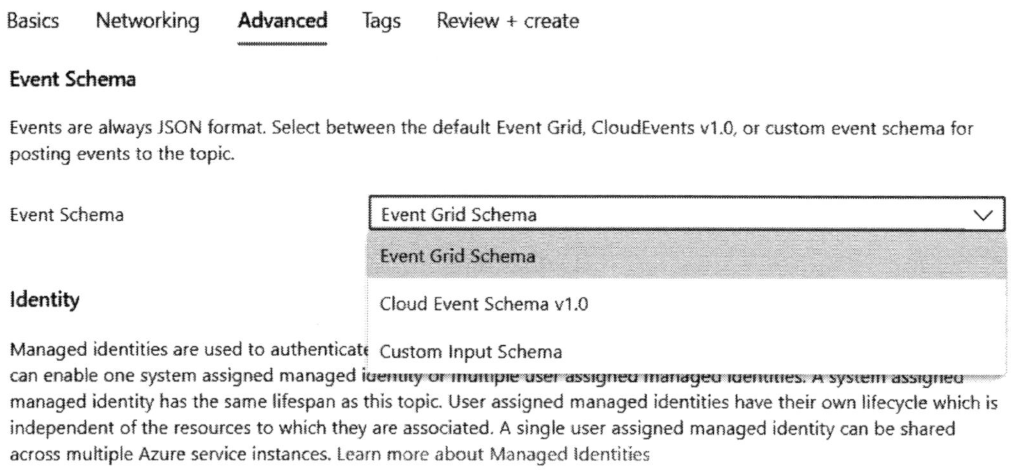

Basics   Networking   **Advanced**   Tags   Review + create

Event Schema

Events are always JSON format. Select between the default Event Grid, CloudEvents v1.0, or custom event schema for posting events to the topic.

Event Schema

Event Grid Schema	∨

Event Grid Schema

Cloud Event Schema v1.0

Custom Input Schema

Identity

Managed identities are used to authenticate ~~identity or multiple user assigned managed identities. A system assigned~~ can enable one system assigned managed ~~identity or multiple user assigned managed identities. A system assigned~~ managed identity has the same lifespan as this topic. User assigned managed identities have their own lifecycle which is independent of the resources to which they are associated. A single user assigned managed identity can be shared across multiple Azure service instances. Learn more about Managed Identities

Figure 11.12 – Choosing between different event schemas for Event Grid

Depending on your requirement, one of the preceding options might fit better with your apps. While there are no strategic differences in the supported schemas, the choice made when provisioning an instance of Event Grid will impact how other services integrate with it.

Event Grid schema

When using the default schema, you will expect that each event uses the following properties when sending data:

```
[
  {
    "topic": string,
    "subject": string,
    "id": string,
    "eventType": string,
    "eventTime": string,
```

```
    "data":{
      object-unique-to-each-publisher
    },
    "dataVersion": string,
    "metadataVersion": string
  }
]
```

The only unique part will be what is sent in the `data` field—this is the part of an event that is set individually by each event publisher. For example, when Azure Blob Storage sends its event, the `data` object will look like this:

```
"data": {
      "api": "PutBlockList",
      "clientRequestId": "<client-id>",
      "requestId": "<request-id>",
      "eTag": "<etag>",
      "contentType": "application/octet-stream",
      "contentLength": <content-length>,
      "blobType": "BlockBlob",
      „url": „https://<storage-account-name>.blob.core.windows.
net/<container>/<blob>",
      "sequencer": "<sequencer-value>",
      "storageDiagnostics": {
        "batchId": "<batch-id>"
      }
    }
```

Each event for the supported event publishers is described within the documentation (for more information, please see the *Further reading* section).

> **Note**
>
> When using a custom event publisher, you will decide what the event schema will look like. Event Grid does not assume anything related to events sent by external publishers.

If you feel that the default schema is not enough, you can try the second option with the CloudEvents schema.

The CloudEvents schema

The CloudEvents schema is an open specification not related to Azure. Any publisher can implement that schema specification, so it is easier to integrate different systems with each other by ensuring that they follow a common specification. An example event representing the mentioned schema could look like this:

```
{
    "specversion": "1.0",
    "type": "Microsoft.Storage.BlobCreated",
    "source": "/subscriptions<subscription>/
resourceGroups<resource-group>/providers/Microsoft.Storage/
storageAccounts/<account-name>
    "id": "<id>",
    "time": "<time>",
    "subject": "blobServices/default/containers/<container>/
blobs<file>
    "dataschema": "#",
    "data": {
        "api": "PutBlockList",
        "clientRequestId": "<client-id>",
        "requestId": "<request-id>",
        "eTag": "<etag>",
        "contentType": "image/png",
        "contentLength": <content-length>,
        "blobType": "BlockBlob",
        "url": "https://<account-name>.blob.core.windows.
net/<container<file>
        "sequencer": "<sequencer>",
        "storageDiagnostics": {
            "batchId": "<batch-id>"
        }
    }
}
```

As you can see, the CloudEvents schema is very similar to the default Event Grid schema, so even if you have multiple components using different schemas, it should be easy to integrate them. What is more, switching from one schema to another will not be that difficult either. The specification of the CloudEvents schema is available in the *Further reading* section.

Custom schema

When selecting the custom schema option while creating Event Grid, you will see a custom schema configuration view, as shown in the following screenshot:

Custom Schema Configuration

Use the **mapping fields** to map your custom input schema to the Event Grid event schema. For example map 'eventType' in the Event Grid schema to your custom 'type' field by putting 'type' in the mapping field. If a mapping is not provided for 'id' or 'eventTime', a value will be generated and added to each event.

Similarly, use the **default values** to have Event Grid stamp a static default value on to the 'subject', 'eventType', or 'dataVersion' fields when a value is not provided in an event.

Key	Mapping Field	Default Value
subject		
eventType		
dataVersion		
id		New GUID
eventTime		Event publish time

Figure 11.13 – The custom schema configuration tool

For example, the configurator allows you to tell that the **eventType** field should be mapped to an **eventTypeValue** field. This allows you to adjust the schema accordingly and make sure that it can work with your system. The main concept of using the custom schema is backward compatibility—if you have an already working component and changing the schema seems like a lot of work, it is easier to reroute fields using the configurator.

After describing the different event schemas, let's switch our focus to the last topic of this chapter, which is receiving and filtering events.

Receiving and filtering events

As mentioned earlier, if you use Event Grid to publish events to any endpoint triggered by an HTTP trigger, you will have to validate an endpoint. This is not the best solution, but fortunately, it is possible to use Azure Functions with `EventGridTrigger`, which allows us to skip the endpoint validation step when configuring services. This topic itself is quite big, so we will not cover each problem possible. However, I will point you to the specific parts of the documentation, which will help you understand the topic even better.

EventGridTrigger in Azure Functions

In general, the easiest way to integrate Azure Functions with Azure Event Grid is to use `HttpTrigger`:

```
[FunctionName("Function1")]
public static async Task<IActionResult> Run(
    [HttpTrigger(AuthorizationLevel.Anonymous, "get", "post",
Route = null)] HttpRequest req,
    ILogger log)
{
    ...
}
```

This is the most generic setup. It provides direct access to a request message and enables you to control its specific parts. However, there is an alternative to the preceding setup—we can use `EventGridTrigger` instead:

```
[FunctionName("CloudEventTriggerFunction")]
public static void Run(
    ILogger logger,
    [EventGridTrigger] CloudEvent e)
{
    // …
}
```

Here, with `EventGridTrigger`, you can directly access the payload of a request, which is useful if you are not interested in the remaining part of it. Additionally, you do not have to validate an endpoint.

Testing Azure Event Grid and Azure Functions

You are probably thinking about the options for testing Azure Event Grid and Azure Functions locally. In fact, currently, you have two ways of doing this:

- Capturing and resending events to your application
- Using ngrok, which is available at `https://ngrok.com/`, to forward requests to your local computer

The method you choose will depend on your capabilities (for example, ngrok exposes your computer's port, so it can be a security concern), so you will have to figure out by yourself what the best option is. Both methods are described in the link mentioned in the *Further reading* section. The only thing you need to do is to ensure that the request reaches your local endpoint for Event Grid. It will only be available if it is exposed via `EventGridTrigger`:

```
http://localhost:7071/runtime/webhooks/
eventgrid?functionName={FUNCTION_NAME}
```

Here, you can find an example request:

```
http://localhost:7071/runtime/webhooks/
eventgrid?functionName={FUNCTION_NAME}
Host: localhost:7071
Content-Type: application/json
aeg-event-type: Notification
Cache-Control: no-cache

  [
   {
      "subject": "example",
      "id": "1",
      "eventType": "SectionFinished",
      "eventTime": "2018-08-12T07:41:00.9584103Z",

      "data":{
        "section": 3

      },
      "dataVersion": "1",
   }
  ]
```

Note one important thing here—you have to set `aeg-event-type` to `Notification`. If you fail to do so, you will receive an `HTTP 400` response. With such a setup, you can emulate how your function will behave when deployed to Azure.

Filtering events

To set a filter for incoming events, you need to configure it when creating a subscription. Let's go back to one of the commands used earlier in this chapter:

```
includedEventTypes="<event-types>"
```

```
az eventgrid event-subscription create --name <rg-name>
--resource-group myResourceGroup --endpoint <endpoint-URL>
--included-event-types $includedEventTypes
```

By using `–included-event-types`, we can filter events based on the event type presented in the event payload. Each event publisher has a list of events published by it, and in general, an event type looks like this:

- `Microsoft.Resources.ResourceWriteFailure`
- `Microsoft.Storage.BlobCreated`

Of course, if you publish a custom event, its custom type might not follow the naming convention presented in the preceding list. Besides filtering based on the event type, you can filter events based on a subject using the `–subject-begins-with` and `–subject-ends-with` parameters:

```
az eventgrid event-subscription create --resource-id <resource-
id>
   --name <rg-name> --endpoint <endpoint-URL> --subject-ends-
with ".txt"
```

More advanced filtering includes subscriptions with advanced filters, where you use various operators to decide whether an event should be included or not. To do that, you need the `–advanced-filter` parameter. This concept is presented in the *Further reading* section.

Summary

In this chapter, you learned what reactive architecture is and how to use it with Azure Event Grid. You integrated different event producers with event handlers and used custom topics to publish custom events. What is more, now you have the knowledge of how to integrate Azure Event Grid with Azure Functions and test it locally.

This chapter ends the second part of the book, which has been about serverless services and architectures. In the next part, we will cover different storage options and messaging and monitoring services, which will broaden your proficiency with Azure even more.

Questions

Here are some questions to test your knowledge of the important topics in this chapter:

1. What are the supported event schemas in Azure Event Grid?

2. How can you authorize a request to an Event Grid endpoint when posting a custom event?

3. What must be returned when validating an endpoint?

4. When will an endpoint not have to be validated?

5. What happens if an endpoint doesn't return a successful response?

6. How can you filter events in Azure Event Grid?

7. How can you test Event Grid integration with Azure Functions?

Further reading

For more information, please refer to the following resources:

- The official Event Grid documentation: `https://docs.microsoft.com/en-us/azure/event-grid/overview`

- Event filtering: `https://docs.microsoft.com/en-us/azure/event-grid/event-filtering`

- The standard CloudEvents specification: `https://cloudevents.io/`

- Event delivery in Azure Event Grid: `https://docs.microsoft.com/en-us/azure/event-grid/manage-event-delivery`

- Azure Event Grid bindings for Azure Functions: `https://docs.microsoft.com/en-us/azure/azure-functions/functions-bindings-event-grid`

- CloudEventsSchema: `https://github.com/cloudevents/spec/blob/v1.0/spec.md`

Part 3: Storage, Messaging, and Monitoring

PaaS in Azure is not only about App Services or containers. This particular cloud offers much more, especially when talking about different options for storage, messaging solutions, and monitoring. With services such as Event Hubs, Azure Storage, and Application Insights, we're given a complete set of cloud components, which offer great flexibility and simplify the development of complete, scalable, and easy-to-maintain applications.

This part of the book comprises the following chapters:

- *Chapter 12, Using Azure Storage – Tables, Queues, Files, and Blobs*

- *Chapter 13, Big Data Pipeline – Azure Event Hubs*

- *Chapter 14, Real-Time Data Analysis – Azure Stream Analytics*

- *Chapter 15, Enterprise Integration – Azure Service Bus*

- *Chapter 16, Using Application Insights to Monitor Your Applications*

- *Chapter 17, SQL in Azure – Azure SQL*

- *Chapter 18, Big Data Storage – Azure Data Lake*

12

Using Azure Storage – Tables, Queues, Files, and Blobs

Azure Storage is one of the fundamental services that are used across various Azure-based architectures. It is a universal solution that covers various aspects of application development—file hosting, messaging, and data storage.

The following topics will be covered in this chapter:

- Using Azure Storage in a solution
- Storing structured data with Azure Storage tables
- Implementing fully managed file shares with Azure Files
- Using queues with Azure Queue Storage
- Using Azure Storage blobs for object storage

Technical requirements

To perform the exercises in this chapter, you will need the following:

- An Azure subscription
- The **Azure command-line interface (Azure CLI)**
- **Visual Studio Code (VS Code)**
- Azure Storage Explorer, available at `https://azure.microsoft.com/en-us/features/storage-explorer/`
- Azurite if using the latest technology stack—see `https://github.com/azure/azurite`

Using Azure Storage in a solution

Most applications cannot work without a storage solution. This can be any kind of database—relational, document, file, or graph. Most of them require some skills to be able to configure and start working with them. For now, we have covered one storage solution available in Azure—namely, Azure Cosmos DB, which is a serverless database, where the only thing needed was to set a correct throughput value. Of course, Azure offers much more in the way of storage services, of which the most common is Azure Storage. It is a **platform-as-a-service** (**PaaS**) cloud component (though some define it as serverless, mostly because of a lack of servers) that can be used in four different ways. In this chapter, we will cover all of them so that you become familiar with their capabilities and features.

Different Azure Storage services

Azure Storage consists of the following four different services:

- Table storage

- Queue Storage

- Blob Storage

- Azure Files

They all serve different purposes and offer different capabilities and limits. While their names are self-explanatory, you will see that each is a completely different service, and though they can be used in connection with each other, they require a different set of skills to be able to do this efficiently, and you need to use best practices.

Azure Storage offers an additional service called Disk Storage, which is a feature used by virtual machines (**VMs**). Because of that, it will not be covered in this book. Nonetheless, you can find a link to its documentation in the *Further reading* section.

Different types of storage accounts

Some time ago, Azure Storage offered different types of accounts that could be used for different purposes. You could create a general-purpose account for generic work or use a *blob* account for working with files only. That changed recently, and now, when creating a new instance of the service, the only thing to decide is the performance tier. The question, for now, is: what is the difference between the **Standard** and **Premium** tiers—besides pricing, of course? You can define them like so:

- **Standard**: The most common choice with reasonable performance and support for all types of data. These accounts use magnetic disks for storage.

- **Premium**: Accounts with better performance, thanks to the use of **solid-state drive** (**SSD**) disks—recommended for VMs and when you require quick access to data stored on them (or you just have low-latency requirements).

The choice between the **Standard** and **Premium** tiers will impact the overall behavior of your storage account and its capabilities. The most important thing here is the fact that the **Premium** tier enables you to decide what kind of blob tier will be available for you, as outlined here:

- **Block blob**—For heavily utilized applications constantly communicating with a storage solution
- **File share**—Especially useful when you need to share data across the company
- **Page blob**—Used for VM disks

> **Note**
> You cannot change the account tier (kind) after it is created.

In general, if you are searching for predictable performance that is easily adjustable, you should go for the **Premium** tier as it allows for a granular selection of throughput and **input/output operations per second (IOPS)**. Here is a simple comparison of different page blob types with their parameters:

- **P10**: 500 IOPS, throughput 100 **megabytes per second (MB/sec)**, 128 **gigabytes (GB)**, **United States dollars (USD)** $21.68 per month
- **P30**: 7,500 IOPS, throughput 250 MB/sec, 1 **terabyte (TB)**, $148.68 per month
- **P60**: 7,500 IOPS, throughput 250 MB/sec, 8 TB, $1040.64 per month

As you can see, pricing varies greatly, depending on the parameters of the selected page blob type.

Securing Azure Storage

In general, there are two ways of securing access to your storage accounts, as noted here:

- **Azure Active Directory (Azure AD)** with **role-based access control (RBAC)**
- **Shared access signature (SAS)** tokens

Additionally, blobs can be accessed publicly (of course, only if you decide to do so). Depending on your needs, one option or another may cover your requirements—this, of course, depends on the characteristics of your application. Here is the difference between those two methods of securing Azure Storage:

- **RBAC**: This method is used to secure management operations on your accounts. You can restrict access to specific features of a service to only a specific group defined in Azure AD. However, you are unable to use this method to secure a blob or a table (although you can do this indirectly by securing access to a SAS token). This method also includes the use of managed identities, which use an Azure AD token for authentication and authorization based on roles assigned to **service principals (SPs)**.

- **SAS tokens**: These are long strings that store different parameters describing access to a resource. They specify a service type, permissions, and the lifetime of a token, or restrict access to an **Internet Protocol (IP)** address.

Here is an example of a SAS token:

```
https://myaccount.blob.core.windows.net/securecontainer/blob.
txt?sv=2015-04-05&st=2015-04-29T22%3A18%3A26Z&se=2015-04-30T02%
3A23%3A26Z&sr=b&sp=rw&sip=168.1.5.60-168.1.5.70&spr=https&sig=Z
%2FRHIX5Xcg0Mq2rqI3OlWTjEg2tYkboXr1P9ZUXDtkk%3D
```

As you can see, it restricts access to a `blob.txt` file stored as a blob in the `securecontainer` container. It defines parameters, such as service version (`sv`), expiry time (`se`), or the actual signature of a token (`sig`). In general, with SAS tokens, you can restrict access to either an account or a service (and thanks to that, also—for example—to a range of entities in Table storage).

Replication

When using a cloud, you must expect that any service can be down at any time. Although Azure Storage is considered one of the most durable services (because many services in Azure rely on it), it is possible that it will face an outage. To mitigate problems related to such failures, it offers four different kinds of replication, as outlined here:

- **Locally redundant storage (LRS)**: Three copies of your data within the same data center
- **Zone-redundant storage (ZRS)**: Three copies of your data within the same region
- **Geo-redundant storage (GRS)**: Three copies of your data within the same data center plus three copies in another region
- **Read-access GRS (RA-GRS)**: Three copies of your data within the same data center plus three copies in another region, with the ability to read from that region

In addition, the ZRS replication model is extended to the following additional two models:

- **Geo-zone-redundant storage (GZRS)**—Works as a combination of ZRS and GRS. The result is six copies—three in the primary region and three in the secondary region. All the copies are stored across **availability zones (AZs)**.
- **Read-access GZRS (RA-GZRS)**—The same as GZRS but additionally gives you read access in the secondary region.

> **Note**
> It is impossible to change the replication model to/from ZRS/GZRS/RA-GZRS after a storage account is created.

When architecting an application using Azure Storage, you must carefully design its availability requirements. Depending on your expectations, a different model may suit you better.

> **Tip**
>
> When using a model that replicates data to another data center (basically, GRS and RA-GRS), take into account the cost of transferring data between different regions.

You may wonder how durable LRS is compared to other replication models. To define that, you must understand how data is stored within a single data center. In fact, disks for Azure Storage are installed within racks that are part of a bigger concept known as a stamp. Stamps are configured in such a way that they use different power lines and networks, and thanks to such a setup, it is possible to store copies of your data in different fault domains, ensuring that if one fails, the other two will still work. Microsoft states that LRS is designed to provide at least 99.999999999% durability. If that is not enough, you may consider other models.

> **Tip**
>
> When using RA-GRS, do not take for granted the ability to easily write to the secondary region if an outage occurs. While it is possible to initiate a failover manually (in a similar manner as in the case of Azure Cosmos DB), it is still an opt-in decision. In general, the **recovery time objective (RTO)** for Azure Storage consists of both time for Microsoft to decide whether to perform a failover or not and time to change **Domain Name System (DNS)** entries to point to another region.

After this short introduction, let's learn more about various Azure Storage services, starting with Table storage.

Storing structured data with Azure Storage tables

We will start our journey with Azure Storage capabilities by learning something about Table storage. If you want to store unstructured data with almost limitless capacity and with high demands regarding availability and durability, this service is for you. In this section, you will learn how to start developing applications using Table storage and the best practices for storing data and achieving the best performance for both writing and reading it. You will also see how to efficiently query it, and what is important when designing services using this Azure Storage capability.

Creating an Azure Storage service

To get started, we must create an instance of Azure Storage. To do so, please follow these steps:

1. Go to the Azure portal and click on + **Create a resource**. Search for storage account and click on the **Create** button.

2. You will see a multi-step form, where you must configure a new instance of a service. Here is an example of what I chose for the **Basics** tab:

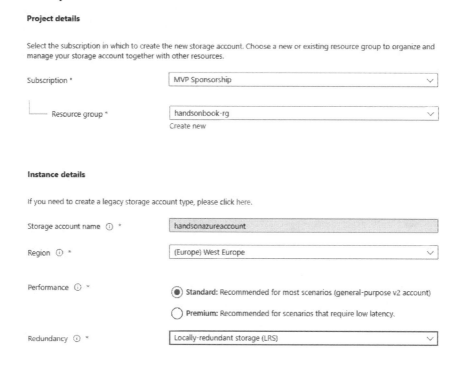

Figure 12.1 – Initial screen of Azure Storage creation wizard

Now, I would like to describe some of the more mystical options available here, as follows:

- **Performance**: It is possible to select either the **Standard** or **Premium** performance tier. As mentioned previously, this impacts the hardware used to provision your service with common magnetic disks for the **Standard** tier and SSDs for the **Premium** tier.

- **Redundancy**: Implies which replication model is used for your account. Remember that ability to select any zone-related model is connected to the availability of AZs in the selected region.

While it is possible to configure much more options related to the different capabilities of Azure Storage, we will skip them for now. All the default options should allow for account creation, so let's click on the **Review + create** button and then on the **Create** button and wait a moment—your account will be created, and soon you will be able to start working with it.

Managing Table storage

When you go to the **Overview** blade, you will see a dashboard with basic information available regarding your account, as illustrated in the following screenshot:

Figure 12.2 – Overview blade for Azure Storage

As you can see, it displays the information you defined while creating it, such as location, performance tier, or replication type. Additionally, when you scroll down, you will see the **Properties** section, where you can see all the basic parameters of the service. Additionally, you can select another tab to get further information, as illustrated here:

Figure 12.3 – Various Azure Storage properties available for the Overview blade

In this section, we are covering Table Storage, so find the **Tables** blade on the left and click on it. Initially, you should see no tables at all, as illustrated in the following screenshot. Of course, this is something we expected, as this instance of the service has been just provisioned. Nonetheless, this is one of the methods to check what is stored within an account:

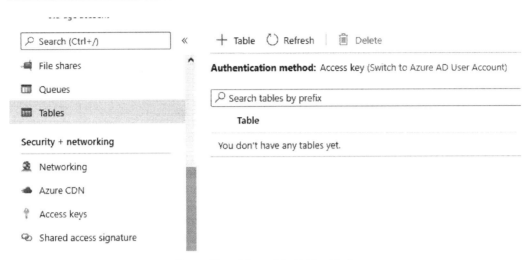

Figure 12.4 – View of the Tables blade

To create a new table, simply click on the + **Table** button—you will be asked to provide a table name, which is all that is needed to get started. As you probably remember, I described Table storage as a capability for storing unstructured data. While the term *table* may imply that this feature works in a similar way to relational databases (which also contain tables), it is instead a key-value storage. Here is the same view after a table is created:

Figure 12.5 – List of tables inside Azure Storage

The preceding screenshot shows an **handson** table and its **Uniform Resource Locator** (**URL**)—you may be wondering what this URL is all about. As there are multiple ways to manage and use Azure services, Azure Storage allows you to use its capabilities using different methods, such as **REpresentational State Transfer** (**REST**), PowerShell, the Azure CLI, or the Azure portal. When using **software development kits** (**SDKs**) and reading their source code, you could find that they are just wrappers around simple a REST **application programming interface** (**API**). This makes this service superbly easy to get started working with on a daily basis. We have talked a little bit about tables' basics—now, it is time to describe their schema.

Storing data in Table storage

Each record in Table storage has a row structure with multiple columns. Each row has the following base columns:

- `PartitionKey`: **Identifier (ID)** of a partition of a row.
- `RowKey`: The row's ID.
- `Timestamp`: This column tells you when a row was recently modified.
- `ETag`: Table storage implements the optimistic concurrency model and uses **entity tags (ETags)** to control whether an entity should be modified or not.

Of course, you are not limited to the columns listed here—you can create any additional columns you want and give each a specified type. However, before we go any further, you must fully understand the implications of such a design. Here, you can find an example of entities stored within a single table:

PartitionKey	RowKey	Timestamp	FirstName	LastName	PhoneNumber
1	jd	2021-12-17T12:31:00.99...	John	Doe	100200300
2	jad	2021-12-17T12:31:17.70...	Jane	Doe	200300400

Figure 12.6 – Data stored inside Table storage

In the preceding example, data is stored within multiple partitions, and though a single table is used, multiple schemas still can work, so there is no need to use additional tables.

PartitionKey

Table storage uses partitions to distribute, load, and handle requests. The number of partition keys within a table impacts the ability to balance them. It is possible to use a single partition per table, but in most cases, this is an invalid approach that will lower the performance of your storage account. Partition keys are limited to 1 **kilobyte (KB)** in size and must be unique within a table (so, once an entity is assigned a partition key, all others that use the same value will be stored in the same storage). They also must be strings.

RowKey

Each row key is a **unique ID (UID)** of a row within a partition (so, you can have rows using the same `RowKey` column value, as long they have a different `PartitionKey` value). More importantly, each table is sorted in ascending order using values of row keys. This requires a smart design when you need, for example, to read only a selection of top rows and do not want to provide their row keys (we will cover that later in this chapter). As with `PartitionKey`, `RowKey` is also limited to 1 KB and must be a string.

Timestamp

This column is maintained server-side and is a `DateTime` value that is changed each time an entity is modified. It is also internally used to provide optimistic concurrency and cannot be modified. Even if you set it, the value will be ignored.

General rules for entities

Table storage has some hard limitations when it comes to storing data, as outlined here:

- The maximum number of columns is 255.

- The maximum size of an entity is 1 MB.

- By default, each entity column is created as a type string—this can be overridden when it is created.

- It is not possible to store `null` as a value—if you do not provide a column value, an entity will be considered as if it does not have it at all.

Querying data in Table storage

To get started with querying data, we need to create a table. You can do this in the Azure portal and can also use the Azure CLI for that, as illustrated in the following code snippet:

```
az storage table create --name [--account-key] [--account-name]
```

> **Note**
> Remember to use the `az login` command if you are starting a new session in your terminal.

We now need to get a connection string, so depending on the storage account you would like to use, you must do one of the following:

- Go to the Azure portal, find your storage account, and copy a connection string from the **Access keys** blade.

- Use the `UseDevelopmentStorage=true` value for connecting with Storage Emulator if you have an instance running locally.

- As Storage Emulator is starting to be considered deprecated, you can use Azurite to emulate a storage account locally. If so, your connection string will look like this:

```
DefaultEndpointsProtocol=http;AccountName=account1;
AccountKey=key1;BlobEndpoint=http://account1.blob.
localhost:10000;QueueEndpoint=http://account1.queue.
```

```
ocalhost:10001;TableEndpoint=http://account1.table.
localhost:10002;
```

When you execute an application, a table should be created without a problem. Now, when we have a table, we would like to insert something into it. To do so, you will need the following code:

```
az storage entity insert [--account-key] [--account-name]
--entity PartitionKey=AAA RowKey=BBB Content=ASDF2 --if-exists
fail [--table-name]
```

The preceding command will insert a new entity passed with the --entity parameter. Note that all the data here is passed using a key=value notation and can be different for each record. Additionally, we are using the --if-exists fail parameter, so the whole command will fail if we try to insert a duplicate record.

The last thing to do is to query a table. Performing such an operation in the Azure CLI is very simple, as we can see here:

```
az storage entity query --table-name MyTable [--account-key]
[--account-name]
```

We just executed a basic query that will return all rows from a table. While it works now, it is not the best idea to query all data within a table using such a query—in most cases, you will use a more sophisticated approach that may include additional parameters available for that command, as illustrated here:

```
az storage entity query --table-name
                        [--accept {full, minimal, none}]
                        [--account-key]
                        [--account-name]
                        [--connection-string]
                        [--filter]
                        [--marker]
                        [--num-results]
                        [--sas-token]
                        [--select]
                        [--subscription]
                        [--timeout]
```

> **Note**
>
> Remember that to achieve the best performance, your queries should include both `PartitionKey` and `RowKey`. Using `PartitionKey` only leads to worse results but is still acceptable. Using only `RowKey` will result in reading the whole partition anyway. Not using those columns will result in reading the whole table.

You can also check what is stored in a table using Azure Storage Explorer, as illustrated in the following screenshot:

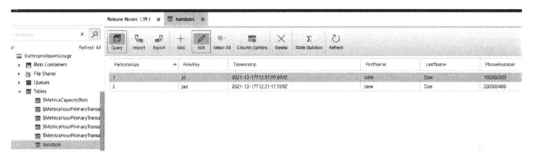

Figure 12.7 – Using Azure Storage Explorer for data exploration

In general, browsing data with that tool can help you quickly check data stored inside a table or add a record without additional tools. For more advanced scenarios (that require smart filtering of data or reporting), a coded approach will be more helpful.

Table API in Azure Cosmos DB

It is possible to leverage the premium offering for Table storage using Azure Cosmos DB. Using that option has the following advantages:

- Automatic and manual failovers

- Secondary indexes (the ability to index against all properties inside a row)

- Independent scaling across multiple regions

- Different consistency levels

- Dedicated throughput per table

While failover is currently available for Azure Storage, the rest of the presented features are available only for Azure Cosmos DB and can be a great solution if you like the simplicity of this service and still want to challenge it against more complicated scenarios. However, leveraging the Table API for Azure Cosmos DB is beyond the scope of this book. To help you explore the topic further, I added some links related to that feature in the *Further reading* section.

Implementing fully managed file shares with Azure Files

When in need of creating a file share that can be accessed by different people, you often must either buy some hardware that will be set up and configured for such functionality or use third-party solutions, which can be hard to customize, or expensive. With Azure Storage, you can quickly develop a solution that is almost limitless in terms of capacity, offers industry-standard protocols, and can be quickly provisioned and ready to use.

Azure Files concepts

Azure Files has some basic concepts that create a whole picture of a service. In fact, it is designed to replace current on-premises file servers in terms of functionality and performance. The main difference between Azure Files and the "old" solution is accessibility (as you can set the access token and make the URL private). What is more, it is **operating system (OS)**-agnostic, allowing you to use the very same file share mounted on different machines using Linux, Windows, or macOS. It—of course—shares other Azure Storage concepts, so you can use it with the same reliability and durability assurance. The main feature of Azure Files is support for the **Server Message Block (SMB)** protocol. This is a very common protocol (and a mature one, as it was designed in the mid-1980s) for sharing computer resources, and is also used for printers and other network devices. We could summarize Azure Files as follows:

- **Fully managed**: This is a full cloud service, where you do not have to worry about the OS or its configuration.

- **Durability and resiliency**: With Azure Files, you do not have to worry about not having access to data stored and securing your resources against power failures and other outages.

- **Common development (dev) tools**: Accessing Azure Files is easy, thanks to the system I/O APIs, appropriate SDKs, or even REST APIs.

Let's now see how we can work with that service.

Working with Azure Files

When you go to the Azure portal and open your Azure Storage instance, you will find the **File shares** blade. This displays a list of available file shares, as seen in the following screenshot:

Figure 12.8 – Available file shares in the Azure portal

From this screen, you can create a new file share by clicking on the + **File share** button. The important thing here is the value of the **Quota** field—this determines the maximum capacity of a file share.

> **Note**
> The maximum size of a file share is 100 **tebibytes** (**TiB**). This requires an **Enable large file shares** option to be enabled on your storage account and limits replication models to LRS and ZRS.

To get information about how to connect to a file share, you can click on the file share and then on the **Connect** button, as illustrated here:

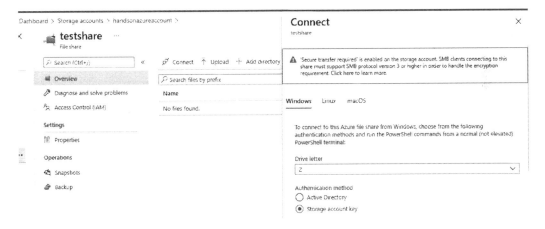

Figure 12.9 – Connection instruction for file share

This will display some short instructions about how it is possible to quickly connect from your computer to a specific file share. Here, you can find an example of a command for Windows written in PowerShell:

```
$connectTestResult = Test-NetConnection -ComputerName
handsonazureaccount.file.core.windows.net -Port 445
if ($connectTestResult.TcpTestSucceeded) {
    # Save the password so the drive will persist on reboot
    cmd.exe /C "cmdkey /add:`"handsonazureaccount.file.core.
windows.net`" /user:`"localhost\handsonazureaccount`" /pass:
`"zAY8PABBFs8L2sbNX++ckztZerSEIpa0RgSqm3WvufQd8kjen
5btJxF2yDJ+MCIF0Qm5tXhof7B4rkpJpt4oww==`""
    # Mount the drive
    New-PSDrive -Name Z -PSProvider FileSystem -Root "\\
handsonazureaccount.file.core.windows.net\testshare" -Persist
} else {
    Write-Error -Message "Unable to reach the Azure storage
account via port 445. Check to make sure your organization or
ISP is not blocking port 445, or use Azure P2S VPN, Azure S2S
VPN, or Express Route to tunnel SMB traffic over a different
port."
}
```

You can specify the letter of a drive using the -Name parameter (in the preceding example, it is Z).

> **Note**
> Mapping a drive is an operation that may require additional permissions—make sure you are running all these commands as an administrator.

The whole setup takes only a few minutes—this is the strength of this service, as normally I would need many hours to set everything up and achieve the same level of portability and reliability. It also gives you unlimited storage capacity—nothing blocks you from attaching multiple file shares and storing all your files on them.

Blob storage versus Azure Files

In fact, both Azure Blob storage and Azure Files have a similar purpose—you create them to store and share files. There are, however, some fundamental differences between them when it comes to use cases. Let's have a look at some examples of how you would use the services here:

- If you want to create a common file share space for your company, you will use Azure Files.

- If you want to have a space for files uploaded by your users via—for example— your website, you will use Blob storage.

- If you want to have your files completely private, you will use Azure Files.

- If you want to configure security on a blob or a container level, you will use Blob storage.

Both services also have different pricing models (for example, Azure Files is much more expensive when it comes to paying for each GB of data).

Using queues with Azure Queue Storage

Azure Storage—besides being a service for storing many kinds of data—can be used also as a queue. Queue Storage is another capability that allows you to quickly develop a solution that requires a simple queue solution and additionally can store in a queue millions of messages without affecting performance. In this section, you will see how to develop applications using Queue Storage and what is important when using this feature. Additionally, I assume that you already have a storage account. If not, look at the *Storing structured data with Azure Storage tables* section, where I described the process of creating an account.

Queue Storage features

In general, Queue Storage has the following two use cases:

- Processing messages asynchronously

- Exchanging communications between different services (Azure Functions, legacy web roles/ worker roles)

It is a very simple queue solution that can store and process messages in any format, limited to 64 KB. The retention time of a message is 7 days—after that, it is lost. The capacity of a queue is basically equal to the capacity of your storage account. In general, you should not worry that you will run out of available space. Queue Storage shares many additional features—such as **virtual networks** (**VNets**), SAS tokens, and much more—with other Azure Storage capabilities. Therefore, we will not reintroduce them in this section.

Developing an application using Queue Storage

To present Queue Storage, I created the following two applications:

- `Producer`
- `Consumer`

Producer will create and push messages, which will then be consumed by Consumer. Here, you can find the code for the Producer app:

```
using Azure.Storage;
using Azure.Storage.Queues;
using Azure.Storage.Queues.Models;

namespace QueueStorage.Producer
{
    internal class Program
    {
        private static async Task Main()
        {
            var queue = new QueueClient("<your-connection-
string>", "<queue-name>");
            await queue.CreateAsync();
            await queue.SendMessageAsync("Hello!");
        }
    }
}
```

And of course, we'll also look at the code for the Consumer app, as follows:

```
using Azure.Storage;
using Azure.Storage.Queues;
using Azure.Storage.Queues.Models;

namespace QueueStorage.Consumer
{
    internal class Program
    {
        private static void Main()
        {
            var queue = new QueueClient(connectionString,
queueName);
```

```
            foreach (var message in (await queue.
ReceiveMessagesAsync(maxMessages: 10)).Value)
            {
                Console.WriteLine($"Message: {message.Body}");
                await queue.DeleteMessageAsync(message.
MessageId, message.PopReceipt);
            }
        }
    }
}
```

When you publish a message to a queue, you can retrieve it at any time—as mentioned previously, you have 7 days to fetch it from a queue. Here, you can see what a message looks like when stored in a queue:

Figure 12.10 – Available messages in Azure Storage Explorer

Remember that you can read a message multiple times—in many scenarios, once read, a message is dequeued and is not available for other consumers. However, it is possible to read multiple streams, though in general, Azure Storage is not the best solution for that. The reason is quite simple—in Azure Storage, when a message is read by a single consumer, it is invisible to others if a lease is in place. This leads to sequential reads—*Consumer B* can only read a message if *Consumer A* is done with it. For parallel processing, Azure Event Hubs is a better choice.

Using Azure Storage blobs for object storage

The last capability of Azure Storage is Blob Storage. In the previous sections, we were using this service to store unstructured data using Table storage, push messages to a queue with Queue Storage, and create file shares, thanks to *Files*. In the last section of this chapter, we will focus on developing solutions that store so-called blobs. You may wonder what exactly a blob is—well, there is no single definition for that. In general, blobs are files of different types, such as text files, images, or audio. Here, you will see how to use them in your applications, how to secure them, and how you can achieve maximum performance.

Blob storage concepts

Before we go deeper into the service, you should understand the basic concepts of Blob Storage. Here, you can find a diagram that clearly defines the three main concepts:

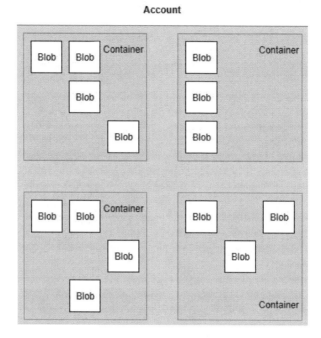

Figure 12.11 – Blob storage concepts

As you can see, we have three different concepts, as follows:

- **Account**: This is basically your storage account and stores all data within Blob Storage. Note that you can only have 250 accounts per region per subscription.

- **Container**: This is a logical entity holding an unlimited number of blobs inside it. An account can have an unlimited number of containers.

- **Blob**: A file stored within a container.

Additionally, there are three different types of blobs:

- **Block blob**: Text or binary data with a maximum size of 4.7 TB. Such a blob is made up of smaller blocks.

- **Append blobs**: A more specific type of blob, which is best for scenarios such as logging data or storing events or transactional logs. They are optimized for append operations.

- **Page blobs**: Designed for storing **virtual hard disk** (**VHD**) files used by VMs.

With the newest version of Storage Accounts (v2), it is possible to use the latest features of this service. One of the most interesting additions is access tiers. Now, it is possible to select whether you would like to use a **Hot** or **Cool** tier. The choice depends on the frequency of accessing your data—if you would like to read it often, **Hot** will be the best choice; otherwise, it is better to use the **Cool** tier or a general-purpose account.

> **Note**
> The tiers are available when modifying the properties of a file uploaded as a blob to the storage account. You cannot select a tier when creating a service.

There is also one more tier: **Archive**, designed for storing blobs that are rarely accessed, although it is available only on the blob level. You're probably wondering about the differences between these tiers. Here, you can find a table that defines their pricing:

	Premium	Hot	Cool	Archive
First 50 terabyte (TB) / month	**$0.195** per GB	**$0.02** per GB	**$0.01** per GB	**$0.0018** per GB
Next 450 TB / month	**$0.195** per GB	**$0.0188** per GB	**$0.01** per GB	**$0.0018** per GB
Over 500 TB / month	**$0.195** per GB	**$0.018** per GB	**$0.01** per GB	**$0.0018** per GB

Figure 12.12 – Azure Blob Storage pricing

In terms of storage, you can see that the **Hot** tier is the most expensive and the rest are much cheaper, especially **Archive**. Now, let's check the price for 10,000 read operations. This is what they would cost under the different tiers:

- **Hot**: $0.006
- **Cool**: $0.013
- **Archive**: $7.8

Ouch—the difference is huge here! Therefore, selecting the correct tier is so important—you may end up with a solution that costs many, many dollars, only because you misused the blob tier.

Inserting data into Blob Storage

Now, we will try to add something to our blob storage. Here, you can find a piece of code that allows you to upload a single file to a container:

```
using Azure.Storage;
using Azure.Storage.Blobs;
```

```csharp
using Azure.Storage.Blobs.Models;

namespace BlobStorage
{
    internal class Program
    {
        private static void Main()
        {
            var container = new
BlobContainerClient(connectionString, "sample");
            await container.CreateAsync();
            try
            {
                var blob = container.GetBlobClient("sample");

                await blob.UploadAsync("path_to_a_local_file");

            }
            finally
            {
                // If you want to delete a container, simply
// uncomment the below line
                // await container.DeleteAsync();
            }
        }
    }
}
```

As in the previous examples, this one looks pretty similar. You will need to follow these steps:

- Firstly, you have to create an instance of BlobContainerClient.

- Then, you need to obtain a reference to a container and create one if none exists.

- Finally, you must get a reference to a blob, and upload some content.

If I open Azure Storage Explorer, I can see that a new blob was uploaded to a container, as illustrated here:

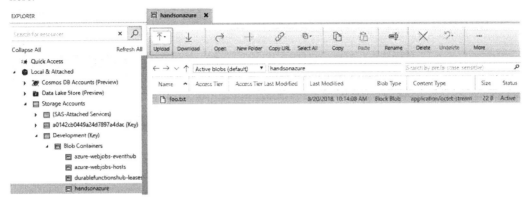

Figure 12.13 – Uploaded blob visible in Azure Storage Explorer

Of course, if I open the file, I will see that it contains the text that I uploaded, as illustrated here:

Figure 12.14 – Content of the uploaded blob

With development activities covered, let's now switch our focus to design-related topics of Blob storage.

Containers and permissions

It is possible to select a proper access level when it comes to accessing a container stored within Blob storage. If you go to the Azure portal and open your Azure Storage service, you will find the **Blobs** blade. Inside it, you can click on the **+ Container** button, which will open a small window, as illustrated here:

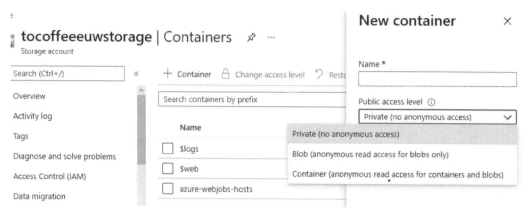

Figure 12.15 – Setting container permissions level

As you can see, besides providing a name for a container, you can select the **Public access level** option for selecting an access model for it. Currently, you have three different options available, as follows:

- **Private**: For no anonymous access

- **Blob**: Anonymous access on a blob level

- **Container**: Anonymous access on a container level to the container itself and blobs within it

You can click on a container you created to see another screen, where you can manage it. I will use it to upload a file to see which other options become available. Here, you can see what it will look like in the portal when a file is uploaded and I click on it:

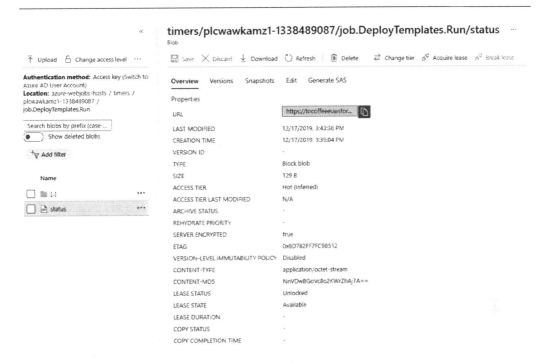

Figure 12.16 – Blob properties

Now, I can see additional metadata regarding a file, managing or acquiring leases, or generating a SAS token.

> **Note**
>
> If you want to make a file read-only, click on the **Acquire lease** button—while it will still be possible to change it, such an action will require you to provide a lease ID.

What is more, there is a **URL** property available that can be used to access a blob directly—for example, using a browser. Here, you can see what it looks like in my case:

```
https://handsonazurestore.blob.core.windows.net/blob/11047_01_01.
PNG
```

Now, you may be wondering what the difference is between **Blob** and **Container** access. To find out, we will use the following code:

```
using Azure.Storage.Blobs;
using Azure.Storage.Blobs.Models;


var blobAccessClient = new BlobContainerClient(new
```

```
Uri("https://xxx.blob.core.windows.net/blobaccess"));
var containerAccessClient = new BlobContainerClient(new
Uri("https://xxx.blob.core.windows.net/containeraccess"));
var listOfFiles = new List<string>();
try
{
    await foreach (BlobItem blobItem in blobAccessClient.
GetBlobsAsync())
    {
        listOfFiles.Add(blobItem.Name);
    }
}
catch (Exception)
{
    Console.WriteLine("Failed to read blob dues to access");
}

try
{
    await foreach (BlobItem blobItem in containerAccessClient.
GetBlobsAsync())
    {
        listOfFiles.Add(blobItem.Name);
    }
}
catch (Exception e)
{
    Console.WriteLine(e.Message);
}
```

I already created two different containers—one with **Blob** access, and the other with **Container** access. If I execute the preceding code for a container with full public access, here is what I will see:

```
D:\TheCloudTheory\HandsOnAzure2.0\Chapter12>dotnet run
Failed to read blob dues to access
```

Figure 12.17 – Failed access due to permissions level allowing us to access individual files only

Now, let's run it for a container that has public access. This is what I will see:

```
D:\TheCloudTheory\HandsOnAzure2.0\Chapter12>dotnet run
Chapter12.csproj
```

Figure 12.18 – Error when accessing non-public container without proper permissions or credentials

As you can see, container-level operations are unavailable when the access level is *blob* or *private*. Of course, if you authorize using—for instance—an access key, you will be able to list all blobs within a container, even if it is private.

Blob storage – additional features

One of the coolest capabilities of Blob storage is the **Soft delete** feature, which allows you to perform an operation called a soft delete. What does this mean? In some cases, you may want to delete a file but have the option to easily revert the deletion within a fixed time. In Blob storage, that option is available via the **Data protection** blade, as illustrated in the following screenshot:

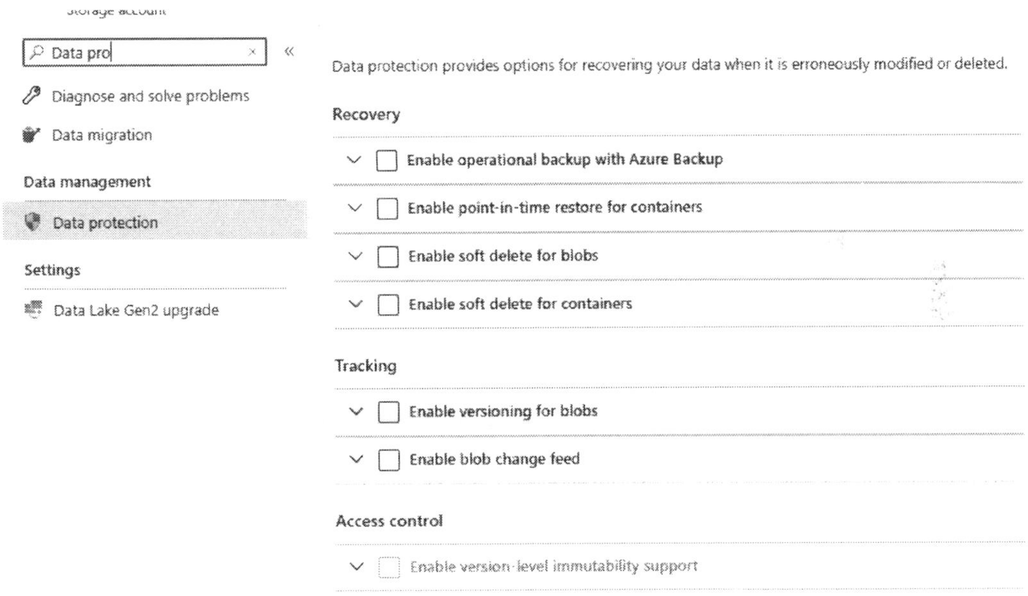

Figure 12.19 – Data protection blade

If you turn it on, any deleted blob will still be available within storage (but not for retrieval or modification) for a set number of days. Blob storage also has plenty of additional features that can be used in various scenarios, such as the following:

- **Azure CDN**: A **content delivery network** (**CDN**) service for serving static content to your customers—we will cover this later in the book.

- **Azure Search**: As already discussed, here, you can easily set your blob storage as a data source for a search engine.

- **Static website**: Instead of provisioning a VM or using Azure App Service, you can leverage Azure Storage as your web-hosting server.

- **Data lake**: Azure Storage can be used as a data lake service with hierarchical namespaces. You can migrate to such a solution at any time (by enabling **Large file shares** in the **Configuration** tab) or create a new account with the feature already enabled.

As you can see, this is a very flexible and useful Azure Storage capability that can be used for file storage, as an Azure Search document store, a logs database, and much, much more.

Summary

In this chapter, you have learned some basics regarding one of the most important services in Azure—Azure Storage. We developed a few solutions for tables, queues, files, and blobs—each enabling you to do different things, from asynchronous message processing to creating file shares. You also read about different redundancy models and how reliable and durable this particular service is. In the *Further reading* section, you will find plenty of additional resources that will allow you to build even more skills for working with this Azure service, such as Table storage patterns, performance targets, and a REST API reference. In the following chapters, you will learn something about data processing services, such as Azure Event Hubs and Azure Stream Analytics.

Questions

Here are some questions to test your knowledge of the important topics in this chapter:

1. Which tiers are available during account creation when selecting **Blob** as an account type?

2. What must you include in a query against Table storage to achieve maximum performance?

3. What are the available redundancy models for storage accounts?

4. What is the difference between blob and file storage?

5. Can you store binary files using Blob storage?

6. How long does a message in Queue Storage live before it is removed?

7. What is the maximum size of a message in Queue Storage?

8. What is the maximum size of the `PartitionKey` column value?

9. Which concurrency model is implemented in Table storage?

10. What is the difference between Azure Files storage and an on-premises filesystem?

Further reading

For more information, refer to the following sources:

- Disk storage: `https://docs.microsoft.com/en-us/azure/virtual-machines/windows/about-disks-and-vhds`

- SAS token reference: `https://docs.microsoft.com/en-us/azure/storage/common/storage-dotnet-shared-access-signature-part-1`

- **Azure Resource Manager** (**ARM**) versus classic deployment: `https://docs.microsoft.com/en-us/azure/azure-resource-manager/resource-manager-deployment-model`

- Table service data model: `https://docs.microsoft.com/en-us/rest/api/storageservices/Understanding-the-Table-Service-Data-Model`

- Blob storage pricing: `https://azure.microsoft.com/en-us/pricing/details/storage/blobs/`

- File storage performance targets: `https://docs.microsoft.com/en-us/azure/storage/files/storage-files-scale-targets`

- Guidelines for Table storage: `https://docs.microsoft.com/en-us/azure/storage/tables/table-storage-design-guidelines`

13

Big Data Pipeline – Azure Event Hubs

Azure Event Hubss is one of the best solutions for introducing an entry point with almost limitless throughput. It's designed for big data workloads and can process millions of messages per second. It offers a very simple configuration, and thanks to the available SDK, you can easily adjust it to almost any solution developed in the cloud. It also integrates natively with other Azure components, making creating a whole platform hosted in the cloud a breeze.

In this chapter, the following topics will be covered:

- Working efficiently with Azure Event Hubss
- Different concepts such as publishers, partitions, **throughput units** (**TUs**), or consumer groups
- Azure Event Hubss security concepts
- Azure Event Hubss capture feature
- Working with events replication and multi-region federation of streams

Technical requirements

To perform the exercises in this chapter, you will need the following:

- A Microsoft Azure subscription
- Visual Studio Code

Azure Event Hubss service and concepts

Nowadays, we gather more and more data, which must be aggregated, processed, and stored somewhere. This implies using services that can handle increasing loads, scale to growing demands, and offer the smallest latency available. All of these requirements are often mentioned when building so-called big data pipelines—parts of a system designed to process as much data as possible, so it is later accessible by tools such as Hadoop, Spark, ML, AI, and more. If you are looking for a service in Azure that can handle millions of messages per second, Azure Event Hubss is the right choice. In this chapter, you will learn the basics of this Azure component and become familiar with messaging solutions in Azure.

Azure Event Hubss concepts

In general, Azure Event Hubss is a simple service that is built on top of two concepts:

- Event publishers
- Event processor

As Azure services are constantly evolving, currently, event processors can be built using one of the following approaches:

- Event processor host – used in legacy SDKs
- Event processor – for the latest SDK

Of course, these are not the only topics we will cover here. However, before we proceed, I would like to focus a little bit on the distinction between a publisher and a processor:

- **Publisher**: This is an entity that sends data to an instance of Azure Event Hubss. It can use one of the two available protocols (HTTP or AMQP) and is unaware of the current Event Hub capabilities.

- **Processor**: This is an entity that reads events from Azure Event Hubss as they become available. It uses AMQP for communication and relies on additional concepts such as consumer groups and partitions.

The following diagram shows how Azure Event Hubss works:

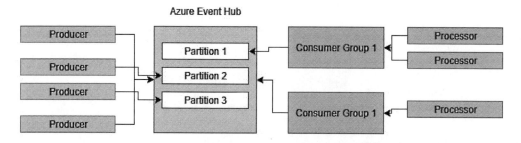

Figure 13.1 – The high-level architecture of Azure Event Hubss

As you can see, there are two more concepts mentioned here:

- **Partition**: Each partition is an independent event log that stores data separately. In general, it is Event Hubs' responsibility to ensure that each event sharing the same partition key is stored within the same partition in order. Of course, you can set this value by yourself—in such a scenario, you must make sure you are not overloading one specific partition.

- **Consumer group**: If you would like to allow separate processors to consume events separately, you must use different consumer groups to do so.

As you can see, Azure Event Hubss does not use things such as instance topics for distributing data—instead, it acts as a single event pipeline that you can read anytime with high throughput. To define this value, Event Hub uses a concept named **throughput units (TUs)**. 1 TU is defined as follows:

- Up to 1 MB/s or 1,000 events for ingress

- Up to 2 MB/s or 4,096 events for egress

> **Note**
>
> Note that Azure Event Hubss shares TUs for all consumer groups you are using. If you have 1 TU and 5 consumer groups, the maximum egress will be divided among all consumers (so, when all 5 read events at the same time, a maximum of 400 events per second will be available).

If you happen to exceed the available limit, Event Hub will start throttling your requests, finally returning `ServerBusyException`. However, this is only true for incoming events—for egress, you just cannot read more than the current TU value allows.

> **Note**
>
> By default, you cannot have more than 20 TUs per Event Hub namespace. However, this is just a soft limit—you can extend it by contacting Azure support.

Now, let's focus a little bit on partitions. Each hub in Event Hubs can have a maximum number of 32 partitions. You might wonder what this implies—in fact, this gives some additional options:

- Because each partition can have a corresponding consumer, by default, you can process messages in parallel using 32 consumers.

- Because you cannot change the number of partitions after the hub's creation, you must carefully design it at the very beginning.

- Using the maximum number of partitions by default is not always the best option—it should reflect the number of readers you are planning to support. If you choose too many, they will start to race to acquire a lease on a partition.

The following diagram shows how data could be stored among different partitions within a hub globally:

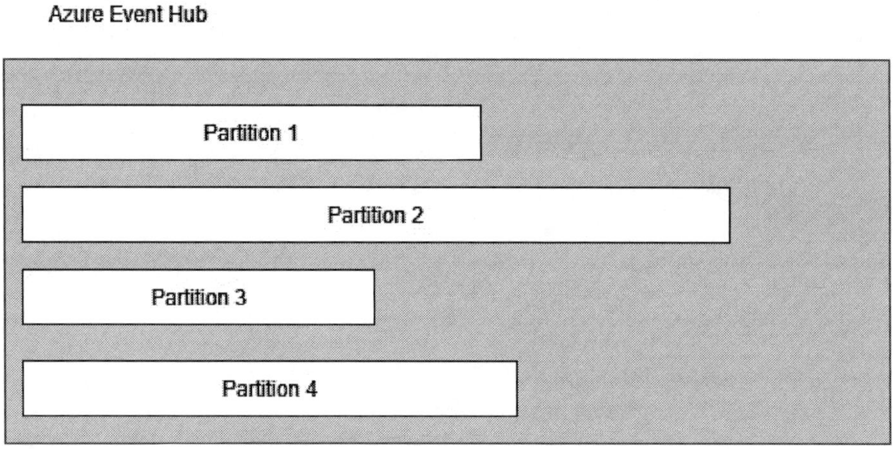

Azure Event Hub

Figure 13.2 – Storing data among multiple partitions

As mentioned earlier, each partition can grow independently—what is more, each one has an individual offset value. So, what is an offset value? Well, you could think about it as a pointer to some specific point within a log—if it stores events numbered from 1 to 10,000 and you have read 1,000, an offset value will be 1,001. In such a case, that means a reader should start reading data from the $1,001^{st}$ event.

> **Note**
>
> In fact, offset and consumer groups are connected with each other conceptually—each consumer group has an individual offset value; that is why, by introducing it, you can read all available logs once more.

However, remember that to set an offset, a consumer must perform a checkpoint. If it fails to do so, the next time it connects, it will read all the data once more. This is very important if you want to avoid processing duplicates—either you must implement a very durable process for processing events, so you can be sure that a checkpoint will be performed even if something fails, or you need to have a mechanism for detecting duplicates.

> **Tip**
>
> If you must do so, you can easily read previous events by providing the offset value you are interested in when starting a processor.

The last thing to consider for now is Azure Event Hubs' retention policy for stored events. By default (or in other words, by using the Basic tier), events can only be stored for 24 hours; after that period, they are lost. Of course, it is possible to extend it by using the Standard tier; you will have an option to do so for up to a maximum of 7 days from event retention. In general, you should avoid using this service as a standard queue or cache—its main purpose is to provide functionality for aggregating thousands of messages per second and pushing them further.

Azure Event Hubss durability

In many scenarios, Azure Event Hubss is one of the main entry points to the system, making it a critical component that should be replicated and highly available. In this service, the geo-disaster recovery feature is available when selecting the Standard tier and requires you to set up and configure the appropriate environment. To do so, you need to understand the following topics:

- **Alias**: Instead of providing multiple connection strings, you can use an alias to make a connection with a single stable one.
- **Failover**: This is the process of initiating a switch between namespaces.
- **Primary/secondary namespace**: When using the Azure Event Hubss geo-disaster recovery feature, you must define which namespace is the primary one and which is the secondary one. The important thing here is that you can send events to both namespaces, but the second one remains passive—that means events from an active namespace are not transferred.

Now, to implement the feature in Event Hub, you can do two things:

- Monitor your primary namespace to detect any anomalies.
- Initiate failover.

Of course, if a disaster occurs, you will have to create a new pairing after finishing a failover.

> **Tip**
> You must understand the difference between an outage, which is when there are temporary problems within a data center, and a disaster, which often means permanent damage and the possible loss of data. The geo-disaster recovery feature is designed for disasters; in the case of an outage, you should implement another way of dealing with it, such as caching data locally.

Working with Azure Event Hubss

Now that you are familiar with some basic concepts, we can proceed and start working with a real instance of Azure Event Hubss. In this section, you will learn how to both create and access Event Hubs in the Azure portal and work with it using its SDK. In fact, using this service is possible both from the portal (as many Azure components seamlessly integrate with it and no additional configuration is required) and by providing custom implementations for consumers that read and process data further.

Creating an Azure Event Hubss instance in the Azure portal

To create an Azure Event Hubss instance, we will start, as in most cases, by clicking on the + **Create a resource** button. Enter Event Hub and select the service from the search results. Here, you can see an example of the configuration of my Event Hub instance:

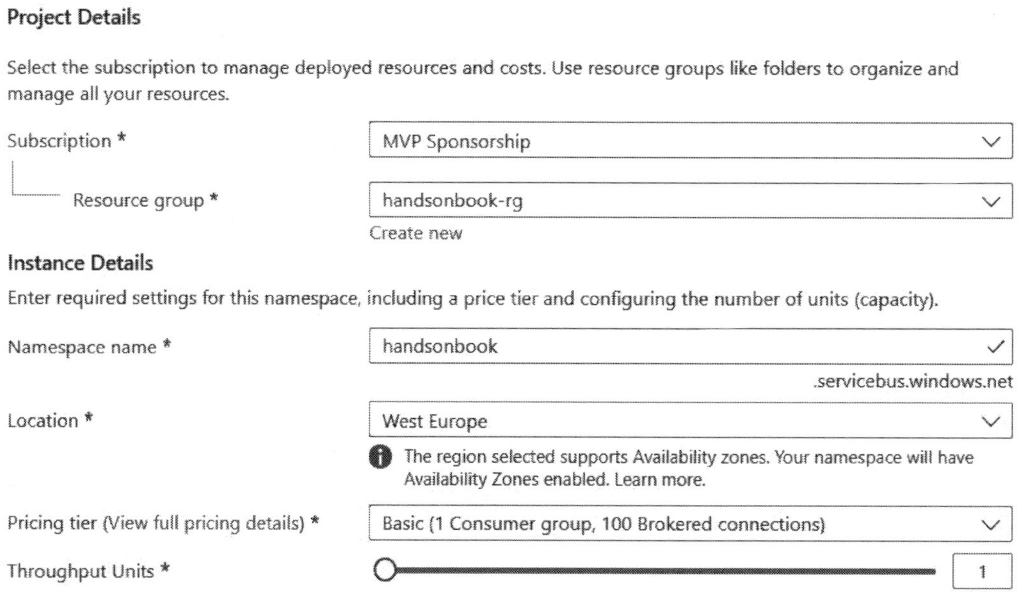

Project Details

Select the subscription to manage deployed resources and costs. Use resource groups like folders to organize and manage all your resources.

Subscription *   MVP Sponsorship

Resource group *   handsonbook-rg

Create new

Instance Details

Enter required settings for this namespace, including a price tier and configuring the number of units (capacity).

Namespace name *   handsonbook

.servicebus.windows.net

Location *   West Europe

ⓘ The region selected supports Availability zones. Your namespace will have Availability Zones enabled. Learn more.

Pricing tier (View full pricing details) *   Basic (1 Consumer group, 100 Brokered connections)

Throughput Units *   1

Figure 13.3 – Creating Azure Event Hubss in Azure portal

Now, let's focus on what we have here:

- **Project Details**: Similar to other Azure services, you always must configure the subscription and resource group where a service will be deployed.

- **Pricing tier**: You can choose between the **Basic**, **Standard**, and **Premium** tiers. In fact, there is also an additional tier—**Dedicated**. However, this is only available if you ask for it directly. The difference between **Basic**, **Standard**, and **Premium** is quite huge in terms of capabilities and throughput; we will cover it later.

- **Location**: This is the region in which Azure Event Hubss will be created.

- **Throughput Units**: This setting defines the throughput of the whole namespace. In Azure, each instance of Event Hub shares available TUs with all of the other hubs in a namespace. You can change the value later, depending on your needs.

> **Note**
> Remember that you are charged for each TU—that means that if you selected the Basic tier and require 10 TUs, you will pay *9.41 EUR * 10 = 94.1* EUR per month!

As you can see, if you select a location where the availability zones are available, then Azure Event Hubss is automatically created with zonal redundancy. This helps when looking for a more reliable solution and does not require any additional configuration.

When you click on the **Create** button, Azure will take care of creating an instance of Azure Event Hubss for you. Now, let's see what an instance of Event Hub looks like when created.

Working with Azure Event Hubss in the portal

The following screenshot shows a brand-new instance of Azure Event Hubss:

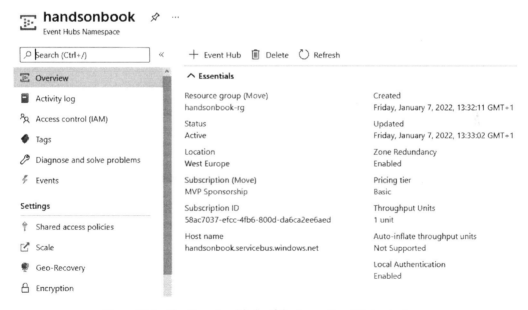

Figure 13.4 – The Overview blade of the Azure Event Hubss instance

As you can see, it contains some basic information such as metrics, metadata, and access to connection strings. Of course, this is the view of a namespace—we have not created any Event Hub instance yet. Before we do so, I would like to focus a little on what we have available now. On the left-hand side, you can find the **Settings** section, which contains additional features:

- **Shared access policies**: In Azure Event Hubs, access policies have two levels—they are either assigned for a namespace or a hub. With them, you can share an access key with a combination of three permissions—*Manage*, *Listen*, and *Send*.

- **Scale**: If you feel that you need more throughput, you can go to this blade and scale a namespace up (or down if you need fewer TUs). From that screen, you can also change the tier—for example, select **Standard** to be able to use **Auto-Inflate**.

- **Geo-recovery**: If you have a requirement to make your Event Hub highly available and you selected the Standard tier, then this blade allows you to initiate pairing with another region.

However, all of those features will bring little value if we do not create a hub, which is responsible for handling all messages. Let's do that now:

1.   Click on the **Event Hubs** blade:

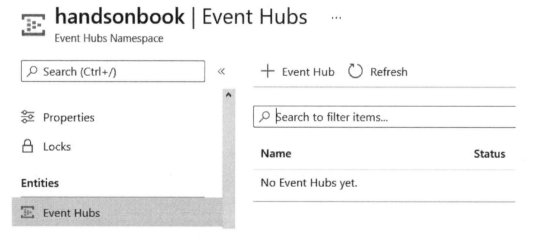

Figure 13.5 – The Event Hubs blade

2.   Click on the + **Event Hub** button to see a form that enables you to configure a new instance of a hub:

Create Event Hub   ...

Event Hubs

Name * ⓘ

| handsonazurehub | ✓ |

Partition Count ⓘ

```
─────────────────────────●──────────────────────────     16
```

Message Retention ⓘ

```
○───────────────────────────────────────────────────      1
```

Capture ⓘ

(On   **Off**)

Figure 13.6 – Creating Event Hub in Azure portal

Note that some fields are currently grayed out. This is because I used the Basic tier for this example; both **Message Retention** (which enables you to extend the period an event is available to a maximum of 7 days) and **Capture** (which will be described later) are features of the Standard tier.

3. Click on the **Create** button to initiate the creation of a hub.

Once a hub has been created, you can click on it and access it, as shown in the following screenshot:

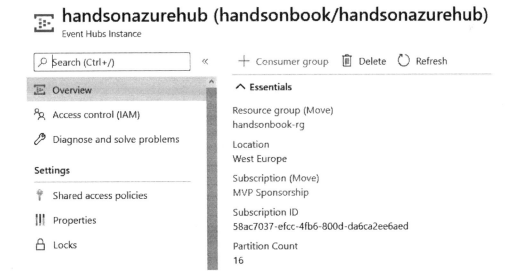

handsonazurehub (handsonbook/handsonazurehub)

Event Hubs Instance

🔍 Search (Ctrl+/) «   + Consumer group   🗑 Delete   ↻ Refresh

📧 Overview   ⌃ Essentials

👥 Access control (IAM)   Resource group (Move)
                                   handsonbook-rg
🖉 Diagnose and solve problems
                                   Location
Settings   West Europe

💡 Shared access policies   Subscription (Move)
                                   MVP Sponsorship
◫ Properties
                                   Subscription ID
🔒 Locks   58ac7037-efcc-4fb6-800d-da6ca2ee6aed

                                   Partition Count
                                   16

Figure 13.7 – The Overview blade of a created hub

Note that this view is a bit different from the view of a namespace; while it also contains some metadata and metrics, available additional features are limited. However, each hub created inside Azure Event Hubs is a real resource that is managed like everything else. It can be managed with the CLI, created with Azure Resource Manager templates, and secured with RBAC.

> **Note**
>
> Note that for the Basic tier, consumer groups are also unavailable. With that tier, only the default group—named $Default—can be used.

Developing applications with Azure Event Hubs

We created and configured our instance of Azure Event Hubs in the Azure portal; now, it is time to work with a concept that I mentioned at the very beginning—Event Processor Host. In this section, you will learn about the following:

- How to send events to Azure Event Hubs

- How to receive events by implementing your own Event Processor Host instance

However, before we start writing some code, you must understand what really underlies such a concept. As opposed to competing consumers, where each consumer uses the same messaging channel, Azure Event Hubs uses the idea of an Event Processor (Host) instance, which is an intelligent agent able to distribute events between different, partitioned consumers. You might wonder how this idea works when implemented; to gain a better understanding, you can see a diagram of the first scenario as follows:

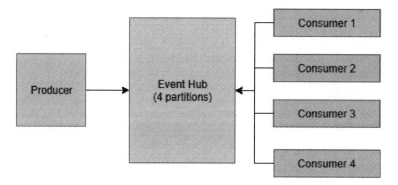

Figure 13.8 – Consuming events from a single hub with four partitions

In this diagram, you can see that there is a single **producer** and four different **consumers**. Each consumer implements IEventProcessor (the legacy SDK) or EventProcessorClient (a new SDK), which makes receiving events possible. Each **consumer** covers one **partition** and acquires a lease on it. Now, let's check another scenario:

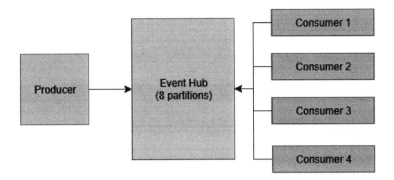

Figure 13.9 – Consuming events from a single hub with eight partitions

The only change here is the number of **partitions**—now the Event Hub has eight. Event Processor Host ensures that the load will be distributed equally, and each **consumer** will consume two **partitions**. To make things even more complicated, there is a third scenario to consider:

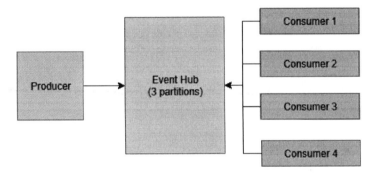

Figure 13.10 – Consuming events from a single hub with three partitions

This time, we have more **consumers** than **partitions** available. In that case, you will notice a situation where one **consumer** does not work as there is no **partition** it can process. Additionally, there is one more caveat in that scenario; because lease duration (the time during which a partition is attached to a specific **consumer**) is finite, an idle **consumer** can expropriate others and take control over a partition. Now, when the concept of Event Processor (Host) is described, we can check how to write some code that can interact with Azure Event Hubs. The following code presents an interface needed when using the legacy SDK:

```
public class EventProcessor : IEventProcessor
{
    public Task CloseAsync(PartitionContext context,
CloseReason reason)
    {
```

```
        }

    public Task OpenAsync(PartitionContext context)
    {
    }

    public Task ProcessErrorAsync(PartitionContext context,
Exception error)
    {
    }

    public Task ProcessEventsAsync(PartitionContext context,
IEnumerable<EventData> messages)
    {
        // Your logic…
        return context.CheckpointAsync();
    }
}
```

The old approach can be compared with the new SDK:

```
static async Task ProcessEventHandler(ProcessEventArgs
eventArgs)
    {
        // Your logic…
        await eventArgs.UpdateCheckpointAsync(eventArgs.
CancellationToken);
    }

    static Task ProcessErrorHandler(ProcessErrorEventArgs
eventArgs)
    {
    }
```

To use any of the preceding code samples, you will need a connection string. To get it, I accessed my hub instance, went to the **Shared access policies** blade, and created a new policy with only the **Send** permission, which will be used for the producer of events:

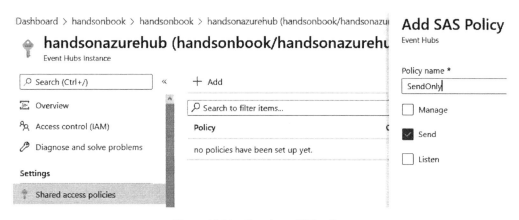

Figure 13.11 – Creating a SAS policy

> **Note**
> There are two identical blades named **Shared access policies**—one is available on the Event Hub namespace level, and the second one (as displayed in *Figure 13.11*) can be accessed directly on the hub level.

When a SAS policy is created, it will display a connection string, which can be used for connection:

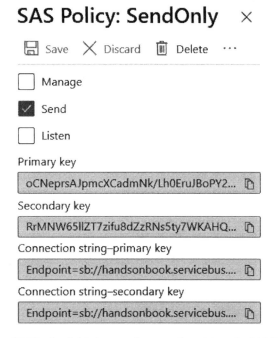

Figure 13.12 – Available keys and connection strings for SAS Policy

We have a connection string for a producer, and now we need a consumer! I created an access policy once more, but this time, only for **Listen**:

Figure 13.13 – ListenOnly SAS Policy

Now, to be able to send events to Event Hubs, you need to create an instance of a producer. For the legacy SDK, you could use the `EventHubClient.CreateFromConnectionString()` method:

```
var connectionStringBuilder = new EventHubsConnectionStringBuil
der("<connection-string-with-send-permission>")
{
    EntityPath = "<event-hub-name>"
};
producerClient = EventHubClient.
CreateFromConnectionString(connectionStringBuilder.ToString());
```

The same can be done for the new SDK (you can install it via NuGet—look for the `Azure.Messaging.EventHubs` package), but this time using `EventHubProducerClient`:

```
var producerClient = new EventHubProducerClient(("<connection-
string-with-send-permission>"), "<event-hub-name>");
```

> **Note**
>
> If your connection string already contains the event hub name, you do not need to pass it to the `EventHubProducerClient` constructor. In that case, just skip the second parameter.

Both the legacy SDK and the new SDK use the `SendAsync()` method to send events, although they require different parameters:

```
# Legacy SDK
await producerClient.SendAsync(new EventData(Encoding.UTF8.
GetBytes("your message")));
```

```
# New SDK
using EventDataBatch eventBatch = await producerClient.
CreateBatchAsync();
eventBatch.TryAdd(new EventData(Encoding.UTF8.GetBytes("your
message")));
await producerClient.SendAsync(eventBatch);
```

Now, let's compare the implementation of the Event Processor instance. For the legacy SDK, you will need to create an instance of `EventProcessorHost`:

```
var eventProcessorHost = new EventProcessorHost(
        "<event-hub-name>",
        PartitionReceiver.DefaultConsumerGroupName,
        "<connection-string-with-listen-permission>",
        StorageConnectionString,
        StorageContainerName);
```

> **Note**
>
> Note that Event Processor Host requires you to create a Storage Account instance. It uses it to internally manage leases and offsets.

Once your processor host has been initialized, you can register it in your code:

```
await eventProcessorHost.
RegisterEventProcessorAsync<YourClassImplementingI
EventProcessor>();
```

The new SDK uses a similar approach but with a different class:

```
Var storageClient = new
BlobContainerClient(blobStorageConnectionString,
blobContainerName);
var processor = new EventProcessorClient(storageClient,
EventHubConsumerClient.DefaultConsumerGroupName, "<connection-
string-with-listen-permission>", eventHubName);

processor.ProcessEventAsync += ProcessEventHandler;
processor.ProcessErrorAsync += ProcessErrorHandler;
await processor.StartProcessingAsync();
```

Here, you can see the log coming from my processor:

```
Registering EventProcessor...
Receiving. Press enter key to stop worker.
MyFirstEventProcessor initialized. Partition: '4', Offset: ''
MyFirstEventProcessor initialized. Partition: '9', Offset: ''
MyFirstEventProcessor initialized. Partition: '11', Offset: ''
MyFirstEventProcessor initialized. Partition: '8', Offset: ''
Message received. Partition: '9', Data: '5e0b2a73-ca9d-418d-
8d47-43c7b7feb17e'
Message received. Partition: '4', Data: '1a09038b-1aeb-4729-
ace0-104f26c7d376'
Message received. Partition: '4', Data: '859cce28-76e1-4a68-
8637-a2349d898e8b'
MyFirstEventProcessor initialized. Partition: '15', Offset: ''
Message received. Partition: '15', Data: '36f13819-46d6-42c9
-8afe-6776264e7aab'
MyFirstEventProcessor initialized. Partition: '1', Offset: ''
MyFirstEventProcessor initialized. Partition: '5', Offset: ''
MyFirstEventProcessor initialized. Partition: '0', Offset: ''
MyFirstEventProcessor initialized. Partition: '7', Offset: ''
MyFirstEventProcessor initialized. Partition: '12', Offset: ''
MyFirstEventProcessor initialized. Partition: '3', Offset: ''
MyFirstEventProcessor initialized. Partition: '14', Offset: ''
MyFirstEventProcessor initialized. Partition: '10', Offset: ''
MyFirstEventProcessor initialized. Partition: '2', Offset: ''
MyFirstEventProcessor initialized. Partition: '6', Offset: ''
MyFirstEventProcessor initialized. Partition: '13', Offset: ''
```

Note how a single receiver handles all 16 partitions I used for this hub. Now you can check what happens if I introduce another consumer:

```
Microsoft.ServiceBus.Messaging.ReceiverDisconnectedException:
New receiver with higher epoch of '4' is created hence current
receiver with epoch '3' is getting disconnected. If you are
recreating the receiver, make sure a higher epoch is used.
TrackingId:628871df00003ffd002d0cc25b7fd487_C1655342710_B13,
SystemTracker:handsonazure:eventhub:handsonazurehub~2047|
$default, Timestamp:8/24/2018 9:49:09 AM
```

```
    at Microsoft.ServiceBus.Common.AsyncResult.End[TAsyncResult]
(IAsyncResult result)
    at Microsoft.ServiceBus.Messaging.MessageReceiver.
RetryReceiveEventDataAsyncResult.TryReceiveEnd(IAsyncResult r,
IEnumerable`1& messages)
    at Microsoft.ServiceBus.Messaging.MessageReceiver.
EndTryReceiveEventData(IAsyncResult result, IEnumerable`1&
messages)
    at Microsoft.ServiceBus.Messaging.
EventHubReceiver.<ReceiveAsync>b__61_1(IAsyncResult result)
    at System.Threading.Tasks.TaskFactory`1.
FromAsyncCoreLogic(IAsyncResult iar, Func`2 endFunction,
Action`1 endAction, Task`1 promise, Boolean
requiresSynchronization)
--- End of stack trace from previous location where exception
was thrown ---
    at System.Runtime.CompilerServices.TaskAwaiter.
ThrowForNonSuccess(Task task)
    at System.Runtime.CompilerServices.TaskAwaiter.
HandleNonSuccessAndDebuggerNotification(Task task)
    at Microsoft.ServiceBus.Common.TaskHelpers.
EndAsyncResult(IAsyncResult asyncResult)
    at Microsoft.ServiceBus.Messaging.
IteratorAsyncResult`1.<>c.<CallTask>b__24_1(TIteratorAsync
Result thisPtr, IAsyncResult r)
    at Microsoft.ServiceBus.Messaging.IteratorAsyncResult`1.
StepCallback(IAsyncResult result)
Processor Shutting Down. Partition '0', Reason: 'LeaseLost'.
```

As you can see, `Partition 0` has been taken by another receiver, which will start processing events from it:

```
Registering EventProcessor...
Receiving. Press enter key to stop worker.
MyFirstEventProcessor initialized. Partition: '0', Offset: ''
Message received. Partition: '0', Data: '3c3bb090-2e0c-4d06-
ad44-1d0ad4a106a7'
Message received. Partition: '0', Data: '54fed07a-a51e-4f36-
8f26-f2ded2da9faa'
Message received. Partition: '0', Data: '69b8b291-8407-466a-
a2c1-0b33a2ef03ad'
```

```
Message received. Partition: '0', Data: 'ec45d759-01bb-41db-
ab51-de469ee5da55'
Message received. Partition: '0', Data: 'fcf41b0e-cd6b-465a-
ac20-100ba13fd6af'
Message received. Partition: '0', Data: '2f05104a-c4a2-4a8f-
8689-957f2dca6c71'
Message received. Partition: '0', Data: '63d77b4c-584f-4db3-
86d0-9f73179ccb9f'
Message received. Partition: '0', Data: '03c70d22-4efa-4bd6-
9c5c-f666c2922931'
Message received. Partition: '0', Data: '96f4c8be-831c-415c-
8aa7-0a5125458f16'
Message received. Partition: '0', Data: 'af2e8a21-d9ce-4256-
a8eb-73483387912c'
Message received. Partition: '0', Data: '73d9f92b-686b-44d1-
b01a-50c0c63426ee'
Message received. Partition: '0', Data: 'bf53ea8f-dd34-405f-
a6a6-0e947ce2473b'
```

It will gradually take control of half of the available partitions until the load has been balanced. Now, let's check how we can federate message processing using Azure Event Hubs and handle the events coming from multiple sites.

Federation – events replication

Most realistic architectures assume that there is more than a single Event Hub instance. This is especially true in all those scenarios where data is aggregated across multiple regions, and you need a way to merge all the streams. There are many patterns that should be considered when implementing more advanced architectures based on Event Hubs:

- The availability of messages across multiple namespaces
- Latency optimization
- The additional validation of messages with optional reduction or enrichment
- Pre-batching messages for further analysis

Now, depending on the scenario, a different approach should be taken. You might consider what technologies there are that can be used to handle those situations. While Azure Event Hubs can be considered a service, which can be integrated even with components that are non-native to Azure, there are two services that can easily help when managing complex architectures.

One of the options is Azure Functions, which can be used for stateless replication. This approach is well-tested and flexible enough to handle even more sophisticated situations. With all available triggers and output bindings, you can quickly develop a solution that will be responsible for copying messages from one namespace to another, so each consumer can fetch data no matter where it was initially published.

The second Azure native solution is Azure Stream Analytics, which will be described in the next chapter. Consider Azure Stream Analytics when you need to consider relations between messages, aggregate them, or perform queries, which can help in filtering.

All the described scenarios can be visualized using the following diagram:

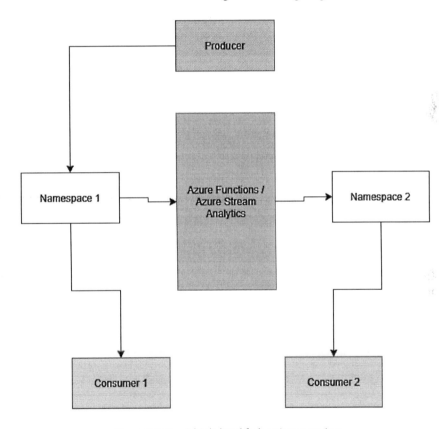

Figure 13.14 – A high-level federation overview

You can find more information about this topic in the *Further reading* section.

Azure Event Hubs security

We have covered some topics regarding working with and developing applications using Azure Event Hubs—now, it is time to learn something more about the security features of this service. In the previous part of this chapter, you used shared access policies, which are the easiest options when you want to restrict access to a hub to some predefined operations (such as listening to events, sending them, or managing Event Hubs). Now I will show you something more about the security model and restricting access to the whole namespace by IP filtering.

Private Link

To connect privately with Azure services, you can use **Azure Private Link**. While the configuration of such a service is beyond the scope of this book, I would like to make a note here about the availability of that integration. For Azure Event Hubs, Private Link is available starting from the Standard tier onward. That means the Basic tier cannot use that kind of connection and must be accessed publicly.

Resource isolation

Only the Premium and Dedicated tiers in Azure Event Hubs guarantee resource isolation. For the Standard and Basic tiers, your infrastructure is shared with other clients.

IP filters and networking

When using a tier greater than Basic, it is possible to restrict access to Azure Event Hubs by introducing IP filters or VNet integration; this feature (as shown in *Figure 13.15*) allows you to secure the whole namespace by knowing which IP addresses should be rejected. By default, Azure Event Hubs allows for connection from any IP address and network:

Figure 13.15 – Default networking configuration

However, if you select the **Selected networks** radio button, you will be able to decide which networks can access your service and also configure the IP filter:

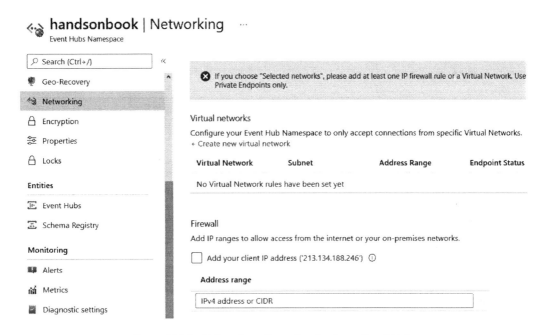

Figure 13.16 – Network configuration for Azure Event Hubs

When I restrict access to my computer's IP, I will get the following message when I try to send an event:

```
25.08.2018 13:11:39 > Sending message: 0a7dd971-6600-458c-816d-
fbbbee0d81cb
25.08.2018 13:11:40 > Exception: Ip has been prevented to
connect to the endpoint. TrackingId:9421f06c-3a1c-4e4e-
8a25-fb76f1cacee6, SystemTracker:AmqpGatewayProvider,
Timestamp:8/25/2018 11:11:36 AM
```

You can choose to either restrict access from some specific IP addresses or allow a particular subset. Note that public access can be completely disabled by using the **Public network access** option:

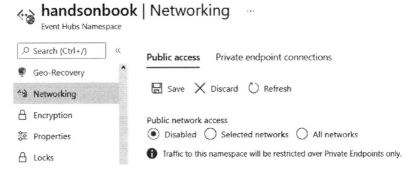

Figure 13.17 – Disabling public access to Azure Event Hubs

However, that option requires the use of private endpoints, which are beyond scope of this book. One thing to remember though is the fact that private endpoints affect the cost of your infrastructure. As you pay for both data flow and the endpoint itself, make sure you understand the implications of using them before applying a new configuration.

Azure Event Hubs Capture feature

There is one feature of Azure Event Hubs that requires an individual section itself to describe it in depth. **Capture** is a functionality that allows you to automatically store events using a predefined storage solution (such as Azure Storage or Azure Data Lake) and process them further. Unfortunately, this feature is often misused as its use cases are not so obvious; additionally, the way it works might sometimes be unclear.

What is an Azure Event Hubs Capture?

In common use cases for Event Hubs, you need a **producer** and a **consumer** to fetch data and process it. Let's consider the following scenario:

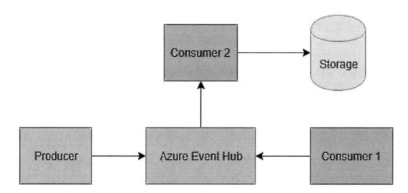

Figure 13.18 – Multiple processing flows for Azure Event Hubs

In this scenario, we have two consumers:

- **Consumer 1** for some generic processing
- **Consumer 2** for archiving events

Additionally, we introduced **storage** for storing a log of events. As you can see, the downside of that solution is the fact that you need to maintain both consumers—two code bases and two instances. With Event Hub Capture, the scenario we are considering now will change slightly:

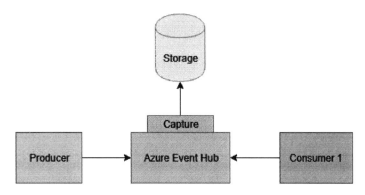

Figure 13.19 – Capture enabled for Azure Event Hubs

Now we no longer require additional consumers, as it will be the responsibility of Event Hub Capture to store data. You might wonder how storing data works in that scenario; in general, it is based on a time window that, when it ends, triggers the capture of data.

This can be easily described using an example. Let's suppose you set your time window to 10 minutes; after that interval, all the data that is stored within Azure Event Hubs will be captured and stored inside a selected database using the **Apache Avro** format.

> **Note**
>
> An important thing is Capture pricing; it costs €0.085/hour per TU. This means that if you have Azure Event Hubs with 1 TU and Capture enabled, you will pay €80 instead of €18. With 2 TUs, it will be €160 instead of €37.

Enabling Event Hub Capture

Event Hub Capture is a feature of an individual Event Hub, not the whole namespace. To enable it, you need to navigate to your hub and search for the **Capture** blade.

Now, when you enable Capture, you will see a full configuration of the feature, which we will try to understand next:

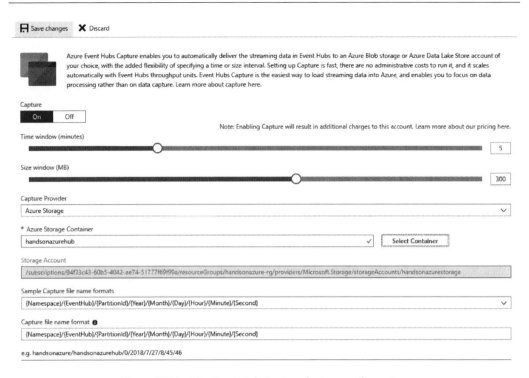

Figure 13.20 – The Event Hub Capture feature configuration

As you can see, it contains the following settings:

- **Time window**: This defines after how many minutes a capture is triggered.

- **Size window**: Alternatively, it is possible to trigger a capture after a window reaches the size limit. Whether it triggers because of time or size depends on which one reaches the limit first.

- **Capture Provider**: You can choose between Azure Storage and Azure Data Lake Store. The choice is yours, as it does not imply any additional features or limits.

- **Azure Storage Container/Data Lake Store**: Depending on your choice, you will have to choose a different kind of container.

- **Capture file name format**: This Event Hub feature has a predefined set of formats for how your files will be stored. Unfortunately, it is impossible to make it fully customizable as it must contain the {Namespace}, {EventHub}, {PartitionId}, {Year}, {Month}, {Day}, {Hour}, {Minute}, and {Second} fields.

Once you are satisfied with your choice, you can save the form. After some time, your producers will send data; you will see that data from each partition is captured:

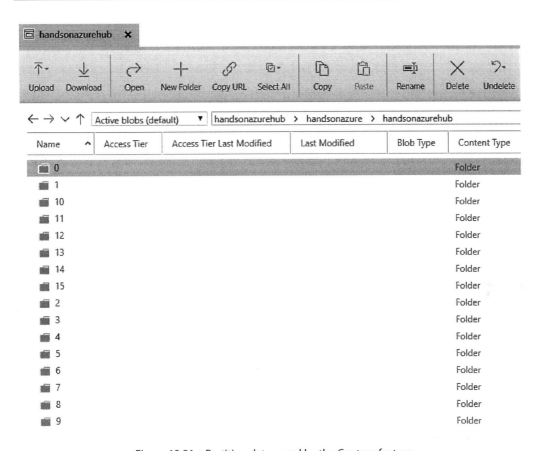

Figure 13.21 – Partition data saved by the Capture feature

What is more, they contain files with data in the following format:

```
Objavro.codecnullavro.
schema{"type":"record","name":"EventData","namespace
":"Microsoft.ServiceBus.
Messaging","fields":[{"name":"SequenceNumber","type
":"long"},{"name":"Offset","type":"string"},{"name":
"EnqueuedTimeUtc","type ":"string"},{"name":"SystemProperties",
"type":{"type":"map","values":["long ","double","string",
"bytes"]}},{"name":"Properties","type":{"type":"map",
"values":["long","double","string","bytes","null"]}},{"name":
"Body","type":[" null","bytes"]}]}
```

This data can be easily converted into JSON:

```json
{
  "definitions" : {
    "record:Microsoft.ServiceBus.Messaging.EventData" : {
      "type" : "object",
      "required" : [ "SequenceNumber", "Offset",
"EnqueuedTimeUtc", "SystemProperties", "Properties", "Body" ],
      "additionalProperties" : false,
      "properties" : {
        "SequenceNumber" : {
          "type" : "integer",
          "minimum" : -9223372036854775808,
          "maximum" : 9223372036854775807
        },
        "Offset" : {
          "type" : "string"
        },
        "EnqueuedTimeUtc" : {
          "type" : "string"
        },
        "SystemProperties" : {
          "type" : "object",
          "additionalProperties" : {
            "oneOf" : [ {
              "type" : "integer",
              "minimum" : -9223372036854775808,
              "maximum" : 9223372036854775807
            }, {
              "type" : "number"
            }, {
              "type" : "string"
            }, {
              "type" : "string",
              "pattern" : "^[\u0000-y]*$"
            } ]
          }
```

```
        },
        "Properties" : {
          "type" : "object",
          "additionalProperties" : {
            "oneOf" : [ {
              "type" : "integer",
              "minimum" : -9223372036854775808,
              "maximum" : 9223372036854775807
            }, {
              "type" : "number"
            }, {
              "type" : "string"
            }, {
              "type" : "string",
              "pattern" : "^[\u0000-y]*$"
            }, {
              "type" : "null"
            } ]
          }
        },
        "Body" : {
          "oneOf" : [ {
            "type" : "null"
          }, {
            "type" : "string",
            "pattern" : "^[\u0000-y]*$"
          } ]
        }
      }
    }
  },
  "$ref" : "#/definitions/record:Microsoft.ServiceBus.
Messaging.EventData"
}
```

As you can see, the Capture feature can be helpful when you need to get snapshots of events automatically. While it can be implemented on your own, it helps to do things natively and avoid implementing a feature that is already available. If you found this interesting, you will find more about Avro in the *Further reading* section.

Summary

In this chapter, you learned many things about Azure Event Hubs—how it works, what partitions are for, and how to leverage more advanced features such as consumer groups or the Event Hub Capture feature. I strongly encourage you to give it a try and play a little bit with this Azure service as it is a powerful tool for processing thousands of events per second. Additionally, it is simple to use and does not require much time to get started.

In the next chapter, you will learn about another service that is used for processing many events and, additionally, learn how to analyze and transform them in near real time—Azure Stream Analytics.

Questions

Here are some questions to test your knowledge of the important topics in this chapter:

1. What are consumer groups for?
2. How many events can be processed in one second using 1 TU?
3. How many partitions should you use for each Event Hub instance?
4. Are TUs assigned to a namespace or a particular Event Hub instance?
5. What are the three different permissions you can assign to an access policy?
6. Can an event publisher listen to incoming events using its token?
7. What happens if you have more consumers than partitions?

Further reading

For more information, please refer to the following sources:

- The full documentation on Event Hub disaster recovery can be found at `https://docs.microsoft.com/en-us/azure/event-hubs/event-hubs-geo-dr`.
- The Apache Avro documentation can be found at `https://avro.apache.org/`.
- The Azure Event Hubs federation overview can be found at `https://docs.microsoft.com/en-us/azure/event-hubs/event-hubs-federation-overview`.

14
Real-Time Data Analysis – Azure Stream Analytics

While some Azure components enable us to deliver data to the cloud, in most cases we also need something that is designed for analyzing and querying streamed data. One such service is Azure Stream Analytics, a real-time data analysis tool that can read all messages sent through – for example—Event Hubs, and transform and save them using one of the predefined outputs. This chapter is structured in a way that will help you start with the analysis of streamed data and should help in getting things done properly.

The following topics will be covered in this chapter:

- Introducing Azure Stream Analytics
- Defining available input and output types
- Querying data using theAzure Stream Analytics query language
- Event ordering, checkpoints, and replays
- Common query patterns

Technical requirements

To perform the exercises in this chapter, you will need the following:

- **Visual Studio Code (VS Code)**
- An Azure subscription
- Azure Stream Analytics tools—see `https://marketplace.visualstudio.com/items?itemName=ms-bigdatatools.vscode-asa`

Introducing Azure Stream Analytics

In the previous chapter, we discussed Azure Event Hubs, which is a solution for receiving and processing thousands of messages per second, by introducing the implementation of event-processor hosts. While it is great for workloads such as big data pipelines or **Internet of Things** (**IoT**) scenarios, it is not a solution to everything, especially if you want to avoid hosting **virtual machines** (**VMs**). Scaling such architectures can be cumbersome and nonintuitive—therefore, there is Azure Stream Analytics, which is an event-processing engine designed for high volumes of data. It fills a gap where other services such as Event Hubs or IoT Hub do not perform well (or where they do so, they require much more skill and/or more sophisticated architecture), particularly for real-time analytics, anomaly detection, and geospatial analytics. It is a great tool that will greatly improve your cloud- and message-processing skills.

Stream ingestions versus stream analysis

To get started, we will compare the following two topics:

- **Stream ingestion**: This is a process where you introduce a service/**application programming interface** (**API**) for receiving messages from your producers. Such a service is designed to ingest data only—it does nothing more (such as transforming or analyzing). To perform any kind of analysis of ingested data, you must introduce your own processors.

- **Stream analysis**: This is a process where you analyze the data. You search for anomalies, duplicates, or malformed data, process it, and push it further to other services for storing, presenting, and triggering other actions.

To make things even clearer, we can look at the following diagram:

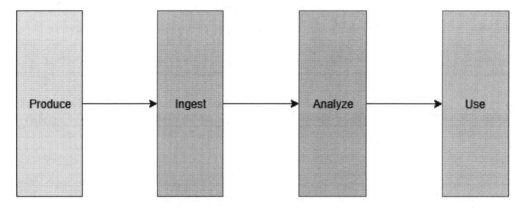

Figure 14.1 – Process of data aggregation and analysis

It shows the four steps of data processing, which are listed here:

- **Produce**: Here, data is produced by different services, devices, and clients.

- **Ingest**: This is when the data is consumed from different sources.

- **Analyze**: During this step, data is analyzed, transformed, and routed to appropriate services and components.

- **Use**: Storing, displaying, and processing data further in other services, such as Power BI, Azure Functions, and many others.

While Azure Event Hubs or Azure IoT Hub is a part of the ingest step, Azure Stream Analytics is responsible for analyzing data.

> **Note**
>
> Note that you are not limited to Azure services when it comes to ingesting data. In such a scenario, you can also use any kind of queue or API, if it is capable of processing thousands of events per second.

Azure Stream Analytics concepts

In Azure Stream Analytics, the most important concept is a **stream**. You can think about it as a flow of many events carrying data—they do not necessarily have to be the same or shared schema. Analyzing such a stream is not a trivial task. If you must decode hundreds of thousands of events, the process has to be quick, robust, and reliable. We will discuss the main concepts of this service to verify whether it can act as our analyzing solution and the main events processor, as follows:

- **Fully managed**: Azure Stream Analytics is a fully managed **platform as a service** (**PaaS**), so you do not have to worry about provisioning resources and scaling it—the runtime will take care of that, so you can focus on providing optimal queries for data analysis.

- **A Structured Query Language (SQL)-based query language**: To analyze data, Azure Stream Analytics uses an SQL-based query language that enables developers to build advanced procedures quickly and extracts from a stream exactly what they want. Additionally, you can bring your own extensions such as **machine learning** (**ML**) solutions or user-defined aggregates to perform extra calculations, using tools unavailable to the service.

- **Performance**: Azure Stream Analytics is focused on **streaming units** (**SUs**) instead of some hardcoded values of **central processing units** (**CPUs**) or memory. This is because it is designed to provide stable performance and recurrent execution time. What is more, thanks to this concept, you can easily scale your solution to meet your demands.

- **Low cost of ownership**: In Azure Stream Analytics, you pay only for what you choose. As pricing depends on the amount of SUs per hour, there is no additional cost to be incorporated into the overall payment.

There are also some extra technical concepts (such as input and output types, checkpoints, and replays) that we will cover in the next parts of this chapter. To see a big picture of the whole pipeline using Azure Stream Analytics, please check out the following diagram:

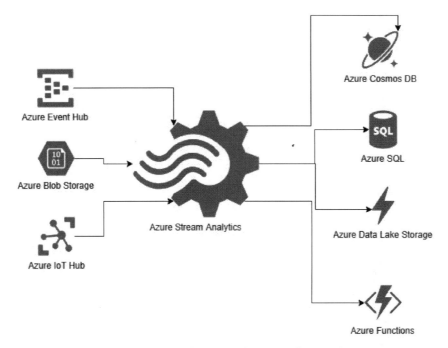

Figure 14.2 – Azure Stream Analytics as a data pipeline

Of course, there could be other references in this diagram (additional services, user functions, and analyzers), but for the sake of simplicity, I did not include them.

Defining available input and output types

Azure Stream Analytics offers seamless integration with some native Azure services, such as Azure Event Hubs, Azure IoT Hub, or Azure Blob Storage. Additionally, it can be easily configured to output data to a SQL database, blob, or even anAzure Data Lake store. To leverage those possibilities, you will have to define both input and output types you are interested in. This allows for data to be easily ingested (in the form of a stream), so a job that you will write can work on thousands of events, analyzing and processing them. In this section, you will learn how to get started with Azure Stream Analytics and define both input and output.

Creating an Azure Stream Analytics instance in the Azure portal

To get started, you will need to create an instance of Azure Stream Analytics. To do so, you must click on + **Create a resource** and search for `Stream Analytics job`. This will display a form where you can enter all the necessary data to create a service, as illustrated in the following screenshot:

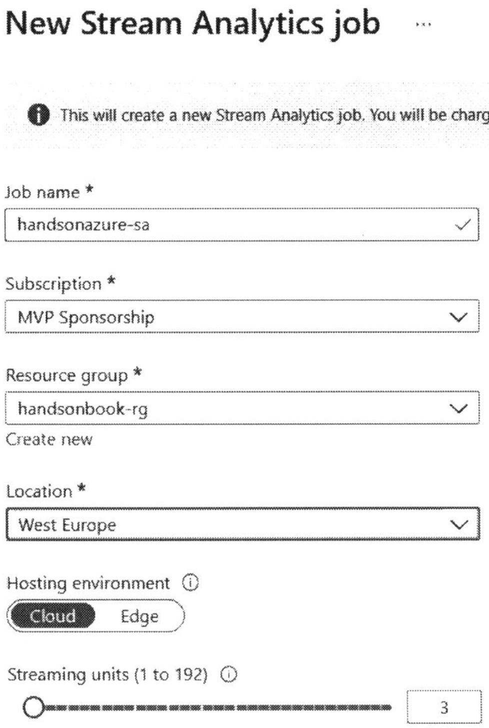

New Stream Analytics job ⋯

ⓘ This will create a new Stream Analytics job. You will be charged according to Azure Stream Analytics billing model. Learn more. →

Job name *

handsonazure-sa ✓

Subscription *

MVP Sponsorship ⌄

Resource group *

handsonbook-rg ⌄

Create new

Location *

West Europe ⌄

Hosting environment ⓘ

Cloud   Edge

Streaming units (1 to 192) ⓘ

3

Figure 14.3 – Creating a Stream Analytics job in the Azure portal

Two fields may not be self-explanatory at this moment, so we'll take a closer look at them here:

- **Hosting environment**: Azure Stream Analytics can be hosted in two ways: as a native Azure service or deployed to an on-premises IoT Edge gateway device. IoT Edge is a topic beyond the scope of this book, so the natural choice will be **Cloud**.

- **Streaming units (1 to 192)**: You must select how many SUs you would like to provision for a job to process your events. The number of required SUs depends on the characteristics of your job and additionally may vary depending on the input type of your choice. There is a link in the *Further reading* section that describes in detail how many SUs you may need for your job.

> **Note**
> Remember that you will pay in **United States dollars (USD)** $0.12/hour for each SU you choose, even when it is not working on a job.

Once you click **Create** and open the **Overview** blade, you will see an empty dashboard, as shown here:

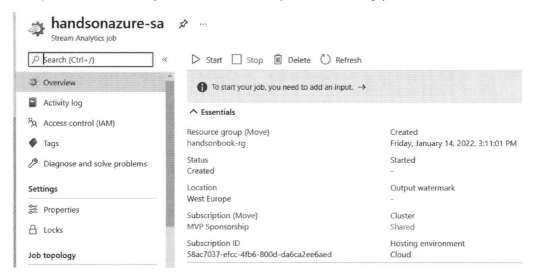

Figure 14.4 – Azure Stream Analytics job overview page

As it is a fresh instance, both the **Inputs** and **Outputs** features for the job are empty for now—we must change this so that we can use them in our query. Both features are available on the left, in the **JOB TOPOLOGY** section, as illustrated here:

Figure 14.5 – The JOB TOPOLOGY section

Let's now proceed to add an input from the **JOB TOPOLOGY** section.

Adding an input

To add an input, click on the **Inputs** blade. This will display an empty screen where you have two possibilities, as outlined here:

- **+ Add stream input**: Here, you can add a link to services that enable you to ingest a stream. The currently available Azure components are Azure Event Hubs, Azure IoT Hub, and Azure Blob Storage. The inputs can live (or not) in the same subscription, and such a connection supports compression (so, you can pass a compressed stream using—for example—`gzip`or `deflate`).

- **+ Add reference input**: Instead of ingesting data from a real-time stream, you can also use Azure Blob Storage or SQL Database and add a reference to it, so you can ingest reference data. In that scenario, Azure Stream Analytics will load the whole data into memory so that it can perform lookups on it. It is an ideal solution for static or slowly changing data and supports data up to the maximum size of 300 **megabytes** (**MB**).

Here, you can find an example of configuring **Event Hub** as an input:

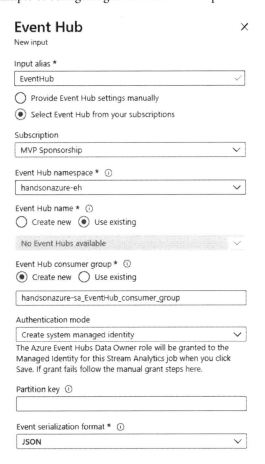

Figure 14.6 – Adding an Event Hub instance as input

Depending on your choices (whether you have an Event Hub instance in your subscription, and selected *authentication* mode), there will be different options available. In the previous example, I configured a new hub to be created inside the existing **Event Hub** namespace and be the source of my data. There are some fields, however, that I would like to cover now, as follows:

- **Event Hub consumer group**: If you would like to make Azure Stream Analytics read data from the very beginning, enter a consumer group here. Note that the creation of a new consumer group requires at least the **Standard** tier for Azure Event Hubs.

- **Event serialization format**: You can choose from **JSON**, **Avro**, and **CSV**. This allows you to deserialize events automatically, based on the used serialization format.

- **Event compression type**: If you are using GZip or Deflate, here you can choose the right option so that the input will be automatically deserialized.

- **Partition key**: If your input is partitioned, you can use that field to link it with your job for better performance.

> **Note**
>
> Note that you need an actual Azure Event Hubs namespace with at least the **Standard** tier to be able to create a hub from Azure Stream Analytics automatically.

Currently, inputs support two ways of authenticating, as follows:

- A system-managed identity, which allows you to configure access to Event Hubs using the standard **role-based access control** (**RBAC**) approach

- A connection string, which requires embedding the Event Hubs policy key

I strongly recommend using the former approach as it is much easier to extend and manage, especially in the case of more advanced architectures.

After filling in all the required fields, you will be able to click on the **Create** button to initialize the creation of a new input. Of course, you can add more than just one input as they will all be available in the input stream, so you will be able to work with incoming events. Before you start your job, you will need at least one output, which we are about to add now.

Adding an output

To add an output, you must click on the **Outputs** blade. It is like the **Inputs** one, but there are different kinds of outputs available, as illustrated in the following screenshot:

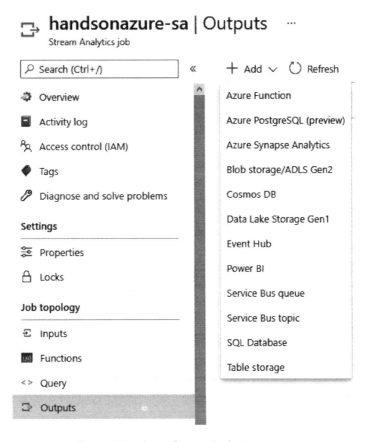

Figure 14.7 – Azure Stream Analytics outputs

As you can see, there are many different types of output available, which makes Azure Stream Analytics so flexible when it comes to pushing ingested data into different services. We can divide them into different categories, as follows:

- **Storage**: SQL database, Blob storage, Table storage, Cosmos DB, and Data Lake Storage

- **Reporting**: Power BI

- **Compute**: Azure Functions

- **Messaging**: Event Hubs, Service Bus

Depending on the category, you will have different options for what you can do with the processed events, as outlined here:

- **Storage**: Storing data for further operations, archiving, and event logs

- **Reporting**: Near-real-time reports

- **Compute**: An easy solution for achieving unlimited integration capabilities
- **Messaging**: Pushing events further for different pipelines and systems

Here, you can find a configuration for integrating Azure Table storage as an output:

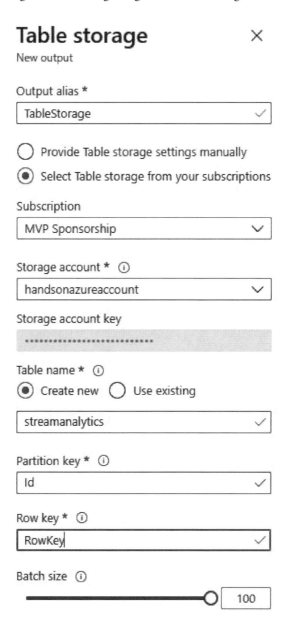

Figure 14.8 – Output configuration for Azure Table storage

Available fields depend heavily on the selected output type, so I will not focus on them in this chapter. You can find a reference to them in the *Further reading* section.

Querying data using theAzure Stream Analytics query language

The strength of Azure Stream Analytics—besides the rich selection of Azure services that seamlessly integrate with it—lies in its query language, which allows you to analyze an input stream easily and output it to a required service. As it is a SQL-like language, it should be intuitive and easy to learn for most developers using this service. Even if you are not familiar with SQL, the many examples available and its simple syntax should make it easy for you.

Writing a query

In the Azure portal, the query window for Azure Stream Analytics can be found either in the **Overview** or **Query** blade. It looks like this:

Figure 14.9 – The Query window in the Overview blade

In the preceding example, you can see a simple SQL-like query that performs the following three actions:

- Selects data from the input using the given alias
- Chooses columns
- Pushes them into a specific output

You can also click on the **Edit query** link to be routed to the **Query** screen, which looks like this:

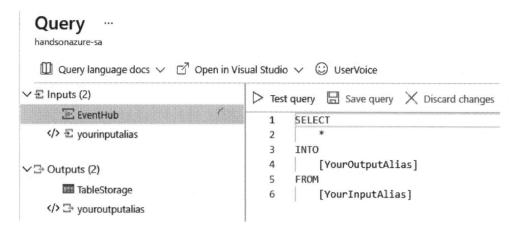

Figure 14.10 – The Query editor screen

As you can see, to be able to work with a query, you will need both an input and an output, as without them you will not be able to save it. In general, a query consists of the following three elements:

- SELECT: Where you are selecting columns from the input you are interested in
- INTO: Where you are telling the engine which output you are interested in
- FROM: Where you are selecting an input from which data should be fetched

Of course, the preceding statements are not the only ones available—you can use plenty of different options, such as GROUP BY, LIKE, or HAVING. It all depends on the input stream and the schema of incoming data. For some jobs, you may only need to perform a quick transformation and extract the necessary columns; for others, you might require more sophisticated syntax for getting exactly what you want. You will find common query patterns in the link in the *Further reading* section. In general, depending on what your input is, you will have access to different columns in the SELECT section. For example, if your input contains a property named Date, you can use SELECT date to push it to your output. Additionally, you can rename input fields using the AS construct option.

Now, to be able to read and write data, we need to insert the defined aliases into our query, as shown in the following screenshot:

Figure 14.11 – Query using both defined aliases

Let's assume that the input has the following structure:

```
{"Id":"165e0206-8198-4f21-8a6d-ad2041031603","Date":"2018-09-
02T12:17:48.3817632+02:00"}
```

To select those fields in the query, we would write something like this:

```
SELECT
    Id,
    Date
INTO
    [TableStorage]
FROM
    [EventHub]
```

This is one of the most basic queries you can use when working with your instance of Azure Stream Analytics. However, the basic constructs are only a few percent of the overall capability of the service. There are also inbuilt functions that can be easily used in each query to enhance it, as follows:

- Mathematical functions, as shown here:

```
SELECT FLOOR(input.x) AS "The FLOOR of the variable x"
FROM input
SELECT SQUARE(input.x) AS "The SQUARE of the variable x"
FROM input
```

- Aggregate functions, as shown here:

```
SELECT COUNT(*) FROM Input
SELECT SUM (Income) FROM Input
SELECT AVG (Income) FROM Input
```

- Analytic functions, as shown here:

```
SELECT ISFIRST(mi, 10) as first FROM Input
```

- Geospatial functions, as shown here:

```
SELECT ST_DISTANCE(input.pos1, input.pos2) FROM input
```

- String functions, as shown here:

```
SELECT SUBSTRING (SerialNumber ,1,3 ), FROM Input
```

In addition to these, there are some more inbuilt functions such as record functions, date/time functions, conversion functions, and array functions. The preceding examples are, of course, not all the available functions—you can find them all in the *Further reading* section. The important thing here is that some functions are deterministic (this means that they always return the same result if the same input values are used) and some are not—this is especially important when handling high loads and trying to avoid possible anomalies.

> **Note**
>
> Remember—you can merge different streams of data and push them to a single output (or vice versa—have a single input and distribute it to multiple outputs). This is a very powerful feature of this service, which makes ingesting and processing data much easier.

With the basics of query language described, let's check how we can work with more advanced features of the service.

Event ordering, checkpoints, and replays

In the previous sections, we covered some basic topics of Azure Stream Analytics: how to configure inputs and outputs, querying data, and using the service. In the last part of this chapter, I will show you its more advanced features such as event ordering, checkpoints, and replays, which ensure that events are processed in the exact way you would expect. These topics are, in fact, common subjects in many different messaging solutions, so you will be able to use knowledge from this chapter in other projects as well.

Event ordering

There are two concepts of events when it comes to their ordering, as follows:

- Application (or event) time
- Arrival time

There is a clear distinction between them, as noted here:

- **Application time**: This is a timestamp when an event was generated on the client (or application) side. It tells you exactly when it occurred.
- **Arrival time**: This is a system timestamp that is not present in the original payload. It tells you when an event was received by a service and picked up for processing.

Depending on the input type, arrival time and application time will be different properties (EventEnqueuedUtcTime or EnqueuedTime for arrival time, whereas application time—in general—will be a generic property). What you must remember is, depending on the selected scenario, you can process events as they come—out of order, or in order but delayed. This can be easily described using the following event sequence:

1. `Arrival: 2018-09-02T12:17:49 Application: 2018-09-02T12:17:48`
2. `Arrival: 2018-09-02T12:17:50 Application: 2018-09-02T12:17:44`
3. `Arrival: 2018-09-02T12:17:51 Application: 2018-09-02T12:17:46`

If you process events as they come into the stream, they will be processed **out of order**—in fact, they occurred in a different order, so there is a possibility that some data will be outdated. The other option is to sort events by application time; in such a scenario, the process will be delayed, but the order will be preserved.

> **Note**
>
> Whether you need to or not, processing events in order depends on the data schema and characteristics of the processed events. Processing them in order is more time-consuming, but sometimes you just cannot do it the other way.

Azure Stream Analytics has an **Event ordering** feature that allows you to decide about what to do with events, which are either out of order or outdated. You can see an overview of this feature in the following screenshot:

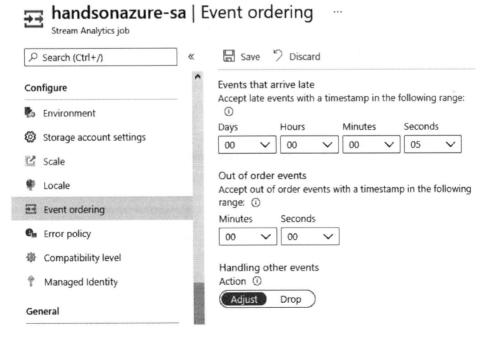

Figure 14.12 – The Event ordering blade

There are two options available, as follows:

- **Events that arrive late**: This one allows you to process outdated events (for which the application time does not match the one processed previously) within a defined time window.

- **Out of order events**: Azure Stream Analytics may consider some of your events to be out of order (this situation could happen, for instance, if your senders' clocks are skewed). Here, you can set a time window during which this situation is acceptable.

Additionally, you can define an action that will be performed if an event either arrived late or was out of order—for **Drop**, it will simply be removed, and if you select **Adjust**, processing will be suspended for some time when such situations occur.

Checkpoints and replays

Azure Stream Analytics is, in fact, a stateful service that can track event-processing progress. This makes it suitable for the following:

- Job recovery

- Stateful query logic

- Different job start modes (**Now**, **Custom**, and **When last stopped**)

Of course, there is a difference between what is possible after the checkpoint and when a replay is necessary. There are situations when the data stored within a checkpoint is not enough, and a whole replay is required; however, this may differ depending on your query. In fact, it depends on the query parallelization factor and can be described using the following formula:

[The input event rate] x [The gap length] / [Number of processing partitions]

The more processors you have, the faster you can recover when something goes wrong. A good rule of thumb is to introduce more SUs in case your job fails and you have to close the gap quickly.

> **Note**
> The important thing to consider when replaying data is the use of window functions in your queries (tumbling, hopping, sliding, or session)—these allow you to process data in different kinds of windows but complicate the replay mechanism.

Let's now check what the common query patterns for Azure Stream Analytics are so that we have a reference for them.

Common query patterns

Many patterns can be used with Azure Stream Analytics, and it is impossible to include them all in this book. However, we will try to cover the most common ones and describe them in terms of syntax.

Multiple outputs

It is possible to read data from the same input and push it to multiple outputs at the same time, as illustrated in the following code snippet:

```
SELECT
    *
INTO
    Output1
FROM
    Input TIMESTAMP BY Time

SELECT
    Column1,
    Column2
INTO
    Output2
FROM
    Input TIMESTAMP BY Time
GROUP BY
    Column1
```

As you can see, that pattern is quite simple as it only requires you to put two SELECT statements in the same query. Azure Stream Analytics takes care of proper processing and distinguishing the streams.

Data aggregation over time

One of the most popular patterns when working on streams is aggregating data over a period. Let's consider the following example:

```
SELECT
    Column1,
    COUNT(*) AS Count
```

```
FROM
     Input TIMESTAMP BY Time
GROUP BY
     Column1,
     TumblingWindow(second, 30)
```

Here, we are grouping data using the `Column1` column and counting items inside those groups for every 30-second period. The `TumblingWindow` function used here is one of the windowing functions. You can read more about these in the *Further reading* section.

Counting unique values

Sometimes, you need to count all unique values that appear in a stream. Here, the pattern is very similar to queries you might have used in relational databases:

```
SELECT
     COUNT(DISTINCT Column1) AS Count_column1,
     System.TIMESTAMP() AS Time
FROM Input TIMESTAMP BY TIME
GROUP BY
     TumblingWindow(second, 2)
```

The preceding query will give you a count of distinct values appearing in a 2-second window.

Summary

In this chapter, we covered Azure Stream Analytics, a service for processing streams of data in near real time. You have learned what the available inputs and outputs are and how to configure them. Furthermore, you were able to write your first query and check how the query language works for analyzing and processing incoming events. If you need a PaaS that can quickly read and transform events and push them to many different Azure services, Azure Stream Analytics is for you. Always consider its capabilities, such as being able to perform a checkpoint and replay data, and make sure that you follow the documentation when building a query. This contains lots of helpful examples that will allow you to quickly start with logic and then extend it depending on your needs.

In the next chapter, we will go through Azure Service Bus, an enterprise-class messaging solution that is, in fact, the foundation of Azure Event Hubs, which we discussed previously.

Questions

Here are some questions to test your knowledge of the important topics in this chapter:

1. What is the payment model for Azure Stream Analytics?

2. What is the difference between a stream and reference output?

3. What is the difference between application and arrival time?

4. For which query construct do you need to select an **identifier** (**ID**) from an input and push it to an output?

5. Can you process different inputs in the same query?

6. When is an event considered out of order?

7. Is it possible to get a substring from a property in a query? If so, which function can be used for that?

Further reading

For more information, refer to the following sources:

- Scaling and SUs: `https://docs.microsoft.com/en-us/azure/stream-analytics/stream-analytics-streaming-unit-consumption`

- Different output types: `https://docs.microsoft.com/en-us/azure/stream-analytics/stream-analytics-define-outputs`

- Common query patterns: `https://docs.microsoft.com/en-us/azure/stream-analytics/stream-analytics-stream-analytics-query-patterns`

- Window functions: `https://docs.microsoft.com/en-us/azure/stream-analytics/stream-analytics-window-functions`

15
Enterprise Integration – Azure Service Bus

To integrate our applications using messaging solutions, we sometimes need something more than a simple pipeline, which offers limited capabilities when it comes to distributing data and filtering it. Topics, filters, and many more features are available in Azure Service Bus, an enterprise-level solution designed for providing a reliable, scalable, and efficient way to send messages to multiple receivers. By going through the chapter, you will be able to understand how you can build messaging solutions with more strict requirements such as ordering, transactions, and reliability.

The following topics will be covered in this chapter:

- Azure Service Bus fundamentals
- Azure Service Bus security
- Advanced features of Azure Service Bus
- Handling outages and disasters

Technical requirements

To perform the exercises in this chapter, you will need the following:

- Access to a Microsoft Azure subscription
- **Visual Studio Code (VS Code)**

Azure Service Bus fundamentals

You have already learned about other messaging solutions, which allow you to ease communication between your services, and all are characterized by different features. In Azure Event Hubs, you were able to process thousands of messages per second, while with Azure Queue Storage, you were given a reliable and durable solution that you could use to work asynchronously on ingested data. In this chapter, we will discuss Azure Service Bus, a multi-tenant cloud messaging service that introduces advanced concepts such as **first-in, first-out** (**FIFO**) messaging, dead lettering, or transactions. It is an enterprise-class cloud component able to integrate many different services and applications. To understand the topic, we will start by comparing available messaging solutions.

Azure Service Bus versus other messaging services

In the previous chapters, we discussed the following services, which allowed us to process messages:

- Azure Event Hubs
- Azure Queue Storage
- Azure Event Grid

They all have some similarities, yet they are designed to serve different features and offer different capabilities. We often use the concepts of events and messages alternately. In fact, there is a slight difference between them, and understanding this is crucial to be able to use different messaging services successfully. Let's have a look at them in more detail here:

- **Event**: This carries the information that something happened—the fact that someone or something produced an event does not imply any expectations regarding how an event should be handled. Events, in general, are lightweight information carriers and do not bring the full data to the receiver.

- **Message**: As opposed to an event, when a producer sends a message, it has some expectation about how it will be handled (so there is a contract between a producer and a consumer). What is more, a message carries the raw data while an event implies that something happened; a message indicates that a component has initialized a communication that should be handled in the usual way.

Now, if you can recall what you have learned about—for example—Azure Event Grid or Azure Event Hubs, they both have the word *event* in their name, but work in quite different ways, as explained here:

- **Azure Event Grid**: This is designed to distribute events and react to changes. It delivers only the metadata, and the actual message must be fetched individually; thus, it can be said that it distributes events.

- **Azure Event Hubs**: This works as a big data pipeline and streams events to other services. Depending on your implementation, it can stream both events and messages.

Now, let's compare Service Bus with the previous two. Here's how it works:

- **Azure Service Bus**: This was created to support critical processes that have high requirements regarding the order of processing and reliability of the messaging service. You can use it when a message cannot be lost or duplicated. It does not work with the concept of events—instead, it allows you to push the whole data, which can be read by a consumer.

While the mentioned services offer a variety of different features and can be easily leveraged in basic and advanced scenarios, Azure offers one more service that can be used to implement communication via queues.

Azure Service Bus and Azure Queue Storage

You may be wondering what the difference between Azure Service Bus and Azure Queue Storage is. In fact, they are both messaging solutions that are reliable, durable, and can handle multiple messages at once. However, looking more closely, you can see they are quite different services, built using different concepts and for different purposes, as outlined here:

- Azure Queue Storage solutions are forced to poll the queue to receive a message— with Azure Service Bus, you can establish a long-polling receive operation via **Transport Control Protocol** (**TCP**).
- In Azure Queue Storage, you can store messages of up to 64 **kilobytes** (**KB**)—Azure Service Bus changes that limit to 256 KB (1 **megabyte** (**MB**) for the Premium tier).
- Azure Service Bus queues can store less data than Azure Queue Storage—up to 80 **gigabytes** (**GB**).
- Azure Service Bus supports consuming batches of messages.
- In Azure Queue Storage, the security model is quite basic—Azure Service Bus supports a **role-based access control** (**RBAC**) model when it comes to securing queues.
- Azure Queue Storage does not support transactional behavior.

As you can see, in Azure Service Bus, many advanced features are available that can be very helpful in applications integrating different systems and applications, and in third-party ones. Of course, those additional features cost extra as they require a more expensive tier. In Azure Service Bus, you have three tiers, as set out here:

- **Basic**: Supports queues and scheduled messages only.
- **Standard**: All features are available.
- **Premium**: The maximum message size is extended to 1 MB, and brokered connections are included in the price. This tier also guarantees higher throughput and better performance.

If you require only the basic functionality (without topics, transactions, or sessions), an Azure Service Bus instance can be even cheaper than using Azure Queue Storage. It all depends on your system requirements.

Azure Service Bus in the Azure portal

To create an instance of Azure Service Bus, you must search for the `Service Bus` service in the marketplace. You will see a short form where you fill in the most crucial information, such as the name of the service, the pricing tier, and its location, as illustrated in the following screenshot:

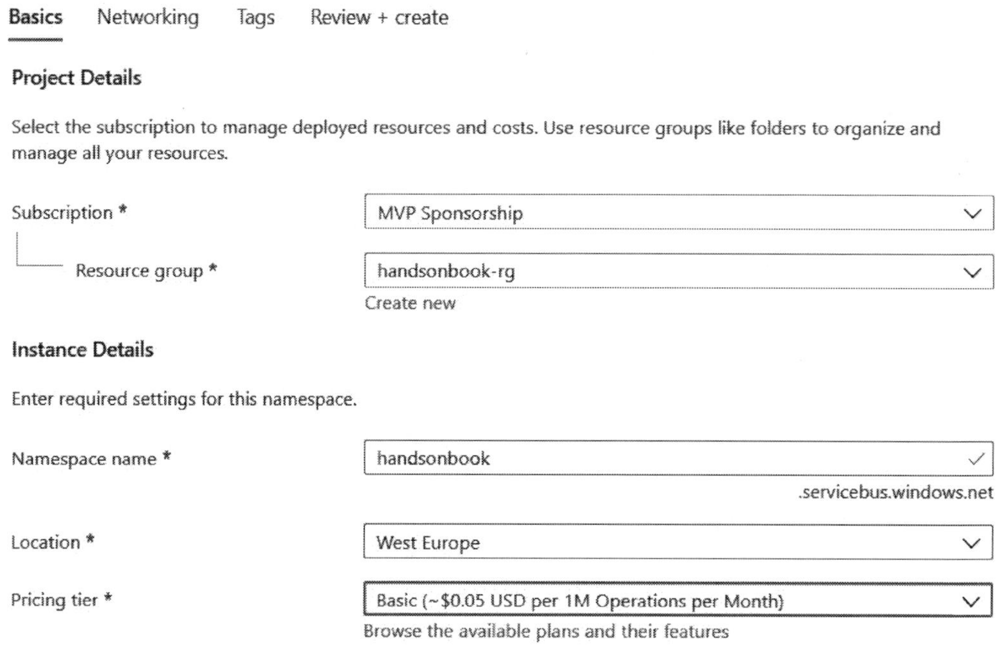

Basics   Networking   Tags   Review + create

Project Details

Select the subscription to manage deployed resources and costs. Use resource groups like folders to organize and manage all your resources.

Subscription *	MVP Sponsorship ⌄
└─── Resource group *	handsonbook-rg ⌄
	Create new

Instance Details

Enter required settings for this namespace.

Namespace name *	handsonbook ✓
	.servicebus.windows.net
Location *	West Europe ⌄
Pricing tier *	Basic (~$0.05 USD per 1M Operations per Month) ⌄
	Browse the available plans and their features

Figure 15.1 – Creating an Azure Service Bus instance in the Azure portal

For now, this is all you must enter—just click on the **Review + create** button and wait a second until a service is created. The **Overview** blade shows a bit more information, but as you can see here, it is very similar to the one you saw when working with Azure Event Hubs:

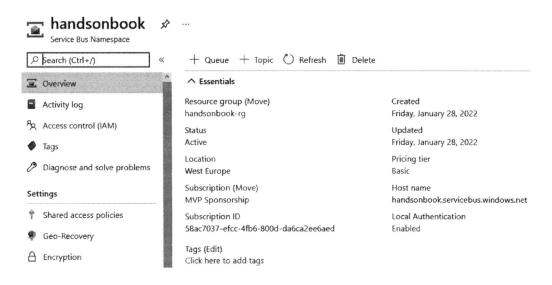

handsonbook
Service Bus Namespace

Search (Ctrl+/)   «   + Queue   + Topic   ↻ Refresh   🗑 Delete

Overview

Activity log   ∧ Essentials

Access control (IAM)   Resource group (Move)   Created
                                handsonbook-rg   Friday, January 28, 2022
Tags
                                Status   Updated
Diagnose and solve problems   Active   Friday, January 28, 2022

Settings   Location   Pricing tier
                                West Europe   Basic
Shared access policies
                                Subscription (Move)   Host name
Geo-Recovery   MVP Sponsorship   handsonbook.servicebus.windows.net

Encryption   Subscription ID   Local Authentication
                                58ac7037-efcc-4fb6-800d-da6ca2ee6aed   Enabled

                                Tags (Edit)
                                Click here to add tags

Figure 15.2 – Overview of Azure Service Bus namespace

In the preceding screenshot, you see that the + **Topic** button is grayed out—this is because I selected the Basic tier for this exercise. By clicking on the + **Queue** button, you will be able to create a new queue, as illustrated here:

Create queue   ✕
Service Bus

Name * ⓘ

myfirstqueue   ✓

Max queue size

1 GB   ⌄

Max delivery count * ⓘ

10

Message time to live ⓘ

Days   Hours   Minutes   Seconds

14   0   0   0

Lock duration ⓘ

Days   Hours   Minutes   Seconds

0   0   0   30

☑ Enable dead lettering on message expiration ⓘ

☑ Enable partitioning ⓘ

Figure 15.3 – Creating a new queue

This is where things get a little bit more complicated. Let's break this down here:

- **Name**: This is the unique name of a queue.

- **Max queue size**: You can decide the maximum size of a queue (as opposed to a fixed size of 80 GB in Azure Queue Storage).

- **Message time to live**: In Azure Queue Storage, the maximum lifetime of a message was 7 days. Here, you can specify the custom lifetime of a message before it is deleted (or moved to a dead-letter queue).

- **Lock duration**: When a message is picked up by a consumer, it is locked for a fixed time period to avoid duplicated reads. Here, you can customize it (up to a maximum of 5 minutes).

- **Enable dead lettering on message expiration**: If a message expires, it is automatically deleted. To push it to a dead-letter queue instead, enable this option.

- **Enable partitioning**: This option detaches a queue from a single messaging store, so in fact, you are ending with multiple queues. This option ensures that even if a store has an outage, the whole queue or a topic does not go down. There are some limitations, however, regarding this feature—one is that with partitioning, you cannot send messages belonging to different sessions in a single transaction. What is more, there is a limit of 100 partitioned queues or topics per namespace.

> **Note**
> Partitioned queues and topics are not supported in the premium tier of Azure Service Bus. Also, when using the Basic tier, you will not have access to sessions.

This is how a queue looks when partitioning is enabled:

Figure 15.4 – Empty queue

As you can see, the maximum size of a queue is displayed as 16 GB—this is because with partitioning enabled, we are ending with 16 partitions, each hosting a queue of the maximum size of 1 GB.

> **Note**
> Because the maximum size of a single queue is set as 5 GB, you can achieve the maximum size of 80 GB by using partitioning. With that feature enabled, the maximum size will be *5 GB * 16 partitions = 80 GB*.

Queues, topics, and relays

Azure Service Bus supports three different kinds of entities, as listed here:

- Queues
- Topics
- Relays

All three give you different options while handling communication.

Queues

A queue is the simplest entity available in the service. You can define it like this:

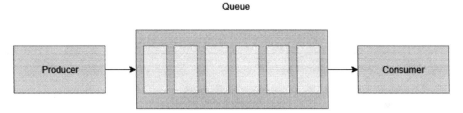

Figure 15.5 – Diagram of a queue

In the preceding example diagram, you can see that we have the following concepts:

- **Producer**: An application or a service that pushes a message to a queue
- **Queue**: A container for messages
- **Consumer**: An application or a service that reads messages from a queue using a pull model

A pull model means that a producer has to ask a queue to receive messages. Of course, there can be multiple producers and multiple consumers—this is where the lock duration feature is especially helpful as it ensures that only a single consumer reads a message at any one time.

Topics

Topics are a slightly different model than queues as they allow you to implement a **publish/subscribe** (**pub/sub**) communication model. When a queue is a point-to-point communication, topics give you an option to distribute different messages to a different queue, as illustrated in the following diagram:

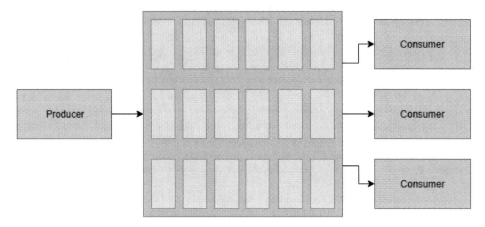

Figure 15.6 – Diagram of a topic

This model makes it possible to filter messages and isolate them, so a consumer reads only those they are interested in.

> **Note**
>
> Remember—topics are not available in the Basic tier; you must use at least the Standard tier.

Relays

Both queues and topics are models that are designed to deliver one-way communication only—a producer sends a message, and a consumer reads it. If you want to implement bidirectional communication, you must use a relay, as illustrated in the following diagram:

Figure 15.7 – Diagram of a relay

Azure Relay is, in fact, a separate service, and we will not cover it in this chapter. There are, however, many great features that you may find helpful in your applications. Let's have a closer look at them here:

- It is designed to securely expose services hosted within a corporate network
- It allows different communication models such as one-directional, pub/sub, and two-way communication
- It does not alter the network as a **virtual private network** (**VPN**) does, making it more stable and scoped to a single application endpoint

Let's now learn about available options when developing solutions with Azure Service Bus.

Azure Service Bus design patterns

Azure Service Bus is often a central point of integration for many different cloud services—it can be used in a variety of scenarios, including data integration, broadcasting information, or even bidirectional communication. As the service is rich in different features, you can use it to implement various responsibilities. You can find many examples of design patterns for Azure Service Bus in the *Further reading* section of this chapter.

Developing solutions with the Azure Service Bus SDK

There is a rich database of many different examples for working with Azure Service Bus, available on GitHub (you can find a link in the *Further reading* section), so we will cover only the basic ones in this chapter.

Before we write some code, we need to understand where a connection string to your instance of Azure Service Bus comes from. The easiest way is to go to the Azure portal, find your Service Bus instance, and access the **Shared access policies** blade, as illustrated in the following screenshot. From there, you will be able to obtain a connection string by using one of the created policies:

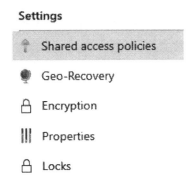

Figure 15.8 – Shared access policies blade

Here, you can find the simplest way to send a message to a queue. This is what the code looks like:

```
using Azure.Messaging.ServiceBus;

namespace HandsOnAzure.ServiceBus
{
    internal class Program
    {
        private static void Main()
        {
            MainAsync().GetAwaiter().GetResult();
        }

        private static async Task MainAsync()
        {
            var client = new
ServiceBusClient(connectionString);
            var sender = client.CreateSender(queueName);
            var message = "This is my message!";

            await sender.SendMessageAsync(new
ServiceBusMessage(message));
        }
    }
}
```

As you can see, all it requires (at least, to get the basic functionality) is to use a `QueueClient`/ `ServiceBusClient` instance. The overall implementation will differ between different versions of the **software development kit** (**SDK**). The newest SDK eases things a bit, as for both queues and topics, you can use `ServiceBusClient.CreateSender()`. After I ran the preceding code three times and checked my queue, this is what I saw in the portal:

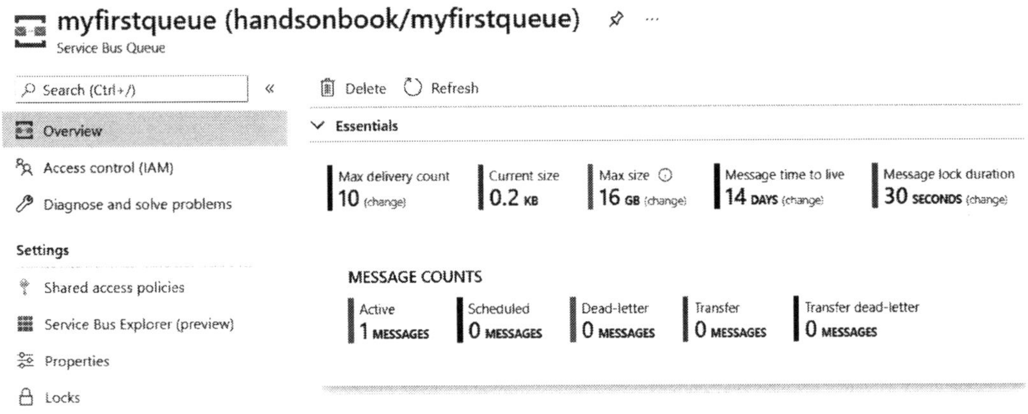

myfirstqueue (handsonbook/myfirstqueue)
Service Bus Queue

Figure 15.9 – A queue with a message in it

As you can see, there is a single active message. That means I have successfully published it, and it is ready to be pulled. There are many different options for pulling a message—here, you can find an example using `PeekAsync`:

```
using System;
using System.Text;
using System.Threading.Tasks;
using Microsoft.Azure.ServiceBus.Core;

namespace HandsOnAzure.ServiceBus.Reader
{
    internal class Program
    {
        private static void Main()
        {
            MainAsync().GetAwaiter().GetResult();

            Console.ReadLine();
        }

        private static async Task MainAsync()
        {
            var receiver =
                new MessageReceiver(
```

```
                    "<connection-string>",
                    "<queue-name>");

            while (true)
            {
                var message = await receiver.PeekAsync();
                if(message == null) continue;

                Console.WriteLine($"New message: [{message.
ScheduledEnqueueTimeUtc}] {Encoding.UTF8.GetString(message.
Body)}");
                await Task.Delay(100);
            }
        }
    }
}
```

However, if you only peek messages, you will not dequeue them. To do that, you have to use `ReceiveAsync`, like so:

```
var message = await receiver.ReceiveAsync();
```

The difference will be visible when you read messages using both methods. `PeekAsync` will not change the state of messages (so they will still be visible as *active*, even if you set the `ReceiveMode` option to `ReceiveAndDelete`). `ReceiveAsync` will use the value of a `ReceiveMode` option and possibly act as an atomic `CompleteAsync` operation.

> **Note**
>
> To mark messages as *read* after using `PeekAsync`, you can use `CompleteAsync`.

Receiving messages using the newer SDK looks a little bit different. There, you will use `ServiceBusClient`, but to receive something from Service Bus, you will need to implement a proper handler. Here's how to do so:

```
var client = new ServiceBusClient(connectionString);
var processor = client.CreateProcessor(queueName, new
ServiceBusProcessorOptions());
processor.ProcessMessageAsync += MessageHandler;
processor.ProcessErrorAsync += ErrorHandler;
```

The handlers can look like this:

```
static async Task MessageHandler(ProcessMessageEventArgs args)
{
    string body = args.Message.Body.ToString();
    Console.WriteLine($"Received: {body}");
    await args.CompleteMessageAsync(args.Message);
}

static Task ErrorHandler(ProcessErrorEventArgs args)
{
    Console.WriteLine(args.Exception.ToString());
    return Task.CompletedTask;
}
```

We will cover more advanced scenarios later in this chapter.

Azure Service Bus security

As Azure Service Bus is described as an enterprise-level cloud service designed for integrating different services, there are serious expectations regarding the security features it offers. Besides shared access tokens, there are new features that allow much more flexible access management.

The first option described will be **Managed Identity** (**MI**), which can be considered current **state-of-the-art** (**SOTA**) when developing solutions based on Microsoft Azure.

MI

MI is a feature of Microsoft Azure cloud that eases authentication between services without storing credentials in your code. A whole description can be found in the link in the *Further reading* section. When it comes to using it with Azure Service Bus, there is no additional blade available—what you need is to just find an identity in the access control (**IAM**) blade, as illustrated in the following screenshot:

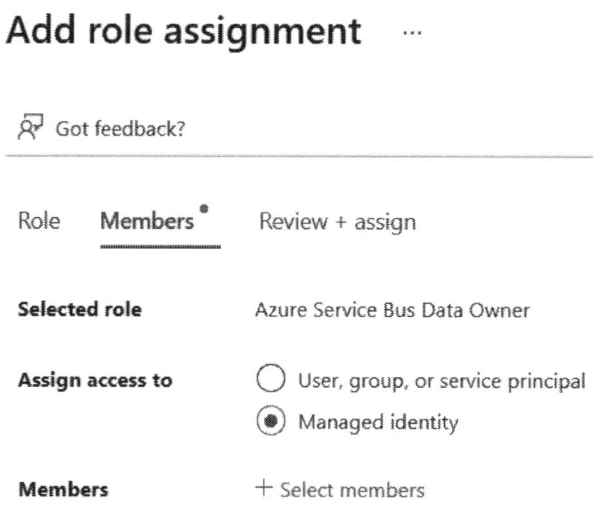

Add role assignment   ...

Ⴝ Got feedback?

Role   Members *   Review + assign

Selected role   Azure Service Bus Data Owner

Assign access to   ◯ User, group, or service principal

                           ⦿ Managed identity

Members   + Select members

Figure 15.10 – Adding role assignment for a resource

Now, instead of using a **shared access signature (SAS)** token or access policy, you can use the following code to authenticate the request:

```
using Azure.Identity;
using Azure.Messaging.ServiceBus;


var client = new ServiceBusClient("namespace-name", new
DefaultAzureCredential());
```

As you can see, the flow becomes much simpler as you do not have to store credentials or keys; instead, you let the provider handle the authentication. The `DefaultAzureCredential` object in that example will take care of proper authentication, including your local credentials if developing an application on your computer.

RBAC

In Azure Service Bus, there is also a possibility to leverage roles defined in **Azure Active Directory (Azure AD)** to grant access to a service. The whole feature relies on the assumption that a user will be able to take responsibility for granting access to a Service Bus instance. The first step is the same as with MI authentication—you must add a user to a service so that they gain access and can start pushing and receiving messages. Full instructions can be found in the *Further reading* section.

> **Note**
>
> With the ability to tell explicitly how a user or an application can access Azure Service Bus, you are given much better control over how messages are published and received. This is a great improvement over Azure Queue Storage, where such features are not available.

There is also a possibility to use RBAC authentication to grant access to a service to another service (if MI is not available). In that scenario, there will be no interactive login required as it is all handled by Azure AD.

> **Note**
>
> Even if interactive login is required, this is not handled by an application, so you can be sure that it will not handle any credentials directly.

Advanced features of Azure Service Bus

We have already covered some of the basics of the Azure Service Bus, such as SDK, the most crucial concepts, and security considerations. Now, we will focus a little bit on more advanced use cases, such as dead lettering, performance, sessions, and transactions. All those topics are crucial when developing a reliable and important service integrating many different applications and systems. Also, remember to look at the Azure Service Bus examples in the *Further reading* section, as this points to a GitHub repository where you can find many different use cases and concepts when using this service.

Dead lettering

In general, dead lettering means that there are messages in a queue considered dead (because there was no receiver code logic interested in pulling them), and you have two options to proceed, as follows:

- Delete them permanently
- Push them to an additional queue, named a dead-letter queue

In Azure Service Bus, you have two options to push a message to a dead-letter queue, as follows:

- Set the maximum lifetime of a message—once it expires, it is automatically moved to a dead-letter queue
- Use the `DeadLetterAsync` method on `MessageReceiver`, as follows:

```
await receiver.DeadLetterAsync("<lock-token>", "<reason>");
```

- Use the `DeadLetterMessageAsync` method in the new SDK available on the `ServiceBusReceiver` object

Here, you can find a complete example for the old SDK, and you can find a lock token:

```
while (true)
{
  var message = await receiver.ReceiveAsync();
  if(message == null) continue;

  Console.WriteLine($"New message: [{message.
ScheduledEnqueueTimeUtc}] {Encoding.UTF8.GetString(message.
Body)}");

  await receiver.DeadLetterAsync(message.SystemProperties.
LockToken, "HandsOnAzure - test");
  await Task.Delay(100);
}
```

Handling dead lettering in the new SDK is even simpler, as we can see here:

```
// message is ServiceBusReceivedMessage object
receiver.DeadLetterMessageAsync(message);
```

Of course, it is possible to fetch messages from a dead-letter queue. To get the name, you can use the following method:

```
var deadLetterQueueName = EntityNameHelper.
FormatDeadLetterPath("<entity-path>");
```

As you can see, using a dead-letter queue in Azure Service Bus is a matter of calling one method that will take care of moving a message to a dead-letter queue. Now, we will focus on learning how we can guarantee a FIFO model when sending and receiving messages.

Sessions

In Azure Service Bus, sessions are used to achieve a FIFO guarantee. In general, the service does not control the relationship between messages, so even if in most cases the order is preserved, it is not guaranteed. To put a message to a session, you must leverage a SessionId property (this applies to both old and new SDKs), as follows:

```
await client.SendAsync(new Message(Encoding.UTF8.
GetBytes(message)) { SessionId = Guid.Empty.ToString()});
await client.SendAsync(new ServiceBusMessage(message)) {
SessionId = Guid.Empty.ToString()});
```

To handle a session on the receiver side, you must use the `RegisterSessionHandler` method on a `QueueClient` instance, like so:

```
var client = new QueueClient("<connection-string>", "<queue-
name>");
client.RegisterSessionHandler((session, message, ct) => Task.
FromResult(new SessionHandler()), args => Task.CompletedTask);
```

Additionally, you will have to implement `ImessageSession`.

The new SDK will require using a `ServiceBusSessionReceiver` object.

Transactions

Transactions in Azure Service Bus are a wide topic referring to many different entities that you can work with in this service, such as the following:

- Clients (`QueueClient`, `TopicClient`, `ServiceBusClient`)
- Messages (by using operations such as `Complete`, `Defer`, `Abandon`, and many more)
- Sessions (`GetState/SetState`)

As you can see, there are no receive operations listed; this is because there is an assumption that they are atomic by design.

> **Note**
>
> In general, there is a requirement for using the `ReceiveMode.PeekLock` mode when pulling messages and opening a transaction scope inside a loop or an `OnMessage` callback. If you want to progress with processing a message, you will need to follow up with a `receiver.CompleteMessageAsync(message)` method.

You can refer to the following code snippet to get a better picture of what we are talking about in this section:

```
var message = receiver.Receive();
using (scope = new TransactionScope())
{
    var newMessage = "some_message"// transfer

    sender.Send(newMessage);
    message.Complete();
```

```
    scope.Complete();
}
```

In the preceding example, a processor (which at the same moment is responsible for producing a message) marks a message as complete, while transferring a new message to another queue. The whole model leverages the auto-forwarding feature of Azure Service Bus. The following code snippet provides an example of a topic:

```
var subscription = new SubscriptionDescription(sourceTopic,
subscriptionName);
subscription.ForwardTo = destinationTopic;
namespaceManager.CreateSubscription(subscription);
```

When a transaction is implemented, you can be sure that committing to a queue log will only happen if the whole transaction succeeds; otherwise, there will be simply no trace of messages that were handled inside it.

Handling outages and disasters

If you make Azure Service Bus the center of your architecture—a service that is responsible for integrating dozens of services and handling communication—you must make sure that it is replicated and invulnerable to disasters. There are two topics to consider here—**disaster recovery** (**DR**) and handling outages. As those terms are completely different concepts, you have to both understand them and be able to implement a solution in case unexpected issues and accidents occur. In the last section of this chapter, you will learn how Azure Service Bus can be made into a durable cloud component on which you and your applications can rely.

DR

When a disaster happens, you may lose a part or all of your data. In general, a disaster is defined as a temporal or permanent loss of the whole service, with no guarantees that it will become available again. Such disasters are floods, earthquakes, and fires, just to name a few. Disasters tend to occur in a single region (the probability of disasters occurring in separate regions simultaneously is very small), so in general, you need two different data centers to implement DR.

> **Note**
> Remember—using two different data centers may not be enough if they are close to each other. You must select two that can satisfy your requirements, but at the same time are as far from each other as possible.

When it comes to implementing DR in Azure Service Bus, the flow is the same as in Azure Event Hubs, as outlined here:

- Create a primary region
- Create a secondary region
- Create a pairing
- Define a trigger for failover

In general, to create a pairing, you need the following code:

```
var client = new ServiceBusManagementClient(creds) {
SubscriptionId = subscriptionId };

var namespace2 =
   await client.Namespaces.CreateOrUpdateAsync(
   "<resource-group-name>",
   "<secondary-namespace>",
   new SBNamespace { ... params ... });

ArmDisasterRecovery drStatus =
   await client.DisasterRecoveryConfigs.CreateOrUpdateAsync(
           "<resource-group-name>",
       "<primary-namespace>",
       "<alias>",
       new ArmDisasterRecovery { PartnerNamespace = namespace2.
Id })
```

The preceding sample uses the `Microsoft.Azure.Management.ServiceBus` NuGet package for operating on a namespace.

Once a pairing is configured and created, it is up to you to trigger and initiate failover. To do so, the following line of code is all you need:

```
client.DisasterRecoveryConfigs.FailOver("<resource-group-
name>", "<secondary-namespace>", "<alias>");
```

> **Note**
>
> Failover is initiated against the secondary region—this is crucial as the primary region may not be available at the time of initiating an operation.

Once failover is finished, you can start handling messages using your secondary region. There is, however, one important thing to remember—in case another outage happens, you want to be able to fail over again. Because of that, it is also very important to set up another secondary namespace (and make the current one your primary namespace) and pair them to be secure again.

Handling outages

While a disaster often means that some part of your data is lost, an outage may be described as a service being temporarily unavailable. This is why once it is resolved, you may want to synchronize both Service Bus namespaces. While this process is automatic, it may take a while. It is stated in the documentation that only 50-100 entities will be transferred per minute. For this reason, you may consider the concept of active/passive replication, which is described in more detail here:

- **Active**: In this approach, you have two active namespaces that actively receive messages. Then, a receiver always receives both—you have to tag them properly with the same **unique identifier** (**UID**) used to detect duplicates (you can use either the `MessageId` property or `Label` property for that).

- **Passive**: Instead of actively using both queues (or topics), you can use the second one only if a message cannot be delivered to the primary namespace. However, this approach has its caveats—it may cause a message delivery delay (or even loss) or duplicates.

Here, you can find an example of passive replication:

```
private async Task SendMessage(BrokeredMessage message1, int
maxSendRetries = 10)
{
  Do
  {
    var message2 = message1.Clone();
    try
    {
      await _activeQueueClient.SendAsync(message1);
      return;
    }
    Catch
    {
      if (--maxSendRetries <= 0)
      {
        throw;
      }
```

```
      lock (_swapMutex)
      {
        var client = _activeQueueClient;
        _activeQueueClient = _backupQueueClient;
        _backupQueueClient = client;
      }

      message1 = message2.Clone();
    }
  }
  while (true);
}
```

As you can see, it clearly shows how a duplicate of a message is passed to a backup queue. An example of active replication is slightly different, shown as follows:

```
var task1 = primaryQueueClient.SendAsync(m1);
var task2 = secondaryQueueClient.SendAsync(m2);

try
{
  await task1;
}
catch (Exception e)
{
  exceptionCount++;
}

try
{
  await task2;
}
catch (Exception e)
{
  exceptionCount++;
}
```

```
if (exceptionCount > 1)
{
   throw new Exception("Send Failure");
}
```

Here, we are sending the same message to both namespaces, even if one of them fails. One more thing that should be considered to handle outages is using partitioned senders (though unavailable in the Premium tier). When using them, you are safe in case of an outage of a single messaging store, and you can still use other partitions to send and receive data. The following example enables partitioning on a topic:

```
var ns = NamespaceManager.
CreateFromConnectionString(myConnectionString);
var td = new TopicDescription(TopicName);
td.EnablePartitioning = true;
ns.CreateTopic(td);
```

No matter which solution you choose to handle service outages, it is important to test the solution. While testing a **platform-as-a-service** (**PaaS**) solution may be a little bit tricky (mostly due to the fact that you do not control the underlying infrastructure), you can still do that either by manually crashing your services (for example, by deleting the Service Bus instance) or introducing a proxy that will catch incoming requests and simulate outage.

Summary

In this short chapter, you learned the basic concepts of Azure Service Bus including queues, topics, the SDK, and more advanced features such as dead lettering, sessions, and transactions. In general, it is a great service for both simple and critical scenarios as it gives you enough flexibility to adjust it to most applications, and at the same time, it is quite easy to learn how to get started. Remember—you can use the Basic tier for the simplest use cases, which gives you a cheap and reliable solution and is a much richer option than Azure Queue Storage. In the next chapter, we will focus on monitoring services with Azure Application Insights.

Questions

Here are some questions to test your knowledge of the important topics in this chapter:

1. What is the difference between a queue and a topic?
2. Can you use topics in the Basic tier?
3. What is the reason for using a dead-letter queue?

4. What are sessions for in Azure Service Bus?

5. What is the maximum size of a queue with partitioning enabled, when a single queue has a maximum size of 1 GB?

6. What is the difference between active and passive replication?

7. How is DR achieved in Azure Service Bus?

Further reading

For more information, refer to the following sources:

- ML overview - `https://docs.microsoft.com/en-us/azure/active-directory/managed-identities-azure-resources/overview`

- RBAC authentication: `https://docs.microsoft.com/en-us/azure/service-bus-messaging/service-bus-role-based-access-control`

- Service Bus samples: `https://github.com/Azure/azure-service-bus/tree/master/samples/DotNet`

- Azure Service Bus design patterns: `https://msdn.microsoft.com/en-us/magazine/mt845652.aspx`

16
Using Application Insights to Monitor Your Applications

Azure is not only about developing an application. Once we have our solution deployed to the cloud, we must somehow monitor and diagnose it. The Azure Application Insights service offers a complete toolset for maintaining your applications, with **software development kits** (**SDKs**) available for multiple languages and platforms, alerts, query languages, and integration with many native Azure services. It simplifies logging in to applications and gets rid of multiple **sources of truth** (**SOTs**) when it comes to analyzing an issue using data from several places.

The following topics will be covered in this chapter:

- Using the Azure Application Insights service
- Monitoring different platforms
- Using the Smart Analytics module
- Automating Azure Application Insights

Technical requirements

To perform the exercises in this chapter, you will need the following:

- An Azure subscription
- **Visual Studio Code** (**VS Code**)

Using the Azure Application Insights service

One of the most important features when developing applications (especially those hosted in the cloud) is the ability to easily monitor them and detect at an early stage any possible issues and flaws. To do so, you need a whole architecture of loggers, storage, and report tools that you must integrate, configure, and maintain daily. This requires an additional set of skills in your team and, of course, takes time—the bigger your application is, the more is required. With Azure Application Insights, all those operations are much simpler: you have a single service and endpoint for logging all required information, and the rest is done for you automatically.

Logging data in the cloud

Let's assume you have the following architecture:

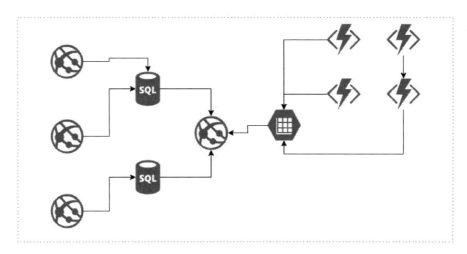

Figure 16.1 – Generic cloud architecture with various services

It contains many different web apps, different storage capabilities (such as a **Structured Query Language** (**SQL**) database or Azure Storage), and Azure Functions. If we want to be able to monitor all those services, we will need the following components:

- A tool for saving logs (which can use different outputs such as storage or a file, possibly multiplatform)
- Storage able to store **gigabytes** (**GB**) of log data
- A dashboard that will get data from the storage and display it using different filters and parameters

When you take all those into account, you may find the following caveats:

- Storing raw data is not enough as you will need a projection view that can be quickly fetched and does not require extra transformations or processing.
- You must find a way to store data that allows users to query at will with different vectors— appending logs may seem great for checking recent records, but for creating an index of dynamic parameters it is not so good.

- You must implement some kind of data retention—most logs have no use after a fixed time period.

- Performance for both applications and the reporting solution should be repeatable and should not change in time (for example, with the increased amount of data stored).

- Having a dedicated team for issue tracking may not be the best allocation of resources—people with reporting and data analyzing skills are much more valuable when they work on actual business data.

The ideal solution for the preceding problems would be a single component capable of doing everything we mentioned earlier, such as the one illustrated in the following diagram:

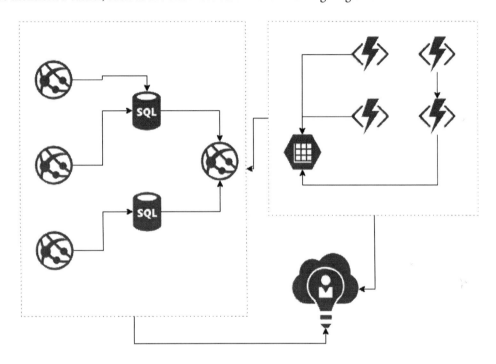

Figure 16.2 – Enriching architecture with a central monitoring component

In Azure, such a component is Azure Application Insights, which we will cover in this chapter.

Azure Application Insights fundamentals

Connecting to the Azure Application Insights service can differ depending on your circumstances. In general, you have multiple possibilities when integrating the service, as outlined here:

- Seamless integration within the portal. No additional steps are required; you just enable and configure a feature—the rest is already implemented.

- Using an appropriate SDK depending on the platform.

- Sending telemetry events directly to the service endpoints.

Depending on the concept you use, a different configuration will be used, as noted here:

- For the portal, you need no extra steps as you are already authenticated, and a resource can be selected—for example, from a drop-down menu.

- For an SDK, you need an instrumentation key or connection string that can be found in the portal—we will cover this topic later in this chapter. As support for instrumentation keys is going to end in 2025, it is recommended to use connection strings from now on.

- For **REpresentational State Transfer (REST) application programming interfaces (APIs)**, there are different options available, such as App ID, a key, or an **Open Authorization 2 (OAuth2)** flow.

> **Note**
>
> Note that, depending on the method of logging used, different features and capabilities may be available. This is especially true for sending custom events or custom logging logic—such actions often will require the use of a dedicated SDK.

Besides some obvious features (such as the ability to log and store information about a request or an exception), Azure Application Insights has many different capabilities implemented, such as the following:

- **Request telemetry**: You can automatically gather information regarding the request count, average latency, and failure rates. If using this service—for example—with Azure App Service, you are given full insights into your web application by just implementing the SDK.

- **Dependencies**: Besides general telemetry, in Azure Application Insights you can find information about how your dependencies (such as Azure Table storage and Azure SQL) perform. This is especially true if you have multiple services integrated and you want to know which one affects latency the most.

- **Exceptions**: Having information about failed requests or dependencies is one thing, but a detailed dashboard displaying aggregated data about errors is much more useful. In Azure Application Insights, you can easily check which type of error is connected to some specific subset of requests. This gives you a much better understanding of what is going on under the hood in your application and where to start fixing it.

- **User telemetry**: Do you want to know exactly how many users you have? Are you interested in what the flow is when they use your application? In Azure Application Insights, additional features give you information about user and session counts, their behavior, and overall activities.

Of course, I have not listed all the available features—there are even more, such as gathering information regarding **Asynchronous JavaScript and XML (AJAX)** calls, page view, and web performance; performance counters (for **virtual machines (VMs)**), and host diagnostics from Docker. In fact, the availability of a feature also depends on the service you have chosen—different telemetry is gathered for Azure Functions and Azure App Service.

> **Note**
>
> You can achieve the same level of granularity of your logs with similar charts and diagnostics available in most services. What changes is the level of effort required—the less integration a service has with Azure Application Insights, the more you must do on your own.

Creating an Azure Application Insights instance in the portal

To create an instance of Azure Application Insights, you must search for the service in the Marketplace.

You will have to fill in the following simple form to proceed:

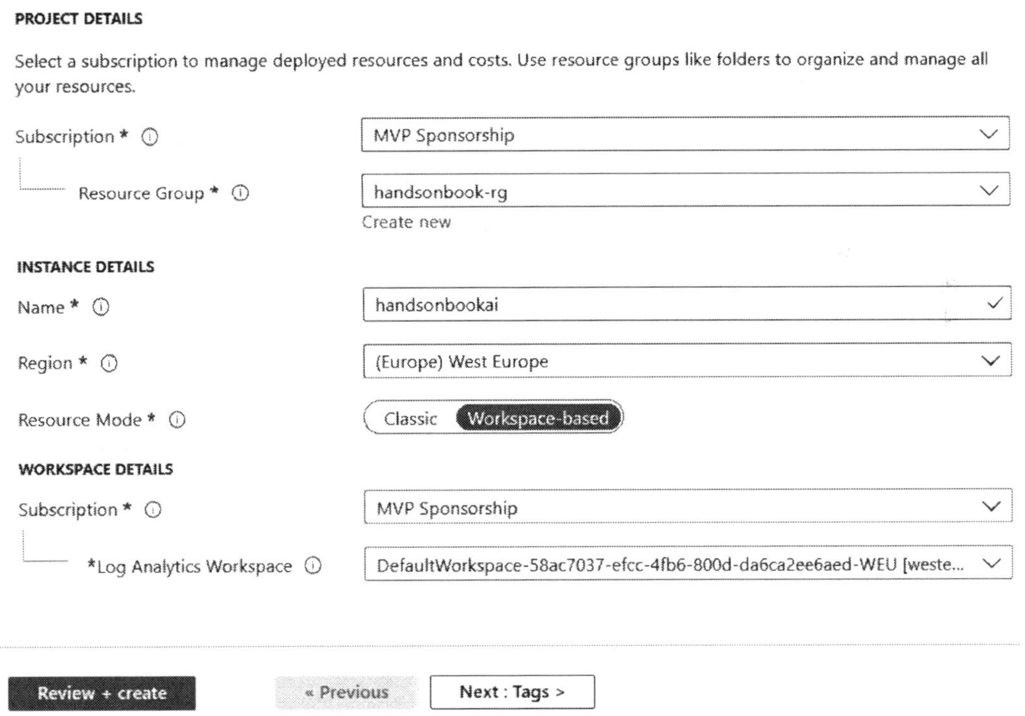

PROJECT DETAILS

Select a subscription to manage deployed resources and costs. Use resource groups like folders to organize and manage all your resources.

Subscription *	MVP Sponsorship
Resource Group *	handsonbook-rg
	Create new

INSTANCE DETAILS

Name *	handsonbookai
Region *	(Europe) West Europe
Resource Mode *	Classic Workspace-based

WORKSPACE DETAILS

Subscription *	MVP Sponsorship
*Log Analytics Workspace	DefaultWorkspace-58ac7037-efcc-4fb6-800d-da6ca2ee6aed-WEU [weste...

Review + create   « Previous   Next : Tags >

Figure 16.3 – Creating an Application Insights instance in the Azure portal

There are two options that will require some definition here, as follows:

- **Resource Mode**—This defines how Application Insights will be deployed. When **Classic** mode is used, Application Insights acts as an individual resource and stores all data within it, with the ability to export it to other services and tools. **Workspace-based** mode introduces seamless integration with Log Analytics, which enhances the overall capabilities of the service and consolidates logging.

- **WORKSPACE DETAILS**—This section is available only when **Workspace-based** resource mode is selected. It allows you to select a Log Analytics workspace used for log aggregation.

> **Note**
>
> **Classic** resource mode will be retired in February 2024, and it is generally advised to go for **Workspace-based** mode. However, migration will also be possible, so if you do not see a reason to go for direct Log Analytics integration, you can still deploy Application Insights in **Classic** mode.

When your instance is configured, the rest of its capabilities depend solely on the services integrated with it and the characteristics of data sent to it.

> **Tip**
>
> Unlike many Azure services, in Azure Application Insights, there is no requirement to have a unique service name for all instances globally—here, you just cannot use the same name for multiple services within a service. This is because it does not use a **Domain Name System** (**DNS**) name to work and connect with other applications.

When you click **Review + create**, the process of deployment will start. It should not take long to provision a new instance of a service, and once it is ready, it will look like this:

Figure 16.4 – Overview blade of Application Insights

As you can see, there is an **Essentials** section containing some common metadata and, more importantly, an instrumentation key and an **identifier (ID)** that uniquely identifies your instance of your service. We will use it to connect to Azure Application Insights—the rest of the feature will be described later in this chapter.

Monitoring different platforms

The strength of Azure Application Insights is its ability to monitor simultaneously from different platforms. You can choose from .NET, Java, Node.js, or even Python or Ruby (however, there are some languages and frameworks officially supported by Application Insights teams, while some are supported by the community). The point is it is platform-agnostic. In fact, when you need the implementation of the communication channel, with an instrumentation key you can easily send data to an instance of a service without additional keys and an extended configuration. In this section, we will focus on sending information from different platforms so that you will be able to start integrating your projects easily on your own.

.NET

In .NET applications, the only thing you have to do to get started is to install the latest NuGet package. Depending on the application type (console/web app), a different package will be used, as outlined here:

- For console applications, a recommended package is `Microsoft.ApplicationInsights.WorkerService` and use of a worker service.
- For web apps, you can use `Microsoft.ApplicationInsights.AspNetCore`.

Now, the initialization of an SDK will also be different depending on what type of application you are building. Console applications can be configured like so:

```
public static IHostBuilder CreateHostBuilder(string[] args) =>
        Host.CreateDefaultBuilder(args)
            .ConfigureServices((hostContext, services) =>
            {
                services.AddHostedService<Worker>();
        services.AddApplicationInsightsTelemetryWorkerService();
            });
```

Then, you can inject a `TelemetryClient` object in your class constructor like so, which gives you access to Application Insights methods:

```
using Microsoft.ApplicationInsights;
using Microsoft.ApplicationInsights.DataContracts;
```

```
public class Worker : BackgroundService
{
    private readonly ILogger<Worker> logger;
    private TelemetryClient telemetryClient;

    public Worker(ILogger<Worker> logger, TelemetryClient tc)
    {
        this.logger = logger;
        this.telemetryClient = tc;
    }

    protected override async Task
ExecuteAsync(CancellationToken stoppingToken)
    {
        while (!stoppingToken.IsCancellationRequested)
        {
            this.logger.LogWarning("Warning!");
            this.logger.LogInformation("Information.");
            this.telemetryClient.TrackEvent("Event");
        }
    }
}
```

Note that the Application Insights SDK automatically collects data sent to the ILogger instance. For additional functionalities, you can use the TelemetryClient instance.

For web apps, the whole configuration is even simpler, as we can see here:

```
public void ConfigureServices(IServiceCollection services)
{
    services.AddApplicationInsightsTelemetry();
    services.AddMvc();
}
```

Once the Application Insights SDK is initialized, it will automatically start collecting data in the same manner as in a console application. Of course, you can extend it further by injecting TelemetryClient into your class and using its methods for better control over data.

> **Note**
> Remember that data collected by the SDK is not set to Azure immediately. Instead, it is collected locally and sent in batches. That behavior can be configured using either a config file or directly in code. See the *Further reading* section for more details.

To give you a better understanding of `TelemetryClient` capabilities, let's take a look here at some available methods:

```
telemetryClient.TrackTrace("Hello World!");
telemetryClient.TrackException(new Exception());
telemetryClient.TrackDependency(new DependencyTelemetry());
```

Of course, there are more methods available—you can find them in the *Further reading* section. Generally speaking, in a .NET application, there is little need to use them explicitly as the SDK will scrape metrics from `ILogger`. Nonetheless, if that is not sufficient, use `TelemetryClient` for all the available features of the SDK.

Before we go to the next platform, there is one more thing to understand. All the code we write for monitoring will be useless until we configure the instrumentation key. There are multiple methods to set this up. For web apps, you can use the `appsettings.json` file, as follows:

```
{
    "ApplicationInsights": {
        "InstrumentationKey": "putinstrumentationkeyhere"
        },
        "Logging": {
            "LogLevel": {
                "Default": "Warning"
            }
        }
}
```

It can also be configured directly in code, like so:

```
var configuration = TelemetryConfiguration.CreateDefault();
configuration.InstrumentationKey = "<instrumentation-key>";
var telemetryClient = new TelemetryClient(configuration);
telemetryClient.TrackTrace("Hello World!");
```

Both methods guarantee the same result, but from a technical point of view, they are no different.

Node.js

To start working with Azure Application Insights in Node.js, you will need the following command:

```
npm install applicationinsights
```

This will install a **Node Package Manager** (**NPM**) package of Application Insights that allows you to work with this service. Here is a full example of the interface of this package:

```
let http = require("http");
let appInsights = require("applicationinsights");

appInsights.setup("<instrumentation-key>");
appInsights.start();
let client = appInsights.defaultClient;

client.trackEvent({name: "my custom event", properties:
{customProperty: "custom property value"}});
client.trackException({exception: new Error("handled exceptions
can be logged with this method")});
client.trackMetric({name: "custom metric", value: 3});
client.trackTrace({message: "trace message"});
client.trackDependency({target:"http://dbname", name:"select
customers proc", data:"SELECT * FROM Customers", duration:231,
resultCode:0, success: true, dependencyTypeName: "ZSQL"});
client.trackRequest({name:"GET /customers", url:"http://
myserver/customers", duration:309, resultCode:200,
success:true});


http.createServer( (req, res) => {
  client.trackNodeHttpRequest({request: req, response: res});
}).listen(1337, "127.0.0.1");

console.log('Server running at http://127.0.0.1:1337/');
```

As you can see, the names of the methods are the same as in the .NET examples. The only difference here is a lack of an automated logs collection. In fact, that feature can be enabled with some additional configuration, as follows:

```
let appInsights = require("applicationinsights");
appInsights.setup("<instrumentation_key>")
```

```
    .setAutoDependencyCorrelation(true)
    .setAutoCollectRequests(true)
    .setAutoCollectPerformance(true, true)
    .setAutoCollectExceptions(true)
    .setAutoCollectDependencies(true)
    .setAutoCollectConsole(true)
    .setUseDiskRetryCaching(true)
    .setSendLiveMetrics(false)
    .setDistributedTracingMode(appInsights.
DistributedTracingModes.AI)
    .start();
```

Depending on the `true`/`false` values, different logs will be automatically collected and sent to your Application Insights instance.

Azure Functions

Azure Application Insights also offers seamless integration with another Azure service—Azure Functions. There are two ways of enabling integration: either turn it on while creating a service or enable it manually by providing an instrumentation key in the app settings.

Here is a form where this feature can be enabled:

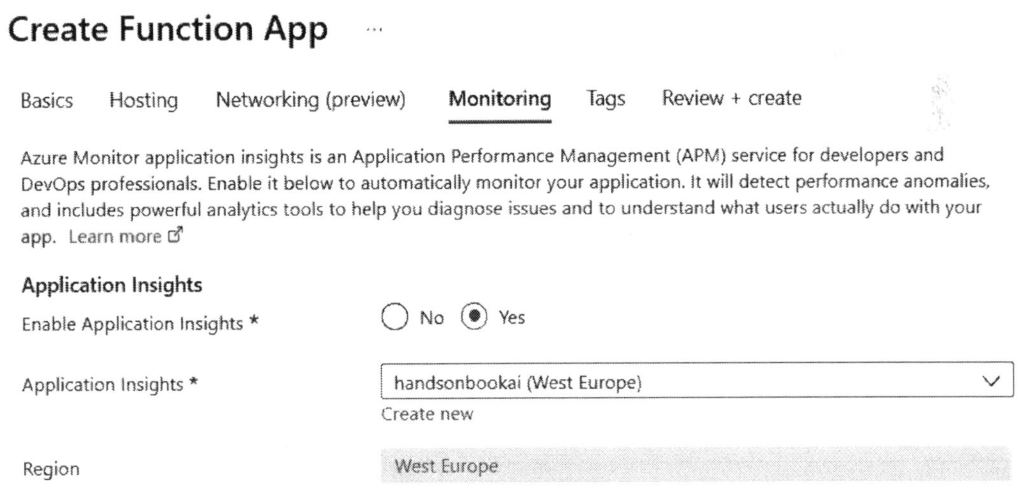

Create Function App ···

| Basics | Hosting | Networking (preview) | **Monitoring** | Tags | Review + create |

Azure Monitor application insights is an Application Performance Management (APM) service for developers and DevOps professionals. Enable it below to automatically monitor your application. It will detect performance anomalies, and includes powerful analytics tools to help you diagnose issues and to understand what users actually do with your app. Learn more ☐

Application Insights

Enable Application Insights *   ○ No ⦿ Yes

Application Insights * | handsonbookai (West Europe)   ∨ |
                                    Create new

Region   West Europe

Figure 16.5 – Enabling Application Insights during function app creation

> **Note**
>
> Application Insights integration can be also enabled on a function app after it is created.

To confirm that integration is enabled, you can go to your function app and select the **Application Insights** blade, which will take you to the following screen:

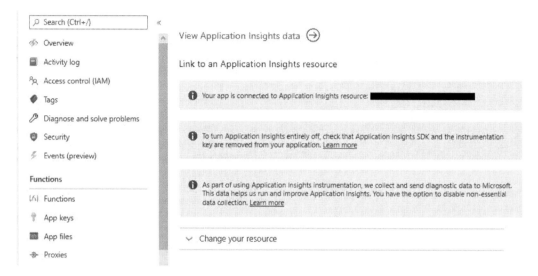

Figure 16.6 – Application Insights tab in Azure Functions

This screen allows you to also change the instance of Application Insights attached to your function app.

With some basics of different platform integration covered, let's now switch to more advanced topics of querying and filtering gathered data.

Using the Logs module

Multiple ways to integrate Azure Application Insights with different services (as well as a custom application) is not the only big feature of this service. Another important and crucial thing is the analytics language available in the Logs module. This is an interactive query language that enables you to explore logged data easily, using a simple and intuitive syntax. Another great thing about it is that you do not need any additional tools to get started—once you store traces, exceptions, or requests, it is available out of the box, and the only thing you need to do is write a query. In this section, we will cover both the query language and the module so that you can start writing your own queries and discover many different dimensions available in stored logs.

Accessing the Logs module

Getting started with the Logs module is easy. Go to the **Overview** blade of your instance of Azure Application Insights and click on the **Logs** button, as highlighted in the following screenshot:

Figure 16.7 – Logs module in the Overview blade

This will display another window showing new options, such as the ability to enter a query, use a pre-defined one, or simply explore the different dimensions available, as illustrated in the following screenshot:

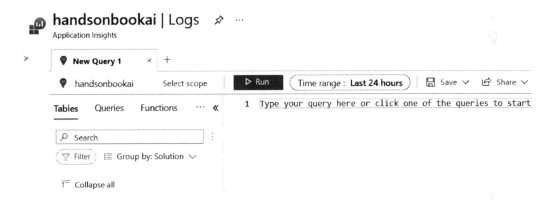

Figure 16.8 – Logs module main window view

Note that if you are accessing that feature for the first time, it will display an additional window with a list of sample queries you can run.

The most important thing here is the query window. This is an interactive feature that enables you to write a query and offers you additional capabilities, such as a syntax validator and suggestions. Let's start with a simple query that displays request counts over the last few days, as follows:

```
requests
| summarize totalCount=sum(itemCount) by bin(timestamp, 30m)
| render timechart
```

As you can see, it has the following three parts:

- `requests`: The dimension you are querying

- `summarize`: A function that defines what you want to get from the dimension

- `render`: An optional function that draws a chart based on the data

Of course, queries can have different structures; you can find one that is a bit more complicated, such as the following:

```
requests
| summarize RequestsCount=sum(itemCount),
AverageDuration=avg(duration), percentiles(duration, 50, 95,
99) by operation_Name
| order by RequestsCount desc
```

As here we are not using the `render` function, there will be no chart—instead, it will display a standard table containing all the available columns. The important thing is the date range for a query, as inside it, you can just filter data. You must select which dates you are interested in. To do so, click on the **Time range** button, next to the **Run** button, and choose the right option from the ones shown here:

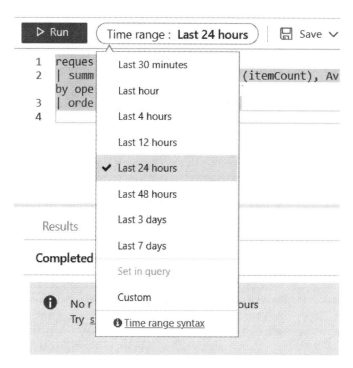

Figure 16.9 – Selecting a time range

> **Note**
> The query language in the Azure Application Logs module is very rich as it defines many different functions for different data types and actions (you can use many different window functions—for example, next()). The relevant reference can be found in the *Further reading* section.

Additionally, you have access to multiple dimensions that contain different data depending on their category or source, as shown in the following screenshot:

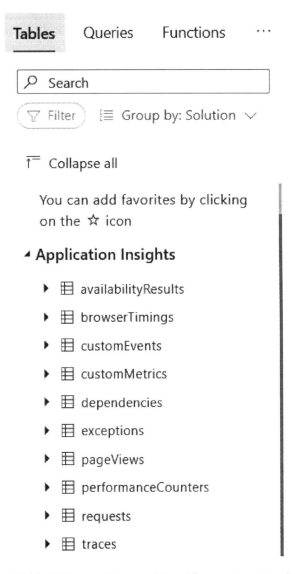

Figure 16.10 – Different tables containing different categories of data

Note that the query syntax and interface are in fact the same as in Azure Monitor. Thanks to that, you do not need to learn another tool to work with your logs across different services and applications.

Let's now switch our focus to the last topic of this chapter, where we will discuss ways to automate things such as alerting in Application Insights.

Automating Azure Application Insights

Monitoring is not something you like to spend time on daily. In fact, the more automated the service is, the better results you can get. It is always easier to let the machine look at different dimensions and find problems based on some preset rules; it will do this quicker and more carefully. In Azure Application Insights, you have many options when it comes to automation: **Azure Resource Manager (ARM)** templates, alerts in the portal, or integrating external services (such as Power Automate). In the last section of this chapter, you will learn how to get started with automation and make sure you focus on development, instead of log analysis and service maintenance. For more information about ARM templates, take a look at *Chapter 25, Tips and Tricks in Azure*, where we are going to discuss that functionality a little bit more.

Alerts

An alert is a feature that enables you to be notified when an anomaly occurs. There are plenty of different possibilities when it comes to setting up an alert, starting with an ARM template. You can see an illustration of this in the following code snippet:

```
{
  "type": "Microsoft.Insights/alertrules",
  "apiVersion": "2016-03-01",
  "name": "string",
  "location": "string",
  "tags": {
    "tagName1": "tagValue1",
    "tagName2": "tagValue2"
  },
  "properties": {
    "action": {
      "odata.type": "string"      },
    "actions": [
      {
        "odata.type": "string"
      }
```

```
    ],
    "condition": {
      "dataSource": {
        "legacyResourceId": "string",
        "metricNamespace": "string",
        "resourceLocation": "string",
        "resourceUri": "string",
        "odata.type": "string"
      },
      "odata.type": "string"
    },
    "description": "string",
    "isEnabled": "bool",
    "name": "string",
    "provisioningState": "string"
  }
}
```

While initially, such an ARM template may be a little bit overwhelming, it can be easily understood when an existing alert is in place. To make things a little bit easier to understand, let's check how to set an alert inside a portal. You can access the **Alerts** blade in the **Monitoring** section, as illustrated in the following screenshot:

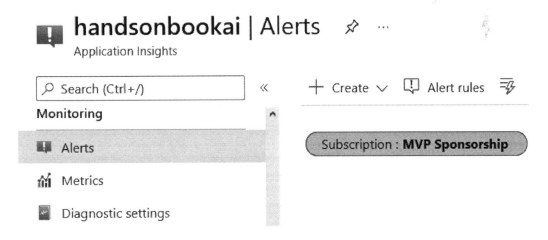

Figure 16.11 – Alerts blade

To get started, you need to click on the + **Create** button and select **Alert rules**. What you will see is a detailed wizard, providing a quick way to set up an alert. The first step, shown here, is selecting a signal:

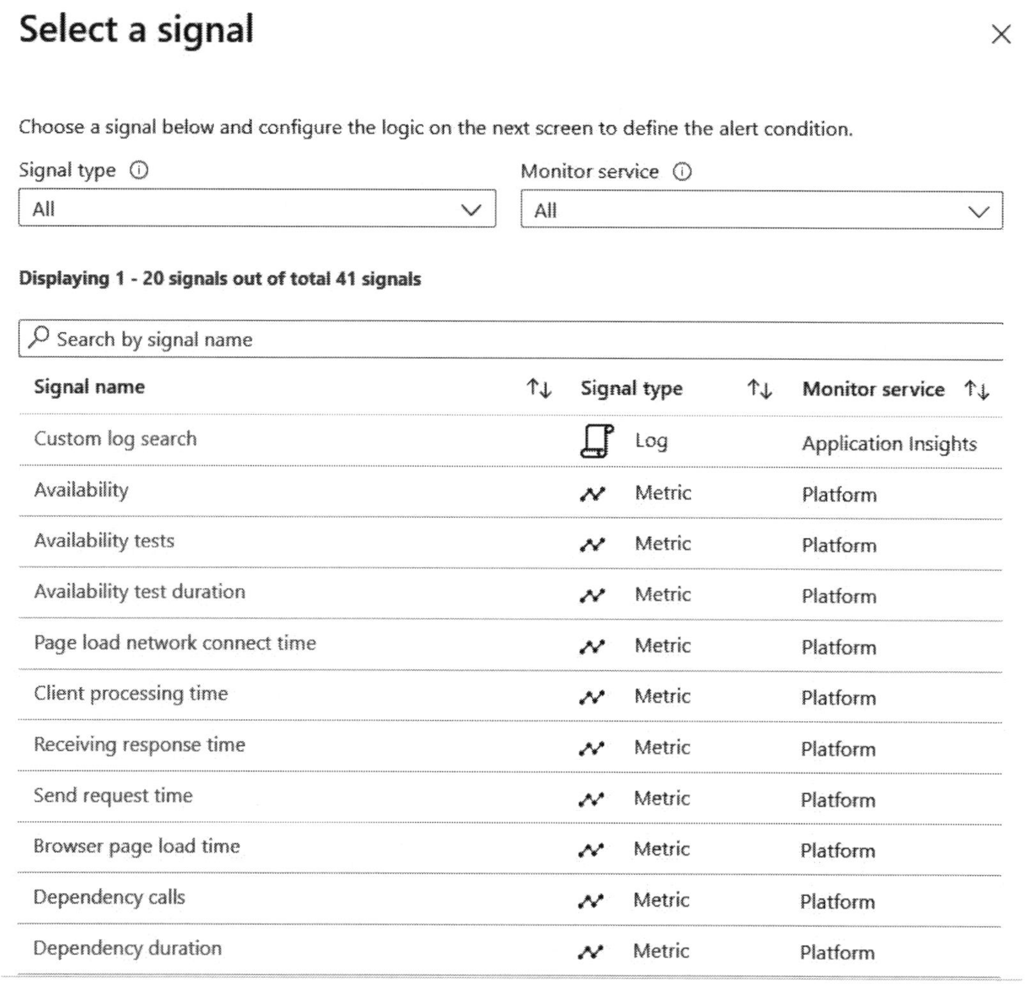

Select a signal   ✕

Choose a signal below and configure the logic on the next screen to define the alert condition.

Signal type ⓘ

| All | ∨ |

Monitor service ⓘ

| All | ∨ |

Displaying 1 - 20 signals out of total 41 signals

🔍 Search by signal name

Signal name ↑↓	Signal type ↑↓	Monitor service ↑↓
Custom log search	📜 Log	Application Insights
Availability	∿ Metric	Platform
Availability tests	∿ Metric	Platform
Availability test duration	∿ Metric	Platform
Page load network connect time	∿ Metric	Platform
Client processing time	∿ Metric	Platform
Receiving response time	∿ Metric	Platform
Send request time	∿ Metric	Platform
Browser page load time	∿ Metric	Platform
Dependency calls	∿ Metric	Platform
Dependency duration	∿ Metric	Platform

Figure 16.12 – Selecting a signal

Once a signal is selected, you need to configure its logic—define its threshold and conditions, as illustrated in the following screenshot:

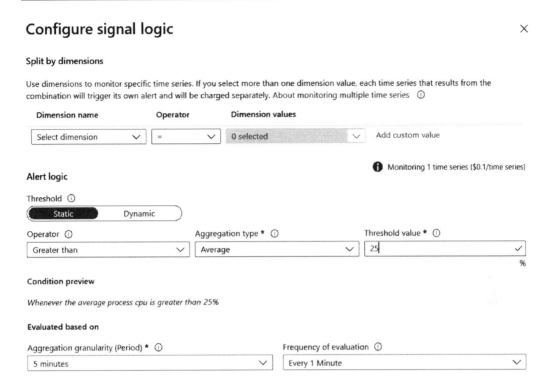

Figure 16.13 – Configuring a signal

Once all conditions are configured, we can continue setting up an alert with defining actions to be taken.

> **Note**
> An alert can be triggered by multiple different conditions. Once one condition is defined, you can add another for it.

Actions can be added directly from the **Actions** tab by clicking on the + **Add action groups** button, as illustrated in the following screenshot:

Create an alert rule ⋯

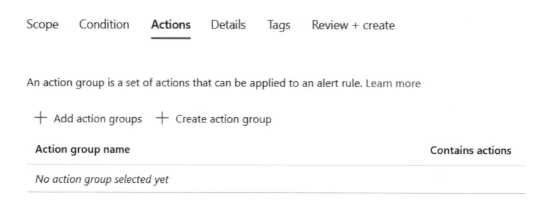

Figure 16.14 – Actions tab

Of course, if you do not have an action group, a new one needs to be created. By default, you have access to one action group created automatically by your Application Insights instance, as we can see here:

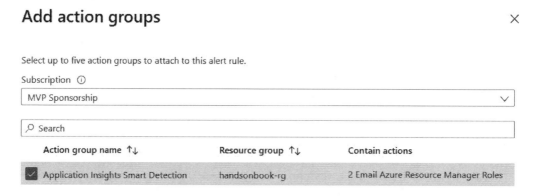

Figure 16.15 – Adding an action group

With the action group selected, the last thing left is defining the characteristics of an alert in the **Details** tab. The following screenshot shows how to do this:

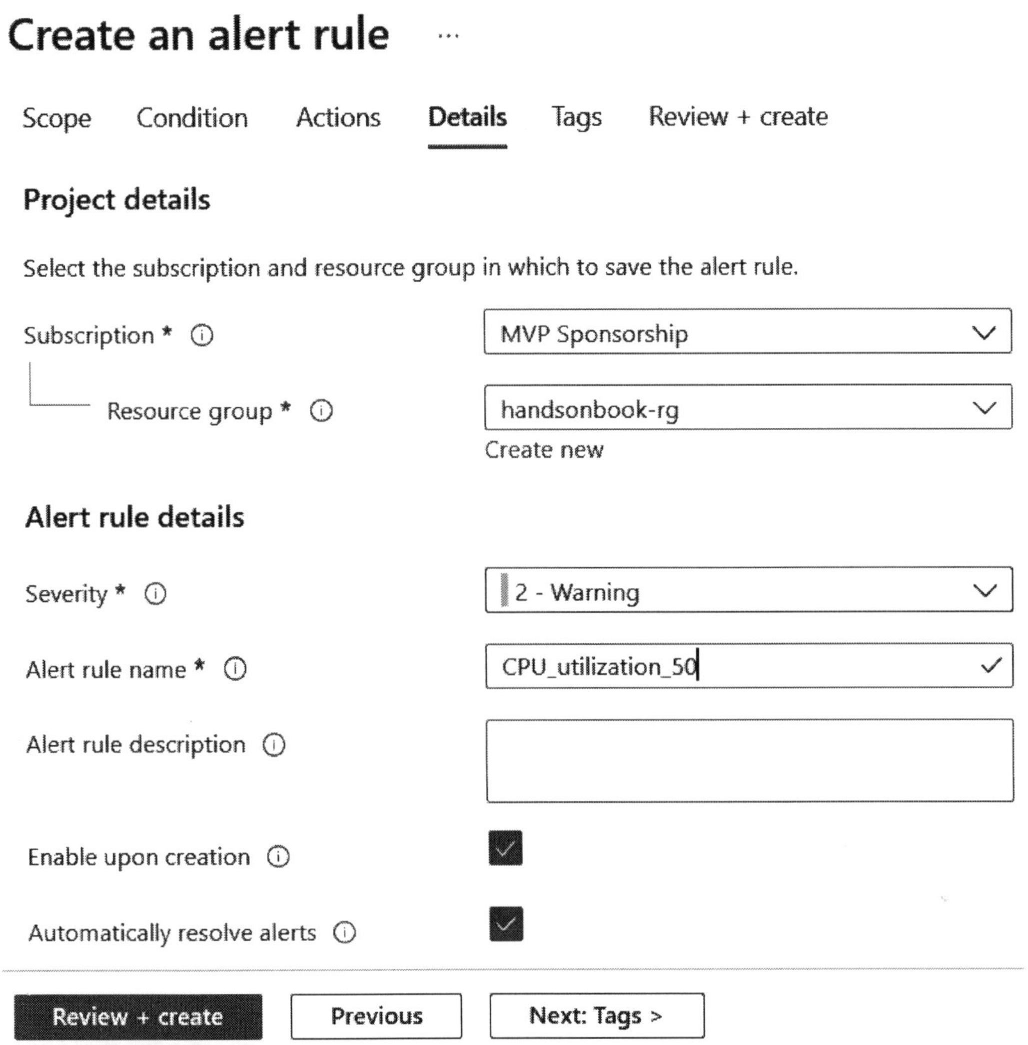

Create an alert rule ...

Scope   Condition   Actions   **Details**   Tags   Review + create

Project details

Select the subscription and resource group in which to save the alert rule.

Subscription * ⓘ

| MVP Sponsorship | ⌄ |

Resource group * ⓘ

| handsonbook-rg | ⌄ |

Create new

Alert rule details

Severity * ⓘ

| 2 - Warning | ⌄ |

Alert rule name * ⓘ

| CPU_utilization_50 | ✓ |

Alert rule description ⓘ

Enable upon creation ⓘ   ☑

Automatically resolve alerts ⓘ   ☑

[Review + create]   [Previous]   [Next: Tags >]

Figure 16.16 – Defining details of an alert

Now, when you click the **Review + create** button and confirm creation, an alert rule will be created. From now on, anytime your metrics reach the alert's threshold, an alert will be triggered.

Summary

In this chapter, you learned about a monitoring solution available for Azure: Azure Application Insights. We covered things such as provisioning a resource, creating an alert, and integrating with other services. This Azure component offers many additional features besides those mentioned in the chapter—there are things such as smart detection, continuous export of data, and detailed usage logs. I strongly encourage you to explore this further on your own, as it greatly simplifies monitoring activities and resolving issues. In the next chapter, we will cover the last Azure service within the scope of this book: Azure SQL, which is a **platform as a service** (**PaaS**), being an Azure version of the well-known database engine.

Questions

Here are some questions to test your knowledge of the important topics in this chapter:

1. What is needed to identify an Azure Application Insights instance and connect to it?
2. Is it possible to use Azure Application Insights inside a Node.js application?
3. How can you query logs stored inside Azure Application Insights?
4. How can you automate creating alerts in the service?
5. Is it possible to use **Short Message Service** (**SMS**) as an action for a triggered alert?

Further reading

For more information, refer to the following sources:

*   TelemetryClient reference: `https://docs.microsoft.com/en-us/dotnet/api/microsoft.applicationinsights.telemetryclient?view=azure-dotnet`
*   Smart Detection: `https://docs.microsoft.com/en-us/azure/azure-monitor/alerts/proactive-diagnostics`
*   Resource Explorer: `https://resources.azure.com/`
*   Sampling in Application Insights: `https://docs.microsoft.com/en-us/azure/azure-monitor/app/sampling`

17

SQL in Azure – Azure SQL

Microsoft SQL Server is one of the most popular databases and is often the core of many popular applications. Thanks to Azure, we can skip the whole cluster setup, installation, and maintenance by using Azure SQL—a cloud version of SQL Server with the same features available. Thanks to flexible pricing, we can select whichever option we want when it comes to both performance and available features. We don't have to worry about geo-replication and storing backups either—all these functionalities can be easily configured and automated in the cloud.

By the end of the chapter, you will have gained fundamental knowledge regarding working with Azure SQL in Azure and learned various built-in features of that service.

The following topics will be covered in this chapter:

- Differences between Microsoft SQL Server and Azure SQL
- Creating and configuring an Azure SQL Database instance
- Working with Azure SQL in the Azure portal
- Security features of Azure SQL
- Scaling Azure SQL
- Monitoring and tuning

Technical requirements

To perform the exercises in this chapter, you will need the following:

- An Azure subscription

Differences between Microsoft SQL Server and Azure SQL

Microsoft SQL Server is a well-known and widely used **Structured Query Language** (**SQL**) database server that has gained much popularity and is considered a default choice for many projects, ranging from very simple websites to enterprise-class services that handle high load and are considered critical for a business. As cloud technologies gain more and more popularity, the natural consequence of such a situation is the expectation that by moving an application to Azure, it is also possible to move its database. To meet such needs, Microsoft has developed Azure SQL Service—a **platform-as-a-service** (**PaaS**) version of Microsoft SQL Server that is managed and upgraded by their teams; the only things you are responsible for are configuration and data management. There is also one more offering from Azure called **SQL Server VMs**, which is one more option for using this database in the cloud. In this section, we will focus on the differences between these two offerings and try to identify different use cases for them.

Azure SQL fundamentals

By using PaaS services in the cloud, you are shifting responsibilities a little bit, in the following ways:

- You are no longer the maintainer of the infrastructure.
- You are no longer responsible for different updates when software is considered.
- By signing a **service-level agreement** (**SLA**) with you, your provider is responsible for making sure that a service is up and running.

Instead, you should focus on the following points:

- Properly configuring a service so that it meets your performance targets and legal requirements
- Integrating different services and applications so that they reflect best practices when it comes to communicating with a service
- Implementing **high availability** (**HA**)/**disaster recovery** (**DR**) scenarios so that an outage or disaster in one region does not impact your systems

By using Microsoft SQL Server, you are fully on your/leased machines, which you must maintain and monitor. While such a case is valid in many scenarios (as there can be some legal requirements that disallow you from storing data outside your own data center or, simply, for some reason, Azure does not provide you with the expected performance you seek), yet in many situations, having a PaaS instance of your SQL database is a big improvement. In fact, you are given a few different options when using this service, including the following:

- A single database with isolated resources

- A pooled database in an elastic pool

- A managed instance, which is the closest model when it comes to comparing it with on-premises SQL Server

The important thing to know is that all new features and updates are deployed to SQL databases hosted within Azure. This gives you an advantage in comparison with traditional Microsoft SQL Server, as you are always up to date: you do not have to schedule updates on your servers on your own.

> **Tip**
>
> The more servers and databases you have, the more complicated and difficult the process of updating them becomes. Take that into account when comparing these two offerings.

Another crucial thing when talking about Azure SQL is its purchasing model. Currently, you have three options, as follows:

- **Database transaction unit (DTU)-based (provisioned)**: A DTU is a mix of computing, memory, and **input/output (I/O)** resources that are given to your database.

- **Virtual core (vCore)-based (serverless)**: A similar model to the provisioned one, it provides auto-scaling and billing per second based on vCores used.

- **vCore-based (provisioned)**: This one simply allows you to select all things on your own (including the number of vCores, the amount of memory, and storage performance).

You may wonder how a DTU reflects the actual hardware; there is a good article that tries to explain these metrics a little bit in the *Further reading* section of this chapter.

> **Tip**
>
> In most cases, using a DTU as the metric is the better choice—very often, it is hard to predict the exact hardware requirements for your application. Use the vCore-based model when you are an advanced SQL Server user and know how many cores or memory you really need.

You may be wondering what the scaling capabilities of Azure SQL Service are. While of course, you can assign more (or fewer) resources to your database, there are scenarios when this makes things much more complicated (or, simply, your application has different demands when it comes to database performance, and such a model simply will not work). To cover those situations, you are given the option to use elastic pools. The concept is simple—normally, you allocate resources to a single database, as depicted in the following screenshot:

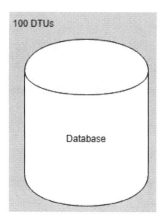

Figure 17.1 – Single database with 100 DTUs assigned

With elastic pools, you change the model a little bit and instead, your pool has resources allocated, as follows:

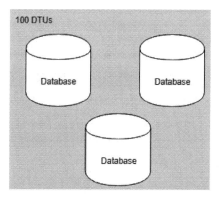

Figure 17.2 – Multiple databases using a single pool

What effect does this change have? Well, this gives you much more flexibility; instead of hosting a huge single database (when it comes to resources allocated), you can easily scale it out so that it can share the load with other instances. What is more, it gives you better control when it comes to costs; you can scale your databases at the same time without the need to control what their individual requirements are.

> **Important Note**
> Scaling Azure SQL is an important topic that initially requires much attention—we will come back to this at the end of this chapter.

Besides performance and different scaling capabilities, Azure SQL gives you many additional features that are very important when considering it as storage for your data. Because an application without information stored in a database is, in most cases, useless, availability considerations are also very important here. Fortunately, Azure SQL has implemented many great features that make it a full-fledged storage option, such as the following:

- **Automatic backups**: In the on-premises world, configuring and managing backups is much more complicated, as it requires you to know the server configuration and find a place to store them. In Azure, things are greatly simplified by integrating automatic backups for Azure Storage for performance and reliability.

- **Geo-replication**: Even if a single region fails, you can still serve data to your customers. With Azure SQL, you can configure a secondary read region that will make sure you can stay online until an outage is resolved.

- **Failover groups**: Instead of implementing failover capabilities and logic on your own, you can rely on what Azure SQL currently provides. This makes creating globally distributed applications much easier as you care only about the configuration and not infrastructure.

> Tip
>
> To know exactly what is different in Azure SQL in comparison with Microsoft SQL Server, refer to the following link:
>
> `https://docs.microsoft.com/en-us/azure/sql-database/sql-database-features`

After that very short introduction to the basic features of Azure SQL, let's now check more advanced topics.

Advanced Azure SQL features

Besides some basic functionalities that ensure Azure SQL is a full version of a relational database on which you can rely and build your system, there are plenty of additional features that make using this service real fun, such as the following:

- **Automatic monitoring and tuning**: How many times, after using a database for several months, have you ended up with a database full of outdated indexes, procedures, and functions? Azure SQL makes things much easier by actively monitoring how you use and maintain your database and advising you whenever an improvement is possible. I find this feature extremely helpful—nowadays, when development is especially rapid and focused on delivering new values to the market, it is easy to get lost and lose track of what should be removed from a database. With the service recommendations for dropping indexes, schema improvements, and query parameterization, I find my storage in much better shape most of the time.

- **Adaptive query processing**: While this feature is also available for SQL Server, having it in Azure SQL is a great addition to other performance recommendations. Basically, when it is enabled, the server engine tries to find the best execution plan for your queries.

- **Security and compliance features**: It is really important to ensure that the data you store is secure and all vulnerabilities are detected as quickly as possible. In Azure SQL, you are given plenty of additional features that try to analyze your data in terms of sensitivity and compliance. There are built-in tools that search for any kinds of anomalies and threats that could affect data integrity or lead to their leak. Additionally, Azure SQL is integrated with the **Azure Active Directory** (**Azure AD**) service and allows for **multi-factor authentication** (**MFA**)—this makes things such as auditing and authorization much easier without additional effort.

> **Note**
>
> The security features for Azure SQL will be described later in this chapter so that you have a whole picture of this service's capabilities that matter.

Let's now learn more about using an alternative SQL service, leveraging SQL Server installed on an Azure **virtual machine** (**VM**).

SQL Server on VMs

If you do not want to go full PaaS, you can create a VM with a SQL Server image already built in. In that option, the performance of the service will rely on the performance of the VM—if you find the database running low on the **central processing unit** (**CPU**) or memory, the only thing you must do is scale up the machine. To create a VM in the portal, search for a SQL Server running on an **operating system** (**OS**) of your choice, as follows:

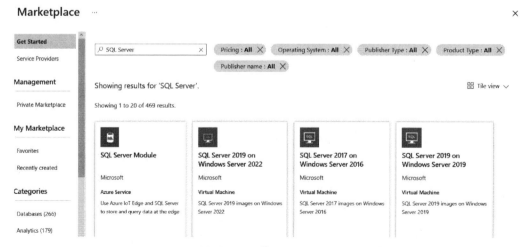

Figure 17.3 – SQL Server offering in Azure Marketplace

By browsing available versions, you will see there are free SQL Server licenses available, and what is more, newer versions can run on Linux machines. Once you select the image you are interested in, you can click on the **Create** button to begin the machine's configuration.

As you can see in the following screenshot, many fields must be filled in to be able to use the service:

Basics   Disks   Networking   Management   Advanced   SQL Server settings   Tags   Review + create

Create a virtual machine that runs Linux or Windows. Select an image from Azure marketplace or use your own customized image. Complete the Basics tab then Review + create to provision a virtual machine with default parameters or review each tab for full customization. Learn more ☐

Project details

Select the subscription to manage deployed resources and costs. Use resource groups like folders to organize and manage all your resources.

Subscription * ⓘ	MVP Sponsorship ▾
└ Resource group * ⓘ	handsonbook-rg ▾
	Create new

Instance details

Virtual machine name * ⓘ	handson-sql-vm ✓
Region * ⓘ	(Europe) West Europe ▾
Availability options ⓘ	No infrastructure redundancy required ▾
Security type ⓘ	Standard ▾
Image * ⓘ	▨ {BYOL} SQL Server 2017 Standard on Windows Server 2019 - Gen1 ▾
	See all images| Configure VM generation
Azure Spot instance ⓘ	☐
Size * ⓘ	Standard_D2s_v3 - 2 vcpus, 8 GiB memory (€130.51/month) ▾
	See all sizes

Figure 17.4 – Details of Azure VM with SQL Server image

This is, of course, related to the **infrastructure-as-a-service** (**IaaS**) model of that way of hosting SQL Server inside Azure. The configuration wizard will advise you about the default size of the VM and other parameters required for the machine. Once the configuration is completed, you will be able to connect to it either via **Remote Desktop Protocol** (**RDP**) or a secured **Secure Shell** (**SSH**) tunnel.

> **Tip**
> Remember to open port 1433 if you want to connect to SQL Server remotely.

Let's now see how we can create and configure an Azure SQL database.

Creating and configuring an Azure SQL Database instance

After reading the beginning of this chapter, you should have a sense of how Azure SQL works and what it offers you. While some theory is always a good thing, it is practice that creates a full picture and allows you to fully understand the topic. In this section, we will focus on creating and configuring an Azure SQL database in the portal and trying to identify all the aforementioned features. You will also see how managing this PaaS service is different from the on-premises version, especially when it comes to using its features.

Creating an Azure SQL Database instance

In the Azure portal, when you search for `Azure SQL`, you will see plenty of different options such as **SQL Database**, **SQL server (logical server)**, or **SQL Elastic database pool**. While they all allow you to create a database, the easiest way to get started with the service is to use **SQL Database**—this will require creating a server, nonetheless. In the following screenshot, you can find a configuration for my server:

Create SQL Database Server ...
Microsoft

Server details

Enter required settings for this server, including providing a name and location. This server will be created in the same subscription and resource group as your database.

Server name *	handsonazure-sql-server ✓
	.database.windows.net
Location *	(Europe) West Europe ✓

Authentication

Select your preferred authentication methods for accessing this server. Create a server admin login and password to access your server with SQL authentication, select only Azure AD authentication Learn more ☑ using an existing Azure AD user, group, or application as Azure AD admin Learn more ☑, or select both SQL and Azure AD authentication.

Authentication method	⦿ Use SQL authentication
	○ Use only Azure Active Directory (Azure AD) authentication
	○ Use both SQL and Azure AD authentication
Server admin login *	handson ✓
Password *	·········· ✓
Confirm password *	·········· ✓

Figure 17.5 – SQL database server configuration

The following screenshot shows the configuration for my database:

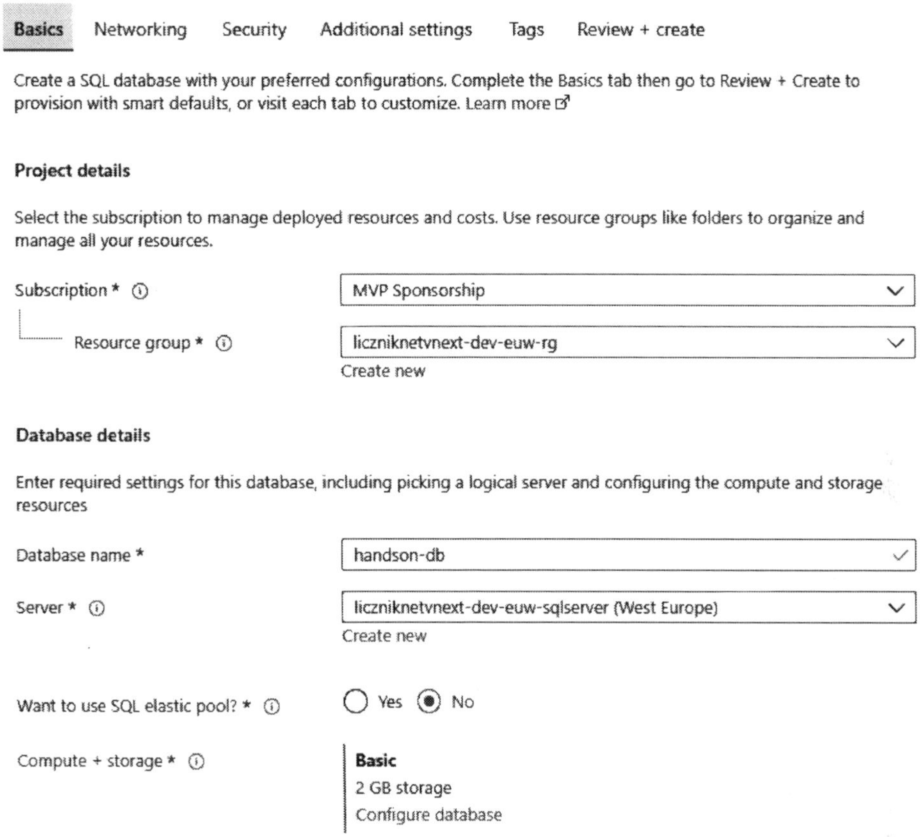

| Basics | Networking | Security | Additional settings | Tags | Review + create |

Create a SQL database with your preferred configurations. Complete the Basics tab then go to Review + Create to provision with smart defaults, or visit each tab to customize. Learn more ☐'

Project details

Select the subscription to manage deployed resources and costs. Use resource groups like folders to organize and manage all your resources.

Subscription * ⓘ   MVP Sponsorship

Resource group * ⓘ   liczniknetvnext-dev-euw-rg
                               Create new

Database details

Enter required settings for this database, including picking a logical server and configuring the compute and storage resources

Database name *   handson-db

Server * ⓘ   liczniknetvnext-dev-euw-sqlserver (West Europe)
                               Create new

Want to use SQL elastic pool? * ⓘ   ○ Yes   ● No

Compute + storage * ⓘ   **Basic**
                               2 GB storage
                               Configure database

Figure 17.6 – SQL database configuration

Let's click on **Configure database** and see what are our options for setting up pricing.

For now, we can skip the **Networking** and **Security** tabs and go directly to **Additional settings**. The important thing here is to select the source—you have three options here, as follows:

- **None**: In most cases, this will be the first option you are interested in
- **Sample**: This will create a sample database called AdventureWorksLT with example data
- **Backup**: A great option if you want to provision a database from an available backup

For the **Blank database** option, you will also have the possibility to select a collation; in that dropdown, select the option that is correct for your data. We will also focus a little bit on the pricing configuration, as shown in the following screenshot:

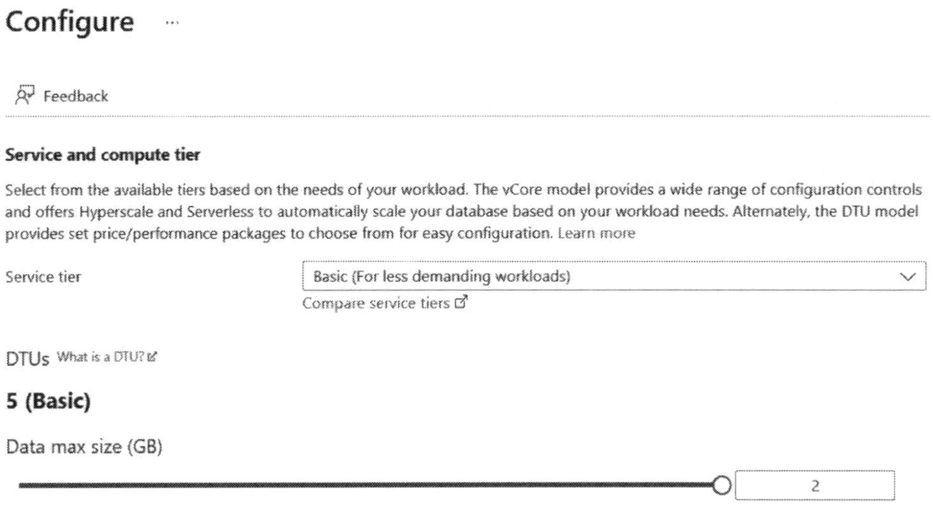

Configure   ...

⟨ Feedback

Service and compute tier

Select from the available tiers based on the needs of your workload. The vCore model provides a wide range of configuration controls and offers Hyperscale and Serverless to automatically scale your database based on your workload needs. Alternately, the DTU model provides set price/performance packages to choose from for easy configuration. Learn more

Service tier   Basic (For less demanding workloads)   ∨

Compare service tiers ⧉

DTUs What is a DTU? ⧉

5 (Basic)

Data max size (GB)

○─── 2

Figure 17.7 – Pricing configuration

As you can see, when using the DTU-based purchasing model, you decide on how many DTUs and the database size you need (for the **Basic** tier, there is no slider for DTU selection). In general, you have available three different tiers, as follows:

- **Basic**: For smaller workloads
- **Standard**: This offers the best balance between cost and performance
- **Premium**: For all workloads that require massive performance capabilities

Depending on the tier, you will be offered either a fixed DTU amount (for **Basic**) or you will have to select the amount you are interested in, as illustrated in the following screenshot:

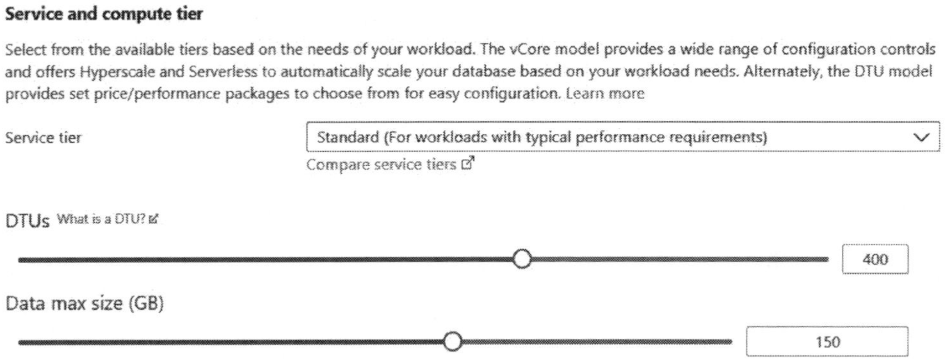

Service and compute tier

Select from the available tiers based on the needs of your workload. The vCore model provides a wide range of configuration controls and offers Hyperscale and Serverless to automatically scale your database based on your workload needs. Alternately, the DTU model provides set price/performance packages to choose from for easy configuration. Learn more

Service tier   Standard (For workloads with typical performance requirements)   ∨

Compare service tiers ⧉

DTUs What is a DTU? ⧉

───────────────────────────────○─────────────── 400

Data max size (GB)

─────────────────────○───────────────────────── 150

Figure 17.8 – DTU and database size selection

> **Tip**
>
> The important thing here is the fact that most of your database costs are resource-allocated—remember to select the biggest database size you can (for example, in the **Standard** tier and with 400 DTUs selected, there is no difference in the pricing between 100 **megabytes** (**MB**) and 250 **gigabytes** (**GB**)).

Of course, you can also switch between a DTU-based model and vCores selection, as illustrated here:

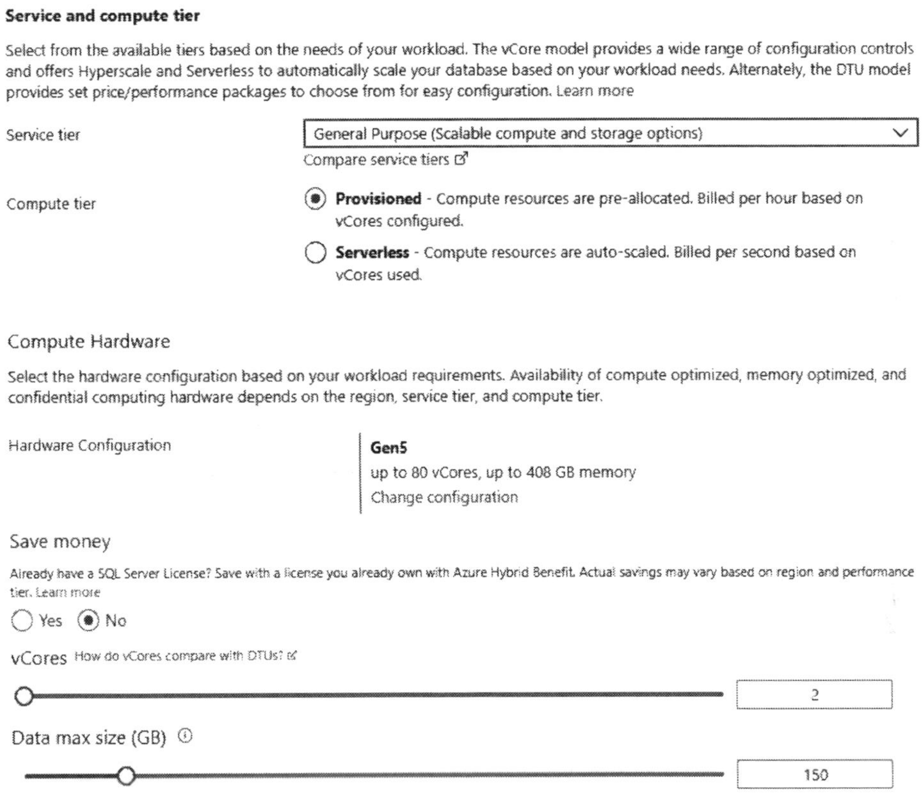

Service and compute tier

Select from the available tiers based on the needs of your workload. The vCore model provides a wide range of configuration controls and offers Hyperscale and Serverless to automatically scale your database based on your workload needs. Alternately, the DTU model provides set price/performance packages to choose from for easy configuration. Learn more

Service tier

> General Purpose (Scalable compute and storage options)   ⌄
>
> Compare service tiers ⌕

Compute tier

> ● **Provisioned** - Compute resources are pre-allocated. Billed per hour based on vCores configured.
>
> ○ **Serverless** - Compute resources are auto-scaled. Billed per second based on vCores used.

Compute Hardware

Select the hardware configuration based on your workload requirements. Availability of compute optimized, memory optimized, and confidential computing hardware depends on the region, service tier, and compute tier.

Hardware Configuration

> **Gen5**
> up to 80 vCores, up to 408 GB memory
> Change configuration

Save money

Already have a SQL Server License? Save with a license you already own with Azure Hybrid Benefit. Actual savings may vary based on region and performance tier. Learn more

○ Yes ● No

vCores How do vCores compare with DTUs? ⌕

> ○———————————————————— | 2 |

Data max size (GB) ⓘ

> ——○———————————————— | 150 |

Figure 17.9 – Database configuration for vCore purchasing model

When using vCores, selecting the **Data max size** option does affect the pricing. What is more, you have three different tiers available here, as follows:

- **General Purpose**: The best choice for most common scenarios without specific needs when it comes to resiliency and traffic

- **Business Critical**: This tier offers better performance and lower latency (and is significantly more expensive)

- **Hyperscale**: Unlimited storage scaling with database size.

When you are satisfied with your configuration, you can click on the **Apply** button to save the configuration and then **Review + Create** so that the provisioning process will start. When it is finished, you can access your resource by going to the **Overview** blade where basic information is available, as illustrated in the following screenshot:

Figure 17.10 – New SQL database Overview blade

We will now try to go through most of the features so that you have a better understanding of how to work with this service.

Azure SQL features in the portal

We will start with the **Compute + storage** blade—when you click on this, you will see that it allows you to set both the tier and the pricing model of your database. This option is especially helpful when you want to improve the performance of your database; you can easily change the amount of DTUs or vCores allocated for it, so it can work with queries much quicker.

> **Tip**
> As I mentioned before, configuring a single database will work for simpler scenarios, where you can easily monitor it and the performance requirements do not rapidly change. In all other cases, the better option is to use elastic pools.

When you go to the **Replicas** blade, you will see a screen where is possible to create a new geo replica. This feature is especially helpful if you need to secure your database from regional failures and aim for HA. You can see what this screen looks like here:

Figure 17.11 – Replicas screen

From this screen, you can quickly create a secondary region that allows you to perform a failover when you need it. To do so, click on the **Create replica** button, which will display the following screen:

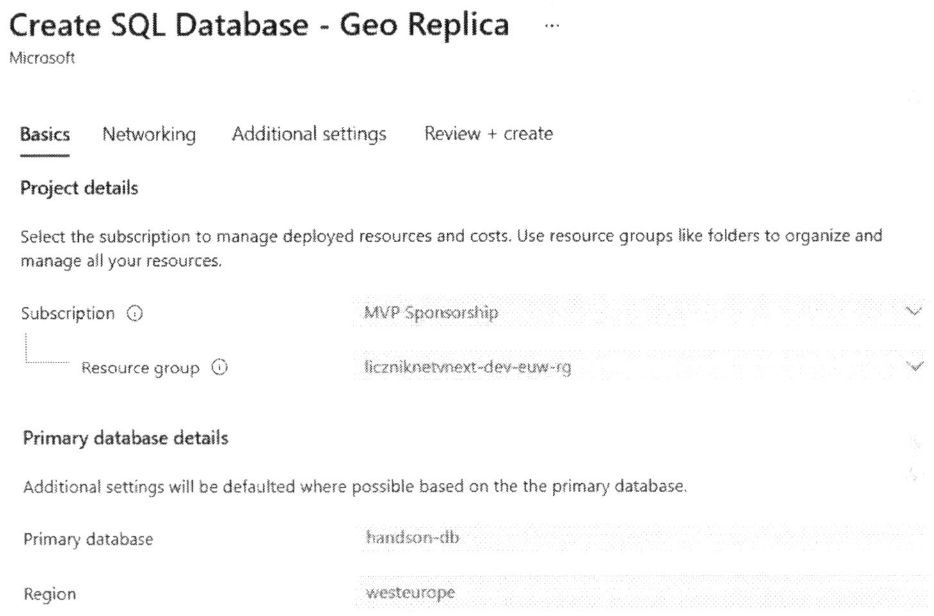

Create SQL Database - Geo Replica
Microsoft

Basics   Networking   Additional settings   Review + create

Project details

Select the subscription to manage deployed resources and costs. Use resource groups like folders to organize and manage all your resources.

Subscription ⓘ   MVP Sponsorship

    Resource group ⓘ   liczniknetvnext-dev-euw-rg

Primary database details

Additional settings will be defaulted where possible based on the the primary database.

Primary database   handson-db

Region   westeurope

Figure 17.12 – Creating a new replica

Note that most of the fields are grayed out and disabled. This is because they are used only for information purposes. What you need is to enter replica details in the **Database details** section, as follows:

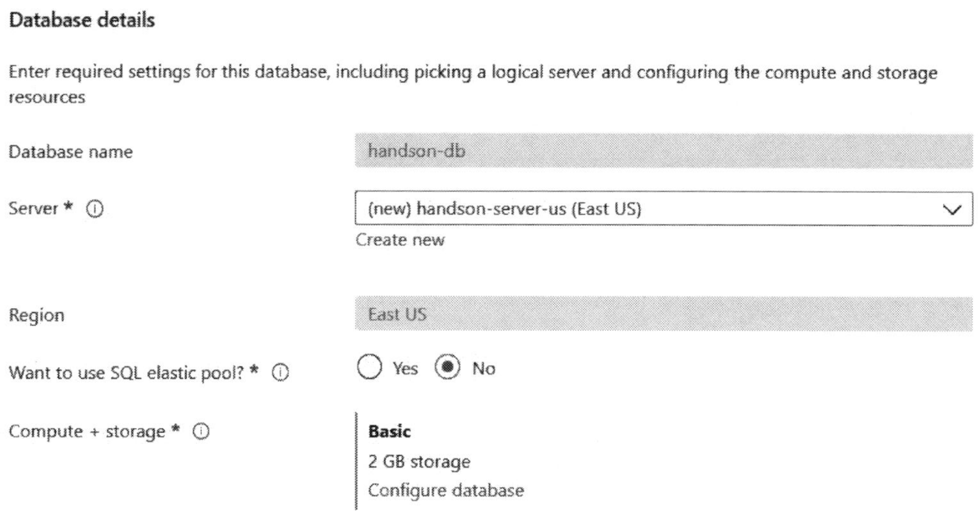

Database details

Enter required settings for this database, including picking a logical server and configuring the compute and storage resources

Database name	handson-db
Server * ⓘ	(new) handson-server-us (East US) ⌄
	Create new
Region	East US
Want to use SQL elastic pool? * ⓘ	◯ Yes ⦿ No
Compute + storage * ⓘ	**Basic** 2 GB storage Configure database

Figure 17.13 – Entering replica details

As you can see, creating a replica will create a new database attached to an additional SQL Server instance managed by Azure. Both replica and primary databases can differ in size and performance.

> **Note**
> The database size for the replica and its performance depend on your replication model. If the replica is served as a passive component, it can be less performant than the primary one. However, in an active-active model, all databases should guarantee the same level of performance.

Once a replica is created, you should see a similar view to mine here:

Name ↑↓	Server ↑↓	Region ↑↓	Failover policy ↑↓	Pricing tier ↑↓	Replica state ↑↓
⌄ **Primary**					
handson-db	liczniknetvnext-dev-euw⋯	West Europe	None	Basic	Online
⌄ **Geo replicas**					
handson-db	handson-server-us	East US		Basic	Readable

Figure 17.14 – Primary database with replica

Now, if you proceed to the **Connection strings** blade, you will see a template for a connection string for different environments, as follows:

Figure 17.15 – Connection string for Azure SQL Database

You will also be able to download different drivers for **ADO.NET**, **JDBC**, **ODBC**, or **PHP**.

> **Note**
> Remember that the service presents only a template for your connection string—you will have to set your username and password to make it work.

Currently, we are exploring a SQL database in Azure—let's check exactly what SQL Server looks like currently. You can find this out by clicking on the server's name on the **Overview** blade. Initially, the screen will look the same, but you will quickly realize that it offers many different features, as we can see here:

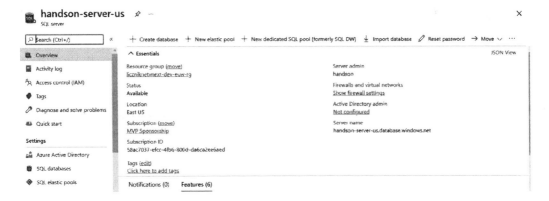

Figure 17.16 – Azure SQL Server overview

Unfortunately, we will not be able to go through all the features, but I will try to describe most of them for you. When we look at the features on the left, we will see the following blades:

- **Failover groups**: To introduce automatic failover, you must create a failover group. A group consists of a primary and secondary server that have a defined failover policy and grace period—a setting that defines the time between outage detection and the actual failover.

- **Backups**: To configure backups for your server (for example, to enable **long-term retention (LTR)**), you can access this blade. It also displays all available backups.

- **Azure Active Directory**: It is possible to set an admin for your server using a user which is defined within your AD users. Of course, you can set more than a single user for that—the trick is to use a group instead of an individual account.

- **SQL databases**: To quickly access a database that is served by this server, use this blade.

- **SQL elastic pools**: Similarly to **SQL databases**, this blade displays available elastic pools. To create a new pool, go to the **Overview** blade and click on the + **New elastic pool** button.

- **Deleted databases**: Even if a database is removed from a service, you will still have a chance to restore it. In such a scenario, consult this blade for all databases available to be restored.

- **Import/Export history**: All import and export operations on your databases will be displayed here. This is a great auditing tool, so you will not miss a situation when somebody exported your data without notice.

- **DTU quota**: If you are interested in seeing the quota of DTUs/vCores for your server, you can access this blade.

As you can see, many functionalities of Azure SQL are similar to on-premises installations of SQL Server or other databases you may be familiar with. In general, the managed version of SQL Server (called Azure SQL Database) should represent the same look and feel as unmanaged versions. However, there can be bigger differences, such as in security features, which we are about to cover.

Security features of Azure SQL

When it comes to Azure SQL features, there are multiple different options you can use to make your solution secure. Things such as firewalls, full operation auditing, and data encryption are the common capabilities of this service and are available even for the **Basic** tier. In this section, we will focus on learning the aforementioned capabilities so that your instance is secured and immune to most threats.

Firewall

When browsing your SQL database, you probably noticed the **Set server firewall** button that is available on the **Overview** blade, as shown here:

Figure 17.17 – Set server firewall button available on Overview blade of SQL database

This is the easiest way to set a firewall rule that allows traffic to Azure SQL.

> **Note**
>
> In Azure SQL, all traffic is initially rejected—you must whitelist all **Internet Protocol addresses** (**IPs**) of computers that should be allowed to communicate with the server.

Before we start configuring the firewall, you must understand why we really need it. Here is what happens if I try to connect to my server using Microsoft **SQL Server Management Studio** (**SSMS**):

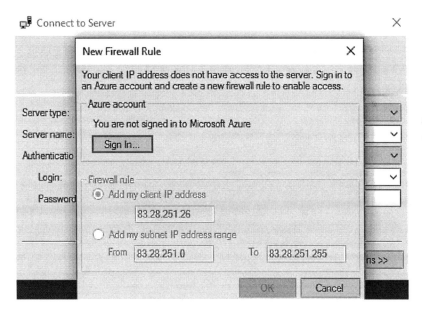

Figure 17.18 – Connecting to Azure SQL Database with no firewall rules applied

As you can see, it automatically detects that my IP is not whitelisted, hence the server refuses to communicate with me. What we need here is to add a particular IP address so that communication will be allowed.

In the portal, you can add the rule by clicking on the **Set server firewall** button—this will then display a screen where you can explicitly set an IP address that should be able to communicate with the server, as illustrated in the following screenshot:

Figure 17.19 – Whitelisting IP address for Azure SQL Server

From this screen, you can also prevent the Azure service from communicating with your instance of Azure SQL. Additionally, you can add a **virtual network** (**VNet**) integration here (using service endpoints/private endpoints). Thanks to that feature, you can create a whole ecosystem with your applications and databases so that they are protected from accessing it with a very strict set of rules.

Microsoft Defender for SQL

Microsoft Defender for SQL is a part of Microsoft Defender for Cloud, which by default is not enabled for your service. Currently, it allows for a free trial of 30 days, during which you can test whether this capability is for you. You can enable it using the **Microsoft Defender for Cloud** blade, as illustrated here:

Figure 17.20 – Accessing Microsoft Defender for SQL

It consists of the following two separate features:

- **Vulnerability Assessment**: A simple solution for discovering, tracking, and remediating database vulnerabilities

- **Advanced Thread Protection**: A feature that actively monitors your database for suspicious activities and logs them for you

Once enabled, it will take care of monitoring your database and verifying operations performed against it.

Data classification

By accessing the **Data Discovery & Classification** blade, you will have access to another Azure SQL functionality that can help you in securing data stored inside your database, as depicted here:

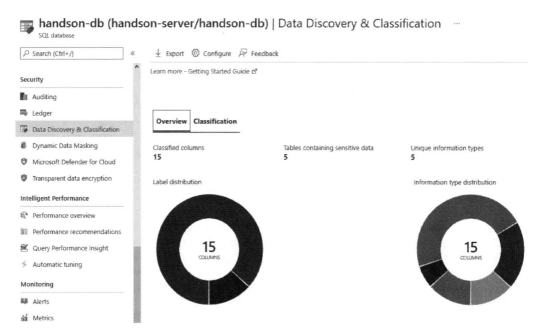

Figure 17.21 – Data classified by Azure SQL

By going to the **Classification** tab, you will see a table that contains all classifications saved by you or another person working with the database, as illustrated in the following screenshot:

Overview   Classification

15 classified columns

Schema: 2 selected ⌄	Table: 5 selected ⌄	Filter by column	Information type: 5 selected ⌄	Sensitivity label: 2 selected ⌄	
Schema	Table	Column	Information type	Sensitivity label	
SalesLT	SalesOrderHeader	TaxAmt	Financial ⌄	Confidential ⌄	🗑
SalesLT	SalesOrderHeader	CreditCardApprovalCode	Credit Card ⌄	Confidential ⌄	🗑
SalesLT	SalesOrderHeader	AccountNumber	Financial ⌄	Confidential ⌄	🗑
SalesLT	CustomerAddress	AddressType	Contact Info ⌄	Confidential ⌄	🗑
SalesLT	Address	PostalCode	Contact Info ⌄	Confidential ⌄	🗑
SalesLT	Address	City	Contact Info ⌄	Confidential ⌄	🗑
SalesLT	Address	AddressLine2	Contact Info ⌄	Confidential ⌄	🗑
SalesLT	Address	AddressLine1	Contact Info ⌄	Confidential ⌄	🗑
dbo	ErrorLog	UserName	Credentials ⌄	Confidential ⌄	🗑
SalesLT	Customer	PasswordSalt	Credentials ⌄	Confidential ⌄	🗑
SalesLT	Customer	PasswordHash	Credentials ⌄	Confidential ⌄	🗑

Figure 17.22 – Classifications added for data inside the database

Azure SQL can automatically detect the data type and declare its sensitivity label. Then, it displays a summary that gives you an overall picture of the shape of the data stored in the database.

> **Tip**
> This feature is a great tool for analyzing big databases for compliance with new regulations—use it when in doubt as to whether you are storing some sensitive data.

Let's now check out the auditing features of Azure SQL.

Auditing

If you want to know exactly what happens inside your server, you must enable auditing. The following screenshot shows how to do this:

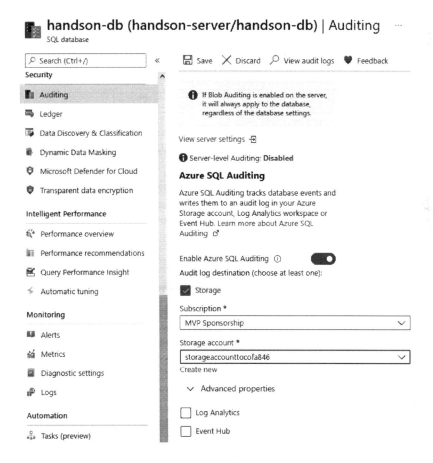

Figure 17.23 – Enabling auditing

This will log all operations within the selected storage (if, of course, you selected the **Storage** option). Currently, there are three different options for storing auditing logs, as follows:

- **Storage**
- **Log Analytics**
- **Event Hub**

While **Storage** is a little bit of a static option, you can use the remaining two for more dynamic integrations (especially when using Azure Event Hubs). Once auditing is enabled, you can see all logged operations as well when you click on the **View audit logs** button, as illustrated in the following screenshot:

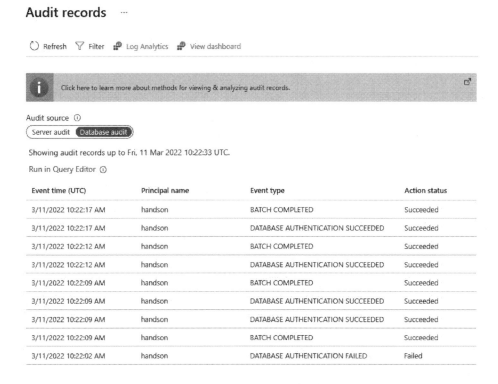

Figure 17.24 – Auditing log of Azure SQL Database

Thanks to integration with external sources, you can easily integrate your database audit with other security tools you are using.

Dynamic Data Masking

Sometimes, you want to allow somebody to read data inside a database, yet at the same time, you do not want them to read more sensitive data (such as birth date, addresses, or surnames). In Azure SQL, there is a feature for that named **Dynamic Data Masking**, as illustrated here:

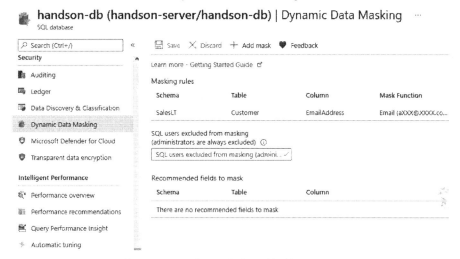

Figure 17.25 – Dynamic Data Masking screen

There are two ways to add a mask—either use the recommendation or click on the + **Add Mask** button to add it manually. The latter option will take you to the following screen:

Figure 17.26 – Adding a masking rule

What you will have to do is select **Schema**, **Table**, **Column**, and **Masking field format** values—once you configure these and save the rule, users who are not administrators will see masked values instead. The following screenshot shows values for an admin:

Title	FirstName	MiddleName	LastName	Suffix	CompanyName	SalesPerson	EmailAddress
Mr.	Orlando	N.	Gee	NULL	A Bike Store	adventure-works\pamela0	orlando0@adventure-works.com
Mr.	Keith	NULL	Harris	NULL	Progressive Sports	adventure-works\david8	keith0@adventure-works.com
Ms.	Donna	F.	Carreras	NULL	Advanced Bike Components	adventure-works\jillian0	donna0@adventure-works.com
Ms.	Janet	M.	Gates	NULL	Modular Cycle Systems	adventure-works\jillian0	janet1@adventure-works.com
Mr.	Lucy	NULL	Harrington	NULL	Metropolitan Sports Supply	adventure-works\shu0	lucy0@adventure-works.com
Ms.	Rosmarie	J.	Carroll	NULL	Aerobic Exercise Company	adventure-works\linda3	rosmarie0@adventure-works.com
Mr.	Dominic	P.	Gash	NULL	Associated Bikes	adventure-works\shu0	dominic0@adventure-works.com
Ms.	Kathleen	M.	Garza	NULL	Rural Cycle Emporium	adventure-works\josé1	kathleen0@adventure-works.com
Ms.	Katherine	NULL	Harding	NULL	Sharp Bikes	adventure-works\josé1	katherine0@adventure-works.com
Mr.	Johnny	A.	Caprio	Jr.	Bikes and Motorbikes	adventure-works\garrett1	johnny0@adventure-works.com
Mr.	Christopher	R.	Beck	Jr.	Bulk Discount Store	adventure-works\jae0	christopher1@adventure-works.com
Mr.	David	J.	Liu	NULL	Catalog Store	adventure-works\michael9	david20@adventure-works.com
Mr.	John	A.	Beaver	NULL	Center Cycle Shop	adventure-works\pamela0	john8@adventure-works.com
Ms.	Jean	P.	Handley	NULL	Central Discount Store	adventure-works\david8	jean1@adventure-works.com
NULL	Jinghao	NULL	Liu	NULL	Chic Department Stores	adventure-works\jillian0	jinghao1@adventure-works.com
Ms.	Linda	E.	Burnett	NULL	Travel Systems	adventure-works\jillian0	linda4@adventure-works.com

Figure 17.27 – Reading database as an admin with data masking enabled

The following screenshot shows values for a user without admin rights:

Title	FirstName	MiddleName	LastName	Suffix	CompanyName	SalesPerson	EmailAddress	Phone
Mr.	Orlando	N.	xxxx	NULL	A Bike Store	adventure-works\pamela0	xxxx	245-555-0173
Mr.	Keith	NULL	xxxx	NULL	Progressive Sports	adventure-works\david8	xxxx	170-555-0127
Ms.	Donna	F.	xxxx	NULL	Advanced Bike Components	adventure-works\jillian0	xxxx	279-555-0130
Ms.	Janet	M.	xxxx	NULL	Modular Cycle Systems	adventure-works\jillian0	xxxx	710-555-0173
Mr.	Lucy	NULL	xxxx	NULL	Metropolitan Sports Supply	adventure-works\shu0	xxxx	828-555-0186
Ms.	Rosmarie	J.	xxxx	NULL	Aerobic Exercise Company	adventure-works\linda3	xxxx	244-555-0112
Mr.	Dominic	P.	xxxx	NULL	Associated Bikes	adventure-works\shu0	xxxx	192-555-0173
Ms.	Kathleen	M.	xxxx	NULL	Rural Cycle Emporium	adventure-works\josé1	xxxx	150-555-0127
Ms.	Katherine	NULL	xxxx	NULL	Sharp Bikes	adventure-works\josé1	xxxx	926-555-0159
Mr.	Johnny	A.	xxxx	Jr.	Bikes and Motorbikes	adventure-works\garrett1	xxxx	112-555-0191
Mr.	Christopher	R.	xxxx	Jr.	Bulk Discount Store	adventure-works\jae0	xxxx	1 (11) 500 555-0132
Mr.	David	J.	xxxx	NULL	Catalog Store	adventure-works\michael9	xxxx	440-555-0132
Mr.	John	A.	xxxx	NULL	Center Cycle Shop	adventure-works\pamela0	xxxx	521-555-0195
Ms.	Jean	P.	xxxx	NULL	Central Discount Store	adventure-works\david8	xxxx	582-555-0113
NULL	Jinghao	NULL	xxxx	NULL	Chic Department Stores	adventure-works\jillian0	xxxx	928-555-0116
Ms.	Linda	E.	xxxx	NULL	Travel Systems	adventure-works\jillian0	xxxx	121-555-0121

Figure 17.28 – Reading database as a user with data masking enabled

As you can see, `LastName` and `Email` are masked for a non-admin user.

The built-in features of Azure SQL can be really helpful when building advanced systems that require a stricter approach to data integrity and security. We will now see how scaling works for Azure SQL and how to use it in a standard daily scenario.

Scaling Azure SQL

The required performance of your database may differ depending on the time and current state of your application. This is when scaling is all-important—you can adjust cost and available resources depending on the needs of your service. In Azure SQL, there are multiple different scenarios that you will need to consider: whether you wish to use a single database or an elastic pool, whether you need to scale out reads, or whether you need all features available everywhere. In this short section, I will show you how to quickly proceed with your decision and where you can find scaling tools.

Single database

As we mentioned previously, with a single database, scaling is simple—you just need to go to the **Compute + storage** blade and select the new tier you are interested in. You can easily decide whether you need to scale a database up by watching its performance, as demonstrated in the following screenshot:

Figure 17.29 – Monitoring database performance

If you see constant spikes or, simply, utilization of the database is becoming dangerously close to the maximum values, it is always a good decision to give it a few more DTUs or other resources.

> **Tip**
> Remember—you can set alerts when utilization hits upper limits, so there are some ways to automate the process.

Elastic pool

With an elastic pool enabled, things change a little bit—instead of operating on, for example, a DTU for a single database, you can select an elastic pool, which introduces a slightly different model of an elastic DTU. You can see an illustration of this in the following screenshot:

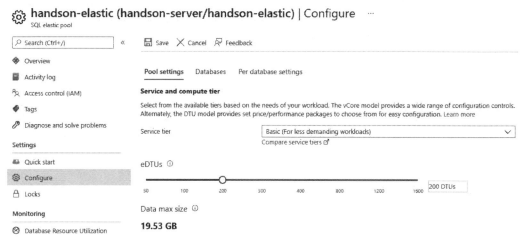

Figure 17.30 – Scaling an elastic pool

In that model, you scale your database using an elastic pool configuration instead. For a single database, you will be able to only change the maximum data size available (which is also limited to the value set by the pool).

Read scale-out

Sometimes, you only need to scale reads for your database. Such a situation occurs when you would rather serve content than modify it (for example, you have a very popular portal that is managed from a single place but is served globally). In Azure SQL, there is a possibility to scale out only a part of the service—the one responsible for managing reads for you.

> **Note**
> You need the **Premium/Business Critical/Hyperscale** tier to get this feature working.

To enable read scale-out on your database, you can use the **REpresentational State Transfer** (**REST**) **application programming interface** (**API**), as illustrated in the following code snippet:

```
HTTP PUT
URL: https://management.azure.com/subscriptions/
```

```
{SubscriptionId}/resourceGroups/{GroupName}/providers/
Microsoft.Sql/servers/{ServerName}/databases/
{DatabaseName}?api-version= 2014-04-01-preview
Body: {
    "properties": {
        "readScale":"Enabled"
    }
}
```

Alternatively, you can use PowerShell, as follows:

```
Set-AzSqlDatabase -ResourceGroupName <resourceGroupName>
-ServerName <serverName> -DatabaseName <databaseName>
-ReadScale Enabled
```

Remembering that Azure SQL can be scaled out for reads only can be helpful when dealing with database bottlenecks as this can save you from upgrading the whole server and will thus save you some money.

Sharding

The last way to scale your database is to use **sharding**. As opposed to elastic pools, by using sharding, you allocate individual resources to each of your databases. It is also one of the models for horizontal scaling (so you provision another database rather than scale up the existing one).

> **Note**
>
> You can also use sharding for elastic pools by using the Elastic Database split-merge tool:
>
> `https://docs.microsoft.com/en-us/azure/sql-database/sql-database-elastic-scale-overview-split-and-merge`

In general, you will use sharding if the following applies:

- You have too much data to be able to handle it with an individual instance
- You want to load-balance requests
- You want to geo-distribute your data

The important thing here is the requirement that the data structure for each shard must be the same. You can find full documentation on sharding in Azure SQL in the *Further reading* section of this chapter.

In general, that approach is much more complicated than simply scaling up/out as it involves careful designing of your database and making sure that data is consistent.

Monitoring and tuning

The last item we cover in this chapter will be the monitoring and tuning of Azure SQL. Because databases are often the heart of many applications, it is crucial to have a quick way to diagnose any issues regarding performance or usage, and easily tweak things if needed. Azure SQL uses multiple different features that you can leverage to get insights from your instance.

Monitoring

To monitor your SQL database, you can use alerts, which should be familiar to you (assuming you have read the previous chapter, *Chapter 16*, *Using Application Insights to Monitor Your Applications*). You can access this functionality by clicking on the **Alerts** blade, as illustrated here:

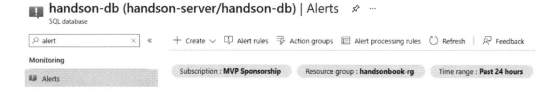

Figure 17.31 – Alerts blade for Azure SQL

You can use Azure SQL alerts to cover the following things:

- Insufficient performance (metric)
- Invalid queries (metric)
- Configuration issues (metric)
- Overall service health (metric)
- Incoming maintenance activities (activity log)
- Actual service issues (activity log)
- Service health recommendations (activity log)

Tuning

There is a whole group of features, called **Intelligent Performance**, that allow you to monitor and tune your SQL database performance, as shown in the following screenshot:

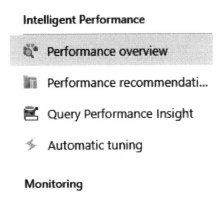

Figure 17.32 – Intelligent Performance section

Let's check out **Performance recommendations** for now, as follows:

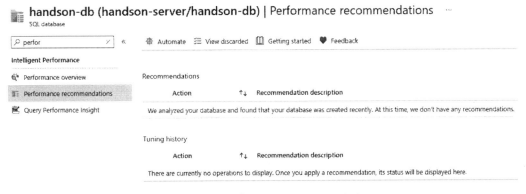

Figure 17.33 – Performance recommendations

While this feature is initially empty, it displays different recommendations while working with Azure SQL. The important thing here is that we can automate things—just click on the **Automate** button to display another screen where you can select what you are interested in, as illustrated in the following screenshot:

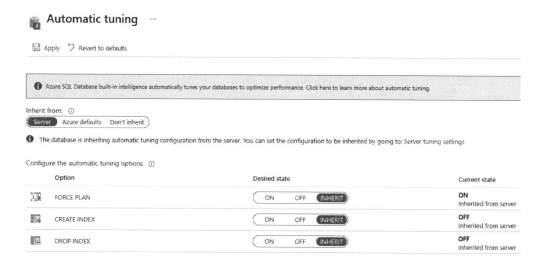

Figure 17.34 – Configuring tuning automation

This screen is, in fact, the **Automatic tuning** blade presented earlier. You can use it to automate things such as managing indexes or forcing a query plan.

Summary

Azure SQL is a very complex and extended service that works in a similar way to its on-premises version, Microsoft SQL Server. While being a full PaaS Azure component, it still allows for many advanced operations such as sharding, multi-tenancy, AD integration or failover, and geo-replication. Besides being hosted in within a cloud provider's infrastructure, you can still use it in the same way you would a standalone version of SQL Server.

In the next chapter, we will cover the last PaaS service mentioned in this book, which is **Azure Data Lake Storage** (**ADLS**).

Questions

Here are some questions to test your knowledge of the important topics in this chapter:

1. What is different in terms of update policy between Azure SQL and Microsoft SQL Server?

2. What is sharding?

3. You created a new SQL database in Azure SQL, but the server refuses to connect to it. What could be the issue here?

4. What are the two available purchasing models for Azure SQL?

5. What is an elastic pool?

6. What is the difference between a DTU and an **elastic DTU (eDTU)**?

7. How can you mask a particular field in Azure SQL?

8. Which audit log destinations are available?

Further reading

For more information, refer to the following sources:

*   How to understand DTUs: `https://sqlperformance.com/2017/03/azure/what-the-heck-is-a-dtu`

*   Performance recommendations: `https://docs.microsoft.com/en-us/azure/sql-database/sql-database-advisor`

*   Adaptive query processing: `https://docs.microsoft.com/pl-pl/sql/relational-databases/performance/adaptive-query-processing?view=sql-server-2017`

*   Securing SQL Database: `https://docs.microsoft.com/en-us/azure/sql-database/sql-database-security-overview`

*   Read scale-out: `https://docs.microsoft.com/en-us/azure/sql-database/sql-database-read-scale-out`

*   Sharding: `https://docs.microsoft.com/en-us/azure/sql-database/sql-database-elastic-scale-introduction`

18

Big Data Storage – Azure Data Lake

Sometimes, we must store unlimited amounts of data. That scenario covers most big data platforms, where having even a soft limit for the maximum capacity could cause problems with the active development and maintenance of our application. Thanks to **Azure Data Lake**, we have limitless possibilities when it comes to storing both structured and unstructured data, all with an efficient security model and great performance. Thanks to this chapter, you will learn the technical basics of building your very own data lake, including things such as the overall capabilities of the service, its security features, and its similarity to Azure Storage.

The following topics will be covered in this chapter:

- Understanding **Azure Data Lake Storage (ADLS)**
- Storing data in ADLS Gen2
- Security features of ADLS Gen2
- Best practices for working with ADLS

Technical requirements

To perform the exercises in this chapter, you will need the following:

- Access to an Azure subscription

Understanding ADLS

When considering your storage solution, you must consider the amount of data you want to store. Depending on your answer, you may choose a different option from the services available in Azure – Azure Storage, Azure SQL, or Azure Cosmos DB. There is also a variety of databases available as images for **virtual machines** (**VMs**) (such as Cassandra or MongoDB); the ecosystem is quite rich, so everyone can find what they are looking for. A problem arises when you do not have an upper limit for data stored or, considering the characteristics of today's applications, that amount grows so rapidly that there is no possibility to declare a safe limit, which we will never hit. For those kinds of scenarios, there is a separate kind of storage named data lakes. These allow you to store data in its natural format, so it does not imply any kind of structure over information stored. In Azure, a solution for that kind of problem is named ADLS; in this chapter, you will learn the basics of this service, which allows you to dive deeper into the service and adjust it to your needs.

ADLS fundamentals

ADLS is called a hyperscale repository for data for a reason—there is no limit when it comes to storing files. It can have any format, be any size, and store information structured differently. This is also a great model for big data analytics as you can store files in a way that is best for your processing services (some prefer a small number of big files; some prefer many small files—choose what suits you the most). This is not possible for other storage solutions such as relational, NoSQL, or graph databases, as they always have some restrictions when it comes to saving unstructured data.

> **Important Note**
>
> Azure currently offers two versions of ADLS – Gen1 and Gen2. As Gen1 will be retired in 2024, this chapter covers only Gen2, which is conceptually quite different compared to Gen1.

Fundamentally, ADLS leverages all the concepts of Azure Storage. This implies things such as redundancy— while Gen1 supported only the **locally redundant storage** (**LRS**) model of replication, with Gen2 you can use all the replication models supported by the base service. In fact, the main feature—which changes when Azure Data Lake is enabled for Azure Storage—is its use of hierarchical namespaces.

Hierarchical namespaces are designed to guarantee appropriate performance and scalability. They connect the flexibility of Azure Storage with filesystem semantics, which is useful when building big data systems and analysis.

There are two key features of hierarchical namespaces, as follows:

- **Atomic directory manipulation**: As Azure Storage does not offer a capability of physical directories (it operates on virtual folders, which are created based on embedding slashes in your filename), performing an analysis of filtered files is not easy as you need to browse all files uploaded to your account. Hierarchical namespaces allow you to operate only on a parent-directory level, improving the overall performance.

- **Filesystem look and feel**: Hierarchical namespaces act as a typical filesystem. This means all tools, developers, and users can interact with them as with any other filesystem interface.

However, always consider whether you really need hierarchical namespaces at all. Azure Storage (mainly Blob Storage) can work just fine without them if you are not working on actual data lake implementation. This includes common file storage implementation, backups, and so on.

Important Note
Once enabled, hierarchical namespaces cannot be disabled.

Above all the things mentioned before, remember that ADLS Gen2 is compatible on the **Hadoop Distributed File System** (**HDFS**)—this allows for seamless integration with many **open source software** (**OSS**) tools, such as the following:

- Apache Hive
- Apache Storm
- Apache Spark
- MapReduce
- Apache Pig

  And many more...!

This gives you a much better ecosystem tool-wise and can be a dealbreaker when compared to other services acting as data lakes.

When it comes to accessing files stored inside an instance of ADLS, it leverages the **Portable Operating System Interface** (**POSIX**)-style permissions model; you basically operate on three different permissions, which can be applied to a file or a folder, as follows:

- **Read (R)**: For reading data
- **Write (W)**: For writing data
- **Execute (E)**: Applicable to a folder, used to give read/write permissions in a folder context (such as creating children or listing files)

We will cover more security concepts in the *Security* section. For now, let's see how we can create a new instance of the ADLS service using the Azure portal.

Creating an ADLS instance

To create an ADLS instance, you will need to search for `Azure Storage` in the portal, fill in the basics, and then check the **Enable hierarchical namespace** feature checkbox on the **Advanced** tab, as illustrated in the following screenshot:

Figure 18.1 – Enabling hierarchical namespaces

If you have an existing Azure Storage instance, you can try to upgrade it to ADLS Gen2 using the ADLS Gen2 upgrade feature, as illustrated in the following screenshot:

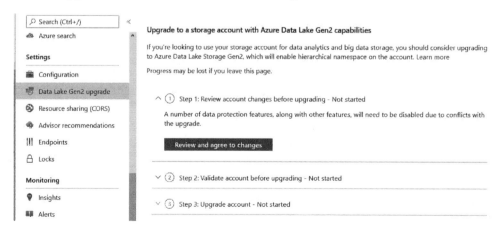

Figure 18.2 – Upgrading Azure Storage to ADLS Gen2

Remember that such an operation will affect operations on your Storage Account instance, so it should be performed with care.

> **Note**
> ADLS Gen2 is compatible with general-purpose **version 2 (v2)** accounts and premium block blobs.

When you click on the **Create** button, your service will be provisioned—you can access it to see an overview, as follows:

Figure 18.3 – Overview of ADLS Gen2

As you can see, it offers the same view as a standard Storage Account. You still have access to most of the basic features of that account—the only change is in the **Properties** tab, where you have a **Data Lake Storage** section now instead of **Blob Storage**, as illustrated in the following screenshot:

Data Lake Storage

Hierarchical namespace	Enabled
Default access tier	Hot
Blob public access	Enabled
Blob soft delete	Enabled (7 days)
Container soft delete	Enabled (7 days)
Versioning	Disabled
Change feed	Disabled
NFS v3	Disabled
SFTP	Disabled

Figure 18.4 – Data Lake Storage properties

Besides that, all the other features are in place, and you can configure them as in Azure Storage. After that brief introduction, let's see how ADLS can store our data and what needs to be done to communicate with it.

Storing data in ADLS Gen2

Because ADLS Gen2 is all about storing data, in this section of the chapter, you will see how you can store different files, use permissions to restrict access to them, and organize your instance. The important thing to remember here is the fact that you are not limited to using big data tools to store or access data stored within a service—if you manage to communicate with the ADLS protocol, you can easily operate on files using C#, JavaScript, or any other kind of programming language.

The first thing to cover will be using the Azure portal to navigate through our files.

Using the Azure portal for navigation

To get started with working with files in the Azure portal, you will have to click on the **Storage browser** button, as illustrated in the following screenshot:

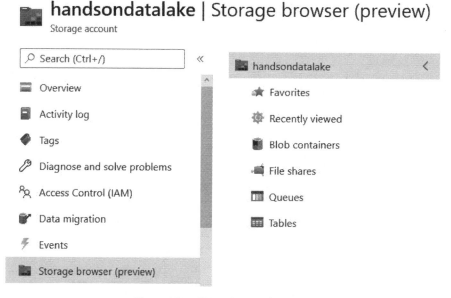

Figure 18.5 – Using Storage browser

Once you click on it, you will see a new screen where you are given many different options for creating a folder, uploading files, or changing access properties. While this tool is not the best way to manage thousands of files, it gives you some insight into what is stored and how. To be able to manage data in ADLS Gen2, simply click on **Blob containers**, as illustrated in the following screenshot:

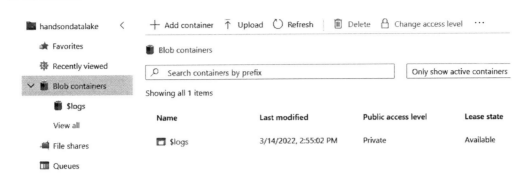

Figure 18.6 – Blob containers

> **Tip**
>
> The downside of the **user interface** (**UI**) available in the portal is the fact that it tends to hang, especially if you have hundreds of files. Some options (such as deleting a folder) also tend to fail if you have stored **gigabytes** (**GB**) of data. In that scenario, it is better to use a **software development kit** (**SDK**).

If you take a closer look, you can see that the overall UI and **user experience** (**UX**) are the same as in Azure Storage—uploading files and managing containers work the same as in the base version of the service. If you want to learn about this in more detail, look at *Chapter 12, Using Azure Storage – Tables, Queues, Files, and Blobs*, where we discuss different features of Azure Storage. More differences can be found when we go to the **Containers** tab, as shown in the following screenshot:

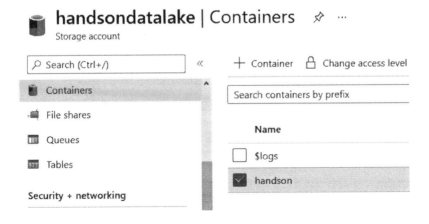

Figure 18.7 – The Containers tab

At the beginning of this chapter, I mentioned that ADLS Gen2 uses a slightly different model for giving access to files, which is based on the POSIX model. You can access this by going to the **Manage ACL** view, as illustrated in the following screenshot:

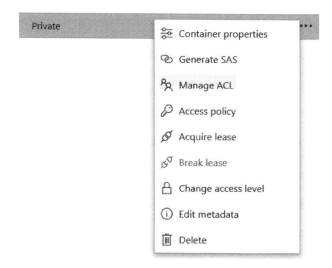

Figure 18.8 – The Manage ACL menu option

This view allows you to easily understand who can read or write something to a directory, as indicated in the following screenshot:

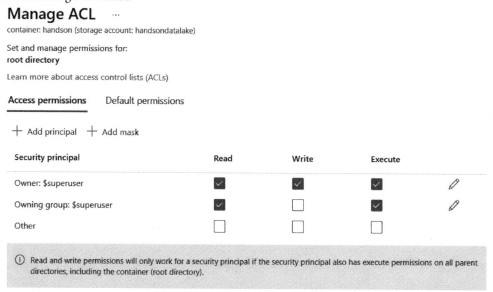

Figure 18.9 – Configuring access to a directory

The same view is available when you find an individual file and decide to overwrite permissions, which are given on a directory level, as shown in the following screenshot:

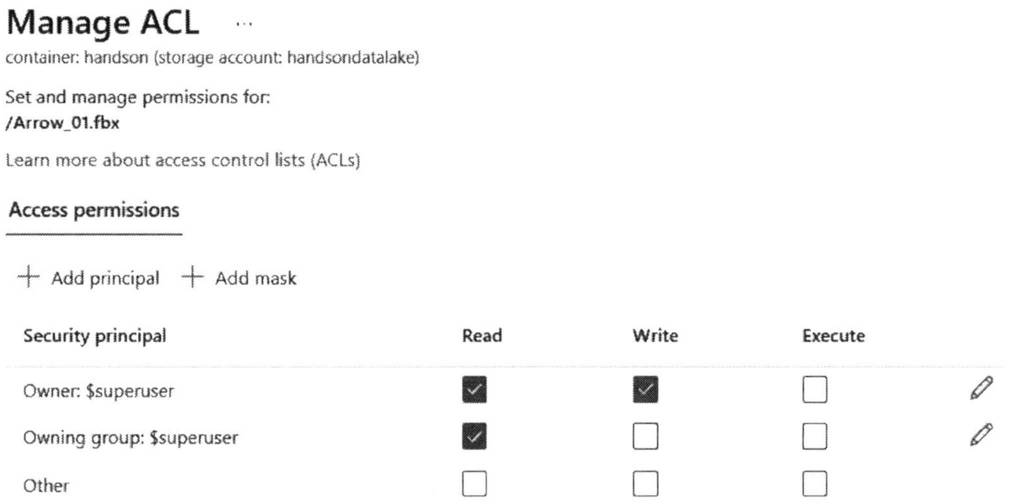

Manage ACL   ...

container: handson (storage account: handsondatalake)

Set and manage permissions for:
/Arrow_01.fbx

Learn more about access control lists (ACLs)

Access permissions

+ Add principal   + Add mask

Security principal	Read	Write	Execute	
Owner: $superuser	✓	✓	☐	✏
Owning group: $superuser	✓	☐	☐	✏
Other	☐	☐	☐	

Figure 18.10 – Configuring access to a file

By default, only you can access a file or a folder. To add a new user or a group, you can click on the + **Add principal** button. As you can see, managing permissions via the portal is really simple and does not require additional operations. With that topic covered, we can go to the next part and see how an SDK can help achieve the same as the Azure portal.

Using SDKs

The most flexible (and the most advanced) option to manage files and your ADLS instance is using an SDK for a language you are using. Currently, there are three different languages officially supported, as follows:

- .NET
- Java
- Python

For .NET, you need to install the `Azure.Storage.Files.DataLake` package—for example—using the following command:

```
dotnet add package Azure.Storage.Files.DataLake -v 12.6.0 -s
https://pkgs.dev.azure.com/azure-sdk/public/_packaging/azure-
sdk-for-net/nuget/v3/index.json
```

For Python, you can leverage `pip`, like so:

```
pip install azure-storage-file-datalake
```

Finally, Java can use different package managers. Here is an example for Maven:

```
<dependency>
  <groupId>com.azure</groupId>
  <artifactId>azure-storage-file-datalake</artifactId>
  <version>12.8.0</version>
</dependency>
```

There is also the possibility of using a **REpresentational State Transfer** (**REST**) **application programming interface** (**API**), so basically, you can connect to it using any language you want.

To connect to a service, you need a client—the actual code depends on the authentication method. Currently, there are two ways of authenticating:

- Using the account key
- Using **Azure Active Directory** (**Azure AD**)

Here, you can see how an ADLS client is obtained for .NET:

```
// Azure AD
// Install Azure.Identity NuGet package to get access to
ClientSecretCredential() object
public static DataLakeServiceClient GetDataLakeServiceClient(
    String accountName, String clientID, string clientSecret,
string tenantID)
{
    var credential = new ClientSecretCredential(
        tenantID, clientID, clientSecret, new
TokenCredentialOptions());
    var dfsUri = "https://" + accountName + ".dfs.core.windows.
net";

    return new DataLakeServiceClient(new Uri(dfsUri),
credential);
}

// Account key
```

```
public static DataLakeServiceClient GetDataLakeServiceClient(
    string accountName, string accountKey)
{
    var sharedKeyCredential =
        new StorageSharedKeyCredential(accountName,
accountKey);
    var dfsUri = "https://" + accountName + ".dfs.core.windows.
net";

    return new DataLakeServiceClient
        (new Uri(dfsUri), sharedKeyCredential);
}
```

Here, you can find an example of two methods written in .NET, which create a directory and upload a file to it:

```
public async Task<DataLakeDirectoryClient> CreateDirectory
    (DataLakeServiceClient serviceClient, string
fileSystemName)
{
    var fileSystemClient =
        serviceClient.GetFileSystemClient(fileSystemName);
    var directoryClient =
        await fileSystemClient.CreateDirectoryAsync("my-
directory");

    return await directoryClient.Value.
CreateSubDirectoryAsync("my-subdirectory");
}


public async Task UploadFile(DataLakeFileSystemClient
fileSystemClient)
{
    var directoryClient =
        fileSystemClient.GetDirectoryClient("my-directory");
    var fileClient = await directoryClient.
CreateFileAsync("uploaded-file.txt");
    var fileStream =File.OpenRead("<path-to-local-file>");
```

```
    var fileSize = fileStream.Length;


    await fileClient.Value.AppendAsync(fileStream, offset: 0);
    await fileClient.Value.FlushAsync(position: fileSize);
}
```

You can find more examples and code snippets in the *Further reading* section.

> **Tip**
>
> The important thing about using SDKs is the ability to abstract many operations and automate them—you can easily delete files recursively or dynamically create them. Such operations are unavailable when using UIs, and most serious project developers would rather code stuff than rely on manual file management.

Let's now revisit the security features available for ADLS Gen2.

Security features of ADLS Gen2

ADLS Gen2 offers almost the same security model as Azure Storage. In fact, the only difference is the **access control list** (**ACL**) feature, which can be used to define access to directories and files. In this section, we will cover the security features available and describe them in detail so that you can use them right away.

Authentication and authorization

To authenticate who or what can access data stored, ADLS Gen2 uses Azure AD to know what the current entity accessing data is. To authorize it, it leverages both **role-based access control** (**RBAC**) to secure the resource itself, and a POSIX ACL to secure data.

It is important to understand the distinction between these two terms, so let's have a closer look here:

- **Authentication**: This determines who or what tries to access a particular resource.
- **Authorization**: This secures a resource by limiting access to it to those who have been assigned a particular set of permissions.

> **Note**
>
> It is important to remember that if you have multiple subscriptions hosting different resources that would like to access ADLS, you have to assign the same Azure AD instance to all of them—if you fail to do so, some will not be able to access data, as only users and services defined within a directory assigned to ADLS can be authenticated and given access to it.

Let's check the difference between the RBAC and POSIX models.

RBAC

RBAC controls who can access an Azure resource. It is a separate set of roles and permissions that has nothing to do with the data stored. To check out this feature, click on the **Access Control (IAM)** blade, as illustrated in the following screenshot:

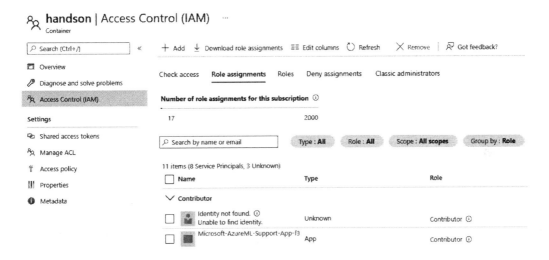

Figure 18.11 – RBAC configuration for a container

In the preceding screenshot, you can see the configuration of RBAC set up on a container level. The same can be done when configuring your instance of a service. When considering RBAC, you have two levels of configuration for ADLS Gen2, as follows:

- **Resource level**, which defines who (or what) can configure an instance of the service
- **Container level**, used for limiting access to containers storing your data

When securing your resource, you can use different roles available for your account, as illustrated in the following screenshot:

Name ↑↓	Description ↑↓
Owner	Grants full access to manage all resources, including the ability to assign roles in Azure RBAC.
Contributor	Grants full access to manage all resources, but does not allow you to assign roles in Azure RBAC, manage assignments in Azure Blu...
Reader	View all resources, but does not allow you to make any changes.
Avere Contributor	Can create and manage an Avere vFXT cluster.
Avere Operator	Used by the Avere vFXT cluster to manage the cluster
Backup Contributor	Lets you manage backup service,but can't create vaults and give access to others
Backup Operator	Lets you manage backup services, except removal of backup, vault creation and giving access to others
Custom Reader	View everything in the subscription and also open support tickets.
Custom Reader 2	Second custom role
DevTest Labs User	Lets you connect, start, restart, and shutdown your virtual machines in your Azure DevTest Labs.
Disk Snapshot Contributor	Provides permission to backup vault to manage disk snapshots.
Log Analytics Contributor	Log Analytics Contributor can read all monitoring data and edit monitoring settings. Editing monitoring settings includes adding t...
Log Analytics Reader	Log Analytics Reader can view and search all monitoring data as well as and view monitoring settings, including viewing the config...
Logic App Contributor	Lets you manage logic app, but not access to them.
Managed Application Contributor Role	Allows for creating managed application resources.

Figure 18.12 – Subset of roles available for RBAC configuration

Using the **Access Control (IAM)** blade, you can easily control who can access your instance of ADLS and how—use it any time you want to change permissions or the set of users/services accessing it.

> **Tip**
>
> A good idea is to manage groups rather than individual entities—this allows you to add/remove a user or an entity in one place (Azure AD) instead of browsing resources and their RBAC.

While RBAC can be useful for limiting access to resources (in other words, the management plane), they serve little purpose when implementing business logic connected to data.

POSIX ACL

As described previously, you can manage access to data stored within your instance of ADLS by providing a set of permissions defined as **R**, **W**, and **E**. They are part of the POSIX ACL model that is a feature of HDFS, which is part of the engine of this Azure service. If you have used—for example—**File Transfer Protocol** (**FTP**) servers, you probably have worked with filesystem permissions; they were described as numbers or strings containing the letters r, w, x, and the character -. Here is an example:

- -rwx------ is equal to 0700 and declares read, write, and execute permissions only for the owner.

- `-rwxrwxrwx` is equal to `0777` and declares `read`, `write`, and `execute` permissions for everyone.

- `-rw-rw-rw-` is equal to `0666` and declares `read` and `write` permissions for everyone.

ACL can be configured on a directory or file level. You can find more about the POSIX ACL model in the *Further reading* section.

Let's now check network isolation features, which are crucial in all enterprise and secure environments.

Network isolation

In ADLS Gen2, network isolation is configured in the same way as traditional Azure Storage, as illustrated here:

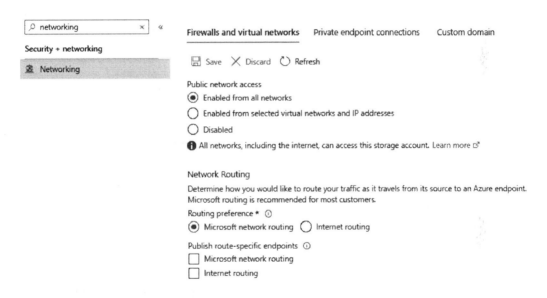

Figure 18.13 – Configuring networking for ADLS

The important thing here is the ability to block other Azure services from accessing your data—this can be helpful if you have requirements that force you to disallow anyone from reading any information stored in ADLS.

We have now completed most of the technical stuff related to ADLS. The last topic for this chapter will be covering some good practices and gotchas that can be helpful for working with the service.

Best practices for working with ADLS

ADLS is a bit different when it comes to accessing data stored and performing read and writes. As this service is designed for storing **petabytes** (**PB**) of data, it is important to know the best practices for doing so, to avoid problems such as the need to reorganize all files or slow reads/writes. This also includes security features (as discussed earlier), as this is an important part of the whole solution. In this section, we will focus on multiple pieces of advice regarding ADLS to help you use it consciously and leverage the best practices.

Performance

One important feature of many storage solutions is their performance. In general, we expect that our databases will work without a problem whether the load is low or high and a single record is big or small. When it comes to ADLS, you must consider the following factors:

- **Using the Premium tier**: As opposed to general-purpose accounts, the **Premium** tier in Azure Storage uses **solid-state drive** (**SSD**) disks for better performance and lower latency. If your application requires access to data with higher performance targets, this is the way to go.

- **Data ingestion optimization**: Always make sure that your infrastructure supports working on high volumes of data. In practice, this means that you should ensure the network will not be a bottleneck, your VMs use SSD disks for lower latency regarding **input/output** (**I/O**), and so on. Microsoft recommends that when Azure VMs are considered, you should go for Azure D14 VMs or better.

- **Network connection**: To make sure that everything is optimized both performance- and cost-wise, deploy your infrastructure and application to the same region so that most of the traffic stays within the same data center.

- **Parallel processing**: Try to perform as many reads and writes as possible to ADLS Gen2 in the same timeframe. This ensures that you are using all the throughput you are given.

- **Use an appropriate file format**: Instead of storing data as **JavaScript Object Notation** (**JSON**) or **comma-separated values** (**CSV**) files, try to use formats such as Avro, Parquet, or **Optimized Row Columnar** (**ORC**). They have a compressed, embedded schema in each file and are machine-readable.

Security

We discussed this topic a little previously, but here, we summarize it. When using ADLS and considering its security features (such as authentication, authorization, and access to files), it is important to remember the following things:

- **Prefer groups over users/services**: While, initially, it is easier to assign an individual user to a resource or a folder, you will quickly face problems when the number of people interested in data starts to grow rapidly. Therefore, it is better to use Azure AD groups to both determine RBAC access to the resource itself and a POSIX ACL for files and folders. It also improves the performance of the solution, as it is quicker to check whether an entity belongs to a group than to traverse through a long list of users.

- **A minimum set of permissions**: As in other services, always start with a minimum set of permissions required by someone who accesses your instance of ADLS. Do not assign a `write` permission to somebody who only reads data or `execute` to a service that reads only a single file in a folder.

- **Enable the firewall**: In general, you do not want to allow anyone to access data stored inside ADLS. To secure your solution so that only a subset of IP addresses can access information, enable the firewall so that anyone outside the list will be rejected.

Resiliency

It is crucial to ensure that your data is stored in a safe manner and will not be lost in the case of any issue inside the data center. As mentioned at the beginning of this chapter, ADLS Gen2 can leverage standard replication options for Azure Storage. This is a great improvement over Gen1, though you should still consider cost when going for geo-replication. When lots of data is replicated, you should always include outbound traffic in your calculations.

Data structure

You will choose a different data structure for different use scenarios—for **Internet of Things** (**IoT**) data, it will be very granular, as shown here:

```
{Vector1}/{Vector2}/{Vector3}/{YYYY}/{MM}/{DD}/{HH}/{mm}
```

On the other hand, for storing user data, the structure may be completely different, as we can see here:

```
{AppName}/{UserId}/{YYYY}/{MM}/{DD}
```

It all depends on your current requirements. The data structure is extremely important when you plan to perform an analysis on the files stored—it directly affects the size of files and their number, which can further affect the possible toolset for your activities.

> **Tip**
> Another important thing here is the legal requirements—if you use any kind of sensitive data as a folder or a filename, you will have to be able to perform a cleanup efficiently if a user tells you that they want to be forgotten or asks for an account to be removed.

Summary

In this chapter, you have learned a bit about ADLS, an Azure service designed to store an almost unlimited amount of data without affecting its structure. We have covered things such as data structure, security features, and best practices, so you should be able to get started on your own and build your very first solution based on this Azure component. Bear in mind that what can easily replace Blob Storage—for example—all depends on your requirements and expectations. If you're looking for a more flexible security model, better performance, and better limits, ADLS is for you. This ends this part of the book, which included services for storing data, monitoring services, and performing communication between them.

In the next chapter, you will learn more about scaling, performance, and maintainability in Azure.

Questions

Here are some questions to test your knowledge of the important topics in this chapter:

1. Which security model is better—managing security groups or individual entities, and why?
2. What is the difference between RBAC and a POSIX ACL?
3. Which data structure is better—a single folder containing thousands of files or a hierarchy of folders containing several files each?
4. Can ADLS be used with any programming language?
5. What is the difference between ADLS Gen2 and Azure Storage?
6. How do you ensure that your solution based on ADLS is geo-redundant?

Further reading

For more information, refer to the following sources:

- Blob Storage features supported by ADLS Gen2: `https://docs.microsoft.com/en-us/azure/storage/blobs/storage-feature-support-in-storage-accounts`

- ACLs: `https://docs.microsoft.com/en-us/azure/storage/blobs/data-lake-storage-access-control`

- Best practices: `https://docs.microsoft.com/en-us/azure/storage/blobs/data-lake-storage-best-practices`

- Java reference: `https://docs.microsoft.com/en-us/java/api/overview/azure/storage-file-datalake-readme?view=azure-java-stable`

- Python reference: `https://azuresdkdocs.blob.core.windows.net/$web/python/azure-storage-file-datalake/12.0.0b5/index.html`

- .NET reference: `https://docs.microsoft.com/en-us/dotnet/api/azure.storage.files.datalake?view=azure-dotnet`

- Query acceleration reference: `https://docs.microsoft.com/en-us/azure/storage/blobs/data-lake-storage-query-acceleration`

Part 4:
Performance, Scalability, and Maintainability

The last part of the book covers more advanced scenarios regarding performance, the scalability of applications in the Azure cloud, and best practices for maintaining them. Summing up all the knowledge from previous chapters is necessary for a deeper understanding of how Azure works and how to make the most of it.

This part of the book comprises the following chapters:

- *Chapter 19, Scaling Azure Applications*
- *Chapter 20, Serving Static Content Using Azure CDN*
- *Chapter 21, Managing APIs with Azure API Management*
- *Chapter 22, Building a Scalable Entry Point for Your Service with Azure Front Door*
- *Chapter 23, Azure Application Gateway as a Web Traffic Load Balancer*
- *Chapter 24, Distributing Load with Azure Traffic Manager*
- *Chapter 25, Tips and Tricks in Azure*

19

Scaling Azure Applications

We cannot talk about reliable and stable applications in the cloud without scaling. While this process may have seemed a bit complicated and cumbersome in models such as **infrastructure as a service (IaaS)** or on-premises, Azure provides many ways to multiply our applications quickly, and without downtime.

The following topics will be covered in this chapter:

- Autoscaling, scaling up, scaling out
- Scaling Azure App Service
- Scaling Azure Functions
- Scaling Azure Cosmos DB
- Scaling Azure Event Hubs

Technical requirements

To perform the exercises from this chapter, you will need the following:

- Access to an Azure subscription

Autoscaling, scaling up, scaling out

The cloud is all about scaling—it is one of the most important advantages of such a setup over an on-premises setup. The ability to rapidly adapt to new demands when it comes to incoming traffic, and the flexibility a cloud offers, enable you to create more stable services that are less prone to unexpected load spikes and insufficient hardware performance. In this chapter, we will focus a little bit on diving deeper into the scaling topic, to build a deep understanding of how different services behave in Azure, and how you can ensure that the scaling feature is automated and requires as little attention as possible.

Autoscaling

You can define the autoscaling feature of many services as follows:

Autoscaling is a feature that allows a service, a machine, or an application to automatically scale up or out based on predefined parameters, such as central processing unit (CPU) utilization, memory used, or artificial factors, such as throughput units (TUs), or worker utilization.

In general, it can be described using the algorithm shown in the following diagram:

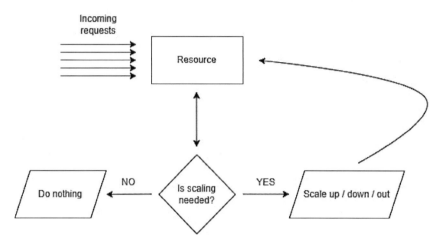

Figure 19.1 – Basic autoscaling algorithm

The preceding diagram can be described as follows:

1. A resource accepts incoming requests as normal.

2. Simultaneously, there is an entity that monitors a resource—it checks it against the scaling rules and decides whether a scaling operation is required.

3. An entity takes a decision regarding scaling—it can scale a resource up/down or out, depending on the settings.

Of course, besides pros, scaling has its downsides, including the following:

*   It may render your application unresponsive.

*   It requires additional resources for load balancing (if scaling out).

*   It takes time, depending on the scaling characteristics. It is, therefore, crucial to plan such action at the design stage.

*   In many cases, it causes your solution to be many times more expensive.

How a service scales depends solely on the service itself. Let's look at some examples here:

- Azure Event Hubs can be scaled manually/automatically (using the auto-inflate feature). You can assign more TUs to an instance to enable it to accept more messages. Automatic scaling down is not implemented.

- Azure App Service can be scaled both manually and automatically (it depends on the tier you have chosen). You have multiple different parameters available, and scaling down is also performed automatically.

- Azure Cosmos DB relies on the **request units** (**RUs**) assigned to an instance. With the **Autopilot** feature introduced, it can dynamically adjust its performance based on incoming traffic.

- Azure SQL has different provisioning models—you can use either **database transaction units** (**DTUs**), **virtual cores** (**vCores**), or elastic pools. Depending on the model, it will scale different parameters.

- Azure Functions service scales automatically using an internal mechanism of workers and the scale controller for the consumption model. When a Premium/App Service plan model is used, autoscaling is done in the same way as in Azure App Service.

- Azure Storage does not support scaling as it does not offer parameters requiring dynamic adjustments.

As you can see, there is no single solution for scaling your services in Azure—you must implement a working solution for each component individually. The rule of thumb is that the less control over a resource you have, the more automated the scaling will be. While for IaaS scenarios, you must operate the number of **virtual machines** (**VMs**), in **platform-as-a-service** (**PaaS**) scenarios, you will end up with vCores or other units. Here, you can find different cloud models ordered from left to right in terms of the scaling complexity (where **IaaS** has the most complex model):

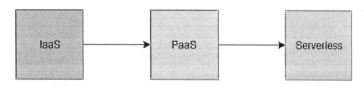

Figure 19.2 – Scaling complexity in the cloud (starting with the most difficult model)

Scaling up and scaling out

There are two different types of scaling (at least when it comes to Azure), as outlined here:

- **Scaling up**: Which upgrades hardware/a tier
- **Scaling out**: Which adds instances of a service

Scaling up can be presented as follows:

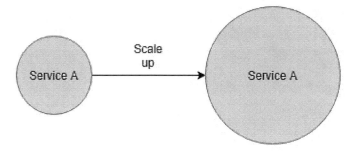

Figure 19.3 – Scaling-up visualization

While for comparison, scaling out is presented as follows:

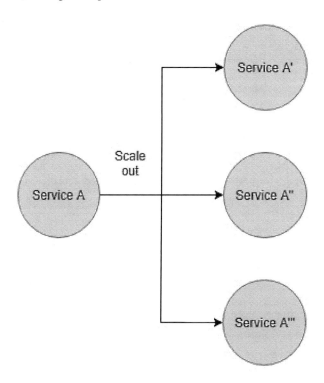

Figure 19.4 – Scaling-out visualization

So, in the first scenario (scaling up), you will get better performance from a single instance, while scaling out will allow you to parallelize your work. The use cases are different in both options and are basically dependent on the workload you are planning to run. These are some examples:

- If your code is sequential and there is no option to multiply it, use scaling up.

- If your code requires much compute power in a unit of time rather than dividing it into multiple machines, use scaling up.

- If you have a way to load-balance your load, use scaling out.

- If you can perform the same work on multiple machines without risk of collision, use scaling out.

Using scaling out can be compared to multithreading—but of course, on a much bigger scale. In fact, the problems are quite similar. If your machine has multiple cores and they can execute your code at the same time, you must introduce very similar constraints.

> **Note**
> Common problems of scaling out are often caused by access to the state—whether it is shared via any kind of storage or distributed among many machines. Make sure you are aware of this before using this feature.

In Azure, multiple services scale out/up differently. We will focus on three of them to get a better understanding of the topic.

Scaling Azure App Service

We started our journey through Microsoft Azure by learning some basics of Azure App Service. This is a very common PaaS component that is widely used among many Azure users, both for very simple websites and complex systems requiring high performance and reliability. To make sure that your web app is always on or to check if it is under pressure, you must implement scaling rules. When it comes to this service, you have two options—either using manual scaling (and implementing an alert so that you know when such an action should happen) or an autoscale feature, which makes things much easier in terms of maintenance. In this section, we will cover and compare both.

Manual scaling

Manual scaling is a feature that is available starting from the **Basic** tier—it is not available for free or shared ones. Depending on the actual tier chosen, there will be a different number of instances that can be used for your Azure App Service.

Here, you can find how things look like for the **B2** tier:

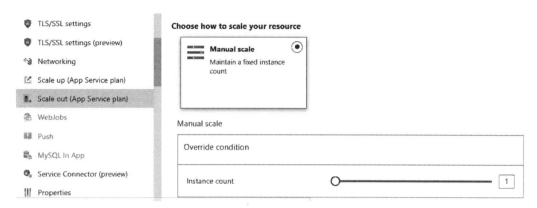

Figure 19.5 – Manual scaling for Azure App Service

In the preceding configuration, the maximum number of instances available is set to 3. However, if I scale up to the **Standard** tier, the result looks like this:

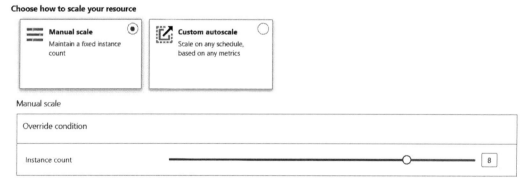

Figure 19.6 – Scale-out options for Standard tier in Azure App Service

Things look quite different—two features have changed, as noted here:

- I can set the **Instance count** value to the maximum number of **10.**
- Autoscaling can be enabled.

> **Note**
>
> Scaling up to the **Premium** tier (**version 3**, or **v3**) will allow you to set the maximum number of **30** instances for your App Service.

Let's now compare manual scaling with autoscaling.

Autoscaling

While manual scaling can be fine for less demanding websites and systems (as they do not require quick actions when something happens), when your application is—for example—a popular e-commerce shop, you want things to happen quickly, including scaling out. Let's try to enable autoscaling for now—it will display a form that enables you to manage these settings, as illustrated in the following screenshot:

Custom autoscale

Autoscale setting name *	handsonazure-Autoscale-889
Resource group	handsonbook-rg

Default *   Auto created scale condition ✎

Delete warning	ⓘ The very last or default recurrence rule cannot be deleted. Instead, you can disable autoscale to turn off autoscale.
Scale mode	⦿ Scale based on a metric ◯ Scale to a specific instance count
Rules	ⓘ No metric rules defined; click Add a rule to scale out and scale in your instances based on rules. For example: 'Add a rule that increases instance count by 1 when CPU percentage is above 70%'. If you save the setting without any rules defined, no scaling will occur. ＋ Add a rule
Instance limits	Minimum ⓘ Maximum ⓘ Default ⓘ 1 1 1
Schedule	**This scale condition is executed when none of the other scale condition(s) match**

Figure 19.7 – Autoscaling options for Azure App Service

In fact, you have two options here, as follows:

- **Scale based on a metric**: This allows you to select a metric that will be a trigger for autoscaling.

- **Scale to a specific instance count**: Executed by default (so should be used along with scaling based on a metric).

To configure **Scale based on a metric**, you will need a rule. You can add this by clicking on the **+ Add a rule** link. Doing so will display another form (which is far more complex than the current one), where you can select all that is interesting to you. The form looks like this:

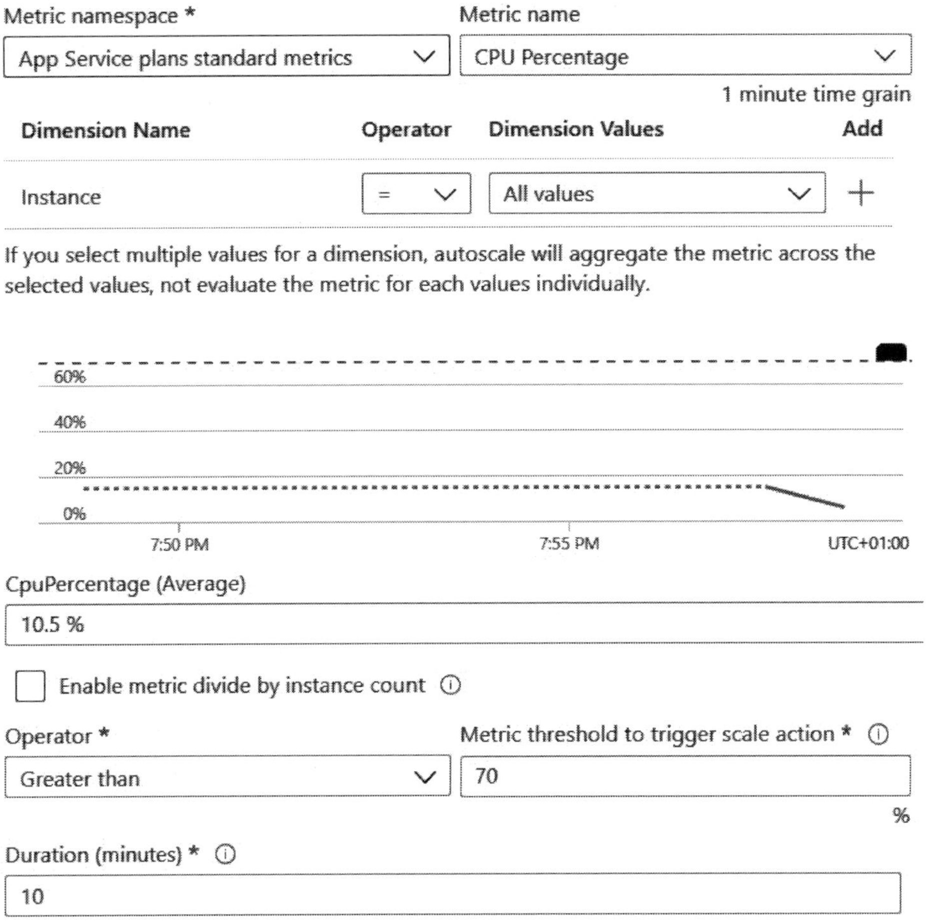

Figure 19.8 – Adding a rule

In the preceding screenshot, you can see a rule that will trigger autoscaling when CPU utilization exceeds 70% over a 10-minute period. Once all conditions are met, the runtime will add another instance to the App Service. What is more, if the conditions are true after another 5 minutes (**Cool down (minutes)** period), the scaling-out operation will be triggered once more. This will happen if the maximum number of instances that you have set is hit.

> **Note**
>
> Remember that you can set more than a single rule for your application. What is more, it seems like a good idea to create a decreasing count by rule, which will remove additional instances if the load gets back to normal.

Once your rule is added, you can click **Save** to confirm your changes—now, your application will be scaled out anytime a rule is considered active. Before we go further, I would like to show you two more things. Look at the following screenshot:

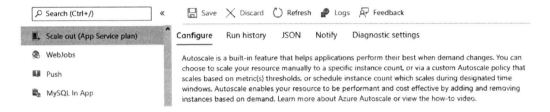

Figure 19.9 – Scale-out panel for Azure App Service

You probably noticed two additional sections on the **Scale out** blade: **JSON** and **Notify**. These give you some additional options when it comes to managing a service, as outlined here:

- **JSON**: This generates a **JavaScript Object Notation** (**JSON**) template that can be used with **Azure Resource Manager** (**ARM**) templates for automatic provisioning of your resource. It will automatically add scaling rules when a service is created.

- **Notify**: This enables you to automatically send a notification to administrators of the resource in Azure, to notify them when something wrong happens there.

Here, you can find a JSON example that was generated for my rules:

```
{
    "location": "West Europe",
    "tags": {},
    "properties": {
        "name": "handsonazure-Autoscale-889",
        "enabled": false,
        "predictiveAutoscalePolicy": {
            "scaleMode": "Disabled"
        },
        "targetResourceUri": "…",
        "profiles": [
```

```
        {
            "name": "Auto created scale condition",
            "capacity": {
                "minimum": "1",
                "maximum": "1",
                "default": "1"
            },
            "rules": [
                {
                    "scaleAction": {
                        "direction": "Increase",
                        "type": "ChangeCount",
                        "value": "1",
                        "cooldown": "PT5M"
                    },
                    "metricTrigger": {
                        "metricName": "CpuPercentage",
                        "metricNamespace": "microsoft.web/
serverfarms",
                        "metricResourceUri": ...
                    }
                }
            ]
        }
    ],
    "notifications": [],
    "targetResourceLocation": "West Europe"
    },
    "id": "..."
    "name": "handsonazure-Autoscale-889",
    "type": "Microsoft.Insights/autoscaleSettings"
}
```

As you can see, it can easily be adjusted to your needs and put in your code repository for further use and automation.

With the topic of scaling Azure App Service complete, let's now extend our knowledge and see how we can work with Azure Functions in terms of changing the number of working instances.

Scaling Azure Functions

When using PaaS services, you can configure how your application will behave when CPU utilization hits the maximum allowed value, or the number of requests exceeds the threshold. However, Azure offers services in other models—one of the most interesting is serverless architecture, which abstracts control even more in favor of easier configuration, minimum maintenance, and the ability to focus on delivering a business value.

In this section, you will see the differences between Azure App Service and Azure Functions when it comes to scaling, both from a technical and conceptual point of view.

Scaling serverless applications

When you are using serverless services (such as Azure Functions, Azure Cosmos DB, or Azure Event Grid), you have limited options when it comes to configuring the feature. Here are some examples:

- In Azure Functions, you rely on the pricing model (consumption plan versus App Service plan).
- In Azure Cosmos DB, you modify the number of RUs.
- In Azure Event Grid, you have no way of defining how the service will scale.

This is all caused by the fact that you do not control the application host—the underlying service engine is completely detached from your application and there is no possibility to directly modify it. What you can do is control it indirectly, either by changing the number of **processing units** (**PUs**) or via available configuration options, which can be interpreted and applied.

> **Note**
> Serverless architecture is meant to be a model where you are isolated from the runtime (and, in some cases, even from the cloud vendor). If the lack of control does not play well for you, it is better to try PaaS or IaaS models and services.

Let's now dive into the details of the Azure Functions scaling mechanism.

Azure Functions scaling behavior

In Azure Functions, there is no possibility to scale up, at least for the consumption plan. Of course, when using the App Service plan, you can scale it up and get better hardware, but it does not affect the service itself. Instead, it creates more resources to consume. On the other hand, you cannot scale out manually—the only possibility is to let Azure Functions scale automatically. To do so, this service implements the concept of a scale controller. This is an internal feature that constantly monitors how particular workers hosting the function's runtime behave, and if one of them seems to be overloaded, another machine is added to the set.

> **Note**
>
> Azure Functions scaling behavior is quite sophisticated and only partially described, as it contains parts that are either open sourced or not available publicly. I will try to describe it in detail in this chapter so that you are aware of the exact algorithm for making a scaling decision.

Before your instance of Azure Functions will make a scaling decision, it will check the following:

- **Scaling interval**: Scaling only happens after a specific interval has passed.

- **Current workers number**: If the number of workers (running the function's hosts) exceeds the configured maximum, a decision will be made to remove one from the working set.

- **Load factor**: If the load factor approaches the maximum value, a new worker will be added. Alternatively, if the load factor drops, one worker will be removed.

- **Busy worker ratio**: If the number of busy workers exceeds the configured maximum, another worker will be added to the set.

- **Free workers**: If the number of free workers is greater than the defined maximum, one of them will be removed from the working set.

Defined values for the preceding actions can be found here:

```
public const int DefaultMaxWorkers = 100;
public const int DefaultBusyWorkerLoadFactor = 80;
public const double DefaultMaxBusyWorkerRatio = 0.8;
public const int DefaultFreeWorkerLoadFactor = 20;
public const double DefaultMaxFreeWorkerRatio = 0.3;
public static readonly TimeSpan DefaultWorkerUpdateInterval =
TimeSpan.FromSeconds(10);
public static readonly TimeSpan DefaultWorkerPingInterval =
TimeSpan.FromSeconds(300);
public static readonly TimeSpan DefaultScaleCheckInterval =
TimeSpan.FromSeconds(10);
public static readonly TimeSpan DefaultManagerCheckInterval =
TimeSpan.FromSeconds(60);
public static readonly TimeSpan DefaultStaleWorkerCheckInterval
= TimeSpan.FromSeconds(120);
```

> **Note**
>
> The preceding values come from the GitHub repository of Azure Functions Host. They may be changed after a while, but if you are interested, look at the following project: `https://github.com/Azure/azure-functions-host`.

Additionally, you can control the maximum number of instances by providing the `WEBSITE_MAX_DYNAMIC_APPLICATION_SCALE_OUT` value in the **Application settings** option of your Function App, as illustrated in the following screenshot:

Name	Value	Source
APPINSIGHTS_INSTRUMENTATIONKEY	Hidden value. Click to show value	App Service Config
AzureWebJobsStorage	Hidden value. Click to show value	App Service Config
FUNCTIONS_EXTENSION_VERSION	Hidden value. Click to show value	App Service Config
FUNCTIONS_WORKER_RUNTIME	Hidden value. Click to show value	App Service Config
LicznikNETDatabaseConnectionString	Hidden value. Click to show value	App Service Config
WEBSITE_ENABLE_SYNC_UPDATE_SITE	Hidden value. Click to show value	App Service Config
WEBSITE_MAX_DYNAMIC_APPLICATION_SCA	Hidden value. Click to show value	App Service Config
WEBSITES_ENABLE_APP_SERVICE_STORAGE	Hidden value. Click to show value	App Service Config

Figure 19.10 – Configuring the maximum number of workers for Azure Functions

What is more, if you connect the instance of your function app to an instance of Azure Application Insights, you will be able to verify how many workers it has by checking the **Live Metrics Stream** feature, as illustrated in the following screenshot:

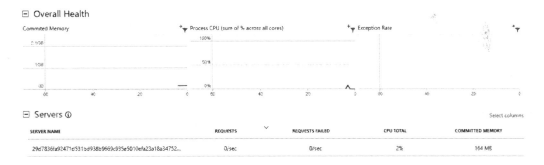

Figure 19.11 – Checking active Azure Functions hosts using Azure Application Insights

With Azure Functions scaling details described, we will now switch our focus to Azure Cosmos DB.

Scaling Azure Cosmos DB

Scaling in Azure Cosmos DB works in a different way depending on your capacity mode, as illustrated in the following screenshot:

Instance Details

Account Name *   handsoncosmos

Location *   (Europe) West Europe

Capacity mode ⓘ   ◉ Provisioned throughput ◯ Serverless

Figure 19.12 – Selecting capacity mode in Azure Cosmos DB

The difference is quite crucial as, depending on the selected mode, Azure Cosmos DB will be scaled differently, as outlined here:

- For **Provisioned throughput**, you manually select provisioned capacity for your containers. If you want to incorporate some automation, you can use the **Autopilot** feature for dynamic capacity selection.

- **Serverless** mode automatically manages available throughput for your containers.

As both capacity modes offer completely different logic for handling database load, you need to analyze the behavior of your application and apply what seems to suit it the most. For example, if you feel that you are unable to predict its performance, **Serverless** mode is a better fit. If you need geo-distribution, then you are left with only one mode as serverless Azure Cosmos DB does not support it. Another big limit is applied for storage per container—in **Serverless** mode, you are allowed to host only 50 **gigabytes** (**GB**) of data in each one. As you can see, the correct mode must be chosen carefully to get the most from your instance of the database.

Autoscaling for provisioned throughput

The **Autoscale** feature can be enabled for each container created in Azure Cosmos DB, as illustrated in the following screenshot:

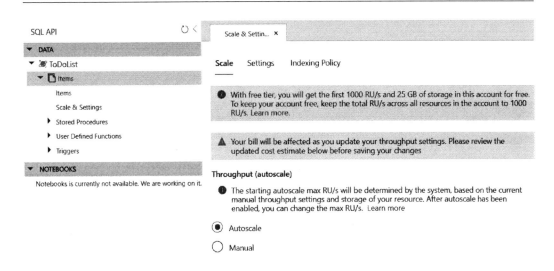

Figure 19.13 – Enabling Autoscale in Azure Cosmos DB container

Once enabled, Azure Cosmos DB will allow you to adjust the maximum number of RUs that can be used by the container, as illustrated in the following screenshot:

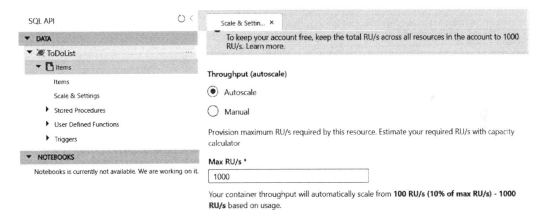

Figure 19.14 – Autoscale enabled for a container

With **Autoscale**, Azure Cosmos DB takes care of monitoring the usage of a container and modifying its throughput depending on actual metrics. The **Max RU/s** parameter can be also altered using the Azure Cosmos DB **software development kit (SDK)**, as follows:

```
// Requires Microsoft.Azure.Cosmos -Version 3.26.1
await container.ReplaceThroughputAsync(ThroughputProperties.
CreateAutoscaleThroughput(autoscaleMaxThroughput));
```

The same can be done, for example, in Java. The following code snippet illustrates how to do this:

```
// <dependency>
//    <groupId>com.azure</groupId>
//    <artifactId>azure-cosmos</artifactId>
//    <version>4.27.0</version>
// </dependency>

container.replaceThroughput(ThroughputProperties.
createAutoscaledThroughput(autoscaleMaxThroughput));
```

The last topic we will cover is scaling options for Azure Event Hubs.

Scaling Azure Event Hubs

As mentioned earlier, Azure Event Hubs is based on TUs. These tell you how many messages Azure Event Hubs can handle. For 1 TU, you will have the following available:

- Up to 1 **megabyte (MB)**/1,000 events per second for ingress
- Up to 2 MB/4,096 events for egress

Once exceeded, your instance of Azure Event Hubs will start failing by returning HTTP 429 status codes.

What we have just said is true only if you are using the **Standard** tier for your Azure Event Hubs instance. When provisioned using the **Premium** tier, the capacity of that service is defined using PUs. While much more expensive, a **Premium** instance of Azure Event Hubs with 1 PU can handle 5-10 MB of ingress and 10-20 MB for egress.

In Azure Event Hubs, you can handle all messages in parallel using partitions. The more partitions you have, the more consumers you can host. Generally speaking, this directly affects your ability to handle more traffic. If each consumer can work on its own partition without creating a bottleneck, they will linearly scale by adding more TUs/PUs.

Azure Event Hubs offers an automation mode for scaling TUs by using the **Auto-inflate** feature. Its mechanics are quite simple—you start with a minimum number of TUs, which allow your application to work without creating bottlenecks. When **Auto-inflate** is enabled, Azure Event Hubs will automatically add more throughput to handle more data. The only thing that should be taken care of is scaling down—unfortunately, **Auto-inflate** will not deflate your Event Hubs instances when traffic goes back to normal.

Summary

In this chapter, we covered the scaling of various services. You saw how this operation works for different application models—sometimes, you scale service instances and VMs, or simply, you do not control it and let the runtime do it for you. In fact, scaling services in the cloud is much easier than when using your own servers. You do not have to reconfigure load balancers, firewalls, routers, and servers. When using the scaling feature, always try to automate the process—manual scaling works only for very simple scenarios and tends to keep your servers underutilized.

In the next two chapters, we will cover two additional Azure services, **Azure Content Delivery Network** (**Azure CDN**) and Azure Traffic Manager, which help in keeping your applications available, even under heavy load.

Questions

Here are some questions to test your knowledge of the important topics in this chapter:

1. What is the difference between scaling up and scaling out?
2. What are the use cases for scaling out?
3. Is scaling up available in serverless services?
4. Does scaling out in Azure App Service affect the pricing of the service?
5. What are the cons of manual scaling?
6. What do you do if you want to automatically scale your Azure App Service instance when CPU utilization reaches 80%?

Further reading

For more information, refer to the following sources:

- Azure SDKs: `https://docs.microsoft.com/en-us/azure/index#pivot=sdkstools&panel=sdkstools-all`

- Azure Event Hubs scalability: `https://docs.microsoft.com/en-us/azure/event-hubs/event-hubs-scalability`

- Best practices for Autoscale: `https://docs.microsoft.com/en-us/azure/azure-monitor/autoscale/autoscale-best-practices`

20

Serving Static Content Using Azure CDN

Hosting many static files, especially when we're developing a highly popular application, is a serious task that impacts both the performance of our web service and the overall **user experience** (**UX**). If we load images, files, or documents too slowly, our customers may choose one of our competitors that provides similar features but performs better. Thanks to cloud services such as Azure **Content Delivery Network** (**CDN**), we're able to handle high-bandwidth content quickly, due to integration with Azure Storage and using components native to Azure.

The following topics will be covered in this chapter:

- Azure CDN fundamentals
- Optimization and caching
- Developing applications using Azure CDN

Technical requirements

To perform the exercises from this chapter, you will need the following:

- An Azure subscription

Azure CDN fundamentals

If you are hosting a popular website that contains many static files, you may wonder what the best way is to optimize serving them to your users. When searching for a solution, you must take into consideration many different factors–**Hypertext Transfer Protocol** (**HTTP**) specification, browser capabilities, your server performance, network latencies, and so on. The whole problem is far from being trivial and requires significant resources to be implemented in the right way. To overcome the listed difficulties, the idea of CDNs was developed. A CDN encapsulates the concept of a complex service that takes care of delivering content to everyone who browses your website. In this chapter, you will learn about Azure CDN, which is an Azure component that is designed to be a fast and reliable solution for all the listed problems.

Let's start by describing the process of working with CDNs and integrating them with an application.

Working with CDNs

When a user accesses your website, it must fetch all the static content that is provided for a specific page. This implies the following actions:

1. A browser must request all images, files, and scripts that are required by a web page.

2. The requests must be queued, as there is a limit on how many requests to a single domain a browser can perform.

3. In most cases, a page must be rendered gradually as content is fetched from the server.

4. A server can throttle requests if it is currently overloaded.

5. A browser must respect all implemented caching mechanisms—of course, if your website tells it how to do it.

We can describe the whole process as follows:

Figure 20.1 – A communication diagram with static files and single server

In the preceding scenario, each request from a **user** is routed directly to the **website**. It then connects with the **server** to fetch the data. Of course, we can imagine a situation where files are hosted by separate servers, as demonstrated in the following diagram:

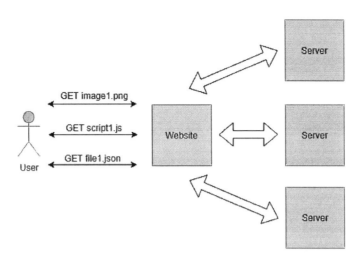

Figure 20.2 – A communication diagram with static files and multiple servers

Such an alternative can improve performance a little bit (as servers will be identified using different domain names), but it complicates maintenance and configuration. What is more, such a setup is not the right solution if you struggle with network latencies (as an additional server will not make a difference). While we are discussing different architectures, you are probably starting to imagine one more setup that may make a difference.

A proxy between a **website** and the **server** that is responsible for proper caching can be easily scaled up and is highly available, as can be seen in the following diagram:

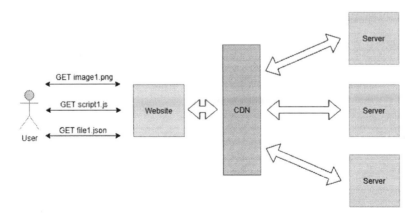

Figure 20.3 – A communication diagram with static files, multiple servers, and aCDN in place

CDNs are exactly the proxy that we are talking about. They provide the following functionalities:

- They can be easily scaled up/out if the load exceeds our expectations.

- They can cache requests, so the end servers are not utilized too much.

- They respect the cache-control header, so it is easy to provide the **time-to-live** (TTL) of a resource.

- They improve the responsiveness of your website by serving content to multiple users simultaneously.

Later in this chapter, you will learn how to leverage such services by using Azure CDN. For now, let's check how an Azure CDN can be created in the Azure portal.

Creating an Azure CDN in the portal

The process of creating an Azure CDN is like all the other services that you are working with when reading this book. To get started, you must click on the + **Create a resource** button and search for `Front Door and CDN profiles`. When you click the **Create** button, you will see a comparison of available offerings, including **Azure Front Door** and other options such as **classic**, **Verizon**, and **Akamai**. We will go for the **classic** (Microsoft) option, as you can see in the following screenshot:

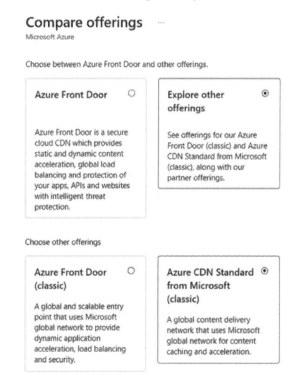

Figure 20.4 – Selected options for the classic CDN

When you proceed by clicking once again the **Create** button, you will see a form where you can enter all the required information regarding the new service, as illustrated in the following screenshot:

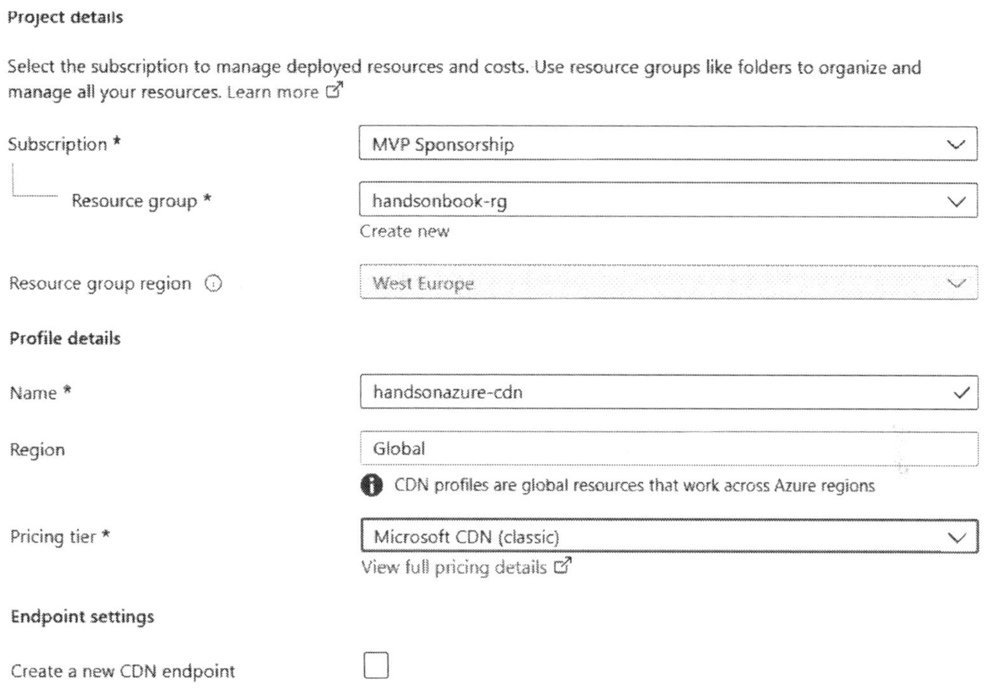

Project details

Select the subscription to manage deployed resources and costs. Use resource groups like folders to organize and manage all your resources. Learn more ☐

| Subscription * | MVP Sponsorship | ⌄ |

| Resource group * | handsonbook-rg | ⌄ |
Create new

| Resource group region ⓘ | West Europe | ⌄ |

Profile details

| Name * | handsonazure-cdn | ✓ |

| Region | Global |
ⓘ CDN profiles are global resources that work across Azure regions

| Pricing tier * | Microsoft CDN (classic) | ⌄ |
View full pricing details ☐

Endpoint settings

| Create a new CDN endpoint | ☐ |

Figure 20.5 – Creating an Azure CDN in the Azure portal

There are two things worth mentioning here, as follows:

- **Pricing tier**: Pricing tiers look a little bit different compared to other Azure services, as you no longer have the **Basic**, **Standard**, and **Premium** options to choose from. Here, you can decide which product you will be using—you can select one from a list containing providers such as **Verizon**, **Akamai**, and **Microsoft**. They offer different features, such as dynamic site acceleration, video streaming optimization, and asset pre-loading. A full list can be found in the *Further reading* section for this chapter.

- **Create a new CDN endpoint**: If you know what your origin (an endpoint that will cache the resources) will be, you can create it right now for the whole service.

To quickly check what is available in the pricing tier, you can click on the **View full pricing details** link—this will redirect you to a documentation page where all the details regarding different versions of the service will be provided.

For Azure CDN, you pay for each **gigabyte** (**GB**) of outbound data transfer, and depending on the selected provider, the price can differ almost fivefold. Therefore, when designing a solution based on Azure CDN, you should carefully read the pricing details. There are also additional features available such as data transfer acceleration, which can greatly improve the performance of your application, though they cost extra.

When you click on the **Create** button, the service creation process will start. Once it finishes, you can access your very own instance of Azure CDN, as illustrated in the following screenshot:

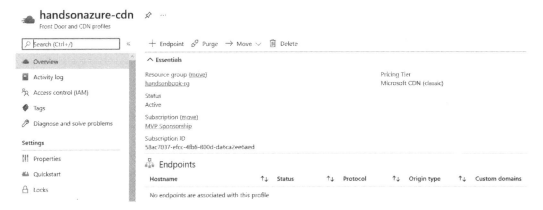

Figure 20.6 – Overview of Azure CDN

Let's now click on the + **Endpoint** button to create a new endpoint. As mentioned before, an endpoint is the element of a CDN that caches the data and serves it for a particular purpose. Here, you can find an example setup:

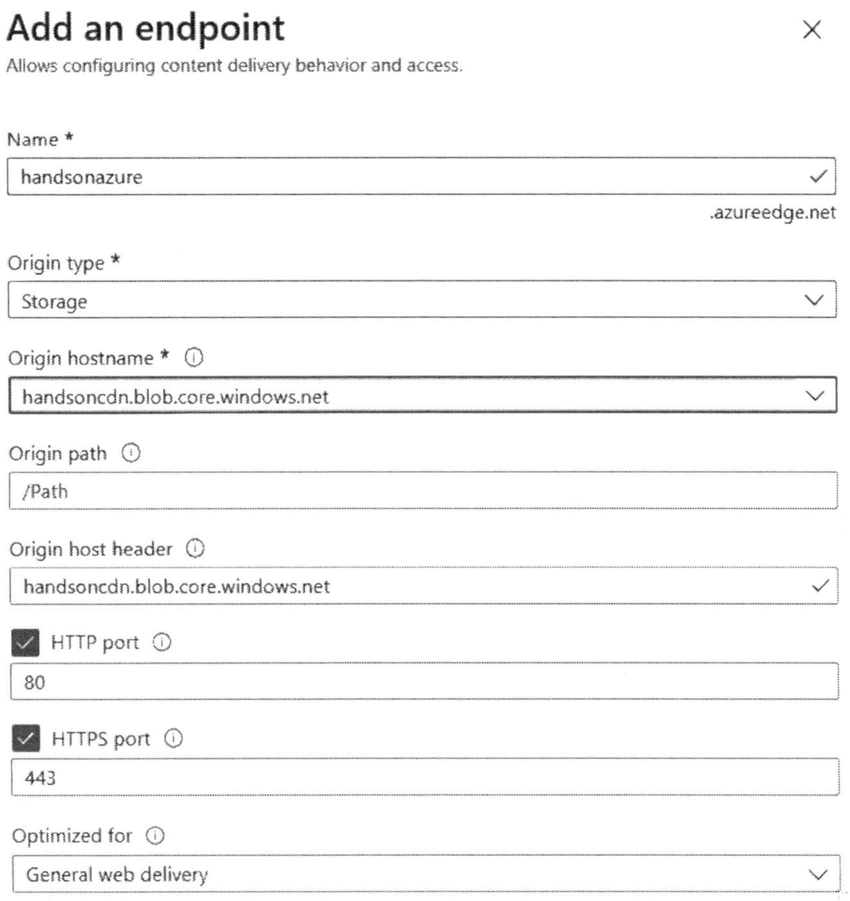

Add an endpoint   ✕

Allows configuring content delivery behavior and access.

Name *

handsonazure	✓

.azureedge.net

Origin type *

Storage	⌄

Origin hostname * ⓘ

handsoncdn.blob.core.windows.net	⌄

Origin path ⓘ

/Path

Origin host header ⓘ

handsoncdn.blob.core.windows.net	✓

☑ HTTP port ⓘ

80

☑ HTTPS port ⓘ

443

Optimized for ⓘ

General web delivery	⌄

Figure 20.7 – Configuration of a new endpoint

As you can see, I selected **Storage** as the **Origin type** value. To be able to do so, you must have an instance of Azure Storage in the same resource group as your CDN. You can also select other available types, such as **Cloud Service**, **Web App**, or a **Custom Origin** type. Once you add an endpoint, you will be able to manage it by clicking on it on the **Overview** tab.

We created a CDN service using Azure CDN—let's now do a comparison using Azure Front Door as our solution.

Optimization and caching

CDNs are all about optimizing the content and caching it. In that way, they improve the performance of your website and the UX. In the previous section, you learned a little bit about the concept of CDNs and configured your instance of Azure CDN. Now, we will try to learn some more advanced features, such as compression, caching rules, and optimization.

Configuring an endpoint

To access the endpoint configuration, click on it on the **Overview** blade, which will take you to the following screen:

Figure 20.8 – Endpoint available on the Overview blade

This will display a new screen, where you can find all information regarding that particular CDN endpoint, such as its hostname, available protocols, and configured rules for content optimization. In fact, the screen looks very similar to the previous one—it just offers some additional options, as we can see here:

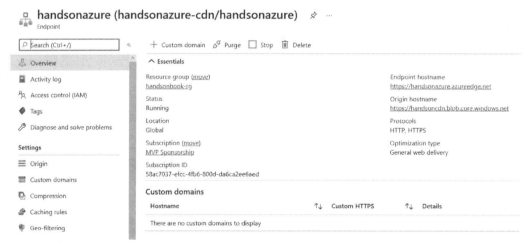

Figure 20.9 – Overview of an endpoint in Azure CDN

Now, we will discuss different features available for an endpoint.

Compression

One of the basic features of CDNs is **Compression**—this allows you to compress different file types on the fly, such as lowering their size and reducing network latency:

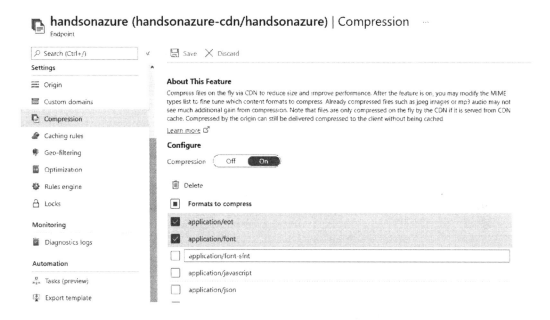

Figure 20.10 – Selecting Multipurpose Internet Mail Extensions (MIME) types for compression

When you enable it, you can select the MIME types you are interested in. You can also add new ones if you plan to support any.

> **Note**
> Remember that a file must be cached by a CDN to be compressed on the fly.

Adding a custom type will be crucial if your application supports any file type that is not listed in the list. Once added, you can simply select it and let Azure CDN handle it once cached.

Caching rules

By default, CDN caches content based on the Cache-Control header you provide. However, you can explicitly define how it should behave if one of the following applies:

- A header is missing

- A query string is introduced

- A particular *match condition* is met

By default, Azure CDN offers you a limited list of behaviors when a query string is considered, as illustrated in the following screenshot:

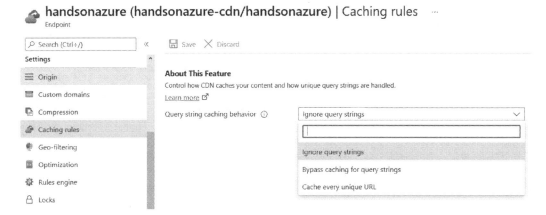

Figure 20.11 – Default caching rules

Fortunately, you can control the behavior of the service using custom caching rules, as illustrated in the following screenshot:

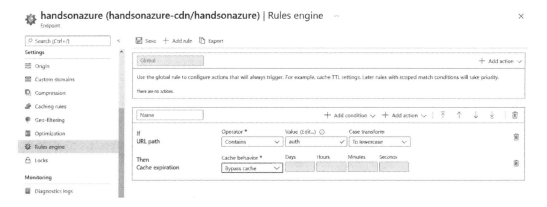

Figure 20.12 – Configuring custom caching rules with Rules engine

By using **Rules engine**, you can configure any behavior you want for your system. For example, if you feel there are some paths that should be excluded from the cache, this is the place to do that. The same applies to the logic behind headers, or even payloads sent via the request body.

Geo-filtering

Sometimes, you need to block or allow content for specific countries. Such a feature might be problematic without a CDN—you must control programmatically who can access a given image or a file based on the geo-location. With Azure CDN, you can enable it within seconds, as illustrated in the following screenshot:

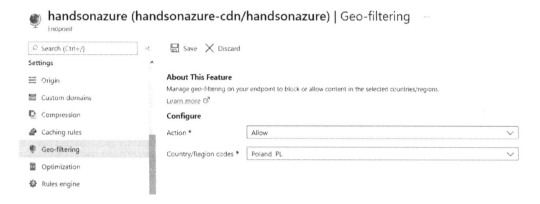

Figure 20.13 – Configuring geo-filtering

On the **Geo-filtering** blade, you can configure different rules blocking or allowing access to a folder or a particular file inside a CDN for a particular country.

The last part of this chapter is related to integrating Azure CDN with an application. We are going to see how managed Azure services can leverage what Azure CDN offers to them and what that integration changes from a source-code point of view.

Developing applications using Azure CDN

Azure CDN itself does not give you anything special—it just caches content and takes responsibility for serving it without delays. The important thing, however, is to know how you can use it in your applications. In Azure, integrating Azure CDN with—for example—Azure App Service—is a piece of cake. It only takes a few mouse clicks to get your CDN working with your existing web applications. In the last section of this chapter, you will see what is required to get the integration set up and ready to improve your website's performance.

Configuring Azure App Service with Azure CDN

To configure Azure App Service to work with your instance of Azure CDN, you will need to go to the **Networking** blade, as shown in the following screenshot. This gives you the ability to enable different web app features, including a CDN:

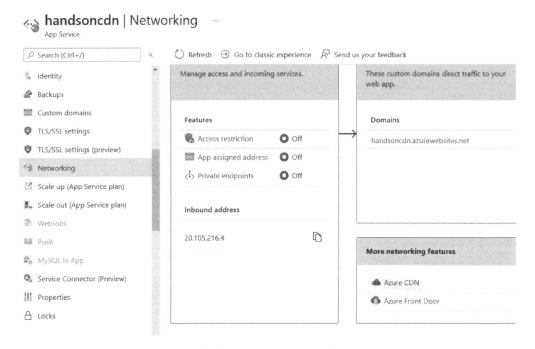

Figure 20.14 – The Networking tab for Azure App Service with Azure CDN

When you click on **Azure CDN**, you will see another screen where you can configure the link between Azure App Service and Azure CDN.

> **Note**
> Azure CDN will automatically start caching static files that can be found on your site. It is a good idea to publish your application at this moment so that you will not have to wait for the process to end later.

In fact, you have two options to proceed now, as follows:

- Use the existing CDN profile (if you performed the exercises from the previous section of this chapter, you should have your CDN already created and ready to work).

- Create a brand-new profile.

In the following screenshot, you can find my configuration (I chose an existing endpoint to speed things up):

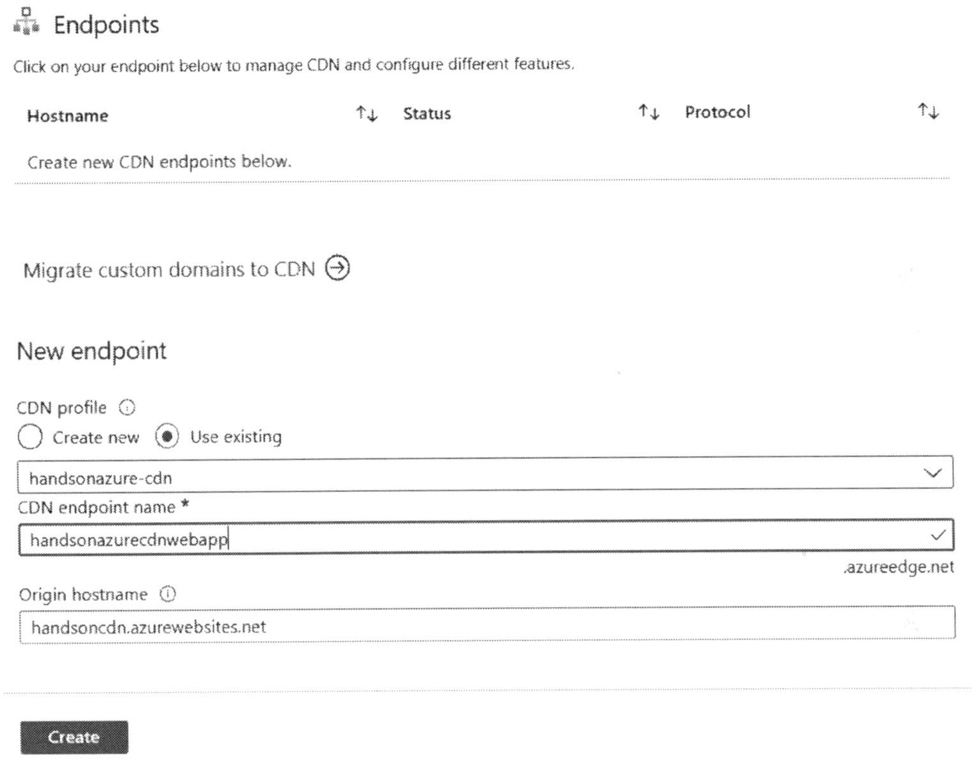

Endpoints

Click on your endpoint below to manage CDN and configure different features.

Hostname	↑↓	Status	↑↓	Protocol	↑↓
Create new CDN endpoints below.					

Migrate custom domains to CDN →

New endpoint

CDN profile ⓘ
◯ Create new ⦿ Use existing

handsonazure-cdn	∨

CDN endpoint name *

handsonazurecdnwebapp	✓

.azureedge.net

Origin hostname ⓘ

handsoncdn.azurewebsites.net	

Create

Figure 20.15 – Configuring an endpoint for Azure CDN and Azure App Service

Once your endpoint is created, you can check whether it works. To do so, you can check—for example—the source of your application, as I did here:

```
<!DOCTYPE html>
<html lang="en">
▼<head>
    <meta charset="utf-8">
    <meta name="viewport" content="width=device-width, initial-scale=1.0">
    <meta http-equiv="X-UA-Compatible" content="IE=edge">
    <title>Microsoft Azure App Service - Welcome</title>
    <link rel="shortcut icon" href="https://appservice.azureedge.net/images/app-service/v4/favicon.ico"
    type="image/x-icon">
    <link href="https://appservice.azureedge.net/css/app-service/v4/bootstrap.min.css" rel="stylesheet"
    crossorigin="anonymous">
  ▶<style>...</style>
    <script src="https://appservice.azureedge.net/js/app-service/v4/loc.min.js" crossorigin="anonymou
    s"></script>
  ▶<script type="text/javascript">...</script>
    </head>
▼<body> == $0
  ▶<nav class="navbar">...</nav> flex
  ▼<div class="container-fluid mr-2 mt-5 pt-5">
    ▶<div class="row">...</div> flex
    ▶<div class="row mt-4">...</div> flex
    </div>
    </body>
</html>
```

Figure 20.16 – Source of an application running on Azure App Service with Azure CDN

As you can see, with the CDN configured, the source of my application is automatically altered—all static content is served using my Azure CDN endpoint instead of my server. This will improve overall load times for my files and let customers access the website quicker.

Summary

In this chapter, you learned what CDNs are and how they may help you in achieving better performance and an improved UX for your web applications. We have configured an Azure CDN instance and saw how to optimize serving content by compressing it. After reading this chapter, you should be able to filter content for countries and develop proper caching rules so that you can define how your instance will behave.

In the next chapters, we are going to cover more advanced topics related to load balancing and **application programming interface** (**API**) management with services such as Azure Traffic Manager, Azure Front Door, and Azure API Management.

Questions

Here are some questions to test your knowledge of the important topics covered in this chapter:

1. Which problems does the use of Azure CDN solve?
2. What are the available CDN providers for Azure CDN?
3. What is the origin of a CDN?
4. How does compression work in Azure CDN?
5. What is the default TTL of content stored within Azure CDN?

Further reading

For more information, refer to the following source:

- CDN features: `https://docs.microsoft.com/en-us/azure/cdn/cdn-features`

21
Managing APIs with Azure API Management

The more applications you have, the more important it becomes to understand their interfaces. Multiple public endpoints managed in various places make administration and development tricky and error-prone. To address **application programming interface** (**API**)-heavy architecture issues, Microsoft Azure offers Azure API Management—a modern and flexible API gateway.

Understanding how to manage multiple APIs on an Azure level becomes more and more important for all systems that were recently created or are undergoing a design phase. This is caused by both an increasing number of working services and a more complex architecture that requires a service to centralize API management.

The following topics will be covered in this chapter:

- The main concepts of Azure API Management
- Guidelines for designing APIs
- The basics of Azure API Management policies with examples
- Automated management of the service

Technical requirements

To perform the exercises in this chapter, you will need the following:

- An Azure subscription

The main concepts of Azure API Management

Before we get started with Azure API Management as a service, let's briefly discuss the purpose of this service. In many **information technology** (**IT**) systems, there are various APIs that are often built by different teams using different technologies. Each of these APIs must authenticate requests, track them, and possibly implement a sophisticated way to handle retries, caching, or thresholding. While doing all these independently may not seem like a bad idea, in most scenarios, it will be considered a bad practice.

The reason for avoiding doing such operations individually in each service is simple–we want to avoid duplication. It is not only relevant for the code base—where architecture is designed, the overall aim is to reuse available components if possible. If there is a way to centralize mentioned features, we should always leverage it.

This is where services such as Azure API Management come into play—they act as a centralized service for managing various APIs across multiple environments. You can treat them as a way of solving more *general* problems, such as the following:

- API discovery
- Centralized security
- Centralized API management
- **Single point of entry** (**SPOE**) for a company's APIs

Azure API Management has three main concepts that we need to understand before going forward, as outlined here:

- **API gateway**, which is a proxy passing requests further to all the backends
- **Management plane** used for configuration of the service, setting up policies, and managing users
- **Developer portal**

All combined make Azure API Management.

API gateway

Most of the logic of the Azure API Management service is done within an API gateway. This is quite a busy component as it is responsible for multiple things, including the following:

- When you configure your API to have a quota or rate limit, the API gateway is responsible for enforcing it.
- It validates credentials (such as **JavaScript Object Notation** (**JSON**) **Web Token** (**JWT**) tokens and API keys).

- It caches request data if caching is configured for your API.

- As all the logging and tracing is done within the API gateway, it is also the main component for reporting and troubleshooting.

As you can see, the API gateway will be one of the most important components for us as many features available for Azure API Management are implemented inside it.

> **Note**
>
> An API gateway has two modes of deployment—managed and self-hosted. When a self-hosted mode is used, you can deploy it directly into the same network as your other services. This enables you to improve traffic and be compliant with any legal requirements.

While in most cases we will not interact with the API gateway directly, it will still be a crucial component of the whole ecosystem.

Management plane

To configure Azure API Management, we will use the management plane. Simply put, this is a layer of the service that handles requests coming from administrators to set up various settings. This component allows us to not only manage Azure API Management itself but also to import APIs using specifications (such as OpenAPI) and set up policies. We cannot perform management tasks without connecting with that layer.

Developer portal

A developer portal is a website that is automatically generated and can be easily customized. Its main purpose is to host things such as documentation of your APIs and interact with them using an interactive console. Using the portal is optional—you can connect to APIs proxied with Azure API Management with traditional tools (including **command-line interface** (**CLI**) tools, custom code, or even browsers). On the other hand, it simplifies the distribution of APIs to end users.

With some fundaments explained, let's learn more about designing APIs and onboarding them to the cloud with Azure API Management.

Guidelines for designing APIs

When designing an API, you need to consider the following aspects:

- Who is the consumer (is this an internal/external API)?

- Which protocol will be used for connection and information exchange?

- How will authentication be performed (if any)?

- What are the performance goals of the API?

- Do you need additional features such as throttling/caching/**conditional access** (**CA**)?

- Are you planning to monetize your API?

Depending on your answer, the use of Azure API Management may or may not be justified. A general rule of introducing such a service depends on your business capabilities and requirements. That said, we always need to challenge our choice against requirements and overall goals.

As it is now possible to host Azure API Management in serverless mode (meaning you pay only for usage), this is still a service mostly beneficial for bigger companies that can leverage its capabilities and see value in centralizing the management of APIs. As Azure API Management is much more complicated in terms of administration and proper design than developer-oriented services (such as Azure App Service or Azure Container Instances), the decision to provision it should involve consulting with other potential users.

It is difficult to determine when deployment of Azure API Management seems like a good idea (because numbers will be different for each company), but we can materialize some general guidelines helpful when making a choice, as follows:

- If there are several APIs in design/already deployed, it seems like a good idea to connect to them through a single proxy.

- Instead of authenticating each service, it may be beneficial to implement it in a single place and just pass requests through the service.

- When working on inventory for a company, putting all the APIs into Azure API Management will improve the discoverability of services.

- Deploying Azure API Management sooner rather than later will also help in potential migration and ensure that all teams can start using its features from the very beginning.

Initially, Azure API Management may look like an overhead, but in many scenarios, it will bring benefits right from the start. The approach is like using reservations in Azure for things such as **virtual machines** (**VMs**)—while you should use them from the very beginning, many people avoid them until they have several machines under their command, thus losing the opportunity to start saving money from day one.

Using Azure API Management also affects the way an API is designed from a code point of view. Normally, we should consider a way to inject additional functionalities for each request coming to our API. Those functionalities are sometimes quite complex and are what increase the technical debt of each service's code base and enforce development teams to maintain them. If a proxy is introduced to handle such logic, each service focuses on the business value it brings without additional responsibilities.

Ultimately, we end up with a healthier ecosystem—each component has its own responsibilities and we do not reinvent the wheel. Let's now check how Azure API Management is deployed and how we can deploy a custom policy handling all requests.

Basics of Azure API Management policies with examples

In this section, we will focus on provisioning our own Azure API Management instance with a policy deployed. Before we start on the practical aspects, let's define what a *policy* is.

As Azure API Management acts as a proxy for each request, it can apply various checks and enforcements for them. In other words, if we want to verify the contents of a request, validate it, block it, or apply a rate limit, a policy is exactly what we need.

> **Note**
>
> Azure API Management allows for the deployment of both in-built and custom policies. In-built policies can also be changed to speed up the deployment of custom ones.

Policy schema

Each policy has a fixed schema that we can extend based on desired logic, as illustrated in the following code snippet:

```
<policies>
  <inbound>
    <!-- logic applied for incoming requests -->
  </inbound>
  <backend>
    <!-- logic applied before passing a request downstream -->
  </backend>
  <outbound>
    <!-- logic applied for each response -->
  </outbound>
  <on-error>
    <!-- handling errors -->
  </on-error>
</policies>
```

As you can see, a policy is a simple **Extensible Markup Language** (**XML**) document where we can put the logic for both inbound and outbound communication. Depending on the direction of the communication, a policy will be applied for different actors, as follows:

- When using a `<inbound>` block, we are handling incoming traffic directly.
- When using a `<backend>` block, we apply logic after the `<inbound>` block is evaluated.
- When using a `<outbound>` block, we operate on data sent by the API itself.

There is also a `<on-error>` block, which is helpful when we want to handle any errors that may happen in other blocks.

What we can do inside a policy depends on the function used. For example, if we want to add a header to a request, we can use a `<set-header>` policy, like this:

```
<policies>
    <inbound>
        <base />
        <set-header name="my-custom-header" exists-
action="override">
            <value>My custom value</value>
        </set-header>
    </inbound>
</policies>
```

This simple policy will add a `my-custom-header` header to each request reaching our backend. Another example would be some validation policy that checks whether a request contains a header with a valid value. To do that, we can use a `<check-header>` policy, like so:

```
<policies>
    <inbound>
        <base />
        <check-header name="Authorization" failed-check-
httpcode="401" failed-check-error-message="Not authorized"
ignore-case="false">
```

```
            <value>my-super-secret-code</value>
        </check-header>
    </inbound>
</policies>
```

The preceding example policy checks whether a request contains an Authorization header and whether it has a my-super-secret code value. If the check fails, HTTP 401 is returned. Now, let's check how policies are configured inside the service.

Provisioning the Azure API Management service

Azure API Management is provisioned in the same manner as other Azure services. To do that using the Azure portal, you can use the + **Create a resource** button and search for API Management, as illustrated in the following screenshot. Then, just click the **Create** button to see a wizard appear:

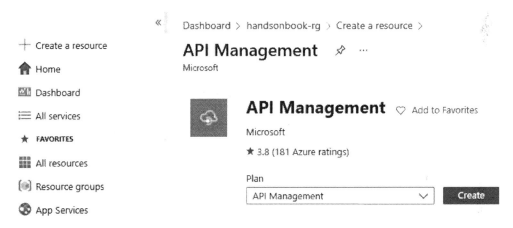

Figure 21.1 – Selecting Azure API Management in Azure Marketplace

Provisioning an instance of Azure API Management is not difficult, but it requires a few steps to complete. The first thing needed is configuring the basics of the service, as follows:

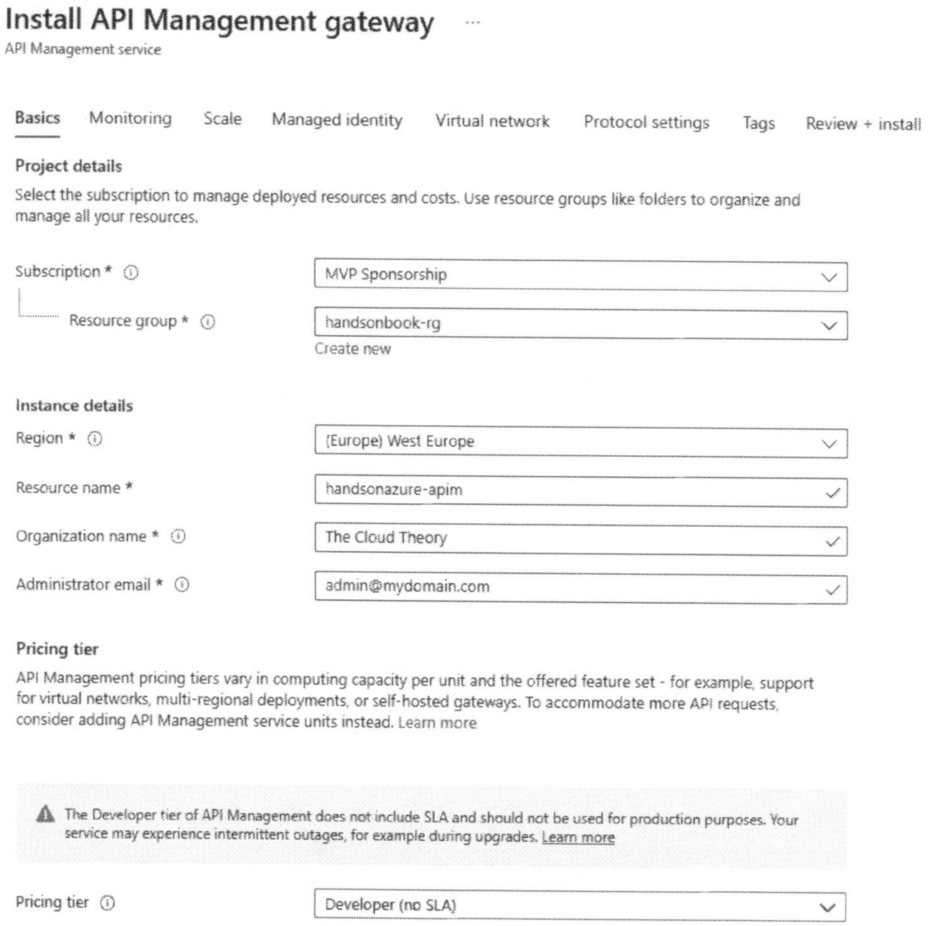

Install API Management gateway ...
API Management service

| Basics | Monitoring | Scale | Managed identity | Virtual network | Protocol settings | Tags | Review + install |

Project details

Select the subscription to manage deployed resources and costs. Use resource groups like folders to organize and manage all your resources.

Subscription * ⓘ — MVP Sponsorship

⌐ Resource group * ⓘ — handsonbook-rg
Create new

Instance details

Region * ⓘ — (Europe) West Europe

Resource name * — handsonazure-apim

Organization name * ⓘ — The Cloud Theory

Administrator email * ⓘ — admin@mydomain.com

Pricing tier

API Management pricing tiers vary in computing capacity per unit and the offered feature set - for example, support for virtual networks, multi-regional deployments, or self-hosted gateways. To accommodate more API requests, consider adding API Management service units instead. Learn more

⚠ The Developer tier of API Management does not include SLA and should not be used for production purposes. Your service may experience intermittent outages, for example during upgrades. Learn more

Pricing tier ⓘ — Developer (no SLA)

Figure 21.2 – Configuring the basics

The **Basics** tab asks for some standard information such as subscription, resource group, and instance name. We need to also enter the organization name and email address of an administrator. Those values should reflect the actual owner of Azure API Management. If you are creating an instance just for prototyping, you can enter any value here. For all other scenarios, make sure that those values are correct.

An important choice here is the pricing tier. Azure API Management offers five different tiers to choose from, as follows:

- **Developer**
- **Basic**
- **Standard**
- **Premium**
- **Consumption**

Each tier offers different features and **service-level agreements** (**SLAs**), so the actual choice depends on the purpose of the provisioned instance.

> **Note**
>
> The **Developer** tier for Azure API Management offers no SLA. It is a great choice for testing but should not be used for production scenarios.

All pricing tiers apart from **Consumption** are priced based on the time a service is deployed. The **Consumption** tier offers pricing in a *pay-as-you-go* model, meaning it scales with usage. Its scaling capabilities are also different as an instance deployed using that pricing tier scales automatically, depending on incoming traffic.

While Azure API Management offers some additional configuration options (such as integration with Azure Application Insights, **virtual network** (**VNet**) integration, and automated managed identity creation), we will skip these in this chapter and go directly to the **Review + Create** tab for a final check. Once the check is complete, click on the **Create** button to start provisioning your instance. This may take a while, so be patient—in some cases, it may take up to 2 hours!

> **Tip**
>
> While the **Consumption** tier may be tempting, before choosing it, make sure you have checked all the differences between it and fixed pricing. Besides scaling differences, the **Consumption** tier is considered shared, meaning it lacks isolation capabilities offered by other tiers.

Once your instance is successfully provisioned, we can configure our first policy. To do so, we need to access the **APIs** tab within an instance of Azure API Management, as illustrated in the following screenshot:

Figure 21.3 – Accessing the APIs tab

Inside that tab, you will have an option to import a new API or access an Echo API, which is a predefined API created with each new Azure API Management instance. When you click on **Echo API**, you will get access to its configuration view, as illustrated in the following screenshot:

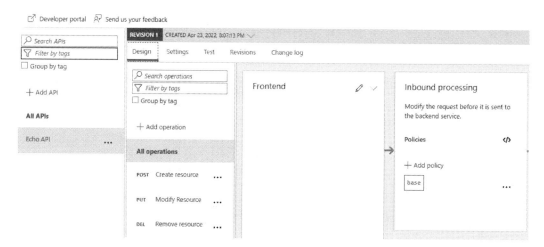

Figure 21.4 – Echo API configuration view

As you can see, here, we can configure things such as available operations, API specifications, and policies for both inbound and outbound communication. This is the place where our policies can be configured.

> **Note**
> Each API in Azure API Management is defined by its schema. While changes can be done mostly via the **user interface** (**UI**), under the hood APIs use a strict specification that can be altered at any moment.

If you click on the + **Add policy** button for inbound processing, you will see a screen where we can select a policy for incoming requests. Let's set up a policy that will add a header when a request is processed. To do that, use the **Set headers** policy from the available list, as illustrated in the following screenshot:

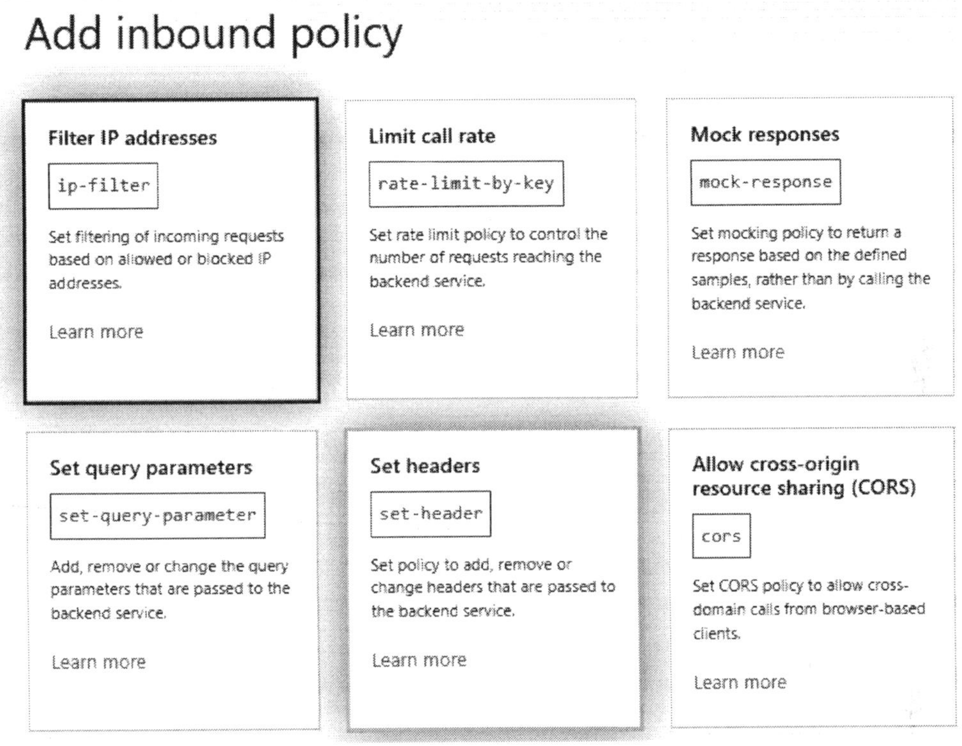

Add inbound policy

Filter IP addresses

`ip-filter`

Set filtering of incoming requests based on allowed or blocked IP addresses.

Learn more

Limit call rate

`rate-limit-by-key`

Set rate limit policy to control the number of requests reaching the backend service.

Learn more

Mock responses

`mock-response`

Set mocking policy to return a response based on the defined samples, rather than by calling the backend service.

Learn more

Set query parameters

`set-query-parameter`

Add, remove or change the query parameters that are passed to the backend service.

Learn more

Set headers

`set-header`

Set policy to add, remove or change headers that are passed to the backend service.

Learn more

Allow cross-origin resource sharing (CORS)

`cors`

Set CORS policy to allow cross-domain calls from browser-based clients.

Learn more

Figure 21.5 – Selecting a policy

The described policy allows you to either add, change, or remove a header for an incoming request. This is helpful—for example—when each request must be decorated with an additional header, but you do not want to do that on an application level. The reason for that is simple—such operations can be done centrally as they are required by central teams handling things such as logging and monitoring. Doing that on an application level is possible but is often difficult as in most scenarios, changing an application's code requires a new release. What is more, adding such a header only after a request reaches the application could be useless as most of the traces are lost.

The following screenshot demonstrates how to add a policy in the Azure API Management service:

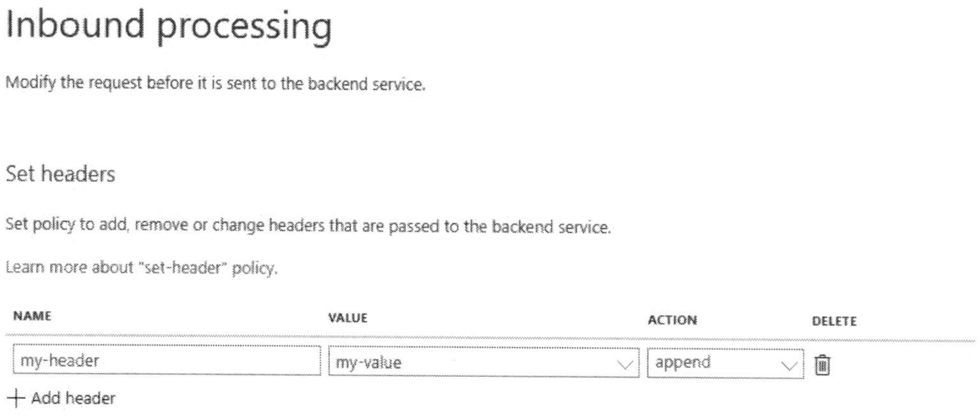

Inbound processing

Modify the request before it is sent to the backend service.

Set headers

Set policy to add, remove or change headers that are passed to the backend service.

Learn more about "set-header" policy.

NAME	VALUE	ACTION	DELETE
my-header	my-value	append	🗑

+ Add header

Figure 21.6 – Adding a policy in Azure API Management

You can add many policies for various operations if needed and combine them depending on your needs. There is a full reference of policies that are available for the service—you can find this in the *Further reading* section for this chapter.

Let's now see what automated management of Azure API Management looks like.

Automated management of the service

Azure API Management is a service that, in many scenarios, requires manual intervention to add a new API, product, or policy. However, certain activities can be automated and ease management tasks when managing the service.

To manage your instance and perform automation tasks, you need access to proper operations through an interface that can be used in a script or application code. Fortunately, Azure API Management offers access to its API via PowerShell commands. For example, if you want to create a user, you can use the following commands:

```
$context = New-AzApiManagementContext -ResourceGroupName
"resource-group" -ServiceName "name-of-your-instance"

$user = New-AzApiManagementUser -Context $context -FirstName
"first-name" -LastName "last-name" -Password "password" -State
"Active" -Note "custom-note" -Email "user-email"
```

As you can see, to perform any operation on your instance of the service, you need a context object. A context object is obtained via the `New-AzApiManagementContext` command, which requires both the name of your instance of Azure API Management and its resource group. Another example command that we could use imports an API, as illustrated in the following code snippet:

```
$context = New-AzApiManagementContext -ResourceGroupName
"resource-group" -ServiceName "name-of-your-instance"
$api = Import-AzApiManagementApi -Context $context
-SpecificationUrl "swagger-url" -SpecificationFormat Swagger
-Path "api-path"
```

The preceding command imports an API schema written using the Swagger format. There are also additional options available such as **Web Application Description Language** (**WADL**) or OpenAPI, so you can adjust the command depending on your needs. If you wish to use them, you need to change the value of the `SpecificationFormat` parameter, as follows:

- Use `Wadl` for WADL.
- Use `Swagger` if you have your API specification prepared in the Swagger format.
- Use `OpenApi` if the specification you use is OpenAPI.

Additionally, you can decide whether a specification will be fetched from a local file or a remotely available **Uniform Resource Locator** (**URL**). To do this, you must select either the `SpecificationPath` or `SpecificationUrl` parameter, which are described in more detail here:

- `SpecificationPath` is used to point to a local file.
- `SpecificationUrl` is helpful when an API is already present on a web server.

Either way, your API will be imported if all parameters are entered correctly.

> **Note**
> When using `SpecificationPath`, your API is not required to be available. This allows you to configure it upfront before the code is deployed to a web server.

We talked a little bit about managing Azure API Management using Azure PowerShell but we must still understand how to run those commands. As the service does not offer inbuilt ways to automate operations, another hosting option for those scripts must be considered. As the only requirement here is access to PowerShell, there are several possibilities to select from, such as the following:

- You can run those scripts manually from your computer.
- Scripts can be hosted on a VM and run with a task scheduler.

- You can create a Docker image and then run containers using any container-hosting platform (this could be Kubernetes, Azure Container Instances, or Docker Compose).

- You can run Azure functions written in PowerShell and use them to execute mentioned commands.

As you can see, there is a variety of different options available—everything depends on actual requirements and technical needs. You can also consider using Azure Automation (which is not covered in this book) as a managed platform for running automation tasks related to your infrastructure. See the *Further reading* section for a commands reference and a better picture of what is possible with that PowerShell module.

Summary

In this chapter, we covered Azure API Management as a proxy service that can act as a discovery service and entry point for APIs developed by your organization. We learned some fundamental concepts and browsed some policies that can be used to control how a request is handled and passed to configured backends.

This chapter starts the last part of the book, where we discuss multiple options for traffic management, routing, load balancing, and controlling ingress. Make sure to check the next two chapters for a whole picture of those services in relation to **platform-as-a-service** (**PaaS**) components.

Questions

Here are some questions to test your knowledge of the important topics covered in this chapter:

1. Which available specifications for an API in Azure API Management can you import?
2. Which component in Azure API Management is responsible for handling incoming requests?
3. Can you add a policy for outbound communication?
4. Which tool is used to automate management tasks for Azure API Management?
5. Can you remove a header using a policy in Azure API Management?
6. Can you implement throttling using Azure API Management?

Further reading

For more information, refer to the following sources:

- API Management PowerShell reference: `https://docs.microsoft.com/en-us/powershell/module/az.apimanagement`

- Self-hosted gateway feature: `https://docs.microsoft.com/en-us/azure/api-management/self-hosted-gateway-overview`

- VNet integration: `https://docs.microsoft.com/en-us/azure/api-management/virtual-network-concepts?tabs=stv2`

- Policies overview: `https://docs.microsoft.com/en-us/azure/api-management/set-edit-policies?tabs=form`

- Azure Automation: `https://docs.microsoft.com/en-us/azure/automation/overview`

22

Building a Scalable Entry Point for Your Service with Azure Front Door

Building a highly scalable and worldwide application requires experience and the right toolset. Connecting clients from various areas and offering them the very same level of performance and functionalities is often one of the key requirements of an application. With Azure Front Door, you can connect your services with high-performing edge locations, load-balance with ease, and control traffic via firewalls and custom forwarding rules.

Understanding global load-balancing options such as Azure Front Door will help you build scalable architectures and applications that can reach customers across the globe.

The following topics will be covered in this chapter:

- When to use Azure Front Door
- Load balancing with Azure Front Door
- Implementing **Uniform Resource Locator** (**URL**) rewrites and redirects

Technical requirements

To perform the exercises in this chapter, you will need the following:

- An Azure subscription

When to use Azure Front Door

When building a scalable application, you must always consider how data will be delivered to your customers. Files, **application programming interfaces** (**APIs**), and web pages should always be available and—possibly—cached to improve performance and lower latency. When global reach is considered, you need to find a reliable service that not only serves static content but also allows for integration with a backbone network and works as the first line of defense against common attacks.

Azure Front Door is a unique solution for traffic management as it is deployed to Azure edge locations and leverages the backbone network of Microsoft to help route all requests in an optimal manner. The overall idea is presented in the following diagram:

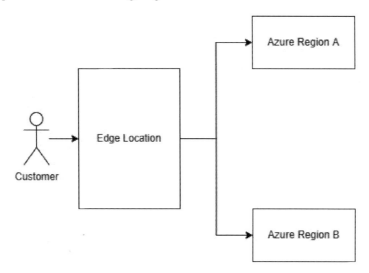

Figure 22.1 – General routing concept for Azure Front Door

As you can see, when Azure Front Door is deployed and used in your communication path, the customer firstly connects with it, and then the connection is handled by the service instance itself. This allows for achieving optimal performance as Azure Front Door becomes responsible not only for routing but also for additional operations such as maintaining connections, verifying requests against **Open Web Application Security Project** (**OWASP**) rules, and handling **Secure Sockets Layer** (**SSL**).

> **Note**
>
> Azure Front Door can handle SSL connections and act as a termination point of certificate validation. In other words, you can offload SSL handling to it so that your services do not have to do that by themselves.

As Azure Front Door is considered a load balancer, you should always consider its capabilities and challenge them against other available solutions. Here is a short summary of different options and their features:

- If you need to manage traffic on a global level, choose between Azure Front Door and Azure Traffic Manager.

- For regional traffic management, Azure Application Gateway and Azure Load Balancer are viable options.

- When **Hypertext Transfer Protocol (HTTP)/HTTP Secure (HTTPS)** traffic is considered, use Azure Traffic Manager or Azure Load Balancer for HTTP and Azure Front Door/Azure Application Gateway for HTTPS.

- Remember that each load-balancing option works on a different layer—Azure Traffic Manager is a **Domain Name System (DNS)**-based load balancer, both Azure Front Door and Azure Application Gateway use Layer 7 for their work, while Azure Load Balancer acts as a Layer 4 load-balancing option.

- Teach your architecture to select a service that you can integrate easily with. Azure Load Balancer can be easily integrated with a cluster of **virtual machines (VMs)**, while Azure Front Door and Azure Application Gateway are perfect choices for web applications.

- Some options can work in tandem with each other. For example, when using **Azure Kubernetes Service (AKS)**, you can use Azure Front Door as a global load balancer and then Azure Application Gateway as an ingress controller. A similar setup is possible when hosting your applications directly on VMs—then, Azure Application Gateway would be replaced with Azure Load Balancer.

As there are several combinations available, I strongly recommend checking the reference architectures in the *Further reading* section. This will help you understand the pros and cons of all the solutions and can be used as starting point for building your own solution.

Let's now check how load balancing is configured with Azure Front Door.

Load balancing with Azure Front Door

In Azure Front Door, load balancing is configured using three connected components, as follows:

- Frontends
- Backend pools
- Routing rules

Each component can be added individually and reused for improved flexibility. Before we dive into the details, we need to provision our own instance of the service so that we can start configuring it. Here's what we should do:

1. In the Azure portal, click on the + **Create a resource** button and search for `Front Door`. The option to select is **Front Door and CDN profiles**, as illustrated in the following screenshot:

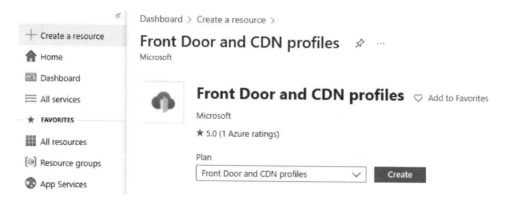

Figure 22.2 – Using Azure Marketplace for Azure Front Door provisioning

2. Now, click the **Create** button so the next screen is displayed with a few options available, as we can see here:

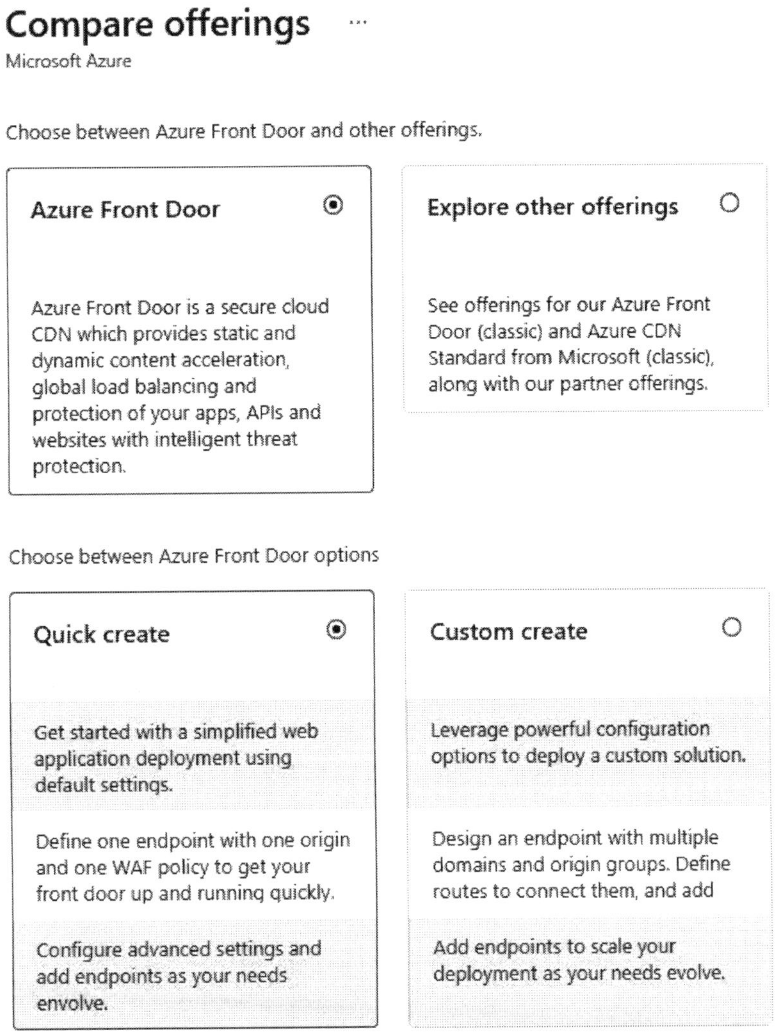

Compare offerings   ...

Microsoft Azure

Choose between Azure Front Door and other offerings.

Azure Front Door ⊙

Azure Front Door is a secure cloud CDN which provides static and dynamic content acceleration, global load balancing and protection of your apps, APIs and websites with intelligent threat protection.

Explore other offerings ○

See offerings for our Azure Front Door (classic) and Azure CDN Standard from Microsoft (classic), along with our partner offerings.

Choose between Azure Front Door options

Quick create ⊙

Get started with a simplified web application deployment using default settings.

Define one endpoint with one origin and one WAF policy to get your front door up and running quickly.

Configure advanced settings and add endpoints as your needs envolve.

Custom create ○

Leverage powerful configuration options to deploy a custom solution.

Design an endpoint with multiple domains and origin groups. Define routes to connect them, and add

Add endpoints to scale your deployment as your needs evolve.

Figure 22.3 – Selecting an offering

3. As you can see, we can either create an Azure Front Door instance here or choose an alternative offering made by Microsoft and its partners. For that exercise, use the default options (**Azure Front Door** and **Quick create**). After proceeding, you will see a default screen containing common configuration options for Azure services, as illustrated in the following screenshot:

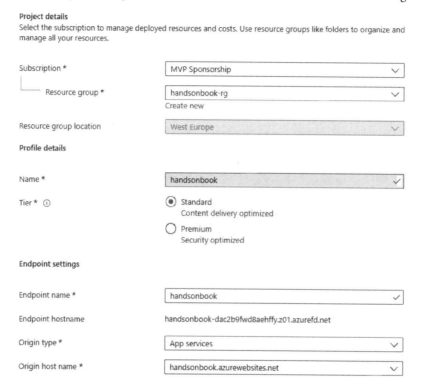

Figure 22.4 – Configuring basic options of Azure Front Door

For now, the most important thing is configuring an endpoint. As we have not described that concept yet, let's stop for a moment to explain this.

When Azure Front Door is configured, it needs to route requests somewhere. There are multiple options available—it could be Azure Storage, a static web app, Azure App Service, another load balancer (Azure Traffic Manager, Azure Application Gateway), or a simple public **Internet Protocol** (**IP**) address. Endpoints are the fundamental configuration option for that service as they define a destination for incoming requests.

> **Tip**
>
> If you do not have an available endpoint, you can create any supported service in parallel and then select it in the form shown in *Figure 22.4*. It does not have to be a production-grade service to start working with Azure Front Door.

4. As we selected **Quick create** here, we do not have many things to configure besides the endpoint. There is a possibility to enable caching or create a **Web Application Firewall** (**WAF**) policy, but we will skip that for now. Once you have entered all the required information, click on the **Review + create** button and start the provisioning of your instance.

When you access an instance of Azure Front Door, you will find the **Front Door manager** functionality, which allows for adding additional endpoints if needed. In the following screenshot, you can see an illustration of this functionality:

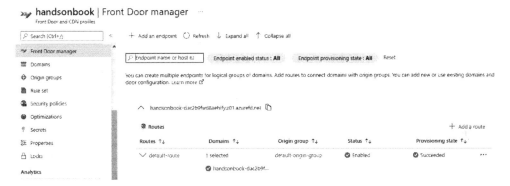

Figure 22.5 – Front Door manager

There is, however, one thing that needs clarification. When we configured our instance using the creation wizard, it asked us to enter endpoint details. What was hidden from us was the fact that under the hood, such a configuration creates more than an endpoint, as explained here:

*   By selecting **Origin type**, we chose what kind of origin will be configured.
*   A default route was created.

5. Now, when we want to configure an additional backend (such as—for example—Azure Storage), we need to use the **Origin groups** feature, as shown in the following screenshot:

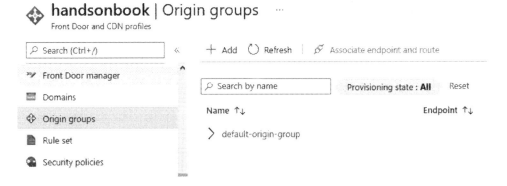

Figure 22.6 – Origin groups feature

6. By clicking on the + **Add** button, you will see an advanced form where you can not only enter origin details but also configure health probes and load-balancing settings, as illustrated in the following screenshot:

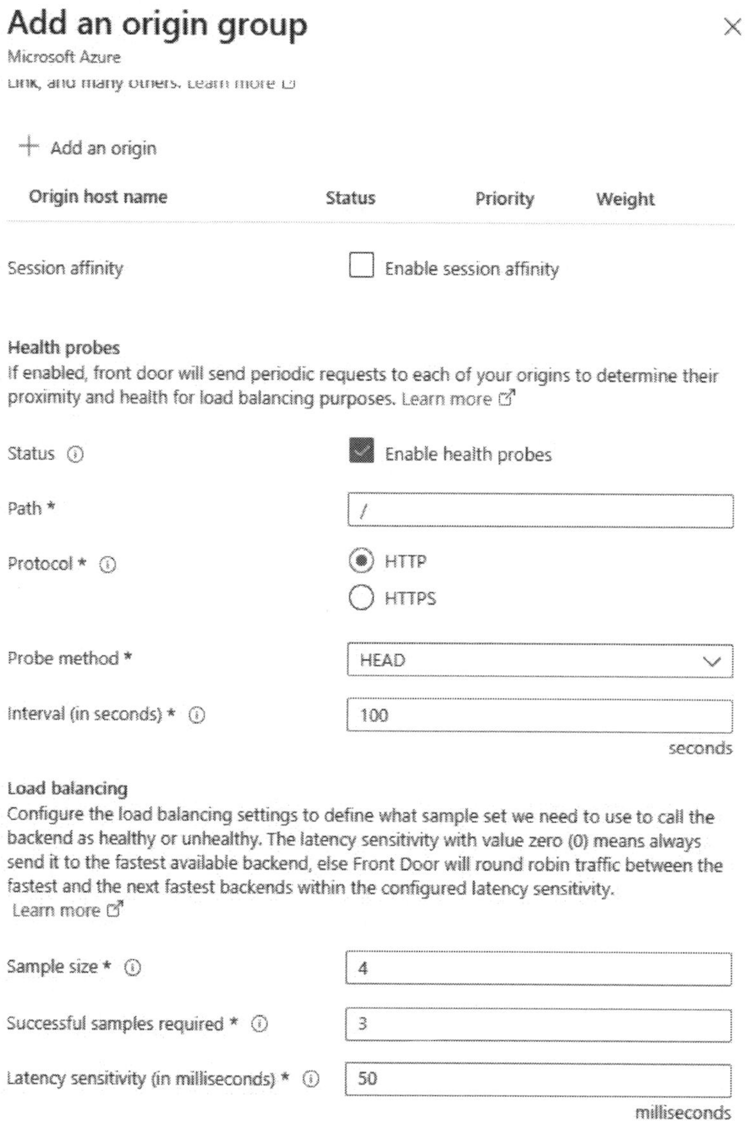

Add an origin group

Microsoft Azure

Link, and many others. Learn more ◻

+ Add an origin

Origin host name	Status	Priority	Weight

Session affinity   ☐ Enable session affinity

Health probes
If enabled, front door will send periodic requests to each of your origins to determine their proximity and health for load balancing purposes. Learn more ◻

Status ⓘ   ☑ Enable health probes

Path *   [/]

Protocol * ⓘ   ⦿ HTTP
                          ○ HTTPS

Probe method *   [HEAD   ⌄]

Interval (in seconds) * ⓘ [100   ]
                                              seconds

Load balancing
Configure the load balancing settings to define what sample set we need to use to call the backend as healthy or unhealthy. The latency sensitivity with value zero (0) means always send it to the fastest available backend, else Front Door will round robin traffic between the fastest and the next fastest backends within the configured latency sensitivity.
Learn more ◻

Sample size * ⓘ   [4   ]

Successful samples required * ⓘ   [3   ]

Latency sensitivity (in milliseconds) * ⓘ   [50   ]
                                              milliseconds

Figure 22.7 – Configuring an endpoint

7. As a default origin is already created, we can select it to check its configuration. To do that, go to the screen presented in *Figure 22.6* and click on `default-origin-group`. This will then display a new screen where you can update its settings if needed, as illustrated in the following screenshot:

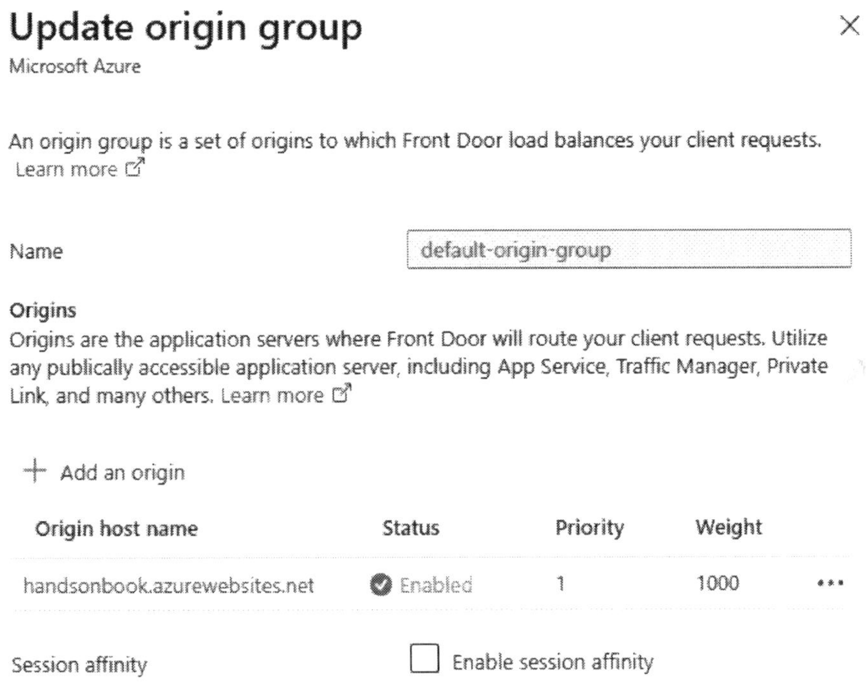

Update origin group   ✕
Microsoft Azure

An origin group is a set of origins to which Front Door load balances your client requests.
Learn more ☑

Name | default-origin-group |

Origins
Origins are the application servers where Front Door will route your client requests. Utilize any publically accessible application server, including App Service, Traffic Manager, Private Link, and many others. Learn more ☑

＋ Add an origin

Origin host name	Status	Priority	Weight	
handsonbook.azurewebsites.net	✅ Enabled	1	1000	•••

Session affinity   ☐ Enable session affinity

Figure 22.8 – Updating an origin group

Note that here, we are talking about origin groups. This means that we can configure multiple servers using the same configuration, possibly related to the same application (such as both API and storage for static files). By adding multiple origins, we can ensure Azure Front Door will treat them as a single entity.

Tip
Using a single origin group, you can configure multiple origins for the same application hosted with different web servers. This will ensure Azure Front Door can load-balance requests across them, ensuring their availability.

8. Coming back to **Front Door manager**, let's define a new route for the added endpoint. To do that, click on the + **Add a route** button visible in *Figure 22.5*. A new screen will be displayed, enabling you to map a domain and add an origin group, as illustrated in the following screenshot:

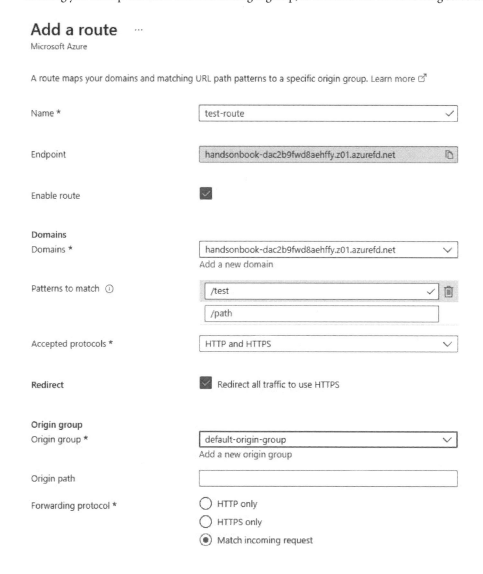

Figure 22.9 – Adding a route

When adding a route, make sure it does not overlap with currently existing routes. As we have a default route added that maps / for a given endpoint, we need to change the route pattern. *Figure 22.9* presents that change by using the /test route instead.

A route can be added for a given endpoint even if you are reusing an origin group. This makes a hierarchy of traffic management, as origins can be grouped and created upfront and then reused by different routes and endpoints. The overall setup depends on your architecture, but that capability allows for handling even complex setups where multiple applications use the same components for things such as a **content delivery network** (**CDN**), authentication, or logging.

When a route is added, you should see it in the list of endpoint routes, as illustrated here:

Figure 22.10 – Two routes added for a single endpoint

Now, we can summarize the whole configuration, as follows:

- To configure an endpoint, we need at least one origin group.

- An origin group is a collection of at least one origin, being a supported service.

- Origin groups can be reused across endpoints when routes are configured, so duplication is avoided.

- A route is a map between a given URL and an origin group. Different routes can be configured even if they point to the same origin group.

- You can map a custom domain to an endpoint so that Azure Front Door can use it for handling incoming connections.

With the basics of routing configuration covered, let's now check how URL rewrites and redirects are implemented.

Implementing URL rewrites and redirects

Besides standard load balancing and probing of endpoints, Azure Front Door allows for additional operations to be performed against incoming requests. If we need, we can either rewrite a request or redirect it to a selected backend without offloading those operations to a connecting client. To do that, here's what we should do:

1. First, we need to go to the **Rule set** feature, as illustrated in the following screenshot:

Figure 22.11 – Rule set feature

2. From this tab, we can add a new ruleset by clicking on the + **Add** button. Rulesets allow for applying additional logic based on a given set of conditions (of course, this is an optional step—we can just skip it and go directly for available actions). URL rewrites and redirects are available by clicking on + **Add an action**, as illustrated in the following screenshot:

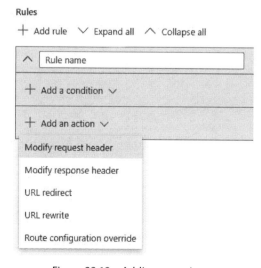

Figure 22.12 – Adding an action

3. Selecting any of the available actions will add them to the whole configuration (a ruleset is a collection of conditions and actions, so it can contain multiple elements). Here, you can see a two-step configuration using both redirect and rewrite:

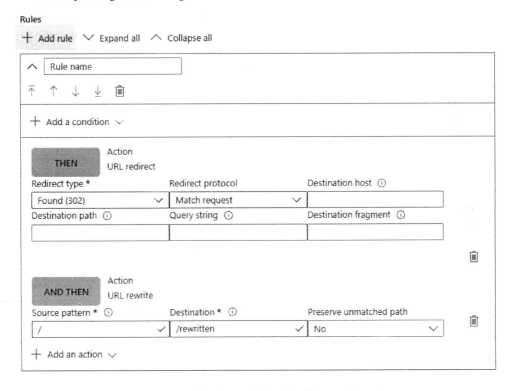

Figure 22.13 – A ruleset with both redirect and rewrite

4. However, when you try to save that configuration, you will get an error saying both rewrite and redirect cannot be used in the same rule. To overcome that problem, create two separate rules, as follows:

Figure 22.14 – Two separate rules

5. Added rulesets can be associated with routes in the Front Door designer. When you go back to a configured route or create a new one, you can select rules at the very bottom of the configuration, as illustrated in the following screenshot:

Figure 22.15 – Selecting a rule

Rules can be reused across different routes—if needed—in the same manner as origin groups. This allows you to reuse logic and avoid duplicated work. While all those configurations may look a bit complex initially, take your time and check all the available options. By carefully preparing all the elements, you can easily create an advanced configuration and handle many different applications with a single Azure Front Door instance.

Summary

This chapter covered Azure Front Door as one of the load-balancing solutions offered by Microsoft Azure. We learned about things such as origins, routes, and rules, which can be applied and configured together. We talked also about other options available for load balancing and the possible advantages of using them.

As mentioned previously in this book, Azure Front Door is not the only service that allows load balancing requests. In the next chapter, we will cover Azure Application Gateway as an alternative solution for handling our web application traffic.

Questions

Here are some questions to test your knowledge of the important topics covered in this chapter:

1. On which layer does Azure Front Door work and handle incoming requests?
2. Can you configure a custom domain for Azure Front Door?
3. Can you reuse rulesets across different routes?
4. What are origin groups?
5. Can you configure Azure Storage as an origin for an endpoint?

Further reading

For more information, refer to the following sources:

- Load-balancing overview: `https://docs.microsoft.com/en-us/azure/architecture/guide/technology-choices/load-balancing-overview`
- Load balancing VMs with Azure Load Balancer: `https://docs.microsoft.com/en-us/azure/load-balancer/quickstart-load-balancer-standard-public-portal`
- Improving availability with Azure Front Door: `https://docs.microsoft.com/en-us/azure/architecture/example-scenario/signalr/#azure-front-door`

- Load balancing with Azure Application Gateway: `https://docs.microsoft.com/en-us/azure/architecture/high-availability/ref-arch-iaas-web-and-db`

- Multi-tier application with Azure Traffic Manager: `https://docs.microsoft.com/en-us/azure/architecture/example-scenario/infrastructure/multi-tier-app-disaster-recovery`

23

Azure Application Gateway as a Web Traffic Load Balancer

Many load-balancing solutions operate on Layer 4 in the OSI model. This means that they cannot make any decisions based on HTTP, which carries information relating to the URL or headers. With Azure Application Gateway, you can extend your current architecture with a service that offers features such as **Web Application Firewall** (**WAF**), static IPs, and zone redundancy.

By going through this chapter, you will learn another way of load balancing requests. In the previous chapter, we learned about a global load balancer – Azure Front Door. Azure Application Gateway can be used as either a separate solution or another element of your architecture that is connected to your applications in a tighter way.

The following topics will be covered in this chapter:

- Azure Application Gateway features
- Configuring routing
- Integrating with web applications
- URL rewriting and redirects

Technical requirements

To perform the exercises in this chapter, you will need the following:

- An Azure subscription

Azure Application Gateway features

When hosting a web application, we always need to consider how it will be exposed to the public internet. While exposing them directly will likely work for all cases, there are things that should be discussed before deciding:

- **Load balancing** – how we are going to distribute traffic between existing instances
- **Security** – handling malicious and malformed requests
- **SSL offloading** – do we need to handle HTTPS directly on our web server?

In general, a web application that is directly exposed to external traffic is a viable choice only for smaller web pages. If our architecture requires a more sophisticated approach (for example, we are going to have multiple instances hosted across various regions), we will need an additional component to handle incoming requests.

Now, let us consider how traffic should be handled. If we are going to decide whether a request is correct or incorrect depending on its payload, we need a component that can handle traffic coming through OSI Layer 7. In other words, we need something that can read an HTTP request and understand it. Standard Azure Load Balancer, very often used in connection with Azure **Virtual Machines** (**VMs**), will not satisfy that requirement as it works only on OSI Layer 4 (TCP/UDP). To be able to do that, we need Azure Application Gateway.

To explain the whole concept better, let us look at the following diagram (*Figure 23.1*):

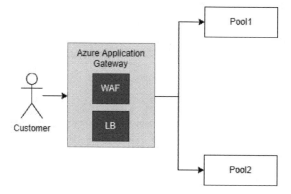

Figure 23.1 – Simplified diagram of Azure Application Gateway communication

The diagram shows three important concepts of Azure Application Gateway:

- **WAF**
- **LB** (**Load Balancer**)
- **Pool**

We will introduce them one by one for a better understanding of the service.

WAF

To secure your web application against common attacks, the concept of WAF was forged. WAF is a centralized service, which helps in protecting services against known exploits and vulnerabilities. Under the hood, WAF is based on OWASP core rulesets, which include mitigation paths for attacks such as SQL injection, **Cross-Site Scripting** (**XSS**), and shell injection.

While WAF cannot secure you from all possible attacks, it greatly improves the security of your application and gives you more time to introduce additional layers of security. It is also a common pattern for web security, plus it is based on a well-known set of rules, which are used across hundreds of applications.

> **Note**
> WAF in Azure is a part of different services, which can be configured independently. You can use it in Azure Application Gateway, Azure Front Door, and Azure CDN. While general capabilities stay the same, its configuration will be different for each of the listed services.

Remember that in Azure Application Gateway, WAF is a separate feature (a separate tier), which is billed differently than the basic version of the service. Here is a comparison:

- $0.26 per hour for the Standard tier
- $0.468 per hour for WAF

As you can see, there is quite a huge difference between those two tiers in terms of pricing – on the other hand, if you think about securing a web application endpoint, even if you use standard Azure Application Gateway, you will need to host WAF somewhere else.

Load balancing

Azure Application Gateway acts as a load balancer working on OSI Layer 7, meaning it can understand HTTP requests and make decisions based on a request's payload. Under the hood, the concept is based on *pools*, which are your web servers handling requests. For example, let us assume you have two separate logical routes:

- `/app`
- `/images`

The first one is handled by one backend, which hosts your web app. The second one is configured to access CDN or a similar kind of server, which returns cached images. As Azure Application Gateway understands the differences between those requests, it can forward them to the appropriate backends. We will talk more about this feature later in the chapter.

Multiple-site hosting

Many load balancing solutions require configuring a single domain, which is then used for further configuration of connected backends. In Azure Application Gateway, you can attach multiple domains to the same instance of the service, meaning you can use it as a central gateway to your infrastructure, which load balances all the requests coming to it. The same applies to the use of subdomains.

Rewriting URLs and headers

Similar to Azure Front Door, Azure Application Gateway can rewrite both URLs and headers. This is helpful when you want to remove headers, which should not be passed to applications, add a new one centrally, or redirect each request to an additional backend for further verification. It also allows for a more advanced setup with the use of conditional rewrites allowing you to implement additional logic for the process.

While those are not all the features available, let us now see how Azure Application Gateway is provisioned and how we can configure its basic feature – routing.

Configuring routing

To enable load balancing with Azure Application Gateway, we need to configure routing. To explain that concept a little bit – we need a way to connect our frontend (the part of the architecture responsible for handling incoming requests) with backends (services hosting our application logic). We will explain that concept using the Azure portal and the Azure Application Gateway configurator.

In the Azure portal, click on + **Create a resource** and search for Application Gateway, then click on the **Create** button to start the process:

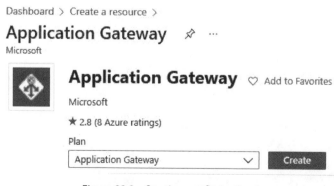

Figure 23.2 – Starting configuration

The basic configuration of my instance looks as follows. I selected **StandardV2 tier (no WAF)** and created a virtual network directly on that screen (Azure Application Gateway cannot be created without integration with a virtual network):

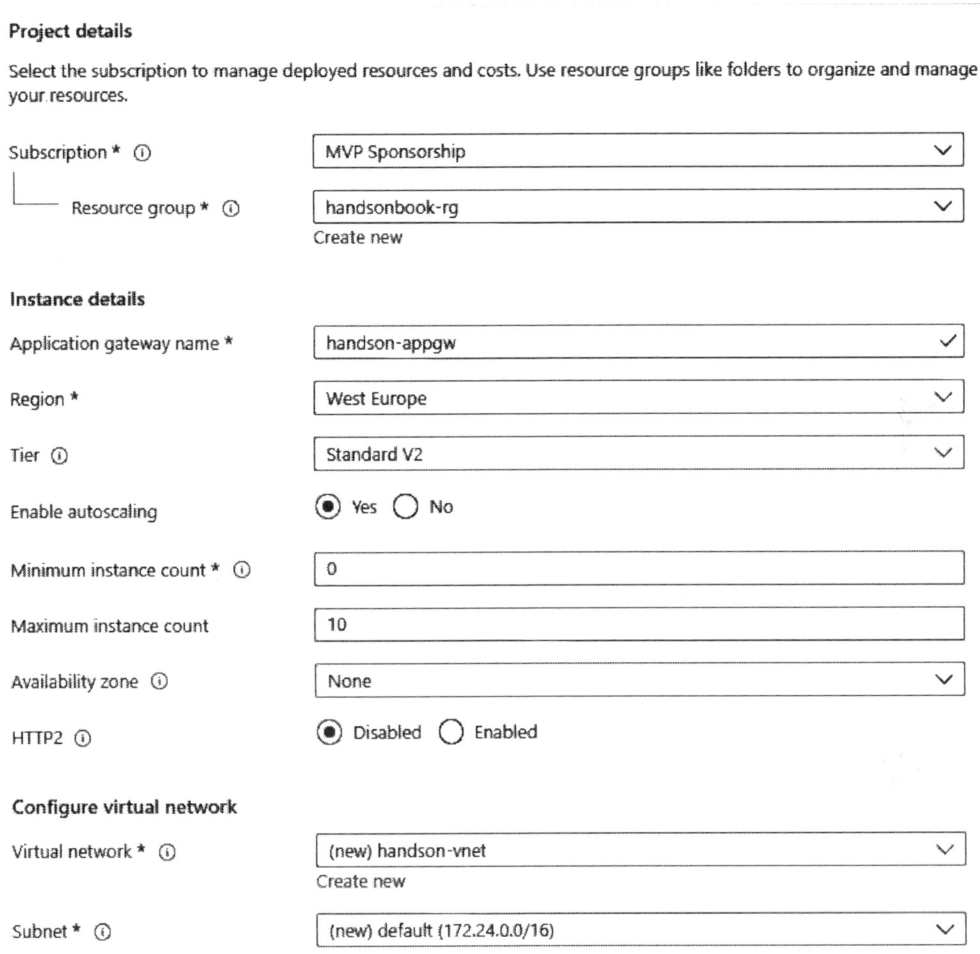

Project details

Select the subscription to manage deployed resources and costs. Use resource groups like folders to organize and manage all your resources.

Subscription * ⓘ	MVP Sponsorship
Resource group * ⓘ	handsonbook-rg
	Create new

Instance details

Application gateway name *	handson-appgw
Region *	West Europe
Tier ⓘ	Standard V2
Enable autoscaling	◉ Yes ○ No
Minimum instance count * ⓘ	0
Maximum instance count	10
Availability zone ⓘ	None
HTTP2 ⓘ	◉ Disabled ○ Enabled

Configure virtual network

Virtual network * ⓘ	(new) handson-vnet
	Create new
Subnet * ⓘ	(new) default (172.24.0.0/16)

Figure 23.3 – Basic configuration

There are additional features that we could enable right now, but we'll skip them as they are not required. However, if you want, you can configure availability zones for your instance (so the availability of the service will be improved) and enable HTTP2 if your client will communicate using that protocol. With the basics configured, let us go to the next tab – **Frontends**.

We need to tell Azure how we want to handle incoming traffic for Azure Application Gateway. We have three choices:

- **Public**
- **Private**
- **Both**

The choice depends on your architecture. If you want to keep traffic private and handle internal requests only, you can go for a private IP. For handling public traffic, we need to have a public IP assigned to our instance of the service.

> **Note**
>
> When **Standard V2 tier** is selected, we cannot select a private IP frontend as it is not supported. For that tier, the options available are a **Public** IP or **Both**.

If you do not have an available IP address, you can click on the **Add new** link for a quick create option. Here, you can see my frontend configuration:

Figure 23.4 – Configured frontend

With the frontend configured, we can do the rest of the configuration. First, we need to configure a backend pool. To keep things short, a backend pool is a collection of resources (backends) that can be linked with Azure Application Gateway and then used for routing. Here, you can see my simple backend pool with a single Azure App Service instance inside it:

Add a backend pool.   ✕

A backend pool is a collection of resources to which your application gateway can send traffic. A backend pool can contain virtual machines, virtual machines scale sets, IP addresses, domain names, or an App Service.

Name *	myfirstpool ✓
Add backend pool without targets	Yes **No**

Backend targets

1 item

Target type	Target	
App Services ⌄	handsonbook ⌄	🗑 ⋯
IP address or FQDN ⌄		

Figure 23.5 – Backend configuration

> **Tip**
> If you do not want to link a backend pool to a backend, you can just create an empty one by switching **Add backend pool without targets** to **Yes**.

The last step of configuring our instance is to connect the dots – our frontend with the backend pool. This is done via routing rules, which can be configured in the **Configuration** tab:

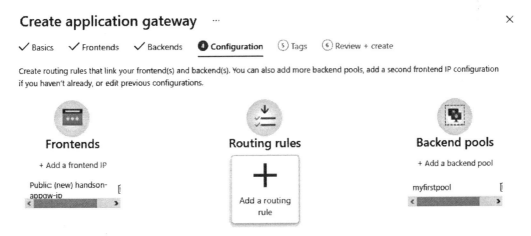

Figure 23.6 – Configuration tab

Let us click on the + **Add a routing rule** button to see what can be done here. The routing rule is quite a complicated concept as it is based on two elements – a listener and a backend target. Here, you can see my listener configured to listen on **HTTP 80**:

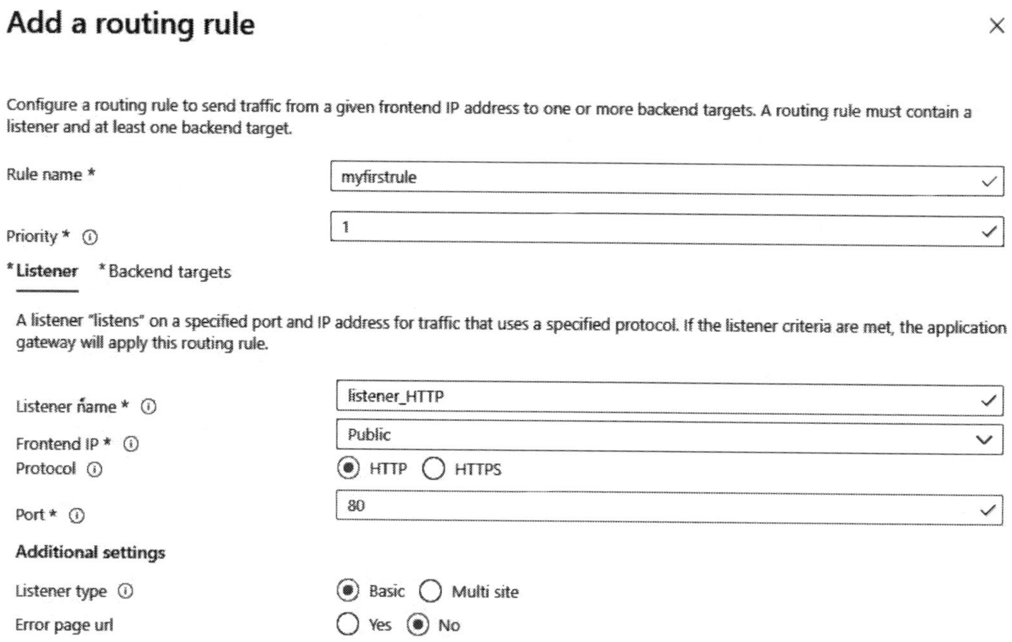

Add a routing rule   ✕

Configure a routing rule to send traffic from a given frontend IP address to one or more backend targets. A routing rule must contain a listener and at least one backend target.

Rule name *	myfirstrule ✓
Priority * ⓘ	1 ✓

*Listener   ***Backend targets**

A listener "listens" on a specified port and IP address for traffic that uses a specified protocol. If the listener criteria are met, the application gateway will apply this routing rule.

Listener name * ⓘ	listener_HTTP ✓
Frontend IP * ⓘ	Public ⌄
Protocol ⓘ	◉ HTTP ◯ HTTPS
Port * ⓘ	80 ✓

Additional settings

Listener type ⓘ	◉ Basic ◯ Multi site
Error page url	◯ Yes ◉ No

Figure 23.7 – Configuring a listener to listen on port 80 for HTTP

I chose a **Basic** listener type as I have a single site, which would be connected to it. For more advanced scenarios (multi-site), you would need to go for the **Multi site** type. With the listener configured, we need to select **Backend targets**, which will be linked to it:

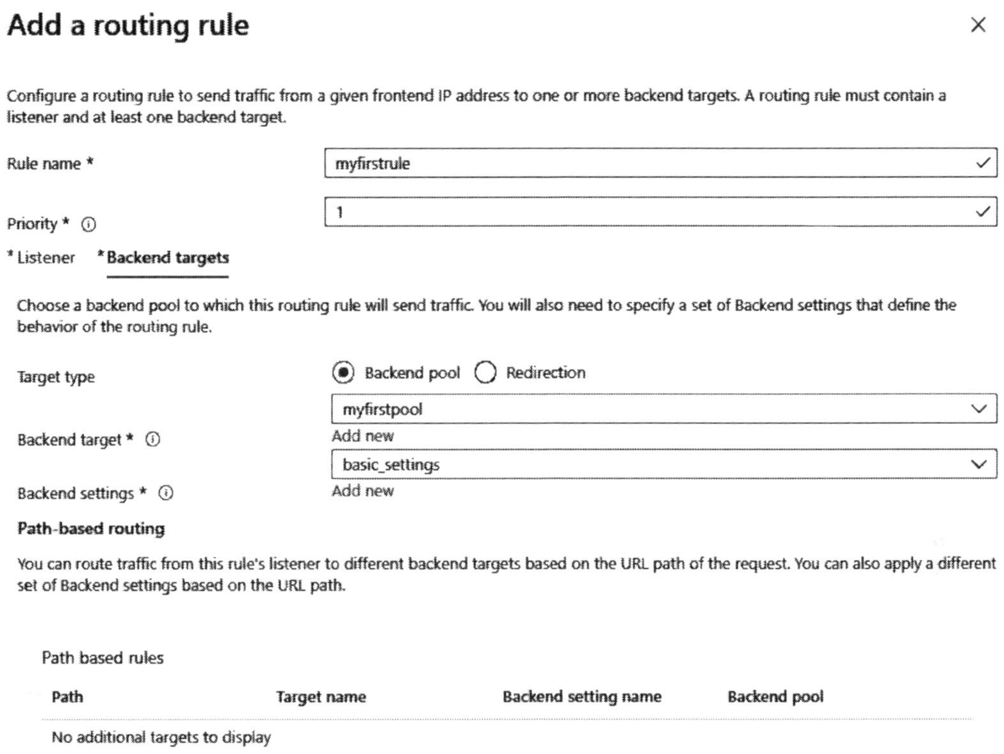

Add a routing rule   ✕

Configure a routing rule to send traffic from a given frontend IP address to one or more backend targets. A routing rule must contain a listener and at least one backend target.

Rule name *

> myfirstrule ✓

Priority * ⓘ

> 1 ✓

* Listener   *** Backend targets**

Choose a backend pool to which this routing rule will send traffic. You will also need to specify a set of Backend settings that define the behavior of the routing rule.

Target type   ⦿ Backend pool ◯ Redirection

> myfirstpool ⌄

Backend target * ⓘ   Add new

> basic_settings ⌄

Backend settings * ⓘ   Add new

Path-based routing

You can route traffic from this rule's listener to different backend targets based on the URL path of the request. You can also apply a different set of Backend settings based on the URL path.

Path based rules

Path	Target name	Backend setting name	Backend pool
No additional targets to display			

Figure 23.8 – Configured routing rule

Additionally, you will need to create a backend setting. This element is responsible for configuring how the backend will be reached – which protocol and port will be used – and additional settings (such as session affinity or path override). You can see a simple configuration here:

Add Backend setting   ✕

← Discard changes and go back to routing rules

Backend settings name * | basic_settings   ✓ |
Backend protocol   ◉ HTTP ○ HTTPS
Backend port * | 80 |

Additional settings

Cookie-based affinity ⓘ   ○ Enable ◉ Disable
Connection draining ⓘ   ○ Enable ◉ Disable
Request time-out (seconds) * ⓘ | 20 |
Override backend path ⓘ | |

Host name

By default, Application Gateway does not change the incoming HTTP host header from the client and sends the header unaltered to the backend. Multi-tenant services like App service or API management rely on a specific host header or SNI extension to resolve to the correct endpoint. Change these settings to overwrite the incoming HTTP host header.

                                  (Yes **No**)
Override with new host name

                                  ○ Pick host name from backend target
                                  ◉ Override with specific domain name
Host name override
Host name | e.g. contoso.com |
                                  (**Yes** No)
Create custom probes

Figure 23.9 – Backend setting configuration

With all the elements correctly set, you can click on the **Review + create** button and start provisioning. Note that it can take some time as Azure Application Gateway consists of multiple underlying components that need to be deployed. Once it is created, you can access your instance – if everything is correct, you should see no errors and be able to use the public IP of the service to access your backend. However, the default configuration can contain some errors that prevent users from accessing the web application. In that scenario, you will see the following error:

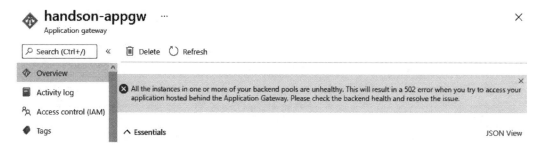

Figure 23.10 – Error indicating that backend pools are incorrectly configured

We will cover adjusting settings in the next section of this chapter.

Integrating with web applications

To connect to your web application, Azure Application Gateway needs to have a proper configuration of the backend. By accessing the **Backend settings** blade, you have access to all the parameters that are used for a connection. If they are incorrect, the backend pool will report **Unhealthy** as the endpoint status and return HTTP 502 as a result. It is important to understand the implications of the parameters used to avoid problems with connectivity.

In the previous sections, we created an instance of Azure Application Gateway using default settings. This can cause problems as, by default, the incoming host header will not be rewritten to match a backend. To change that, go to **Backend settings**, select your settings, and see the **Host name** section:

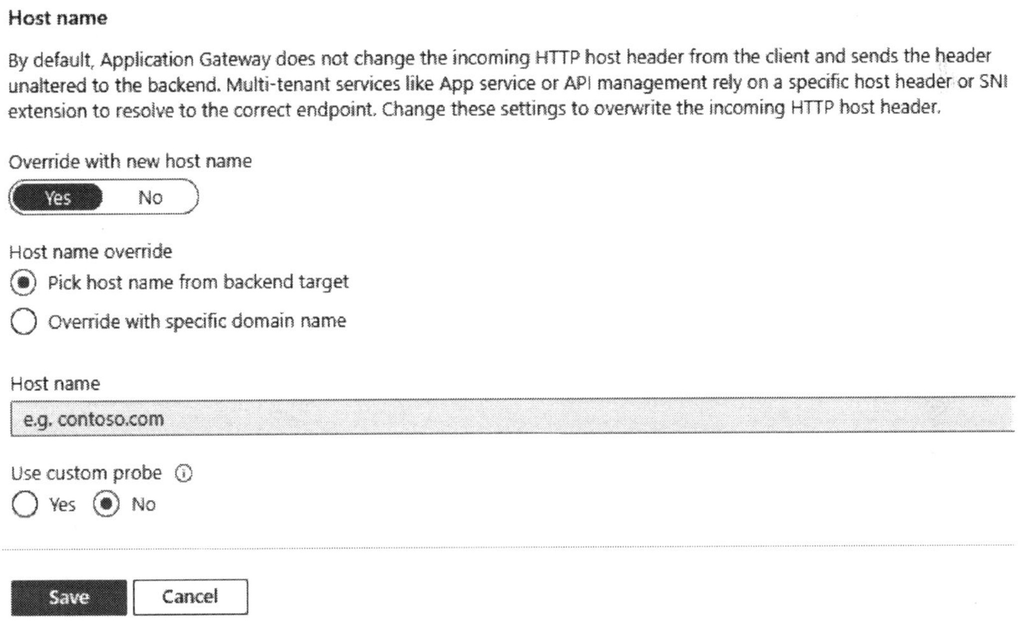

Host name

By default, Application Gateway does not change the incoming HTTP host header from the client and sends the header unaltered to the backend. Multi-tenant services like App service or API management rely on a specific host header or SNI extension to resolve to the correct endpoint. Change these settings to overwrite the incoming HTTP host header.

Override with new host name

[**Yes**   No]

Host name override

(●) Pick host name from backend target

( ) Override with specific domain name

Host name

| e.g. contoso.com |

Use custom probe ⓘ

( ) Yes (●) No

[Save] [Cancel]

Figure 23.11 – Proper configuration of the host name override

To fully integrate our service with Azure App Service, we need to change the **Override with new host name** option to **Yes** and allow it to select a host name from the backend itself. With that enabled, you should be able to access the underlying web page:

Figure 23.12 – Working Azure Application Gateway routing request to Azure App Service

The reason for doing that is quite simple – technically, Azure App Service relies on a host header to resolve it to a correct endpoint. Without overriding it, we are sending Azure Application Gateway's endpoint downstream, which results in an error as it cannot be resolved to match an existing web application endpoint in Azure.

This parameter is not always required as it solely depends on the infrastructure handling a request. If it does not require a host header to be present (or correct), you will not have to change anything on that level.

Let us now see how we can perform rewrites and redirects.

URL rewriting and redirects

As most load balancers work on Layer 7 of the OSI model, Azure Application Gateway is capable of performing rewrites and redirects of incoming requests. That feature is handy if we need to change the desired URL or the underlying resource moved and we could not make that change on the client layer.

To configure rewriting, go to the **Rewrites** blade and click on the **+ Rewrite set** button:

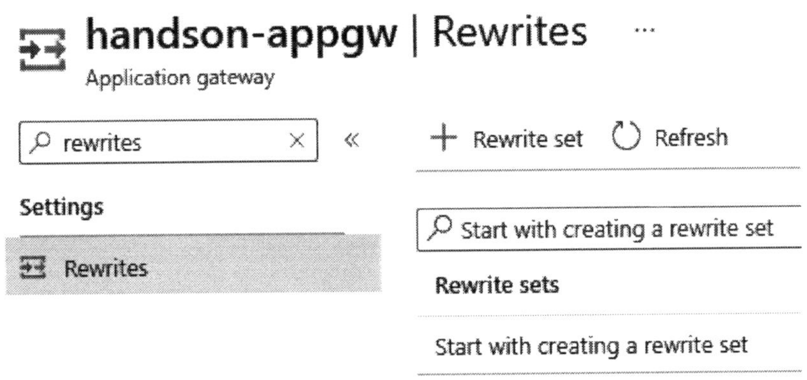

Figure 23.13 – Rewrites blade

Creating a rewrite set requires two actions:

- Giving it a name

- Associating it with existing routing rules

The mentioned configuration may look like this:

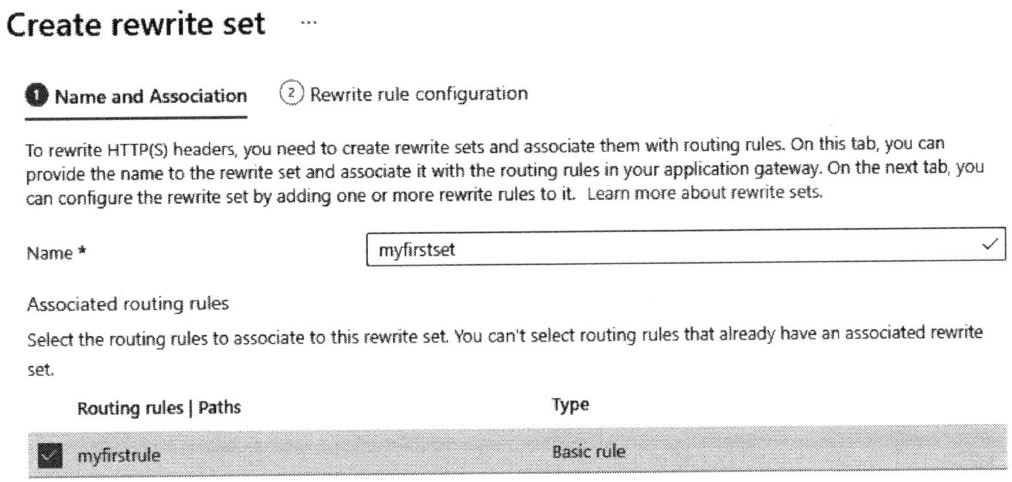

Figure 23.14 – Configuring the name and association of a rewrite set

Then we can go to the next tab and start configuring rewrite rules. By clicking on + **Add rewrite rule**, you will start the process and all the buttons and fields will become enabled. In the beginning, we need to enter both the name of a rule and its sequence, which determines the order of rule execution:

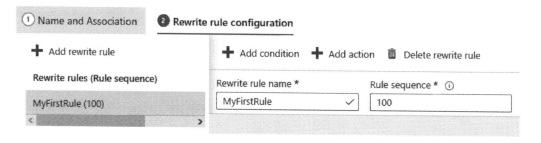

Figure 23.15 – Rule name and sequence number

The next step involves clicking on the + **Add condition** button so our rule will contain two elements:

- A condition
- An action

In other words, the rule's action will be executed only if a request matches the configured condition. On your screen, you should see the following view:

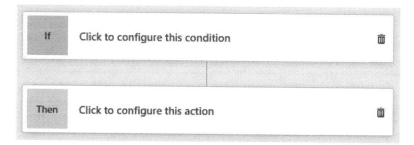

Figure 23.16 – Empty rule with one action and one condition

Let us try to configure a condition first. To do so, click on it, so an extended view will be displayed. There, we can enter all the details needed to decide whether an action should be applied. I configured a condition, which checks for a value of a custom header as follows:

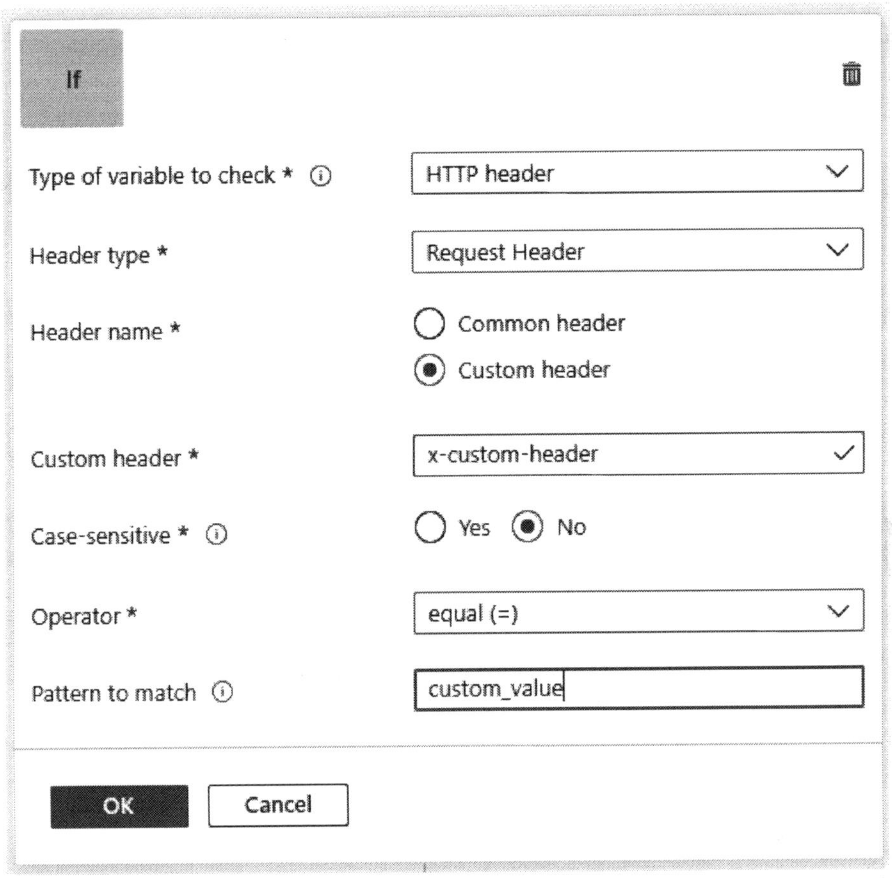

Figure 23.17 – Condition checking for a value of a custom header

As you can see, if a request contains the `x-custom-header` header with the value `custom_value`, the condition will be matched, and the action can be performed. Now let us configure an action:

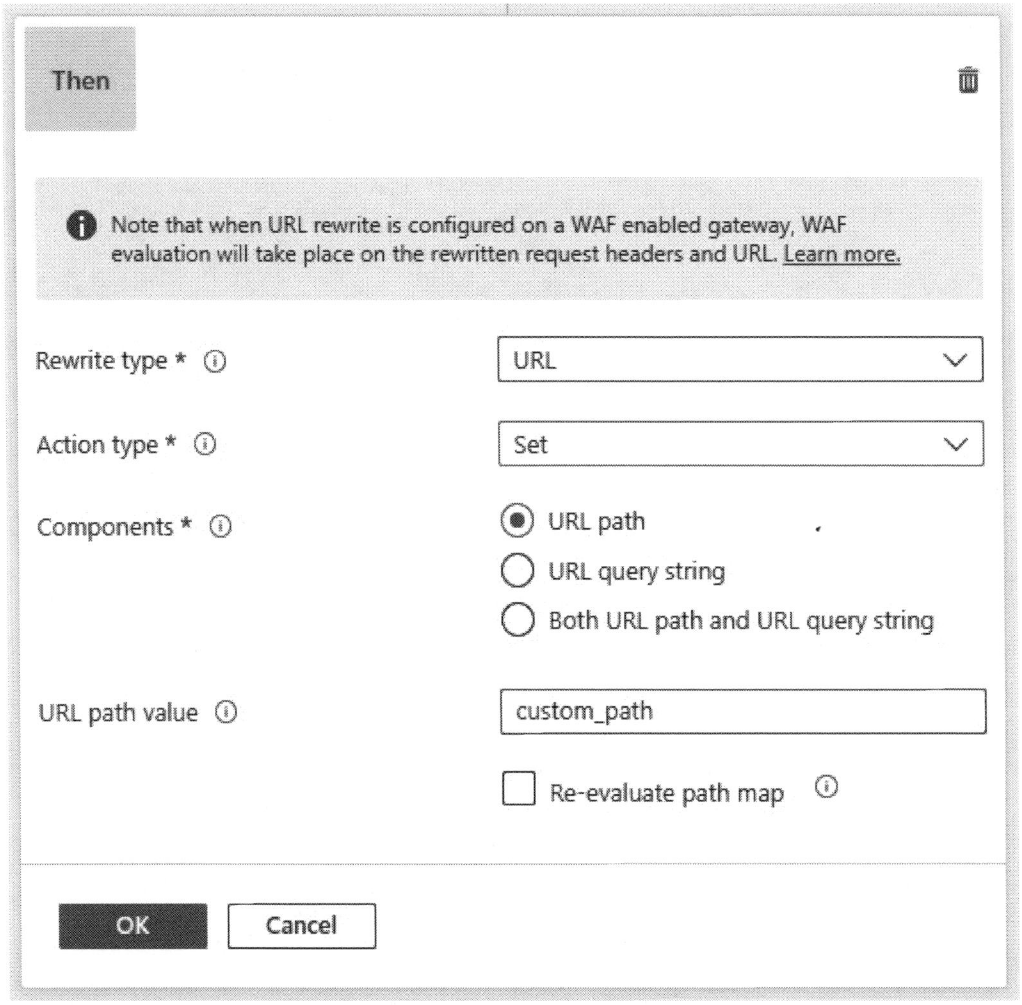

Figure 23.18 – Action configuration for URL rewrite

The action defined in *Figure 23.18*, when applied, will rewrite the request to /custom_path. In general, the possibilities are quite wide-ranging – you can decide to rewrite either a path, a query string, or both. By using **Re-evaluate path map**, you can rewrite a request to a different pool post rewrite. If everything is correct, you can save a rule and test it.

Summary

This was the last chapter describing Azure services and load balancing in particular. It should allow you to further explore the topic as traffic management in Azure is quite a broad subject and, depending on your needs, a different service may be the best fit.

In this chapter, we talked about the basic capabilities of Azure Application Gateway, integration with Azure web applications, and URL rewrite configuration. Compare those features with Azure Front Door, described in the previous chapter, to get a better understanding of the differences.

In the next chapter, we will cover tips and tricks useful when working with Azure. We will also describe automated deployments of infrastructure using an **Infrastructure-as-Code (IaC)** approach with ARM templates and Azure Bicep.

Questions

Here are some questions to test your knowledge of the important topics covered in this chapter:

1. What is WAF?
2. Is WAF enabled in Azure Application Gateway by default?
3. Can you apply a URL rewrite based on a condition?
4. Does Azure Application Gateway work on the same OSI layer as Azure Load Balancer and Azure Front Door?
5. Can you use Azure Application Gateway with private IPs only?

Further reading

For more information, refer to the following source:

- WAF core ruleset: `https://coreruleset.org`

24
Distributing Load with Azure Traffic Manager

Sometimes we want to distribute our load depending on the performance of our backends, or maybe route users to different servers while some are under maintenance. This is not an easy task if we don't have a service that will do this seamlessly and quickly. Thanks to **Azure Traffic Manager** we can improve the availability of our critical applications, distribute traffic when performing large, complex deployments, or perform maintenance without downtime.

The following topics will be covered in this chapter:

- Using Azure Traffic Manager
- Endpoint monitoring

Technical requirements

To perform exercises from this chapter, you will need the following:

- Access to an Azure subscription

Using Azure Traffic Manager

Imagine the following situation—you have an application that must be served globally. To guarantee the best performance for all your customers worldwide, you provision different instances of your service in different regions (one for North America, one for Europe, and one for Africa). There is one problem - you must explicitly tell your customer to access a specific instance of the application, the one that is closest to their location.

While this is, of course, possible (just give the customer the right URL), the solution is not ideal. For example, what if your client goes for a holiday and spends the following two weeks in Europe instead of in Africa? To overcome such problems, in Azure, you can leverage a service named **Azure Traffic Manager**, which takes care of the proper routing of incoming requests and allows you to implement high availability in your application.

Functions of Azure Traffic Manager

You can think of Azure Traffic Manager as a load balancer that works on the DNS level. To understand the concept, please look at the following example. By default, if there is no service such as Azure Traffic Manager, your **customer** uses an endpoint URL to send requests from a **client application** to a **server application**:

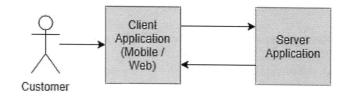

Figure 24.1 – Direct access to an application without a load balancer

If you want to load-balance incoming requests, you must introduce another element of an architecture that will take care of routing them to the proper backend (and possibly ensure that they are healthy):

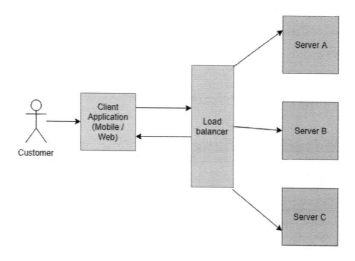

Figure 24.2 – Access to multiple instances of an application using a load balancer

The downside of such a setup is that latency can be introduced. What is more, in that scenario, your client connects via a **load balancer** directly, which does not resolve the problem of globally distributing the entry point.

> **Note**
>
> The preceding example is a common solution when using a reverse proxy, which acts as a gateway to your system.

The described scenario defines a solution, where load balancing is based on distributing traffic based on TCP/UDP, so it is a significantly lower level than DNS. When using Azure Traffic Manager, the flow of a request is completely different:

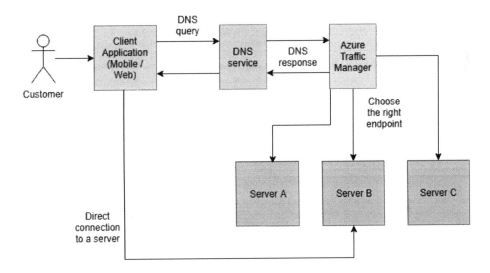

Figure 24.3 – Accessing multiple instances of an application with Azure Traffic Manager

The flow can be described as follows:

1. Send a **DNS query** to a **DNS service** to obtain the address of a server.

2. The **DNS service** is configured in such a way that it points to **Azure Traffic Manager**, instead of pointing to a service directly.

3. **Azure Traffic Manager** chooses the right endpoint based on the query characteristics and returns a **DNS response** containing the address of the proper server.

4. The client receives a **DNS response** and uses it to connect to the right server.

In fact, the client must perform two requests:

- Obtain the URL of a server

- Send the actual request

While it may seem like a bit of an overhead, the impact is imperceptible.

> **Note**
> The advantage of such a solution is the ability to send requests directly to a server. There is no intermediary service that participates in the communication.

Let us now check how quickly we can create Azure Traffic Manager using the Azure portal.

Creating Azure Traffic Manager in the Azure portal

To get started with Azure Traffic Manager in the portal, you must click on the + **Create a resource** button and search for `traffic manager`. Then, from the search results, select **Traffic Manager profile**. You will see a form, where you must enter all required fields to be able to create a service:

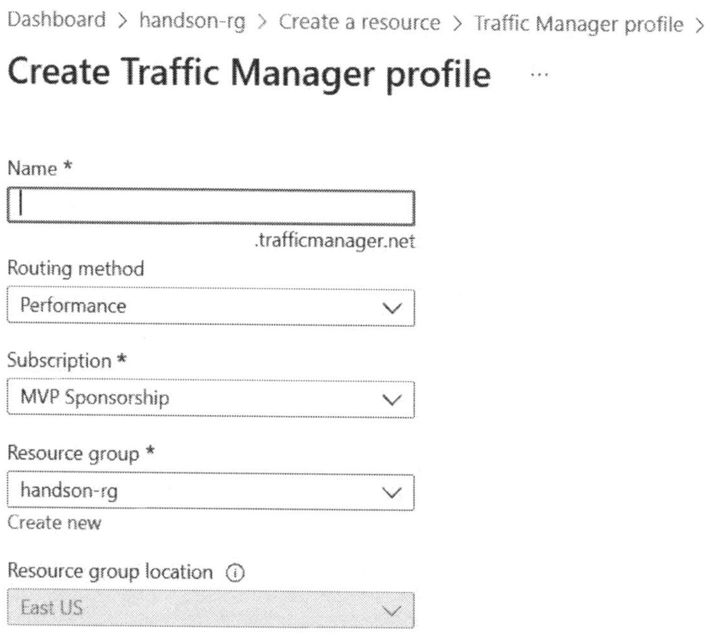

Dashboard > handson-rg > Create a resource > Traffic Manager profile >

Create Traffic Manager profile   ...

Name *

[   ]
                          .trafficmanager.net
Routing method

[Performance   ∨]

Subscription *

[MVP Sponsorship   ∨]

Resource group *

[handson-rg   ∨]
Create new

Resource group location ⓘ

[East US   ∨]

Figure 24.4 – Creating Azure Traffic Manager in the Azure portal

While most of them should be self-explanatory, there is one dropdown that will require our focus, **Routing method**. Here you have six different methods available:

- **Performance**
- **Weighted**
- **Priority**
- **Geographic**
- **MultiValue**
- **Subnet**

Before we describe each one, you have to understand what **Routing method** is exactly. Previously, I mentioned that Azure Traffic Manager decides to which endpoint a user should be routed. This routing operation may give a different result depending on the selected method. Let's consider the following scenarios:

- Instances of your application are distributed globally, and you want to route a user to the closest one.
- Instances of your application offer different performances, and you want to route a user to the one that offers the best user experience.
- You have a primary region that handles all the traffic, and you want to route a user to secondary ones in case of an outage or temporary issues.
- You want to distribute traffic evenly, or according to set weights.
- You want to map user IP addresses to a specific instance.

Depending on the chosen scenario, a different *routing method* should be chosen. Now I will describe them in detail.

Routing method – performance

When using the **performance routing method**, a user will be routed to the endpoint that is the *closest* one. It is important to remember here, that the *closest* endpoint may not be the one that is the closest geographically, as this method takes into consideration performance, not distance. Let us assume that, internally, Azure Traffic Manager stores the following information regarding configured endpoints:

Endpoint	Region	Latency
Server A	West Europe	**12 ms**
Server B	East US 2	67 ms

Figure 24.5 – Example performance of two separate endpoints

In the preceding scenario, the endpoint that performs better is **Server A**. When the performance routing method is selected, the user will be routed to that server.

> **Note**
>
> It is important to remember that with the performance method, Azure Traffic Manager checks the latency of a response, taking into consideration the IP address of the DNS server that sent the request. It is not an IP address of a client.

As performance is not always the best routing method, we can check how to attach weights by using the weighted method of load balancing.

Routing method – weighted

When you want to distribute traffic evenly or based on predefined weights, the **weighted routing method** is what you are looking for. Using that method, you define weights, which are then taken into consideration when deciding where a request should be routed. Let's take into consideration the following table:

Endpoint	Weight	Status
Server A	100	**Online**
Server B	100	Degraded
Server A - staging	5	**Online**

Figure 24.6 – Example status of the configured endpoints

In the preceding example, we have three endpoints, one of which has reporting issues. Although both **Server A** and **Server B** have the same weights, as Server B's status is reported as **Degraded**, it will not be considered as a healthy endpoint, and as a result, a user will not be routed to it. There are two servers left that have different weights. In that situation, Azure Traffic Manager will randomly assign a user to an endpoint with the probability determined by the endpoint's weight. If we imagine that there are 105 requests, 100 of them will be routed to **Server A**, and the rest to the **Server A – staging**.

> **Note**
>
> The weighted routing method is a great option for A/B testing, where you randomly route users to the new instance of your application containing new features. If they like them, you can change the weight and route the rest of the traffic to that instance.

As you can see, with the weighted load balancing method you can easily distribute traffic according to your current requirements. However, if you want a simpler method, you could try using the priority routing method.

Routing method – priority

The **priority routing method** is the most straightforward as it covers a simple scenario where you have a primary region that hosts your application, and you want to ensure that you can easily fail over to the secondary ones in case something is wrong. Let's consider the following scenario:

Server	Priority	Status
Server A	1	**Online**
Server A - secondary	2	Online

Figure 24.7 – Example priorities of endpoints

In the preceding example, all traffic will be routed to Server A for the following reasons:

- Its priority is set to 1
- Its status is considered online

Now something has happened, and the primary replica went down:

Server	Priority	Status
Server A	1	Degraded
Server A - secondary	2	**Online**

Figure 24.8 – Example of changing status of endpoints with priority configured

Because **Server A** is considered unhealthy, all traffic will be routed to the secondary instance until the primary one works again.

> **Note**
> Remember that clients may cache DNS responses, which will extend the period that your endpoint appears unavailable to them.

Priorities allow you to quickly decide which instance should go first when serving requests to your customers. However, they cannot guarantee that they will access the closest region physically. To do that, we need to use the geographic routing method.

Routing method – geographic

Sometimes you need to route a user to a specific region, taking into consideration its location. There are multiple reasons to do so, for example:

- Legal requirements

- Content localization

- Serving an application from a server that is the closest one taking distance into consideration

> **Note**
>
> Do remember that the region that is closest to a user may not be the best one regarding network latency. Do not overuse this routing method to achieve the best user experience.

When using the **geographic routing method**, you assign regions to configured endpoints:

Server	Regions
Server A	France
Server B	Asia
Server C	World

Figure 24.9 – Example relations of servers and regions

Now to route a user to the proper server, Azure Traffic Manager tries to determine its location by reading the IP address of the source DNS server. It starts from state/province (or country/region if the former is not supported) and ends on the **World** value.

> **Note**
>
> When using the geographic routing method, Azure Traffic Manager will return an endpoint whether it is healthy or not. It is important to leverage nested profiles, to extend routing methods further, and achieve high availability.

As you can see, there are some serious considerations when using that method of routing. Make sure you have a plan to mitigate all the potential issues to get the best from it.

Routing method – MultiValue

The **MultiValue routing method** works a little bit differently from other routing methods, as it allows the return of multiple healthy endpoints, and lets the client choose which one should be used. This scenario covers a situation when on the service side, you do not know where to route a user, and simultaneously you want to ensure that a user will be routed to a healthy endpoint.

> **Note**
>
> To make sure that an endpoint can be returned to a user for this routing method, it must be set as *External* and have an IPv4 or IPv6 address assigned.

To complete the list, let us now quickly check how routing can be done based on subnets.

Routing method – subnet

The last routing method is the most sophisticated, as it allows you to map specific IP addresses (or a range of IP addresses) to a specific endpoint.

The use cases for that method may vary if, for example:

- You want to block users using a specific ISP

- You want to route users from a corporate network to an internal instance of an application

- You have branded your application and want to route users from different corporate networks to a particular branded instance

> **Note**
>
> When using the **subnet routing method**, make sure you have covered all possible IP addresses, as failing to do so will result in a NODATA response being returned, resulting in an error being sent to a client.

Once you are satisfied with your choice of a routing method, you can click on the **Create** button to provision a resource in Azure. We will now check how Azure Traffic Manager is configured and managed via the Azure portal.

Working with Azure Traffic Manager in the Azure portal

When you access your instance of Azure Traffic Manager, you will see a default screen containing the overview of the service:

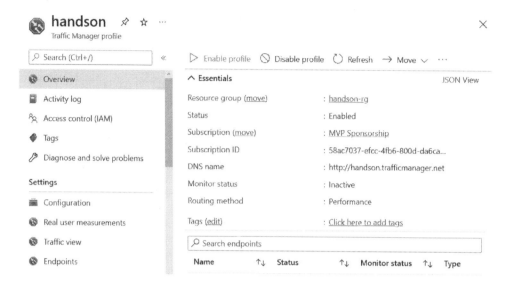

Figure 24.10 – Working instance of Azure Traffic Manager

As there is currently no endpoint attached to this profile, the list of endpoints displayed is empty. Before we add a new one, let's focus a little bit on other service features.

Configuration

When you access the **Configuration** blade, you will see the full configuration of your instance of Azure Traffic Manager:

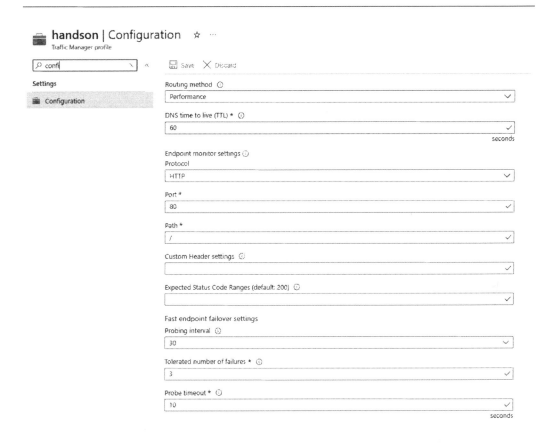

Figure 24.11 – Azure Traffic Manager configuration

It contains things such as **Routing method** (by default it displays the one you chose during service creation), **Endpoint monitor settings**, and **Fast endpoint failover settings**. From this screen, you basically control how Azure Traffic Manager will behave. For instance, let's assume that each of your endpoints has a custom `/status` endpoint that is designed to work with the service. By default, Azure Traffic Manager checks the default endpoint URL (set here as /), so you will have to change the **Path** field as follows:

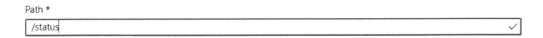

Figure 24.12 – Setting the Pathfield

The same goes for expected status codes. If your endpoints can return a range of HTTP status codes, and each of them should be considered as a success, you are able to enter the range in the **Expected Status Code Ranges** field:

Figure 24.13 – Setting expected status code ranges

You can experiment here with different settings, so they reflect the real scenario you must cover. Once the configuration is complete, we can see how to gather user measurements.

Real user measurements

When using the performance routing method, Azure Traffic Manager checks where DNS requests originate from, and translates the result to an internal table that reflects different network latencies for different end user networks. While this option is perfectly fine for most use cases, sometimes you want to be able to tell Azure Traffic Manager about real latency. With **Real user measurements** features, you can inject JavaScript code into your client endpoints, to send delays to your endpoints directly to this Azure service.

To do so, go to the **Real user measurements** blade and click on the **Generate key** button:

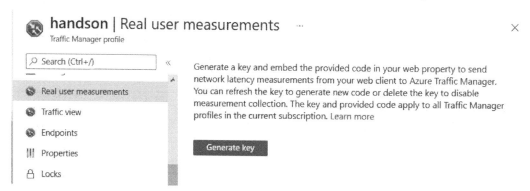

Figure 24.14 – Default view of Real user measurements

Once the key is generated, you will see a slightly different view:

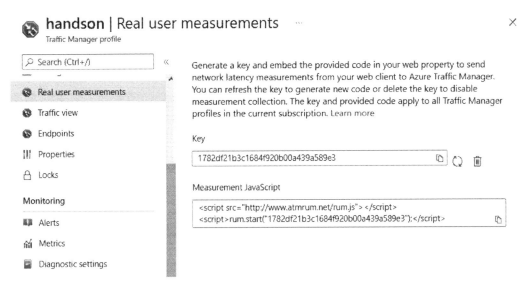

Figure 24.15 – Measurements with a generated key

As you can see, there are two fields:

- **Key**: Stores the generated key

- **Measurement JavaScript**: Holds the script that should be injected into the client application

Once you use the generated script, it will start sending additional information to your instance of Azure Traffic Manager regarding latencies and the client network, which will improve the accuracy of decisions made by the service.

> **Note**
>
> The accuracy improvement is not instant—Azure Traffic Manager must gather lots of data from different networks to improve the performance.

While real user measurements are helpful, they are not the core functionality of Azure Traffic Manager. To be able to load balance traffic, we will need to learn how to configure endpoints.

Endpoints

The main functionality of Azure Traffic Manager is the ability to configure the endpoints it handles. You can access it through the **Endpoints** blade. To add an endpoint, you must click on the + **Add** button and enter the following values:

- **Type**: You can choose between **Azure endpoint**, **External endpoint**, and **Nested endpoint**. The difference impacts the whole form—with **Azure endpoint** you can choose an Azure service, **External endpoint** requires providing a fully qualified domain name or IP, and when you select **Nested endpoint** you can point to another Traffic Manager profile.

- **Name**: Unique name of an endpoint.

- **Target resource type/FQDN or IP/Target resource**: Depending on the **Type** value, you will have to select different values to configure an endpoint.

- **Priority**: Because my routing method is **Priority**, I must enter the correct value for this endpoint. If you select another method, you may find other fields here.

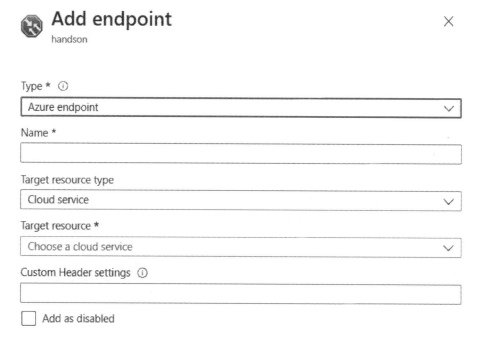

Figure 24.16 – Configuring an endpoint

In the following example, I selected an **Azure endpoint** and pointed the configuration to one of my Azure App Services. I performed the operation twice and added two different endpoints to two instances of my application:

Figure 24.17 – Two separate endpoints added

> **Note**
> Remember that you cannot add to a single Azure Traffic Manager profile service domains that point to the same region.

As you can see, right after adding endpoints, their status is displayed as **Checking endpoint**. This means that Azure Traffic Manager tries to gather information regarding their health. If something is wrong, you will see the **Degraded** status. Otherwise, the status should be marked as **Online**:

Figure 24.18 – Endpoints with one endpoint already online

If you have some problems with Azure Traffic Manager not being able to mark an endpoint as **Online**, make sure you set a correct protocol, path, and port in the configuration. Most errors are caused by invalid configuration of the service.

With the Azure Traffic Manager configuration described, let us now check how we can implement basic monitoring of the service.

Endpoint monitoring

Besides routing traffic to a different endpoint, Azure Traffic Manager offers some additional functionalities when it comes to monitoring. Besides the traditional **Metrics** blade, there is an extra feature available called **Traffic view**, which enables you to monitor traffic. What is more, you can use many different built-in mechanisms (such as `nslookup` in Windows OS), to check the current configuration of the service.

nslookup

To use nslookup, you must run the command line in Windows using your administrator account. Once it is loaded, enter the following command:

```
nslookup <Traffic-Manager-DNS-name>
```

After a moment, it should return a result showing the command resolution:

```
C:\Users\kamil>nslookup handson.trafficmanager.net
Server:  UnKnown
Address: 2001:730:3ed2::53


Non-authoritative answer:
Name:     hosts.butter-prod-euw-functionapp.azurewebsites.net
Address:  20.50.2.9
Aliases:  handson.trafficmanager.net
          butter-prod-euw-functionapp.azurewebsites.net
```

In my case it presented only a single alias, while it was supposed to display two (as I configured two separate endpoints for that instance). The reason for that is the degraded status of the second endpoint – once it came back online, it become available during DNS resolution:

```
C:\Users\kamil>nslookup handson.trafficmanager.net
Server:  UnKnown
Address: 2001:730:3ed2::53


Non-authoritative answer:
Name:     waws-prod-am2-161.cloudapp.net
Address:  52.178.75.200
Aliases:  handson.trafficmanager.net
          tocoffee-functionapp.azurewebsites.net
          waws-prod-am2-161.sip.azurewebsites.windows.net
```

Once everything is up and running, you can incorporate Azure Traffic Manager into your architecture and make sure it is connected to your DNS server. To do that, you will need to simply put a CNAM DNS record into your server:

```
www.yourdomain.com IN CNAME <Traffic-Manager-DNS-name>
```

Once DNS propagation is complete, you will be able to access your website via your instance.

> **Note**
> Remember that you must wait a fixed amount of time before all DNS changes will be propagated. The value can be configured in the **Configuration** blade by changing the **DNS time to live** field.

To finish the topic of Azure Traffic Manager, let us check the **Traffic view** feature.

Traffic view

Traffic view is an additional monitoring feature that enables you to check how the selected routing method works exactly at the DNS level. It gives you extra helpful information such as the following:

- Real latency level
- Volume of traffic
- Users' location

> **Note**
> Remember that this feature takes up to 24 hours to propagate and gather all necessary information.

By default, the screen for this functionality looks like the following:

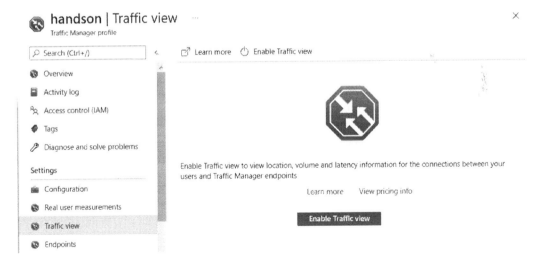

Figure 24.19 – Default view of Traffic view

If you want, you can enable it, but you must remember that, once enabled, it takes up to 24 hours to fully propagate all the information:

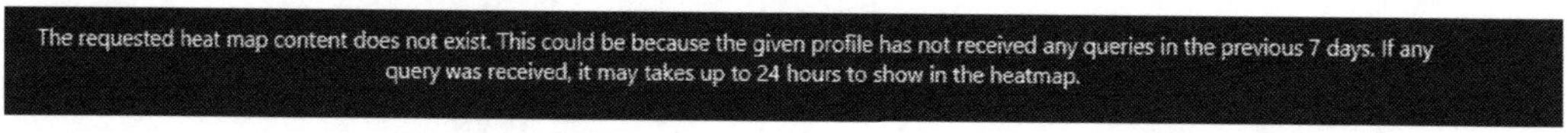

> The requested heat map content does not exist. This could be because the given profile has not received any queries in the previous 7 days. If any query was received, it may takes up to 24 hours to show in the heatmap.

Figure 24.20 – Error status that data for Traffic view has not been fetched yet

Once all the information is downloaded (it requires Azure Traffic Manager to be actively used), you will see a heat map containing how the traffic is distributed.

Summary

In this chapter, we have learned the fundamental concepts of traffic distribution and different routing methods that cover many real use cases that you may well face in your daily work. Now you should understand how this Azure service works and what can be achieved by the proper usage of its features, such as configuration, real user measurements, and monitoring.

In the next (and, unfortunately, the last) chapter, I will show you some useful tips and tricks for working with the Azure portal and different cloud components to improve your skills even further.

Questions

1. What are the supported routing methods in Azure Traffic Manager?
2. How can you use the **Real user measurements** feature?
3. Can you link different Azure Traffic Manager profiles?
4. Is it possible to use an external endpoint?
5. Does a client connect directly to an endpoint returned by Azure Traffic Manager?
6. What is the main difference between a gateway and Azure Traffic Manager?
7. Can Azure Traffic Manager be used to achieve high availability? If so, how?

Further reading

-   Disaster recovery with Azure DNS and Traffic Manager: `https://docs.microsoft.com/en-us/azure/networking/disaster-recovery-dns-traffic-manager`
-   How it works: `https://docs.microsoft.com/en-us/azure/traffic-manager/traffic-manager-how-it-works`

25

Tips and Tricks in Azure

There is always more than only one way to do a particular thing. This statement is especially true in the Azure ecosystem, where we are given multiple tools and shortcuts when provisioning resources, configuring services, and developing applications. This chapter will show you how to enhance productivity even more and shorten the time needed to deliver a working solution. The following topics will be covered in this chapter:

- Using the Azure CLI
- Using Cloud Shell
- Automating infrastructure deployments with ARM templates and Azure Bicep
- Using VS Code for a better developer experience
- Using Continuous Deployment for automated deployments to Azure

Technical requirements

To perform the exercises in this chapter, you will need the following:

- An Azure subscription
- The Azure CLI: `https://docs.microsoft.com/en-us/cli/azure/install-azure-cli`
- VS Code: `https://code.visualstudio.com/download`

Using the Azure CLI

When interacting with Azure resources, you have multiple paths to take to choose from.

- Using the Azure portal
- Leveraging the REST API of Azure Resource Manager

- Using the REST APIs of deployed resources

- Installing the Azure PowerShell module

- Implementing an Infrastructure-as-Code approach

- Installing the Azure CLI

In this chapter, we will focus on understanding the Azure CLI as our main tool for daily tasks as it's detached from the standard Microsoft technology stack and can be easily understood by people using the command-line interface on a daily basis.

> **Note**
>
> While most tasks can be done with both Azure PowerShell and the Azure CLI, there are some minor differences (for example, some SQL database operations can be done only by using Azure PowerShell). Using Azure PowerShell requires at least basic knowledge of PowerShell, thus we're not going to cover it in this book.

The Azure CLI is installed by a simple installer and consists of tens of different modules, each responsible for handling a single Azure resource. To confirm you have the Azure CLI installed, run the following command in your favorite terminal:

```
az
```

This should return a list of modules available for use:

```
Welcome to the cool new Azure CLI!

Use `az --version` to display the current version.
Here are the base commands:

    account           : Manage Azure subscription information.
    acr               : Manage private registries with Azure Container Registries.
    ad                : Manage Azure Active Directory Graph entities needed for Role Based Access
                        Control.
    advisor           : Manage Azure Advisor.
    afd               : Manage Azure Front Door Standard/Premium. For classical Azure Front Door,
                        please refer https://docs.microsoft.com/en-us/cli/azure/network/front-
                        door?view=azure-cli-latest.
    aks               : Manage Azure Kubernetes Services.
    ams               : Manage Azure Media Services resources.
```

Figure 25.1 – Welcome screen of the Azure CLI

The Azure CLI can be run on any machine, which allows for executing programs written in Python. If you have difficulties running it directly from an installer, you can use Docker for that:

```
docker run -it mcr.microsoft.com/azure-cli
```

This will start a Docker container, from which you can sign in to Azure and start managing resources. Signing into your account in the Azure CLI is very simple – just use the following command:

```
az login
```

This should open your browser (or a new tab) and ask you to select an account you would like to use for signing in:

Figure 25.2 – Picking an account when signing in with the Azure CLI

As you can see, even if you have multiple accounts, you can easily switch between them when logging in.

> **Note**
>
> Picking an account is a default screen when your browser has Azure credentials already cached. If it is your first login (or you are using incognito mode), you will be asked for your username before entering a password.

There is one thing we need to mention – there are two different contexts in which you may work in the Azure CLI:

- Account

- Subscription

To switch account, you always need to use `az login` – this is the only way to change the credentials used by the Azure CLI to communicate with Azure. Once signed in, the Azure CLI will display a list of active subscriptions you have access to:

```
[
  {
    "cloudName": "AzureCloud",
    "homeTenantId": "███████████████████████████",
    "id": "58ac7037-efcc-4fb6-800d-da6ca2ee6aed",
    "isDefault": true,
    "managedByTenants": [],
    "name": "MVP Sponsorship",
    "state": "Enabled",
    "tenantId": "███████████████████████████",
    "user": {
      "name": "kamil@███████████",
      "type": "user"
    }
  },
  {
    "cloudName": "AzureCloud",
    "homeTenantId": "███████████████████████████",
    "id": "cf70b558-b930-45e4-9048-ebcefb926adf",
    "isDefault": false,
    "managedByTenants": [],
    "name": "Pay-As-You-Go - Private",
    "state": "Enabled",
    "tenantId": "███████████████████████████",
    "user": {
      "name": "kamil@███████████",
      "type": "user"
    }
  },
```

Figure 25.3 – List of active subscriptions after successful login

Depending on the account selected, you may have access to different subscriptions. Therefore, it's important to remember which account was used to log in to the Azure CLI in order to manage the correct piece of infrastructure.

> **Note**
>
> When using the Azure CLI, you're performing all the operations as *you*. That means that all activity logs will have your username linked to an operation and the whole RBAC access will be scoped to your individual account. Avoid using your personal account with things such as CI/CD setups so you can save yourself from potential security breaches and your account being used to abuse your infrastructure.

Remember that you can use `az login` to sign in as a service principal or managed identity. To do that, use the following commands:

```
az login --service-principal -u <name> -p <secret> --tenant
<tenant-name>
az login --identity # For system-assigned identity
az login --identity -u <identity-name> # For user-assigned
identity
```

There is also a small trick that can save you a lot of time – if you have a resource (such as a virtual machine, web app, function app, or Kubernetes) that has managed identity enabled and assigned to it, you can leverage `az login` with the `-identity` switch without providing any kind of additional credentials. This is because the Azure CLI can interact with managed identity infrastructure and obtain a token on its own.

The last thing I would like to mention is the ability to query the result. You probably noticed that, in some chapters, we were already using Azure CLI commands to perform some operations or get results. Some of those actions generated quite a huge JSON output, which was difficult to read. That is where output formatting and querying come into play. Let us use the following command and result:

```
az network vnet list -g <your-resource-group-name>
```

It will return a result like mine:

```
[
  {
    "addressSpace": {
      "addressPrefixes": [
        "172.16.0.0/16"
      ]
    },
    "bgpCommunities": null,
    "ddosProtectionPlan": null,
    "dhcpOptions": null,
    "enableDdosProtection": false,
    "enableVmProtection": null,
    "encryption": null,
    "etag": "W/\"d1d61d0a-ccac-4a2e-a87e-18ec6344a3db\"",
    "extendedLocation": null,
    "flowTimeoutInMinutes": null,
    "id": "/subscriptions/58ac7037-efcc-4fb6-800d-da6ca2ee6aed/resourceGroups/handsonbook-rg/providers/Microso
ft.Network/virtualNetworks/handson-vnet",
    "ipAllocations": null,
    "location": "westus",
```

Figure 25.4 – Listing available VNets with the Azure CLI

The output is useful for further processing – it is nowhere near being easy to read to the human eye. Let us tweak it a little bit:

```
az network vnet list -g <your-resource-group-name> -o table
```

The result will be much nicer:

Name	ResourceGroup	Location	NumSubnets	Prefixes	DnsServers	DDOSProtection
handson-vnet	handsonbook-rg	westus	1	172.16.0.0/16		False

Figure 25.5 – Listing available VNets as a table

You can experiment with other output formats (such as `tsv`, `yaml`, and so on) to see which seems the best for you. To extract exact information, we can use the `-query` parameter:

```
az network vnet list -g <your-resource-group> -o table --query
"[].addressSpace.addressPrefixes"
```

This will return all address prefixes of all virtual networks inside a selected resource group:

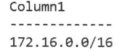

Figure 25.6 – Extracting a field from a result

The syntax is called JMESPath – you can find more information about it in the *Further reading* section. Let us now check the available capabilities of Cloud Shell in Azure.

Using Cloud Shell

Sometimes your computer may not allow for installing multiple developer tools that are useful when interacting with Azure. If that is the case, you can always use an inbuilt tool called Cloud Shell, which gives you an interesting alternative to installing all the software on your machine.

When you sign in to the Azure portal, you can see a small terminal icon in the top-right corner:

Figure 25.7 – Accessing Cloud Shell in the Azure portal

When you click on it, it will display an additional window, where you can start entering various commands:

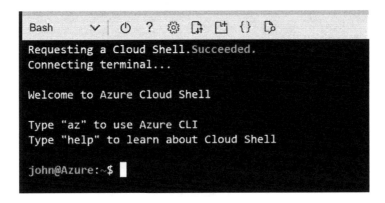

Figure 25.8 – Cloud Shell window

For now, Cloud Shell offers you a rich environment including tools such as the following:

- The Azure CLI
- Terraform
- Docker
- Git
- Runtimes for .NET, Java, Python, and so on

It also contains a simple text editor, which can be useful when creating files or modifying existing ones:

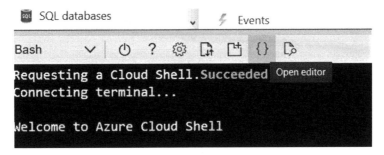

Figure 25.9 – Accessing the text editor

Of course, there are some limitations to what Cloud Shell can do and how it works:

- By default, Cloud Shell uses your account credentials to operate. You can change that with the `az login` command.

- Only a subset of the functionalities of Docker is available as Cloud Shell does not operate in a *full* environment. While you cannot run containers, you can still build, push, and pull them.

- Cloud Shell persists files on an attached file share, meaning files and data can be lost once the underlying storage account is deleted.

The benefits of running Cloud Shell over your local environment include keeping your machine clean and having integrated development environments with Azure and the most recent versions of the whole toolset. You can easily run it as your secondary environment, especially for simpler tasks.

With some basics for CLI tools, let us now check how infrastructure deployments can be automated with tools such as ARM templates and Azure Bicep.

Automating infrastructure deployments with ARM templates and Azure Bicep

When deploying infrastructure to Azure, you can use either a manual or automated approach. A manual approach would include using the Azure portal or the Azure CLI / Azure PowerShell. An automated approach would leverage either CI/CD pipelines calling various commands from CLI tools or using Infrastructure-as-Code. Infrastructure-as-Code is a generic approach that assumes that your infrastructure is scripted using one of the available languages or tools. Those scripts can then be used by you or your automation infrastructure to deploy infrastructure using a *desired state* approach.

Azure already has two native tools that can be used to leverage Infrastructure-as-Code:

- ARM templates

- Azure Bicep

A word from the reviewer

Bicep is a tool that generates an ARM template under the hood and has been written to make managing ARM templates a lot easier. By installing the Bicep CLI, you can then run the following to convert an existing ARM template into a Bicep file:

```
bicep decompile myarmtemplate.json
```

And you can run the following to build an ARM template from a Bicep file (which is handy if you have an existing repo of ARM templates and haven't moved to Bicep yet):

```
bicep build mybycepfile.bicep
```

The other win for Bicep is the code completion, schema validation, and schema version validation that it gives, although there can still be some minor differences in supported resource API versions.

While the names are quite different, these are almost the same tools. The only difference is in the way you write and prepare your scripts. Look at the following examples:

```
param storageLocation string
param storageName string

resource storage 'Microsoft.Storage/storageAccounts@2019-06-01'
= {
  name: storageName
  location: storageLocation
  sku: {
    name: 'Standard_LRS'
  }
  kind: 'StorageV2'
  properties: {}
}
```

What you can see there is a simple script deploying a storage account using Azure Bicep. For comparison, here is the same script but prepared with an ARM template:

```
{
    "$schema": "https://schema.management.azure.com/
schemas/2019-04-01/deploymentTemplate.json#",
    "contentVersion": "1.0.0.0",
    "parameters": {
        "sa_name": {
            "defaultValue": "handsonsa",
            "type": "String"
        }
    },
    "variables": {},
    "resources": [
```

```
        {
            "type": "Microsoft.Storage/storageAccounts",
            "apiVersion": "2021-09-01",
            "name": "[parameters('sa_name')]",
            "location": "westeurope",
            "sku": {
                "name": "Standard_LRS",
                "tier": "Standard"
            },
            "kind": "StorageV2",
            "properties": { }
        }
    ]
}
```

As you can see, those two tools use completely different language to reflect the shape of the infrastructure. Under the hood, both ARM templates and Azure Bicep use the same mechanism – Azure Resource Manager APIs. When starting to develop scripts with those tools, I strongly recommend using Azure Bicep as its goal is to replace ARM templates at some point in the future.

> **Note**
> ARM templates and Azure Bicep are native Azure tools, meaning they guarantee support for all existing resources, very often before they reach the General Availability stage. Third-party tools such as Terraform work differently and, most of the time, are behind the main development stream.

There are some huge advantages of using an Infrastructure-as-Code approach over traditional deployment methods:

- Your code is scripted as text files, meaning it can be reviewed before introducing any changes.
- You can easily incorporate it into your CI/CD pipelines.
- You can quickly deploy your infrastructure to another region or just create a replica, changing only a subset of parameters.
- The process is repeatable, meaning you are guaranteed to achieve the same result with each run.

Both ARM templates and Azure Bicep are deployed using an Azure CLI command:

```
az deployment group create
az deployment sub create
```

```
az deployment mg create
az deployment tenant create
```

In most cases, you will be using the `az deployment group` subgroup to get your resources deployed. The reason for that is quite simple – most deployments happen at the resource group level. The rest of the subgroups (`sub/mg/tenant`) deploy the template using subscriptions/management group/tenant scopes, which are higher in the hierarchy than resource groups.

> **Tip**
>
> You can use higher scopes to deploy your whole infrastructure using a single script. For example, by using management group or tenant scopes, you could deploy your subscription, resource groups, and resources inside them. Such an operation is impossible when deploying a template on a resource group level.

Let us now see how continuous deployment can be designed so you can deploy your applications and your infrastructure as a single unit of work.

Using continuous deployment for automated deployments to Azure

There are two parts to the common CI / CD process:

- Continuous Integration, which is responsible for building your application and integrating it with all the dependencies it uses
- Continuous Deployment, responsible for delivering artifacts created in the previous step

While Continuous Integration is part of a process designed to build your application, Continuous Deployment is a much more generic approach. In general, Azure does not assume anything regarding the technology you use. This means that all the toolsets, parameters, and steps needed are almost the same for all programming languages and runtimes.

> **Note**
>
> Here, we are assuming that all platforms that can be deployed to Azure follow the same patterns and require a similar number of steps to configure an infrastructure correctly so they can run smoothly. This is true for most cases, but still, we need to be prepared for some level of customization.

When working with cloud resources and planning for any kind of delivery of software and infrastructure as a single package, we need to take into consideration the following factors:

- If the whole process is supposed to be automated, we need to make sure that both code and infrastructure can be built and deployed as a unit without manual steps.

- We need to ensure that a proper level of access is assigned to principals running our pipelines – things such as RBAC assignment, access policies, and locks should also be part of the pipeline.

- We need to decide how deployments are validated. Even if infrastructure and software were deployed correctly, we need to make sure they work without issues.

When implementing Continuous Deployment for Azure, tools such as the Azure CLI or Azure PowerShell are especially helpful as they can be easily incorporated into working pipelines without installing an additional toolset.

Let us consider best practices for deploying applications to Azure:

- Use tools such as Azure Bicep, ARM templates, Terraform, or others to script your infrastructure and deploy it before deploying your application.

- Leverage native Azure tools for deploying web apps (avoid using FTP directly).

- Use Azure Key Vault for storing secrets for your apps.

- Use managed identities wherever possible to allow setting access via RBAC.

- Make sure the principal used for deployment is correctly configured and used instead of individual access credentials.

- Introduce E2E tests that validate application deployment after deployment.

Implementing all those elements will improve the way your application and infrastructure deployment work, but it also requires quite a lot of work to connect all the dots. However, this also guarantees the best results as most of the work will be automated with a proper level of access.

Summary

With this short chapter, we have completed the book. By covering topics such as the Azure CLI, ARM templates, and Azure Bicep, you should now have enough knowledge to explore Azure even more on your own. Congratulations, you can consider yourself familiar with the fundamentals of the cloud platform Microsoft provides.

Remember that the best way to learn about Azure resources is to follow documentation and practice various scenarios. Cloud resources are dynamic objects that happen to change quite frequently. To keep the same pace, find some channels where all the news is published – it could be Twitter, LinkedIn, or Microsoft mailing lists. This should help you keep up with all the interesting new capabilities and prepare yourself for possible changes.

Questions

Here are some questions to test your knowledge of the important topics covered in this chapter:

1. What are the different login options for the Azure CLI?

2. Are Azure PowerShell and the Azure CLI the same from a capabilities point of view?

3. Are ARM templates and Azure Bicep compatible under the hood?

4. Is Infrastructure-as-Code part of the Continuous Deployment pattern?

Further reading

For more information, refer to the following sources:

*   JMESPath: `https://jmespath.org`

Index

A

access control list (ACL) 460
Access Restrictions feature 40
ACR Tasks 62-65, 70
active replication 390
activities, Durable Functions 195
ADLS Gen2
  authentication 460
  authorization 460
  Azure portal, using to navigate
    through files 454-457
  data, storing 454
  network isolation 463
  SDKs, using to manage files 457-460
  security features 460
ADLS instance
  creating 452-454
Apache Avro format 345
Apache Lucene
  about 116
  reference link 116
  reference link, for supported
    query operations 121
append blobs 312
Apple Push Notification Service (APNS) 135
Applicability Statement 2 (AS2) 221

application host 158
application programming interfaces (APIs)
  about 522
  designing guidelines 507, 508
applications
  deploying, to Kubernetes cluster 86-90
  deploying, with kubectl 91
  developing, with Azure Event Hub 332-340
  preparing, for deployment 73-77
applications, deploying to Azure
  best practices 584
App Service plan
  creating 8-12
  Dev / Test 9, 31
  Isolated 9, 33
  Isolated V2 34
  Production 9, 32
  selecting 30
ARM templates
  about 410, 479, 580, 581
  infrastructure deployments, automating 580
  using 582
Asynchronous JavaScript and
    XML (AJAX) 399
authentication
  about 460
  configuring, in Azure portal 34

Authentication Context Class
    Reference (ACR) 68
authorization 460
autoscale, Cosmos DB 261, 262
autoscaling
    about 471, 472
    advantages 472
    algorithm, using 472
    disadvantages 472
    examples 473
    scaling out 473
    scaling up 473
availability zones 59
Azure Active Directory (Azure AD)
    about 384
    using, to secure App Service resources 34-38
Azure API Management
    API gateway 506
    concepts 506
    developer portal 506, 507
    management plane 506, 507
Azure API Management policies
    examples 509
    schema 509-511
Azure API Management service
    automated management 516, 517
    provisioning 511-516
Azure Application Gateway
    features 538
    integrating, with web applications 547, 548
    load balancing 538, 539
    multiple-site hosting 540
    security 538
    SSL offloading 538
    URLs and headers, rewriting 540
    Web Application Firewall (WAF) 539

Azure Application Insights service
    alerts 410-415
    automating 410
    capabilities 398
    data, logging in cloud 396, 397
    fundamentals 397-399
    instance, creating in portal 399, 400
    monitoring, from different platforms 401
    monitoring, from .NET 401-403
    monitoring, on Azure Functions 405, 406
    monitoring, on Node.js 404
    using 395, 396
Azure App Service
    about 3, 70, 73, 268
    autoscaling 477-480
    manual scaling 475, 476
    networking, configuring for 38
    scaling 475
Azure App Service plan
    container image, using 78-80
Azure App Service resource
    creating 4
    creating, with Azure portal 4
    creating, with Visual Studio 13-18
    creating, with VS Code 22-25
    deploying 4
    deploying, with Azure CLI 19
    deploying, with ZIP file 19, 20
    securing, with security providers 34
Azure Bicep
    about 580, 581
    infrastructure deployments, automating 580
    using 582
Azure Blob Storage
    about 268
    account 312
    additional features 320

blob 312
concepts 312, 313
container 312
container permissions level 316-318
Data protection blade 319
Soft delete feature 319
Azure CDN
  about 320
  applications, developing 499
  Azure App Service, configuring
    with 500-502
  caching rules 497-499
  Compression 497
  content, caching 496
  content, optimizing 496
  creating, in portal 492-495
  endpoint configuration 496
  fundamentals 490
  geo-filtering 499
  pricing tiers 493
  working with 490-492
Azure CLI
  using 573- 578
Azure Cognitive Search service
  AI, adding to indexing workload 128
  analyzers 121-124
  analyzer selection 124, 125
  cognitive skills, configuring 128-131
  creating 110
  creating, in Azure portal 110-116
  full-text search, performing 116
  indexing 125
Azure container instances 70
Azure Container Registry (ACR)
  deploying, with Azure CLI 49-51
  deploying, with Azure portal 47-49
  hosting, options 46

Azure Cosmos DB
  provisioned throughput, scaling for 484-486
  scaling 484
  Table API 305
Azure Data Lake Storage (ADLS)
  about 450
  best practices 464
  data structure 465
  fundamentals 450-452
  performance 464
  resiliency 465
  security 464, 465
Azure Event Grid
  about 267, 268, 372
  CloudEvents schema 284
  creating, in Azure Portal 274-276
  custom schema option 285
  Event Grid schema 282, 283
  event handlers 272
  event sources 270, 271
  reactive architecture 268-270
  schemas, using 282
  security 277, 278
  services, connecting through 274
  subscription 274
  testing 286, 287
  topics 273
Azure Event Hub
  about 372
  applications, developing with 332-340
  Capture feature 344
  instance, creating in Azure portal 328, 329
  scaling 486, 487
  security 342
  used, for message processing
    federation 340, 341
  working with 328-331

Azure Event Hub Capture
  about 344, 345
  enabling 345-350
Azure Event Hub security
  about 342
  IP filters and networking 342, 343
  Private Link, using 342
  resource isolation 342
Azure Files
  concepts 306
  fully managed file shares, implementing 306
  versus Blob storage 308, 309
  working with 306-308
Azure Front Door
  general routing concept 522
  usage scenarios 522, 523
  using, for load balancing 524-531
Azure Functions
  about 157, 256-268
  bindings 162
  checklist, for scaling 482
  concepts 160
  developing, by configuring local
    environment 165
  EventGridTrigger 286
  features 178
  host.json file 183, 184
  Monitor feature 182
  platform features 179, 180
  pricing models 163
  publish wizard 184, 185
  scaling mechanism 481-483
  security 180-182
  serverless applications, scaling 481
  testing 286, 287
  triggers 162
Azure Functions command
  in Visual Studio Code 166

Azure Functions endpoint
  working with 170, 171
Azure Functions project
  creating 166-168
  in C# 168, 169
Azure Kubernetes Service (AKS)
  about 81, 523
  deployment 84-86
  responsibilities 82, 83
Azure Logic Apps
  about 217, 218
  advantages 220
  B2B integration 233, 234
  connectors 221
  current pricing 221
  integrating, with virtual networks 234, 235
  in Visual Studio Code 230-232
  working 218-220
Azure portal
  function, creating 174-178
  logic apps, creating 224-230
  test notifications, sending 146, 147
  URL 4
Azure Private Link 342
Azure Queue Storage
  application, developing 309-311
  features 309
  queues, using with 309
Azure Resource Manager 100
Azure Search 320
Azure Service Bus
  about 373
  and Azure Queue Storage 373
  basic tier 373
  dead lettering 385, 386
  design patterns 379
  features 385
  fundamentals 372

in Azure portal 374-376

premium tier 373

queues 377

relays 378, 379

security 383

sessions 386, 387

solutions, developing with 379-383

standard tier 373

topics 378

transactions 387

versus other messaging services 372

Azure SQL

about 417, 418

advanced features 421, 422

automatic backups 421

failover groups 421

features, in portal 428-432

fundamentals 418-421

geo-replication 421

monitoring 444

purchasing model 419

security features 432

tuning 444-446

Azure SQL database

configuring 424

creating 424

Azure SQL Database and Azure SQL
    Managed Instance, feature comparison

reference link 421

Azure SQL instance

creating 424-428

Azure SQL, scaling

about 441

elastic pool 442

read scale-out 442, 443

sharding 443

single database 441

Azure Storage

about 293

replication 296, 297

services 294

storage accounts 294, 295

using, in solution 294

Azure Storage blobs

using, for object storage 311

Azure Storage, securing

about 295

RBAC method 295

SAS tokens used 296

Azure Storage service

creating 298, 299

Azure Storage tables

structured data, storing 297

Azure Stream Analytics

about 352

as data pipeline 354

data processing, steps 353

fully managed 353

input and output types 354

instance, creating in Azure portal 355, 356

low cost of ownership 354

performance 353

query patterns 367

stream 353

stream analysis 352

stream ingestion 352

Structured Query Language (SQL)-
    based query language 353

Azure Stream Analytics instance

creating 355, 356

input, adding 357, 358

output, adding 358-361

Azure Stream Analytics query language

used, for querying data 361

used, for writing query 361-363

Azure Traffic Manager
  Configuration blade 564-566
  creating, in Azure portal 558, 559
  Endpoints blade 568, 569
  functions 556-558
  Real user measurements blade 566, 567
  using 555, 556
  working with 564
Azure Web App
  configuring 6, 7
  selecting, from available services 4, 5
Azure WebJobs 157

B

B2B integration
  in Azure Logic Apps 233, 234
bindings, Azure Functions 162
blobs
  append blobs 312
  block blob 312
  page blobs 312
Blob storage
  data, inserting into 313-315
  versus Azure Files 308, 309
block blobs 312
build automation
  enabling 21
built-in connectors
  about 222
  Azure API Management 222
  Azure App Service 222
  Azure Functions 222
  Azure Logic Apps 222
  batch 222
  HTTP 222
  request 222
  schedule 222

C

Capture feature 344
Cassandra 253
central processing units (CPUs) 353
change feed
  about 262
  using, for change tracking 262-265
checkpoints 366
CloudEvents schema 284
Cloud Shell
  limitations 580
  using 578-580
cloud vendors
  responsibilities 158
conditional access (CA) 508
connectionString 142
connectors, Azure Logic Apps
  about 221
  built-in connectors 222
  managed connectors 222
consistency, Cosmos DB 248, 249
Consul
  URL 72
consumer 377
container group
  about 100
  as main unit of work 100-103
container image
  using, in Azure App Service Plan 78-80
container image lifecycle
  high-level diagram 68
Container Instances
  container group 100
  security 104
containerized applications
  hosting, ways 68, 69
containers 67

container throughput 253, 254

content delivery network (CDN) 531

continuous deployment

using, for automated deployments
to Azure 583, 584

Cosmos DB

about 240

autoscale 253, 261, 262

Azure Functions 256, 257

basic information 240, 241

capacity 253

consistency 248, 249

container throughput 253, 254

database level throughput 254, 255

database models 250

data replication 242

features 242

Firewall and virtual networks blade 255, 256

multiple read regions 243

optimization 253

partitioning 246, 247

pricing 243, 245

stored procedures 257-259

throughput 247

triggers 259

User-Defined Function (UDF) 259

Cosmos DB instance

creating, in portal 240-243

Overview blade 241

Cross-Site Scripting (XSS) 539

custom topics 281

D

data

inserting, into Blob storage 313-315

querying, in Table storage 303-305

storing, in ADLS Gen2 454

database level throughput 254, 255

database models, Cosmos DB

about 250

Cassandra 253

graph 251

MongoDB 251

SQL 250

table 252

database transaction units (DTUs) 473

data center (DC) 158

Data Explorer feature 244

data lake 320

dead lettering

about 385

handling 386

Dev/Test App Service plans

about 9, 31

Basic (B1) 31

Free (F1) 31

Shared (D1) 31

dev tools 158

direct connection, for push
notification 136, 137

disaster recovery (DR)

handling 388-390

Disk Storage 294

Durable Functions

about 194

activities 195

dispatcher 198

error handling 203-205

eternal orchestrations 205, 206

external events 202, 203

high availability 212-214

instance management 209, 210

orchestration client 195, 196

orchestration history 196

orchestrations 194

orchestrator function 198
queue 198
singleton orchestrations 206, 207
stateful entities 208
storage 198
task hub 208
template 194
timers 201, 202
versioning 211, 212
working 196-198
Dynamic Data Masking 439, 440

E

endpoint monitoring
  about 569
  nslookup, using 570
  Traffic view feature 571, 572
enrichments 129
enterprise connectors 224
entity functions 208
error handling, Durable Functions 203-205
eternal orchestrations, Durable
        Functions 205, 206
Event Grid schema 282, 283
EventGridTrigger
  in Azure Functions 286
event listener 138
event ordering
  about 364-366
  application time 364
  arrival time 364
  concepts 364
events
  about 372
  filtering 285, 288
  receiving 285
external events, Durable Functions 202, 203

F

File Transfer Protocol (FTP) 462
Firebase Cloud Messaging (FCM) 135
firewall 433, 434
Firewall and virtual networks blade 255, 256
first-in, first-out (FIFO) messaging 372
full-text search, Azure Cognitive Search
  linguistic analysis 121
  performing 116
  request, sending 117-121
fully managed file shares
  implementing, with Azure Files 306
Fully Qualified Domain Name (FQDN) 98
function
  about 161
  creating 171
  creating, with Azure portal 174-178
  creating, with Visual Studio Code 171-173
function app 160
Function-as-a-Service (FaaS) 158
function, components
  function code 162
  function decorator 162
  trigger 162
  trigger data 162
Function file 185-188

G

generic notifications 149
geographic routing method 562
geo-redundant storage (GRS) 296
geo-replication 60-62
geo-zone-redundant storage (GZRS) 296
graph 251
Gremlin 251

H

Hadoop Distributed File System (HDFS) 451
hierarchical namespaces
  about 450
  features 451
high availability, Durable Functions
  about 212
  individual storage approach, using 214
  replicated storage approach, using 214
  shared storage approach, using 212
hubName 142
hyperscale repository 450

I

identity providers (IdPs) 34
image lock 57, 58
images
  about 51
  working with 52-54
index 111
indexing, Azure Cognitive Search
  about 125
  data importing 125
  pull model 127, 128
  push model 125-127
Infrastructure-as-a-Service (IaaS) 4
Infrastructure-as-Code (IaC)
  about 96
  advantages, over traditional
    deployment methods 582
infrastructure deployments
  automating, with ARM templates 580
  automating, with Azure Bicep 580
input/output bindings 188, 189

installations
  about 144
  advantages 144
instance management, Durable
    Functions 209, 210
integration account connectors 224
Internet of Things (IoT) 352, 465
Internet of Things (IoT) hubs 251
Isolated App Service plans
  about 9, 33
  I1V2/I2V2/I3V2 33
Isolated V2 plan 34
Istio
  URL 72

J

JavaScript Object Notation
    (JSON) template 479

K

kubectl
  application, deploying 91
Kubernetes
  about 81
  high-level architecture 81
Kubernetes cluster
  application, deploying to 86-90
Kuma
  URL 72

L

Least Privilege principle 106
linguistic analysis, in Azure Cognitive Search
  performing 121-124

Linkerd
  URL 72
Live Stream blade 164
load balancing
  about 539
  with Azure Front Door 524-531
local environment
  configuring, for developing
    Azure Functions 165
locally redundant storage (LRS) 296, 450
logical partition 246
logic apps
  creating 224
  creating, in Azure portal 224-230
Logs module
  accessing 407-410
  using 406

M

machine learning (ML) 353
managed API connectors 223
managed clusters 82
managed connectors 222
Managed Identity (MI)
  about 383, 384
  setting up 107
manual scaling
  about 475
  versus autoscaling 477
manual trigger 178
message 372
message processing federation
  Azure Event Hub, using for 340, 341
microservices architecture 70, 71
Microsoft Defender for SQL 434, 435

Microsoft SQL Server
  about 417, 418
  on VMs 422, 423
MongoDB 251
MultiValue routing method 563

N

native notifications 149
networking
  configuring, for Azure App Service 38
Networking blade 38
network security 158
network security groups (NSGs) 42
Node.js
  Azure Application Insights, monitoring 404
Notification Hubs
  application design, challenges 134, 135
  notification, sending with SDK 149, 150
  notifications, sending to
    multiple vendors 145
  push notification architecture 136
  rich content notification,
    sending through 150
  test notification, sending 145
  using 134
Notification Hubs device registration
  available registrations, checking 143, 144
  installation, using 139, 144
  notification hub, creating 140, 141
  performing 139
  registration, creating 141-143
  registration, using 139
  tag 139
  template 139
notification services 137, 138
nslookup
  using 570

O

object storage
  Azure Storage blobs, using for 311
on-premises connectors 224
Open Authorization 2 (OAuth2) 398
open source software (OSS) tools 451
operating systems
  about 158
  selecting 26, 27
orchestrations
  about 194
  client 195, 196
  history 196
  limitations 199
  sub-orchestrations 200, 201
  working with 198, 199
outages
  handling 388-392

P

page blobs 312
partition
  about 111
  versus replica 111
partitions, Cosmos DB
  logical 246
  physical 246
passive replication 390
performance consideration, ADLS
  appropriate file format, using 464
  data ingestion optimization 464
  network connection 464
  parallel processing 464
  Premium tier, using 464

performance routing method 559, 560
permissions
  granting, for pulling/pushing images 54-56
physical partition 246
Platform-as-a-Service (PaaS) 4, 164
platform notification services (PNSes)
  about 134
  high-level design 135
platforms
  selecting 28, 29
POSIX ACL 462, 463
POSIX-style permissions model 451
pricing, Cosmos DB 243-245
pricing model 159
pricing models, Azure Functions
  App Service Plan model 163
  Consumption model 163
  Premium plan 163
priority routing method 561
Private Endpoints 40
processing units (PUs) 481
producer 377
Production App Service plans
  about 9, 32
  Premium (P1v2) 32
  Standard (S1) 32
property graph 251
publish/subscribe (pub/sub)
    communication model 378
pull model 127, 377
purchasing model options, Azure SQL
  database transaction unit (DTU)-
    based (provisioned) 419
  vCore-based (provisioned) 419
  virtual core (vCore)-based (serverless) 419
push model 125

push notification architecture
about 136
direct connection 136, 137
queued communication 137
triggered communication 138

Q

query patterns, Azure Stream Analytics
about 367
data aggregation over time 367
multiple outputs 367
unique values, counting 368
queued communication, for
push notification 137
queues
about 377
using, with Azure Queue Storage 309

R

RBAC authentication 384
RBAC, configuration levels for ADLS Gen2
container level 461
resource level 461
reactive architecture 268-270
read-access GRS (RA-GRS) 296
read-access GZRS (RA-GZRS) 296
registration
creating 141-143
registry 51
registry locks 57
relays 378
replays 366
replica
about 111
versus partition 111

replication, Azure Storage
geo-redundant storage (GRS) 296
locally redundant storage (LRS) 296
read-access GRS (RA-GRS) 296
zone-redundant storage (ZRS) 296
repositories
about 51
working with 52-54
repository lock 57
REpresentational State Transfer
(REST) API 139, 458
request units (RUs) 473
rich content notification
about 150
creating 151, 152
sending 151, 152
sending, through Notification Hubs 150
role-based access control
(RBAC) 358, 460-462
routing
configuring 540-547
routing methods
geographic routing method 562
MultiValue routing method 563
performance routing method 559, 560
priority routing method 561
subnet routing method 563
weighted routing method 560
Run from Package feature 21

S

scaling
about 164
Azure App Service 475
Azure Cosmos DB 484-486
Azure Event Hubs 486, 487

Azure Functions 481
  in App Service model 165
  in Consumption model 164
  in Premium plan 165
scaling out
  about 473
  visualization 475
scaling up
  about 473
  visualization 474
SDKs
  generic notifications 149
  native notifications 149
  notification, sending with 149, 150
  reference link 141
  test notifications, sending 148
Search Unit (SU) 111
Secure Sockets Layer (SSL) 251
security, Azure Service Bus
  about 383
  Managed Identity (MI) 383, 384
  RBAC 384
security, Container Instances
  access control 106
  considerations 104
  identity configuration 107
  networking configuration 105
  security areas 104
security features, Azure SQL
  about 432
  auditing 437, 438
  data classification 435-437
  Dynamic Data Masking 439, 440
  firewall 433, 434
  Microsoft Defender for SQL 434, 435
security providers
  used, for securing App Service resources 34
serverless 158

Server Message Block (SMB) protocol 306
Service-Level Agreement (SLA) 242, 513
service mesh architecture 72
services
  configuring 96-99
  integrating 224
  provisioning 96
services, Azure Storage 294
sessions, Azure Service Bus
  about 386
  handling 387
sharding 443
shared access signature (SAS) token
  reference link 145
Single point of entry (SPOE) 506
singleton orchestrations, Durable
      Functions 206, 207
Soft delete feature 319
Software-as-a-Service (SaaS) 4
solid-state drive (SSD) disks 464
split-merge tool
  reference link 443
SQL API 250
SQL Server VMs 418
stable tags 57
stateful entities, Durable Functions
  about 208
  features 208
state-of-the-art (SOTA) 383
static HTML site
  with NGINX, running on Kubernetes 92
static website 320
storage accounts, Azure Storage 294, 295
stored procedures 257-259
stream ingestion
  versus stream analysis 352
structured data
  storing, with Azure Storage tables 297

subnet routing method 563

sub-orchestrations 200, 201

subscription

about 274

creating 278-281

Systems Applications and Products in
Data Processing (SAP) 224

system topics 281

T

table 252

Table API

in Azure Cosmos DB 305

Table storage

data, querying in 303-305

data, storing in 302

general rule, for entities 303

managing 299-301

PartitionKey 302

RowKey 302

timestamp 303

tagging 56, 57

task hub, Durable Functions 208

test notification

sending 145

sending, in Azure portal 146, 147

sending, in SDK 148

throughput, Cosmos DB 247

timers, Durable Functions 201, 202

topic 273, 274, 378

Traffic view feature 571, 572

transactions, Azure Service Bus 387

Transport Control Protocol (TCP) 373

triggered communication, for
push notification 138

triggers

about 259, 260

creating 260

triggers, Azure Functions 162

U

Uniform Resource Locator (URL) 517

unique identifier (UID) 390

unique tags 57

URL redirects

implementing 532-535

performing 548-552

URL rewrites

implementing 532-535

performing 548-552

User-Defined Function (UDF) 259

V

versioning 56

versioning, Durable Functions 211, 212

virtual cores (vCores) 473

virtual networks (VNets) 309

virtual private network (VPN) 379

Visual Studio

Azure App Service resource, creating 13-18

Visual Studio Code

Azure App Service resource, creating 22-25

function, creating 171-173

VNet integration 41, 42, 513

VoiceNets 256

W

Web Application Description
    Language (WADL) 517
Web Application Firewall (WAF) 539
web applications
  Azure Application Gateway,
    integrating with 547, 548
web application settings
  working with 29, 30
web applications, hosting with containers
  factors 69
weighted routing method 560
Windows Notification Service (WNS) 135

Z

ZIP file
  Azure App Service resources,
    deploying 19, 20
zone redundancy 60
zone-redundant storage (ZRS) 296
ZRS replication model
  geo-zone-redundant storage (GZRS) 296
  read-access GZRS (RA-GZRS) 296

Packt.com

Subscribe to our online digital library for full access to over 7,000 books and videos, as well as industry leading tools to help you plan your personal development and advance your career. For more information, please visit our website.

Why subscribe?

- Spend less time learning and more time coding with practical eBooks and Videos from over 4,000 industry professionals

- Improve your learning with Skill Plans built especially for you

- Get a free eBook or video every month

- Fully searchable for easy access to vital information

- Copy and paste, print, and bookmark content

Did you know that Packt offers eBook versions of every book published, with PDF and ePub files available? You can upgrade to the eBook version at packt.com and as a print book customer, you are entitled to a discount on the eBook copy. Get in touch with us at customercare@packtpub.com for more details.

At www.packt.com, you can also read a collection of free technical articles, sign up for a range of free newsletters, and receive exclusive discounts and offers on Packt books and eBooks.

Other Books You May Enjoy

If you enjoyed this book, you may be interested in these other books by Packt:

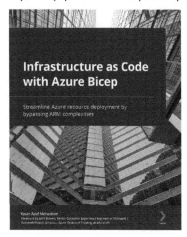

Infrastructure as Code with Azure Bicep

Yaser Adel Mehraban

ISBN: 9781801813747

- Get started with Azure Bicep and install the necessary tools
- Understand the details of how to define resources with Bicep
- Use modules to create templates for different teams in your company
- Optimize templates using expressions, conditions, and loops
- Make customizable templates using parameters, variables, and functions
- Deploy templates locally or from Azure DevOps or GitHub
- Stay on top of your IaC with best practices and industry standards

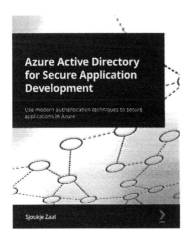

Azure Active Directory for Secure Application Development

Sjoukje Zaal

ISBN: 9781838646509

- Get an overview of Azure AD and set up your Azure AD instance
- Master application configuration and the use of service principals
- Understand new authentication protocols
- Explore the Microsoft Identity libraries
- Use OpenID Connect, OAuth 2.0, and MSAL to make sign-in fully secure
- Build a custom app that leverages the Microsoft Graph API
- Deploy Azure AD B2C to meet your security requirements
- Create user flows and policies in Azure AD B2C

Packt is searching for authors like you

If you're interested in becoming an author for Packt, please visit `authors.packtpub.com` and apply today. We have worked with thousands of developers and tech professionals, just like you, to help them share their insight with the global tech community. You can make a general application, apply for a specific hot topic that we are recruiting an author for, or submit your own idea.

Share Your Thoughts

Now you've finished *Azure for Developers*, we'd love to hear your thoughts! Scan the QR code below to go straight to the Amazon review page for this book and share your feedback or leave a review on the site that you purchased it from.

`https://packt.link/r/1803240091`

Your review is important to us and the tech community and will help us make sure we're delivering excellent quality content.

Made in the USA
Coppell, TX
18 September 2022

83339339R00348